Beginning EJB in Java EE 8

Building Applications with Enterprise JavaBeans

Third Edition

Jonathan Wetherbee
Massimo Nardone
Chirag Rathod
Raghu Kodali

D1226140

Beginning EJB in Java EE 8: Building Applications with Enterprise JavaBeans

Jonathan Wetherbee
San Mateo, California, USA

Massimo Nardone
Helsinki, Finland

Chirag Rathod
Jayanagar I Blk, India

Raghu Kodali
Cupertino, California, USA

ISBN-13 (pbk): 978-1-4842-3572-0
https://doi.org/10.1007/978-1-4842-3573-7

ISBN-13 (electronic): 978-1-4842-3573-7

Library of Congress Control Number: 2018944142

Managing Director, Apress Media LLC: Welmoed Spahr
Acquisitions Editor: Steve Anglin
Development Editor: Matthew Moodie
Coordinating Editor: Mark Powers

Cover designed by eStudioCalamar

Cover image designed by Freepik (www.freepik.com)

Distributed to the book trade worldwide by Springer Science+Business Media New York, 233 Spring Street, 6th Floor, New York, NY 10013. Phone 1-800-SPRINGER, fax (201) 348-4505, e-mail orders-ny@springer-sbm.com, or visit www.springeronline.com. Apress Media, LLC is a California LLC and the sole member (owner) is Springer Science + Business Media Finance Inc (SSBM Finance Inc). SSBM Finance Inc is a **Delaware** corporation.

For information on translations, please e-mail editorial@apress.com; for reprint, paperback, or audio rights, please e-mail bookpermissions@springernature.com.

Apress titles may be purchased in bulk for academic, corporate, or promotional use. eBook versions and licenses are also available for most titles. For more information, reference our Print and eBook Bulk Sales web page at http://www.apress.com/bulk-sales.

Any source code or other supplementary material referenced by the author in this book is available to readers on GitHub via the book's product page, located at www.apress.com/9781484235720. For more detailed information, please visit http://www.apress.com/source-code.

Printed on acid-free paper

Table of Contents

About the Authors

Jonathan Wetherbee is a consulting engineer and tech lead for EJB development tools on Oracle's JDeveloper IDE. He has over 20 years of experience in development at Oracle, working on a variety of O/R mapping tools and overseeing Oracle's core EJB tool set since EJB 1.1. Most recently, Jon has been responsible for the design and development of EJB and JPA data binding solutions for ADF, Oracle's application development framework.

Prior to joining the JDeveloper project, Jon was a product manager for Oracle's CASE (computer-aided software engineering) tools and worked on early object-relational frameworks. He received a patent in 1999 for his work on integrating relational databases in an object-oriented environment. Jon is coauthor of the first edition of this book, *Beginning EJB 3 Application Development: From Novice to Professional* (Apress, 2006), and has published articles online in Java Developer's Journal and Oracle Technical Network. He enjoys speaking and has given talks at conferences and developer groups, including Oracle's iDevelop (Bangalore, Taipei), The Server Side Java Symposium (Barcelona), and various Java user groups. Jon holds a Bachelor of Science degree in cognitive science from Brown University.

Massimo Nardone has more than 24 years of experiences in Security, Web/Mobile development, Cloud, and IT Architecture. His true IT passions are Security and Android.

He has been programming and teaching how to program with Android, Perl, PHP, Java, VB, Python, C/C++ and MySQL for more than 20 years.

He holds a Master of Science degree in Computing Science from the University of Salerno, Italy.

He has worked as a Project Manager, Software Engineer, Research Engineer, Chief Security Architect, Information Security Manager, PCI/SCADA Auditor, and Senior Lead IT Security/Cloud/SCADA Architect for many years.

Technical skills include Security, Android, Cloud, Java, MySQL, Drupal, Cobol, Perl, Web and Mobile development, MongoDB, D3, Joomla, Couchbase, C/C++, WebGL, Python, Pro Rails, Django CMS, Jekyll, Scratch, etc.

He worked as visiting lecturer and supervisor for exercises at the Networking Laboratory of the Helsinki University of Technology (Aalto University). He holds four international patents (PKI, SIP, SAML and Proxy areas).

He currently works as the Chief Information Security Officer (CISO) for Cargotec Oyj, and he is member of the ISACA Finland Chapter Board.

Massimo has reviewed more than 45 IT books for different publishers and is also the coauthor of *Pro JPA 2 in Java EE 8* (Apress, 2018) and *Pro Android Games* (Apress, 2015).

Chirag Rathod is a principal engineer responsible for developing and supporting design-time features for EJB and CDI in Oracle's JDeveloper IDE. He has over 14 years of experience in developing development tools. Prior to joining the JDeveloper IDE team, he helped develop Oracle's flagship products like Oracle SQL*Plus, Oracle Forms, and Oracle Designer. Chirag received a Bachelor of Engineering degree in computer science from The Faculty of Technology and Engineering, Maharaja Sayajirao University.

 **Raghu Kodali** is vice president of Product Management & Strategy at Solix Technologies, where he is responsible for product vision, management, strategy, user design, and interaction. His work includes the next-generation data optimization platform, industry-leading data discovery platform, and enterprise data management-as-a-service, application development using Big Data platforms and cloud. Raghu is coauthor of *Big Data Analytics using Splunk* (Apress, 2013). Prior to Solix, he was with Oracle for 12 years, holding senior management positions responsible for Product Management and Strategy for Oracle Fusion Middleware products. In addition, Raghu was Oracle's SOA Evangelist, leading next-generation Java EE initiatives. Raghu has authored a leading technical reference on Java computing, *Beginning EJB 3 Application Development: From Novice to Professional* (Apress, 2006), published numerous articles on enterprise technologies, and was a contributing author for *Oracle Information Integration, Migration and Consolidation* (PACKT Publishing, 2011).

About the Technical Reviewer

Mario Faliero is a Telecommunications engineer and entrepreneur. He has more than 10 years' experience with radio 1 frequency hardware engineering. Mario has extensive experience in numerical coding, using scripting languages (MATLAB, Python) and compiled languages (C/C++, Java). He has been responsible for the development of electromagnetic assessment tools for space and commercial applications. Mario received his Master's Degree from the University of Siena.

Preface

Dear Reader,

When we conceived the original edition of this book in 2006, the lightweight EJB 3 API was still in its early stages, yet it was clear to us that the EJB specification designers had at last achieved the right blend of power and usability. Coming from the EJB 2.x world, it was like a breath of fresh air, and reminded us of how it felt to discover Java technology after years of programming C and C++. The EJB component, redefined as an ordinary Java class whose metadata could be declared through Java annotations, and enhanced by the introduction of generics, container injection, and interceptors, became the basis for a much more nimble development model: one that gained elegance through simplicity. Enter the new Java Persistence API (JPA), where entities, too, were recast as lightweight Java classes and O/R mapping metadata could be specified through spec-defined annotations, and we suddenly had a comprehensive enterprise component model comprising the latest technologies, all rolled into a worldwide standard. So you can see what got our buzz going.

Fast forward to now, and the release of the EJB 3.2 and JPA 2.1 specs. Spanning over a thousand pages combined, these specifications have matured to address a number of new areas and improve upon their ease of use. Once again we saw an opportunity to translate this latest material into an approachable format that reads well and makes liberal use of examples that you can build, execute, and further explore on your own machine. In this second edition, accompanying the release of Java EE 7, we introduce the EJB 3.2 and JPA 2.1 APIs along with key features in the CDI and JAX-RS specifications through a series of digestible chapters, allowing you to become comfortable with these technologies one topic at a time. Within each chapter we provide executable source code examples that demonstrate how each feature works, and how the pieces fit together. So you don't have to swallow the whole enchilada in one humongous gulp. In the spirit of our Apress Wines Online application, which we use for numerous examples throughout the book, we want you to truly savor and appreciate the richness of the Java EE 7 component ecosystem.

For each technology we provide straightforward examples, but we also strive to explain when and where to use its features and what their strengths and weakness are, and offer insights into best usage practices. Following these topical explorations, we explain how to integrate EJB and related components into a comprehensive Java EE 7 application, and then turn the spotlight on transaction management, performance analysis, deployment, testing in an Embeddable EJB Container, and how to build solid EJB clients.

Our job is to transform you from EJB novice to expert, and we want you to enjoy the ride!

Jonathan Wetherbee, Massimo Nardone, Chirag Rathod, and Raghu Kodali

Who Should Read This Book?

This book is targeted at enterprise software developers who are experienced with Java, have built single tier or multitier applications using earlier versions of EJB or related technologies, and are looking to build enterprise software based on the latest cross-platform industry standards.

As authors of an introductory-level text, we have two main goals:

- Our first goal is to get you comfortable working with the many essential elements of EJB and several closely related technologies so that you can design, build, deploy, execute, and test comprehensive enterprise applications in a Java EE environment. We expect you to be able to come away with a sense of ease with the nuts and bolts required to build and assemble an application based on EJB components.

- Our second goal is to provide you with a broad perspective on the service and persistence tiers of Java EE as a whole and, in particular, on the full range of features offered by EJB. We intend for you to leave this book holding a breadth-first foundation that will serve as a launchpad from which to explore specific areas of the EJB and related specifications in greater depth.

To this end, this book strives to provide an approachable on-ramp to EJB that gets you comfortable with building services and applications that exercise the full breadth of EJB. We deliberately avoid diving deep into many areas of the spec, so that you can get familiar with the overall environment without getting distracted by the minutia of fine-grained options. We believe that this breadth-first foundation—based on a solid understanding of the broad range of features offered by EJB—will put you in the best position to then explore in greater depth, using the specification and other advanced texts as your reference guides, specific areas of the EJB API that are required for your own software development projects.

Acknowledgments

This book is borne of the efforts and insights of people who provided both technical input and pure inspiration throughout its life. In particular, I would like to thank my colleague and principal coauthor of this second edition, Chirag Rathod, for his insight, spirit, and dedication at all stages of the endeavor. Late nights and early mornings are made lighter when a close collaborator is also such a good friend! Raghu Srinivasan and John Bracken were invaluable in design meetings and discussions of EJB and JPA best practices. Chris Carter supported me on my quest, even when it took my attentions away from JDeveloper; he knew that the insights gained from researching and writing this book would surely pay back dividends to the team. And an enjoyable hour and a half with Marina Vatkina discussing the latest state and future directions of EJB 3.2 was both enlightening and timely.

With the technical help from all of the above, writing a book on this topic I hold dear would have been a mere marathon, if it weren't for all of the diversions of everyday life! But for these welcome distractions, I would like to single out a few individuals among many. Adam Beyda and Lauren Webster have given me a lifetime of insight and perspective on what really matters. And Bob Lieb's deep guidance and navigation through the psychological waters of writing a book was essential. Rhonda Jeffrey, Andy Cortwright, Dave Clark, and Marianna Klebanov: thank you for being good sounding boards and wonderful friends during this past year.

My parents, Andrea and Peter Wetherbee, thank you for your love and encouragement and the constant reminder that you are my biggest fans.

In the end, my primary motivation for punching this thing through came from the desire to, once again, spend more time with my children and close friends. That time is now!

—Jon Wetherbee

When Jon Wetherbee asked me if I would be interested in doing a "non-work" related project with him, I had no idea about what I would be getting into. I would like to thank Jon for giving me this wonderful opportunity of coauthoring this second edition. For me he is more than a lead author—he is a friend and guide who led me through the path that resulted in this book.

ACKNOWLEDGMENTS

I would like to thank Srinivasan T. Raman and Chris Carter who not only supported me during this endeavor but also encouraged me. I would have burnt a lot more midnight oil writing this book if Oracle would not have given me time and resources. For this I am grateful to Oracle Corporation.

My parents, Chandrabala and Jayantilal Rathod, thank you for your love. Last but not least I would like to thank my wife Ashwini and daughter Shaylee for making me feel like an "author" who was authoring the next "bestseller."

—Chirag Rathod

Many thanks go to my wonderful family – my wife Pia, and my children Luna, Leo, and Neve for supporting me when working on this book. You are the most beautiful reason of my life.

I want to thank my beloved late mother, Maria Augusta Ciniglio, who always supported and loved me so much. I will love and miss you forever my dearest mom.

I also need to thank my beloved father Giuseppe and my brothers Mario and Roberto for your endless love and for being the best dad and brothers in the world.

To Franco Gentilucci and Maurizio De Marco for being two wonderful friends.

This book is also dedicated to my late dearest cousin Ann Goss. You will be missed.

A special thanks also goes to Catrin Bergholm and Sakari Salomaa for being two wonderful persons and bringing joy to my family.

Thanks a lot to Steve Anglin and Matthew Moodie for giving me the opportunity to work as writer on this book, as well as Mark Powers for doing such a great job during the editorial process and supporting me all the time; and finally Mario Faliero, a good friend and the technical reviewer of this book, for helping me to make a better book.

—Massimo Nardone

CHAPTER 1

Introduction to the EJB 3.2 Architecture & CDI Services

When we set out to write this book, our goal was to present Enterprise JavaBeans (EJB) to developers, with a keen eye toward how this technology can be used in everyday, real-world applications. *JSR-345: Enterprise JavaBeansTM, Version 3.2 EJB Core Contracts and Requirements* is a deep spec that addresses the needs of beginning developers and hardcore power users alike. That's a large audience to satisfy and, as a reference guide, the EJB spec document covers it well. In writing a book about how to *use* EJB, we had to narrow our audience; nonetheless, we believe that we've written a book that will serve the needs of a majority of Java EE developers.

This book is targeted at developers who are experienced with Java, have built single- or multi-tier applications using earlier versions of EJB or other technologies, and are ready to take on the challenges (and rewards) of building enterprise applications using standards-based technology. Recognizing that a combined 1,100 pages of reference material [covering the EJB and Java Persistence API (JPA) specs] can be daunting, we have provided an on-ramp for developers, unfolding EJB one section at a time, and giving you the information and code examples that you need to roll up your sleeves and get to work.

As each chapter unfolds, you will not only learn about a new area of the spec, but you will also learn through specific examples about how to apply it to your own applications. Many of these examples come directly from the comprehensive, end-to-end, Java EE Enterprise Wines Online application constructed in Chapter 7 and Chapter 12, so that you can see how they fit into a bigger picture. You are encouraged to take these examples and run with them. Try them out in your favorite IDE or development environment,

1

© Jonathan Wetherbee, Massimo Nardone, Chirag Rathod, and Raghu Kodali 2018
J. Wetherbee et al., *Beginning EJB in Java EE 8*, https://doi.org/10.1007/978-1-4842-3573-7_1

and change them around and try new things. EJB and the related APIs covered in this book—JPA, Web Services, and Contexts and Dependency Injection (CDI)—offer you a lot with which to work. Once you're comfortable with the basics of building, deploying, and testing, you'll find that EJB components are not only powerful, but also easy to build and use.

Together, the authors of this book have built a number of applications using EJB in concert with other technologies in the Java EE stack, and we have attempted to capture within it advice about the practical patterns we have learned, the strategies we have found successful, and some pitfalls you can avoid. Most chapters in this book are dedicated to exploring specific areas of EJB, but we have also included chapters on Java Persistence API (JPA), Contexts and Dependency Injection (CDI), Web Services, gauging the performance of your EJB applications, and deploying to the Java EE application server of your choice. An introductory "Getting Started" section at the end of this chapter will get you set up to run the many useful sample applications found at the end of each chapter in the book.

We hope this book will serve not only as a reference guide for information on EJB but also as a how-to guide and repository of practical examples to which you can refer back as you build your own applications. Enjoy!

What's New in Java Enterprise Edition (Java EE) 8 Architecture?

This first release of the Java enterprise edition (Java EE) platform is dated June 2013, and by the time I was updating this manuscript Java EE 9 was already published.

Java EE 8 includes updates to core APIs such as Servlet 4.0 and Context and Dependency Injection 2.0 as well as two new APIs—Java API for JSON Binding (JSR 367) and the Java EE Security API (JSR 375).

Java EE, a superset of the Java SE platform, includes over 30 specifications and a runtime environment, which means that Java EE components can take full advantage of all Java SE APIs.

Here is the list of the most important changes in Java EE 8:

- Java EE 8 Platform

- JSON-B 1.0

- JSON-P 1.1

- JAX-RS 2.1
- MVC 1.0
- Java Servlet 4.0
- JSF 2.3
- JMS 2.1
- CDI 2.0
- Java EE Security 1.0
- Java EE Management 2.0
- Concurrency Utilities
- Connector Architecture
- WebSocket
- JPA
- EJB
- JTA
- JCache
- JavaMail

More information about Java EE 8 can be found in the official Java web page: http://www.oracle.com/technetwork/java/javaee/overview/index.html

An Introduction to EJB

In the late 1990s, as Java was bolstered by the emergence of separate technologies (such as RMI, JTA, and CORBA) that addressed the enterprise needs of large-scale applications, a need arose for a business component framework that could unify these technologies and incorporate them under a standard component development model. EJB was born to fill this need. Over the ensuing years, EJB has evolved to encompass numerous features (while judiciously rejecting others), and it has matured into a robust and standard framework for deploying and executing business components in a distributed, multiuser environment.

What Is EJB?

Each release of EJB is managed through the Java Community Process (JCP) as a Java Specification Request (JSR). The latest release, which is covered in this book, is defined by *JSR 345: Enterprise JavaBeans™ 3.2*. EJB JSRs prior to EJB 3.0 covered Persistent components, but since the introduction of JPA, persistence is now managed through its own JSRs. Nonetheless, the two areas complement each other well, and we have included several chapters in this book dedicated largely to JPA.

The EJB 3.2 spec, entitled *JSR 345: Enterprise JavaBeans™, Version 3.2 EJB Core Contracts and Requirements,* together with the class library defined in the EJB 3.2 API, define both a component model and a container framework.

The EJB Component Model

As a component model, EJB defines three object types that developers may build and customize as follows:

- *Session beans* can be stateless, stateful, or singleton, and they perform business service operations. These services may be declaratively configured to operate in distributed, transactional, and access-controlled contexts.

- *Message-driven beans* (MDBs) are invoked asynchronously in response to external events through association with a messaging queue or topic.

Complementing this, the Java Persistence API (JPA) principally defines the following persistent object type:

- *Entities* are objects that have unique identities and represent persistent business data.

Session and message-driven beans are EJBs, and they are often referred to collectively as enterprise *beans.* In earlier versions of EJB, entities were referred to as entity beans, and they also fell into this category. In EJB 3, however, entities are now managed by a persistence provider and not the EJB container, and they are no longer considered enterprise beans. Enhanced message-driven beans contract with a no-methods message listener interface to expose all public methods as message listener methods.

The EJB Container

The EJB container provides the supporting environment in which EJB components operate. This environment offers transaction and security services, pooling and caching of resources, component lifecycle services, concurrency support, and more—all of which we will explore throughout this book. EJB components specify the details of how they wish to interact with their supporting container using EJB-specific metadata that is either captured by the container and applied to the EJB's behavior at runtime, or interpreted at the time an EJB component is deployed to an EJB container and used to construct wrapping. The EJB 3.2 specification also defined the EJB API Groups with clear rules for an EJB Lite Container to support other API groups.

Core Features of the EJB Development Model

Throughout its life, EJB has maintained its focus on delivering components imbued with a handful of core features.

Declarative Metadata

One of the hallmarks of the EJB component model is the ability for developers to specify the behavior of both enterprise beans and entities *declaratively* (as opposed to *programmatically*) using their choice of Java annotations and/or XML descriptors. This greatly simplifies the development process, since much customization can be added to a bean without having to encumber the Java source with service implementation code. To accommodate developer preference and application flexibility, EJB offers developers their choice of both annotations and XML, with the ability to use both methods simultaneously within the same EJB or entity, for specifying behavior in metadata. In cases where the same piece of metadata is defined both in an annotation and in XML, the XML declaration takes precedence in resolving the conflict. Additional benefits of this approach are explored later, in the "EJB 3 Simplified Development Model" section of this chapter.

Configuration by Exception

Coupled with the ability to specify behavior declaratively is the strong use of intelligent defaults in EJB. Much behavior is attached automatically to an EJB or an entity without it being declared explicitly, such as the transactional behavior of session bean methods and the names of the table and columns that map to an entity's persistent data properties. An annotation, or its counterpart in XML, needs to be specified explicitly only when non-default behavior is desired. In the most common cases, where the default behavior is leveraged, this approach leads to very sparse, clean code. This development model is known as *configuration by exception*, because only in exceptional (non-default) cases is it necessary to configure the behavior of the component explicitly.

Scalability

Large-scale applications demand the ability to scale well as the client load increases. The EJB server employs resource pooling to maximize object reuse, utilizes a persistence cache to avoid repeatedly querying or creating the same objects, and implements an optimistic locking strategy in the middle tier to reduce load on the relational database management system (RDBMS) and to avoid concurrency locking issues. The EJB container also manages an EJB's life cycle, allowing dependent resources to be freed up and reused to optimize performance.

Location Transparency

EJBs may be configured for remote access, allowing them to be accessed across a network connection. A client, which may be another EJB, simply requests an instance of a remote EJB, and the local and remote EJB containers transparently manage the communication details.

Transactionality

The Java Transaction API (JTA) defines a standard API for distributed transactions, and the EJB container acts as a JTA transaction manager to EJBs. Since its inception, the EJB spec has defined a standard model for declaratively specifying container-managed transactional behavior on enterprise beans.

Multiuser Security

Method-level access control may be specified declaratively on EJBs, enforcing user- and role-level privileges defined by application server administrators.

Portability

Spec-compliant enterprise beans are deployable to any application server that implements EJB, at least in theory. In practice (and this was particularly true of releases prior to EJB 3), vendors provided their own metadata definitions that enterprise bean developers grew to rely upon, locking them into a particular vendor's implementation. As EJB has matured, it has grown to incorporate many of these formerly platform-specific features, so that EJBs implemented today are far more portable than in the past.

Reusability

EJBs are loosely coupled components. An EJB may be reused and packaged into multiple applications, though it must be bundled with, or have access to, the business interfaces of dependent EJBs.

Persistence

Although no longer covered in the EJB spec, JPA entities are an essential complement to EJB. Entities are persistent domain objects with unique identities. An entity class maps to a database table, and each entity instance is represented by a single row in that table.

Progression of the EJB Spec

Each time a new version of the EJB spec is introduced, it includes new, significant features to address popular demand and adopt emerging technologies. Here is a brief summary of how the EJB spec has progressed since its birth in 1996, or more importantly, since its first commercial implementations in 1998.

EJB 1.0

The initial release, 1.0, began with support for stateful and stateless service objects, called session beans; and optional support for persistent domain objects, called entity beans. For portability, EJBs were made accessible through a special remote interface that offered portability and remotability but incurred the overhead of a remoting infrastructure and pass-by-value semantics.

EJB 1.1

The follow-up release, 1.1, mandated support among vendors for entity beans, and introduced the XML deployment descriptor to replace storing metadata in a special serialized class file.

EJB 2.0

EJB 2.0 addressed the overhead and pass-by-value shortcomings of remote interfaces by introducing the local interface. Only clients running inside the J2EE container could access an EJB through its local interface, but pass-by-reference method calls allowed for more efficient interchanges between components. A new type of EJB was also introduced—the message-driven bean (MDB), which could participate in asynchronous messaging systems. Entity beans gained support for container-managed relationships (CMRs), allowing bean developers to declaratively specify persistent relationships between entity beans that were managed by the EJB container. Also, Enterprise JavaBeans Query Language (EJB QL) was introduced, which gave developers the ability to query entity bean instances using a language that resembled SQL.

EJB 2.1

EJB 2.1 added support for Web Services, allowing a session bean to expose an endpoint interface, and a timer service that allowed EJBs to be invoked at designated times or intervals. EJB 2.1 also provided expanded EJB QL functions, and an XML schema was introduced as a replacement for the DTD that defined the `ejb-jar.xml` deployment descriptor.

EJB 3.0

EJB 3.0 was a major milestone in the evolution of the standard. Introducing a new, simplified development model (see below), EJB components became POJOs (plain old Java objects); an EJB's bean class was no longer required to implement EJB-specific interfaces; and the properties that made a Java class an EJB were factored out into Java annotations or captured externally in the `ejb-jar.xml` deployment descriptor file. With a few basic conditions, any class could become an EJB and leverage the enterprise services offered by an EJB container.

Also new in EJB 3.0, the Entity Beans portion of the spec was replaced by the new JPA spec and, consistent with the new simplified development model, JPA entities were

POJOs as well. JPA entities were also decoupled from the EJB container and could be used independently of EJB, including in a pure Java SE environment.

EJB 3.1

EJB 3.1 further improved upon the simplified development model introduced in EJB 3.0. The no-interface option was now supported for Local EJBs. The Singleton pattern was offered for Session beans along with Asynchronous and enhanced Timer support. EJB Lite—an embeddable subset of the EJB Container's functionality—allowed EJB components to be executed in the same VM as an EJB client.

EJB 3.2

In EJB 3.2, the Asynchronous and enhanced Timer features are added to the EJB Lite subset. Along with other improvements, the bean developer is offered more control over the transactionality of lifecycle interceptor methods, and the rules governing declaration of Local and Remote behavior have been simplified.

The JSR-000345 Enterprise JavaBeansTM 3.2 Final Release can be downloaded from this web page:

`http://download.oracle.com/otndocs/jcp/ejb-3_2-fr-spec/index.html`

The latest EJB 3.2 version release is dated April 10, 2013, and did not change from Java EE 7 to EE 8.

Major changes include the following:

- An option to disable passivation of stateful session beans is enhanced.

- The TimerService API to access all active timers in the EJB module is enhanced.

- The embeddable EJBContainer to implement AutoClosable interface is enhanced.

- The restrictions on javax.ejb.Timer and javax.ejb.TimerHandle that required references to be used only inside a bean were removed.

- The list of standard JMS MDB activation properties is enhanced.

- Support for the optional features in the previous release and moving their description to a separate EJB Optional Features documents was added.

EJB 3 Simplified Development Model

EJB 3.0 was a significant departure from earlier releases. The architects of EJB 3 set out to redesign the development experience; to introduce a greatly simplified development model that would reduce the complexity of the enterprise beans themselves; and, at the same time, incorporate many of the ideas found in peer technologies. The consensus is in: the spec has been widely hailed as having achieved these goals, and in so doing has overcome many of the problems that prevented earlier versions of EJB from becoming widely adopted.

XML and Annotations

If you are familiar with earlier versions of EJB, one of the first things you will notice in EJB 3 is that it is no longer necessary to capture EJB metadata in a deployment descriptor. EJB now lets you store your EJB metadata inside your bean source using Java annotations. This isn't to say that XML deployment descriptors have gone away; they are still alive and well, and many developers prefer them to annotations. Using XML decouples the Java source from the EJB metadata, allowing the same entity or enterprise bean classes to be used in different contexts, where the context-specific information is captured in the XML and doesn't "pollute" the bean class.

Many users, however, will prefer to view their EJB metadata directly in the context of their POJO classes and use annotations. To avoid wading into a religious war (vocal proponents on both sides abound), we suggest that you choose for yourself. A simple rule we follow is this: if we need to decouple our entity and bean classes from their EJB metadata, as when we want to use the same entity classes with two different entity inheritance strategies, we put our metadata in XML. Otherwise, we stick with annotations. Don't forget—you can always mix and match, relying on the firm policy that whenever metadata is specified for an element using both XML and annotations, the XML always wins. This allows any role (see the "EJB Roles" section later in the chapter) downstream of the bean developer to override metadata settings without having to update the Java source, since overrides can be applied exclusively to the XML descriptors.

Note   A more advanced strategy, which we also recommend, is to use annotations only when defining behavior on an enterprise bean or an entity that is truly integral to its definition, such as the relationship type of an entity relationship field, or the transactional requirements of a method on a session bean. Anything that could reasonably be overridden, such as the name of the table to which an entity maps, or the details of a value generator used for populating the primary key on an entity, would go in the XML descriptor, where it can be specified at deploy time by an application assembler, perhaps in consultation with a database administrator. While there is no harm in specifying default values using annotations in the Java source file, this approach recognizes the difference between firm metadata, which ought not to be modified; and loose metadata that may be freely modified without changing the behavior of the enterprise bean or entity.

Dependency Injection

After an EJB is instantiated inside the Java EE container, but before it is handed out to a client, the container may initialize property data on the instance according to rules defined for that enterprise bean. This feature is called *dependency injection*, and it is an example of inversion of control pattern, whereby an external provider initializes the properties of an object instance instead of by the class itself. EJB 3 introduced the use of dependency injection in Java EE and, largely because it caught on so well, this feature has now been given its own spec. The current dependency injection API is managed through *JSR-330: Dependency Injection for Java™*, and the functionality is further extended through *JSR 346: Contexts and Dependency Injection for Java™ EE 1.1*, which we cover in Chapter 10, "Contexts and Dependency Injection."

Note   Injection uses a "push" model to push data out to the bean, and it occurs regardless of whether the bean actually uses the data. If there is a chance that the data will not be used, the bean may elect to avoid incurring the cost of the resource derivation by performing a Java Naming and Directory Interface (JNDI) lookup in Java code to "pull" the data, only if it is actually (or likely to be) used.

Common examples of dependency injection use in EJB are as follows:

- Injecting an `EntityManager` into a session bean for interacting with entities in a persistence unit

- Injecting a `UserTransaction` into a session bean that manages its transaction demarcation

Interceptors: Callback Methods

Both enterprise beans and entities may designate some of their methods, or methods on separate classes, to be called when certain lifecycle events occur. For instance, a session bean may indicate that a certain method should be called after the bean has been instantiated, but before it has been handed off to a client. This method may initialize state information on the bean, or look up resources using JNDI, or any other action it wishes, provided that it does not require a transactional context. Such callback methods are called *interceptors*, and they allow bean developers to participate programmatically in the interaction between an enterprise bean, or an entity, and its container. An important advantage of this pattern (also known as *cross-cutting*) is that a single interceptor may be defined once and then applied to multiple methods, or even multiple EJBs. The EJB 3.2 specification also added an option for the lifecycle callback interceptor methods of stateful session beans to be executed in a transaction context determined by the lifecycle callback method's transaction attribute.

POJO Implementation

EJB 3 took great strides to eliminate the trappings that beset enterprise bean classes and their required interfaces in earlier EJB releases. Similar to complaints over having to define XML metadata to specify even the most basic bean behavior, developers found it burdensome to have to write custom interfaces to handle an enterprise bean's factory support, and inconvenient to require a session bean's interfaces to extend EJB-specific interfaces. All of these limitations were addressed in EJB 3.

Home methods are no longer mandated, although they're still supported. For session beans and MDBs, a default constructor replaces the no-argument `ejbCreate()` method required by earlier EJB specs.

For entities, the `Home` interface is replaced by an `EntityManagerFactory` instance that produces `EntityManager` instances for a JPA persistence unit to manage entity lifecycle operations, including query execution.

Intelligent Use of Defaults

An excellent example of how EJB 3 simplifies the development process is its leveraging of default behavior to provide rich functionality with no coding or declarative metadata required. For instance, by simply marking a POJO with the @Entity annotation, all of its public properties automatically become persistent fields, and the table and column names take on derived values that match the entity and field names. Additional annotations or XML elements are only required when overriding the default behavior of a particular area. Only when the table name does not match the entity name is the @Table annotation required. Great care has been taken to ensure that the default values match the most common usages so that, in the majority of use cases, explicit metadata is not required, leading to leaner, more clutter-free code.

Note   One consequence of relying on default behavior is that the class does not describe its full behavior anywhere, so you need to have a good understanding of the default behavior that is being applied. IDEs can be useful in deriving and displaying the enterprise bean or entity with its fully defaulted values explicitly shown.

Distributed Computing Model

Essential to any enterprise application is the ability to execute tasks and run components in separate Java threads or processes. Through the RMI-based remoting services, clients in an application client tier may access EJBs running in an application server anywhere on the network. The pass-by-value behavior of remote interface methods provides a coarse-grained model designed to reduce network traffic between clients and servers that are loosely connected to each other. Many applications that use EJB do not require remote access, however, and elect to configure their EJBs for local use. This eliminates the overhead of remote access support while continuing to offer the remaining enterprise services.

EJB Roles

The EJB spec defines seven roles for individuals involved in the different stages of defining an enterprise bean or entity, or in providing services and API implementation to enterprise beans. This book is targeted at the three roles involved in defining enterprise beans and their associated metadata. In practice, one or more of these roles may be performed by the same individual, and certain tasks may be performed by one role and overridden by another; but it is useful to understand the logical partitioning of tasks in the EJB development process. We will refer to these roles in various sections throughout the book.

The Enterprise Bean Provider

The Enterprise Bean Provider, also known as the Bean Provider, has the responsibility of defining and implementing the business logic and structure of an enterprise bean. This includes defining the Java class, implementing service methods, specifying transactional and security information declaratively on the bean and its methods, injection or lookup of required resources, and anything else that can be applied to the enterprise bean class.

Applied to JPA entities, the Bean Provider defines the persistent structure of the entity and its relationships with other entities. The provider may define mapping and primary key–generation behavior, but this role is generally limited to defining the logical dependencies and structure of the entity.

The Application Assembler

The Application Assembler combines EJBs into EJB modules and entities into persistence archives, and then it combines these modules together with other Java EE modules to produce an application. This task requires resolving references to logical server resources including references between EJBs. The Application Assembler must work with the interfaces and metadata defined for the EJB and entity components but need not be familiar with the implementation details.

The Deployer

The Deployer takes an application that has been assembled by the Application Assembler and deploys it to a particular application server instance or cluster. The Deployer must resolve all of the external dependencies defined by the EJB component, mapping them to concrete resources installed in the application server environment. In the case of entities, the Deployer may provide or override the details of the live database objects to which the entities will map.

How This Book Is Organized

To orient you to the structure of the remainder of this book, here is a brief summary of each chapter. There is no requirement that you read these chapters in order. Sample programs accompany each chapter, and they may be run independently of one another. Topics are introduced progressively, though, and thus if you find a reference in one chapter to a term or concept that is not defined in that chapter, chances are that it was defined in an earlier chapter of the book.

Chapter 1: Introduction to the EJB 3.2 Architecture & CDI Services

This chapter opens by introducing the book and offering an orientation to EJB. This orientation covers the EJB development framework and component model, the core features of EJB, the history of EJB, the EJB 3 simplified development model, and the EJB distributed computing model. The chapter concludes with a "Getting Started" section to help you install the NetBeans IDE and GlassFish Java EE reference implementation server required to run the many sample applications provided with this book.

Chapter 2: EJB Session Beans

Chapter 2 explores EJB's primary service object: the session bean. Session beans are examined in their many roles: as entity facades, as service components—both with and without state, as singleton or timer-driven objects, and as the primary orchestrators of transaction and security services.

Chapter 3: Entities and the Java Persistence API (JPA)

The Java Persistence API (JPA) is introduced, along with the various persistence services that are available to support entities both within a Java EE container and outside of one. This chapter covers basic O/R mappings, and it introduces the Java Persistence Query Language, or JPQL.

Chapter 4: Advanced Persistence Features

Delving into more advanced persistence concepts, this chapter describes the support offered in JPA for mapping entity inheritance hierarchies. Examples of the three supported inheritance mapping strategies identify the strengths and weaknesses of each approach in order to help you decide which one best suits the particular needs of your application. Among other topics, this chapter also covers complex primary key (PK) mappings, ID generators for autopopulating primary key values using a database sequence or table, locking strategies, and cache management.

Chapter 5: EJB Message-Driven Beans

This chapter describes how you can use MDBs to add asynchronous, event-driven behavior to your application. JMS, Java's messaging API, is explained and demonstrated in this chapter's code examples.

Chapter 6: EJB, Web Services, and Microservices

Session beans provide an excellent implementation for Web Services, and this chapter explores EJB's support for this fine marriage of technologies.

Chapter 7: Integrating Session Beans, Entities, Message-Driven Beans, and Microservices

After covering all of the different component model types individually, Chapter 7 brings them all together in an integrated Java EE application. We think you will find it particularly useful to see how everything fits together to produce a running application.

Chapter 8: Transaction Management

EJB offers rich transaction service support, and it makes it easy for Bean Providers to declaratively specify custom container-provided transactional behavior on an enterprise bean. EJB also allows enterprise beans to opt out of this model and control their own transaction demarcation behavior. This chapter applies two alternative transactional models to a single logical scenario for weighing the benefits of each approach.

Chapter 9: EJB Performance and Testing

This chapter provides an invaluable look at how to gauge the performance of your EJB components in order to help you decide which of the many options EJB offers is right for your application. In addition to explaining how to set up performance tests, we present some performance test cases that we have run, complete with our assessments of the results.

Chapter 10: Contexts and Dependency Injection

Introduced in Java EE 6, Contexts and Dependency Injection (CDI) services augment the component model defined in EJB with a powerful means of injecting resources into your application whose life cycles are contextual and conveniently managed by the server. This chapter introduces CDI and explains how EJB developers can leverage this support to enrich an application's behavior.

Chapter 11: EJB Packaging and Deployment

Assembly and deployment are rolled into this chapter as we cover the tasks required of the Application Assembler and Deployer roles. This chapter discusses packaging EJB and persistence modules, assembling modules in different ways into an enterprise archive (EAR) file, resolving references between modules and between EJBs packaged into different modules, and binding resource requirements to concrete resources installed in the target application server environment.

Chapter 12: EJB Client Applications

In this chapter, we walk you through application architectures and different programming models that you can use to build applications, including the pros and cons of each approach. Once we have done that, we settle on one application architecture—developing Web applications using JavaServer Faces (JSF) technology. We then drill down into the JSF architecture and concepts and focus on integrating JSF user interface components and the JSF navigation model with the EJB/WebService/JPA back-end application that we developed in Chapter 7.

Finally, we also explain how to use a lightweight application client container to execute your session beans in a pure Java SE environment. This lightweight container provides EJBs that execute in its environment with some of the services (such as container injection) that are offered by a true EJB container.

Chapter 13: Testing in an Embeddable EJB Container

In a production deployment, EJB components run in a Java EE environment, inside an application server. For testing purposes, EJB allows you to test your EJB components within a lightweight subset of the EJB Container, known as EJB Lite and implemented as an Embeddable EJB Container, which can run in a pure Java SE environment. This chapter covers a variety of EJB testing scenarios and guides you in using JUnit to test EJB components (and JPA entities) in GlassFish's Embeddable EJB Container.

Getting Started

This section of the chapter will get you ready with the software installation and configuration required to work with the samples in the rest of the book. At the time of this writing, the EJB 3.2 specification was on its way to being finalized. The GlassFish application server had implemented the specification that allowed the developer community to get hands-on experience with the new specification.

GlassFish is an open source application server that implements the newest features of the Java EE platform. In fact, GlassFish is the reference implementation for all of the specifications of the Java EE platform, including the EJB 3.2 specification. Glassfish releases are tracked closely by the NetBeans IDE, ensuring that NetBeans supports the very latest state of the Java EE specifications and making NetBeans the ideal platform for deploying and running the examples in this book. You will find that each successive chapter is accompanied by a NetBeans application project comprised of one or more additional projects representing the EJB, Web, or other modules that demonstrate the features covered in that chapter. Although these sample applications are all configured to run in the GlassFish server, they are portable (by virtue of following the Java EE standards) and may be deployed to the Java EE 8 server of your choice.

Although we built and tested the examples in this book using NetBeans in a Windows 7 environment, the code samples are not operating-system specific, and they can be executed on any system that can run NetBeans and its integrated GlassFish server. Nevertheless, you might have to tweak the environment settings to install and execute NetBeans and its integrated GlassFish server on other operating systems.

Note   You can find more details on the NetBeans IDE and its integrated GlassFish application server at the following website: `http://netbeans.org/features/index.html`

The remaining sections of this chapter will cover the following:

- Installing Java SE Development Kit (JDK)

- Downloading the NetBeans IDE

- Installing NetBeans and its integrated GlassFish server

- Testing NetBeans and GlassFish installation

- Administrating the GlassFish application server

Even if you are familiar with NetBeans and GlassFish, we recommend that you read through the following sections, as running the sample code in the rest of the chapters depends on this setup being done correctly.

Installing Java SE Development Kit (JDK) 8

As first thing we want to make sure we install the Java SE Development Kit (JDK) version 8 from the Java web site:

`http://www.oracle.com/technetwork/pt/java/javase/downloads/jdk8-downloads-2133151.html`

Once Java SE Development Kit (JDK) version 8 is installed you can test if it works by running the command shown in Figure 1-1.

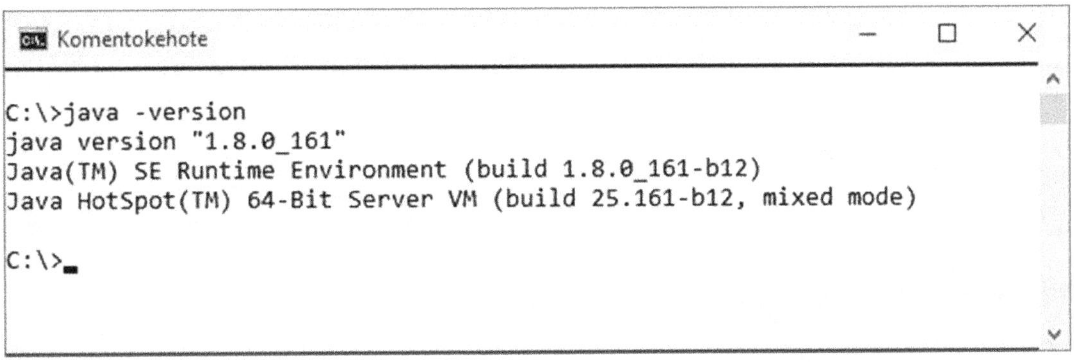

```
Komentokehote                                    —    □    ✕

C:\>java -version
java version "1.8.0_161"
Java(TM) SE Runtime Environment (build 1.8.0_161-b12)
Java HotSpot(TM) 64-Bit Server VM (build 25.161-b12, mixed mode)

C:\>_
```

Figure 1-1. Checking Java version installed

Please notice that there is also a distribution of the JDK 8u161 that includes the Java SE bundle of NetBeans IDE version 8.2:

http://www.oracle.com/technetwork/java/javase/downloads/jdk-netbeans-jsp-142931.html

In this book we installed separately JDK and NetBeans.

Downloading the NetBeans IDE

You can download the latest NetBeans installer from the following location:

http://netbeans.org/downloads/

Make sure that you download the installer with "Java EE" technology, as shown in Figure 1-2. This installer will also contain the required Java SE and GlassFish packages. Ant is included with GlassFish; you can either use it or configure the environment properties to use another installation. The GlassFish project recommends that you use Ant, which is bundled with its install.

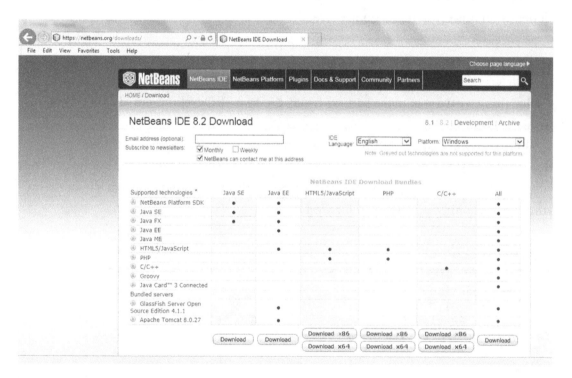

Figure 1-2. *Downloading the NetBeans IDE*

> **Note**   When we started writing this book, the latest NetBeans version was 8.2, which was used to test the setup and the sample code. Remember that multiple installations of NetBeans IDE 5.x, 6.x, and 7.x can coexist with NetBeans IDE 8.2 on the same system. You, actually, don't need to uninstall the earlier versions in order to install or run NetBeans IDE 8.2.

Once the download is complete, you are set to start the installation of NetBeans along with its integrated GlassFish server.

Installing NetBeans IDE and Its Integrated GlassFish Server

Navigate to the directory where the NetBeans IDE installer has been downloaded, and run the installer. The first page of the installer wizard lists the packages that will be installed.

If no Java SE Development Kit (JDK) version is installed you will receive the message shown in Figure 1-3.

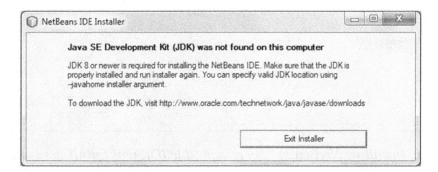

Figure 1-3. *No Java SE Development Kit (JDK) is installed*

If, instead, Java SE Development Kit (JDK) is installed but you see the "No compatible JDK was found" warning message, as shown in Figure 1-4, then you will have to exit the wizard and first download and install the right and compatible Java SE Development Kit 8.

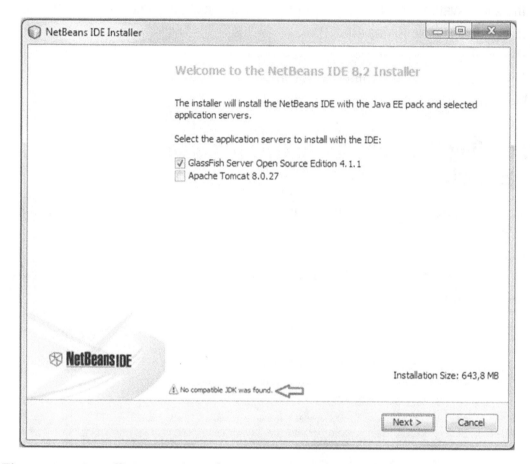

Figure 1-4. *Installing NetBeans. "No compatible JDK was found" warning*

Note   Even if you don't see the "No compatible JDK was found" warning, verify that you have Java Platform (JDK) 8 installed. If you don't have the Java Platform (JDK) 8 installed, then you might get a "javac: invalid target release: 1.8.0" error while executing the samples in this book.

Rerun the NetBeans installer after a compatible JDK version is installed. Verify that the "No compatible JDK found" warning does not reoccur, and traverse the wizard, keeping all of the default values selected. The "Summary" page will list the folders where the NetBeans IDE and the GlassFish application server will be installed. Finish the wizard by pressing the Install button, as shown in Figure 1-5.

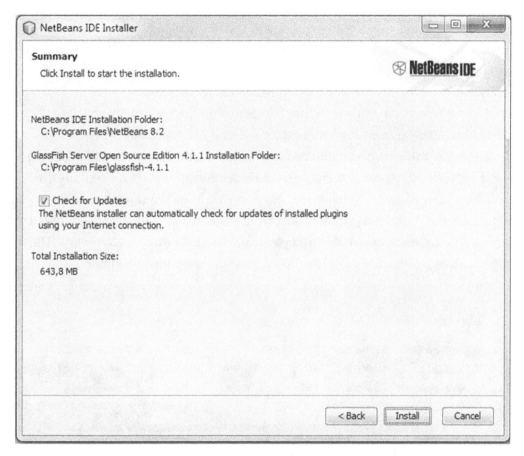

Figure 1-5. Installing the NetBeans IDE and GlassFish application server

After a successful installation, your NetBeans IDE and GlassFish application server will be ready for use. In the upcoming sections, we will show you how to create a simple NetBeans project and verify that the installed GlassFish server is functioning properly.

Testing the NetBeans IDE and GlassFish Installation

Assuming that all of the preceding steps have been executed successfully, you are ready to start the NetBeans IDE and the integrated GlassFish application server. We will also demonstrate a few simple tests to ensure that you are set to run the samples in this book.

Starting NetBeans IDE

The NetBeans IDE provides a graphical environment for creating, deploying, and executing Java EE applications. Administrative tasks like starting and shutting down the GlassFish server domains can also be performed using NetBeans.

Invoke NetBeans, either by selecting "NetBeans" in the Start Menu of your Windows 7 machine or running `C:\Program Files (x86)\NetBeans 8.2\bin\netbeans64.exe` from the command prompt. Note that the exact path will depend on the installation location that is mentioned in Figure 1-3, and for 32-bit systems the executable will be named `netbeans.exe`. If you are running Windows 8 or 10, then you need to press the "Windows" key and start typing "NetBeans." The Apps Search tool will search for the NetBeans executable that you can select to launch the NetBeans IDE.

The NetBeans IDE and GlassFish application server is shown in Figure 1-6.

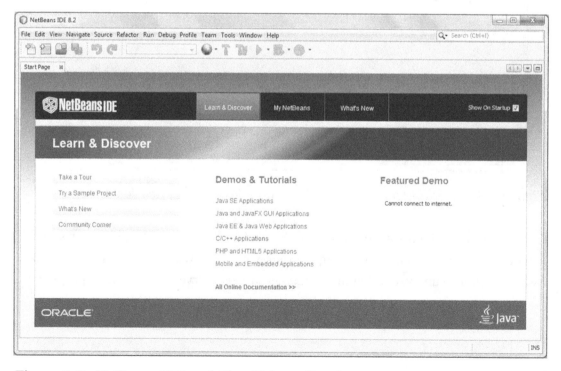

Figure 1-6. *NetBeans IDE and GlassFish application server*

Testing Using Sample Project

Once the NetBeans IDE has opened, we will create a sample project to test the compilation, deployment, and execution aspects of the IDE as well as the application server.

To create a new project, open the New Project wizard by pressing Ctrl-Shift-N. Select the Java Web category and the Web Application project, as shown in Figure 1-7. Traverse the wizard, keeping all of the default values selected, and Finish the wizard.

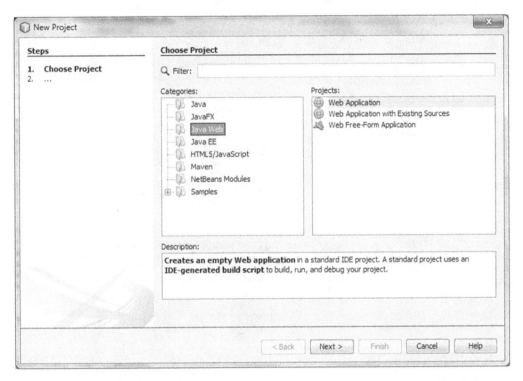

Figure 1-7. *Creating a sample test project*

Create a project named WebApplication1. Next we will create a servlet under the project WebApplication1. To create a servlet, invoke the context menu by right-clicking on the project name in the project navigator. Select the Servlet ... menu that is available under New, as shown in Figure 1-8.

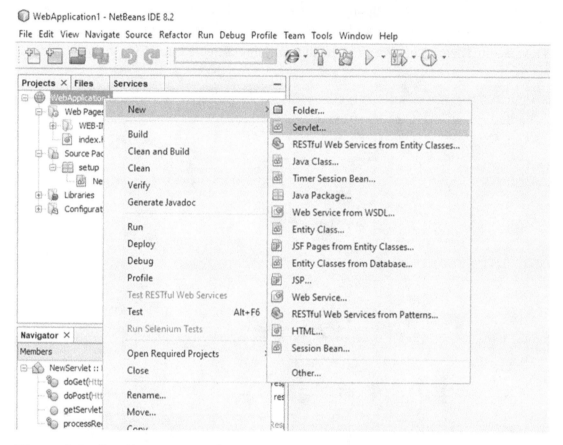

Figure 1-8. *Creating a test servlet*

In the New Servlet wizard, enter a package name and Finish the wizard keeping the other default values, as shown in Figure 1-9. We have used setup as the package name.

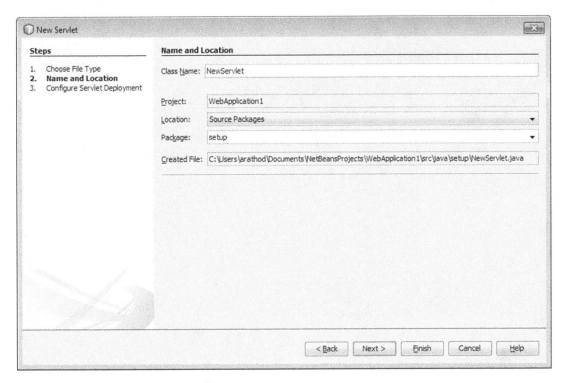

Figure 1-9. *Traversing the New Servlet wizard*

After the NewServlet class is created, we can instantly *run* it by invoking the context menu on the servlet file and selecting the Run File menu option, as shown in Figure 1-10.

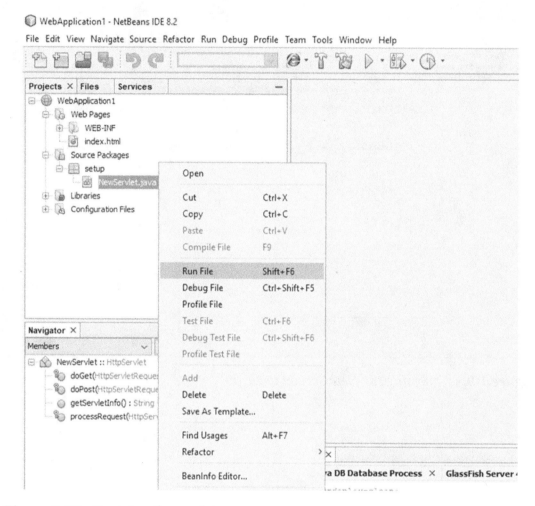

Figure 1-10. *Running the servlet*

When we *run* the servlet, NetBeans will automatically start the integrated GlassFish server.

As part of running the servlet, NetBeans will compile, package, and deploy it to the integrated GlassFish server. After the deployment, NetBeans will automatically open the servlet URL in the default browser, as shown in Figure 1-11.

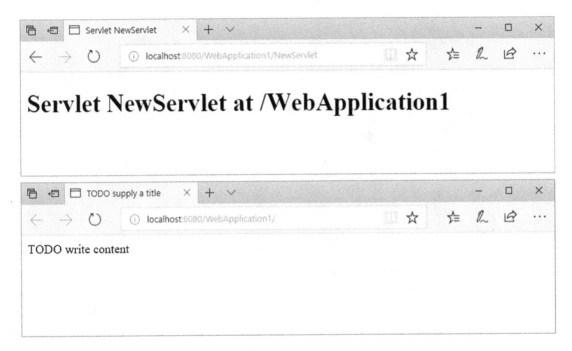

Figure 1-11. *Running the servlet class*

Successful execution of the servlet class means that the installation of NetBeans and the integrated GlassFish server have gone through successfully, and the setup to run the examples presented in this book is ready.

Note   By no means is this section of the chapter a user guide for the GlassFish application server. For more information on GlassFish, see `https://javaee.github.io/glassfish/`

Administrating the GlassFish Application Server

NetBeans provides us with a graphical interface to perform various GlassFish server-related administrative tasks. You can restart, start, and stop the GlassFish server from the Services tab, as shown in Figure 1-12.

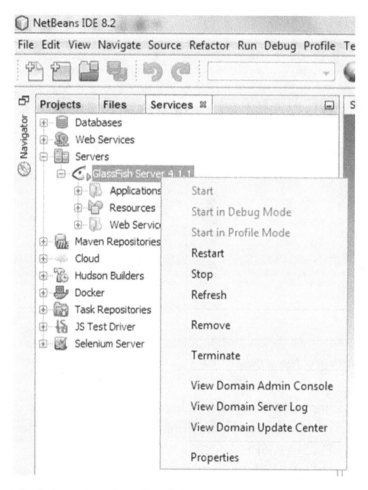

Figure 1-12. *Administrating the Glassfish application server*

Once GlassFish has successfully started, you can test whether the server is able to accept the basic HTTP requests. To do so, open a browser, type in the URL `http://localhost:8080/` and, if the server is up and running, you will be able to see the page shown in Figure 1-13.

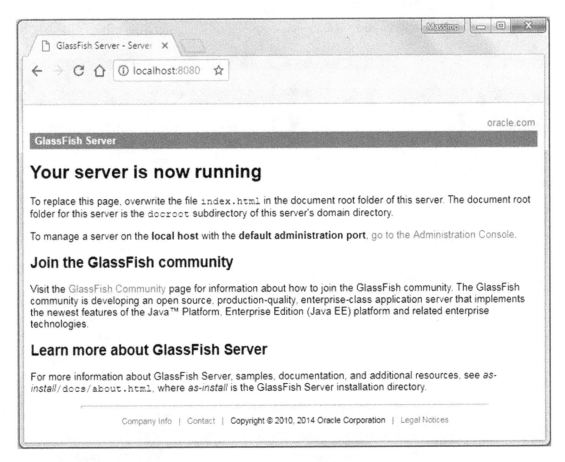

Figure 1-13. *Testing GlassFish server*

Note   Substitute `localhost` with the machine name or IP address if you are trying to access it from a machine other than the one on which GlassFish is installed. If you changed the port number during installation, use that port instead of 8080.

The next step is to test the access to the administration console of the GlassFish server. Make sure that the GlassFish server is up and running, and then select the View Domain Admin Console menu option from the context menu, as shown in Figure 1-12. NetBeans will launch the default browser and open the administrator console. Alternatively, you can type in the URL http://localhost:4848/, and you will be able to see the administration console page, as shown in Figure 1-14.

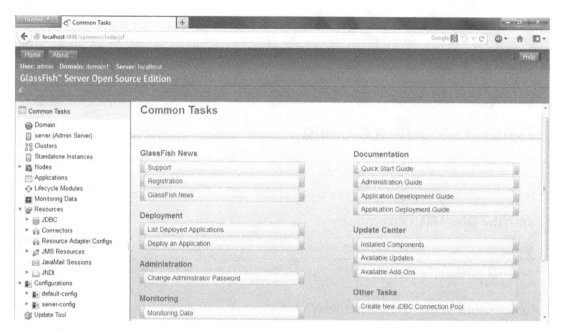

Figure 1-14. *The GlassFish administration console*

Note   Substitute localhost with the machine name or IP address if you are trying to gain access from a machine other than the one on which GlassFish is installed. You will have to enter the username and password on the administration console login page. If you changed the port number during installation, use that port instead of 4848.

Troubleshooting

Even after precisely following the steps mentioned in this chapter and taking the utmost care while installing and configuring the NetBeans IDE along with its integrated GlassFish application server, you may face problems while running the sample code that accompanies this book. This section will try to highlight issues that you may come across and provides information on how to mitigate them.

"No Compatible JDK was found" Warning During Installation

You get a "No compatible JDK was found" warning message on the first page of the NetBeans installer wizard.

Diagnosis

Samples in this book require NetBeans version 8.2 since we utilize Java EE 8. NetBeans 8.2, in turn, requires Java Platform (JDK) 8. You will get a "No compatible JDK was found" warning message if Java Platform (JDK) 8 is not installed on your machine.

Solution

You will have to exit the wizard and install Java Platform (JDK) 8 after downloading it from the following location:

```
http://www.oracle.com/technetwork/java/javase/downloads/index.html
```

Unable to See GlassFish Server's Test Page

You are unable to see the GlassFish server's test page as shown in Figure 1-13 after installing the NetBeans IDE and its integrated GlassFish application server.

Diagnosis

You may not able to see the test page because of the following reasons:

- GlassFish server is not running.

- Browser is unable to resolve the server's hostname.

- Incorrect port number is mentioned in the URL.

Solution

- Start/restart the GlassFish server using the context menu as shown in Figure 1-12.

- Verify that the machine name or the IP address that is used in the URL is correct. You can find your machine's IP address by executing the ipconfig command on your Windows machine's command prompt. If you are using localhost, then verify that the browser is able to resolve it by looping it back to your machine's IP address.

- Verify that the port number used in the URL is correct. This solution is explained in a section that follows.

Unable to Resolve "localhost" Hostname

Your browser or the NetBeans IDE's tester is able to run the GlassFish server's test page using the machine name or the IP address but is unable to resolve the localhost hostname.

Diagnosis

The NetBeans IDE's tester or the browser is unable to *loopback* to your machine using localhost.

Solution

Update the C:\Windows\System32\drivers\etc\hosts file of your Windows machine to add an entry that maps the IP address of your machine to localhost.

```
# localhost name resolution is handled within DNS itself.
# 127.0.0.1          localhost
# ::1                localhost
<IP address of your machine>    localhost
```

Browser is Unable to Connect to "8080" Port

The host name part of your URL is correct, but your browser is unable to connect to the GlassFish application server at port 8080.

Diagnosis

Your browser will be unable to use the 8080 port number for the GlassFish application server if it is used by another application. During installation the configuration tool will first try to assign the 8080 port to the GlassFish application server, but if it detects that the 8080 port number is unavailable, then it will assign a different port number to it.

Solution

You can find the port at which GlassFish application server is running with the following steps:

- Navigate to the Services tab of the NetBeans IDE and invoke the context menu on the GlassFish server node as shown in Figure 1-12.

- Select the Properties menu option to open the Servers dialog.

- Select the GlassFish server instance in the left panel.

- The Location text field, under the Common tab, will show the port number at which the GlassFish application server is running.

Errors While Compiling or Executing Sample Application Projects

You get compilation errors after opening the sample application project, or the sample application project does not execute as expected.

Diagnosis

The samples provided as part of this book are tested with NetBeans version 8.2 and Java Platform (JDK) 8.

You might get the "javac: invalid target release: 1.8" error while compiling the sample application projects provided with this book if the NetBeans IDE is not configured to use Java Platform (JDK) 8.

The sample application code contains *hard-coded* port numbers corresponding to the NetBeans installation on which they were created. The sample will not execute as expected if the port number hard-coded in the sample code is different from your NetBeans installation.

Solution

To resolve the "javac: invalid target release: 1.8" error, you have to verify that NetBeans is using Java Platform (JDK) 8. You may have to install it from the URL mentioned in the earlier sections.

If the sample application is not working as expected, then verify that the port numbers used by the sample code are same as that of your NetBeans installation.

You can consult the Readme.txt file provided with each sample application for additional information.

Unable to Send or Receive the "wine order" Mail

You are unable to send or receive the "wine order" mail while executing the sample application project.

Diagnosis

Few sample projects send out a mail as part of their execution. You may have trouble sending the mail and may not receive it because of the following reasons:

- You have not updated the from and to e-mail addresses in the sample code.

- You are running the sample on a machine that is behind a firewall.

- JMS Resource configuration is incorrect.

- JavaMail Session configuration is incorrect.

Solution

Before you execute the sample application project that sends out a mail, verify that:

- You have created and configured the JMS Resource as shown in Chapter 5.

- You have created and configured the JavaMail Session as shown in Chapter 5.

- You have updated the from and to e-mail addresses in the sample's source code.

- You are not behind a firewall.

You can consult the `Readme.txt` file provided with the sample application of Chapter 5 for information on how to configure `JavaMail Session` properties for popular mail services.

Even after verifying these details, if you are facing problems in sending or receiving the mail, then check the GlassFish server log for any more details on the issue.

Summary

This chapter opened with an introduction to this book and EJB. This orientation covered essential information about the core features of EJB, the EJB framework, and the component model. It included a brief overview of the history of EJB, the EJB 3 simplified development model, and the EJB distributed computing model.

In the "How This Book Is Organized" section, we provided a summary of each chapter to illustrate the general flow of the book, and to help you decide which areas to focus on first, should you wish to read the chapters out of sequence.

The chapter concluded with a "Getting Started" section to help you install and configure the NetBeans IDE and its integrated GlassFish application server, which has the reference implementation of the latest Java EE specifications; and to verify that the installation was successful. Having completed this task, you now have the required software infrastructure to run the code samples in this book and to examine the many features of EJB throughout the subsequent chapters. In the next chapter we will discuss in detail the EJB session beans.

CHAPTER 2

EJB Session Beans

This chapter will discuss EJB session beans, the core business service objects used by EJB client applications. You'll gain an understanding of the simplified EJB session bean model with insights into the following topics:

- Types of session beans—stateful, stateless, and singleton—and when to use each one

- The bean class, business interfaces, and business methods

- Asynchronous methods

- Callback methods

- Interceptors

- Exception handling

- Client view

- Dependency injection with annotations related to session beans

- Timer service

Introduction to Session Beans

Session beans are the most important part of EJB technology because they model the business process of the Java Application and encapsulate a business logic for each process.

Session beans are Java components that run either in stand-alone EJB containers or in EJB containers that are part of standard Java Platform, Enterprise Edition (Java EE) application servers. These Java components are typically used to model a particular user task or use case, such as entering customer information or implementing a process that maintains a conversation state with a client application. Session beans can hold the business logic for many types of applications, such as human resources, order entry,

© Jonathan Wetherbee, Massimo Nardone, Chirag Rathod, and Raghu Kodali 2018
J. Wetherbee et al., *Beginning EJB in Java EE 8*, https://doi.org/10.1007/978-1-4842-3573-7_2

and expense reporting applications. The EJB container provides services to the session bean, and the bean indicates which services it needs using Java annotations and/or XML metadata.

The container will manage the enterprise session beans and provide them with a number of services including security, transaction, thread-safety, etc.

Types of Session Beans

Session beans are of three types:

- *Stateless*: This type of bean does not maintain any conversational state on behalf of a client application.

- *Stateful*: This type of bean maintains a state, and a particular instance of the bean is associated with a specific client request. Stateful beans can be seen as extensions to client programs, which are running on the server.

- *Singleton*: This type of bean is instantiated only once per application. Singleton beans live for the full duration of the application and maintain their state between client invocations.

We will drill down into more specifics of stateless, stateful, and singleton beans in the following sections.

When Do You Use Session Beans?

Session beans are used to write business logic, maintain a conversation state for the client, and model back-end processes or user tasks that perform one or more business operations.

We want to consider using session beans, for instance, when we have a certain methodsor API that doesn't need the container service. In this case the session beans would overhead the container.

Also, Data Access Object (DAO) classes don't need to be session beans because they will be used in the EJB application service layer.

We will see in this book also how Stateless EJB session beans as (DAO), will be implemented with Java Persistence API (JPA).

Typical examples include the following:

- A session bean in a human resources application that creates a new employee and assigns the employee to a particular department

- A session bean in an expense reporting application that creates a new expense report

- A session bean in an order entry application that creates a new order for a particular customer

- A session bean that manages the contents of a shopping cart in an e-commerce application

- A session bean that leverages transaction services in an EJB container (removing the need for an application developer to write the transaction support)

- A session bean used to address deployment requirements when the client applications are not collocated on the same server

- A session bean that leverages the security support provided by the container on the component or method level

- A session bean that implements logging functionality and is shared between different components of an application

Session beans can be used in traditional 2-tier or 3-tier architectures with professional/rich client applications, or in 3-tier web-based applications. These applications can be deployed in different logical and physical tier combinations. In the next section, we will investigate some of the possible combinations.

3-Tier Architecture with Rich Client

Figure 2-1 shows a typical architecture for a session bean in three tiers with a rich client front-end application that has some data entry screens used by end users, such as customer service representatives, bank tellers, and so on. These client applications can be developed using Java Swing technology with the Java Platform, Standard Edition (Java SE), or they can be plain old Java objects (POJOs), which are run from the command line. Generally, the end user launches the client application from his or her desktop, enters some data, and triggers an event by pressing some user interface component, such as a Submit button. The general workflow may look something like this:

1. User action establishes a connection to the session bean running in the EJB container using remote method invocation (RMI).

2. The client application invokes one or more business methods in the session bean.

3. The session bean processes the request and validates data by interacting with databases, enterprise applications, legacy systems, and so on, to perform a certain business operation or task.

4. Finally, the session bean sends a response back to the client application, either through data collections or simple objects that contain acknowledgment messages.

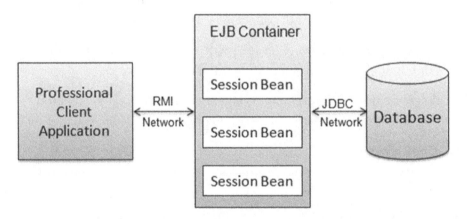

Figure 2-1. *Session beans in a 3-tier architecture with a Rich Client*

3-Tier Architecture for a Web Application

This architecture, as shown in Figure 2-2, is typically front ended by a web application running in the browser of a desktop or laptop computer. These days, other types of client devices, such as smartphones, tablets, cell phones, and telnet devices, are also being used to run these applications. The web application running in a browser or mobile device renders the user interface (data entry screens, submit buttons, and so on) using web technologies such as JavaServer Pages (JSP), JavaServer Faces (JSF), or Java Servlets. Typical user actions, such as entering search criteria or adding certain items to the web application shopping cart, will invoke/call session beans running in an EJB container via one of the aforementioned web technologies. Once the session bean gets invoked, it processes the request and sends a response back to the web application, which formats the response as required and then sends the response on to the requesting client device (browser, smartphone, telnet, and so forth).

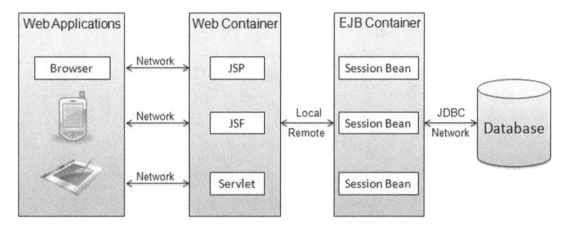

Figure 2-2. *Session beans in a 3-tier architecture with a web application*

In the 3-tier architecture just discussed, the client application (which is the web application) and the session beans can be run within the same instance of an application server (collocated) or from different instances running on the same machine. They can also be run on physically separate machines that have an instance of an application server.

Stateless Session Beans

Stateless session beans are comprised of the following elements:

- A bean class, which contains the business method implementation to be executed

Optionally, one or more business interfaces allow different combinations of the bean's business methods to be presented to client applications. A Stateless session beans pooling is a pool that contains all Stateless session beans instances. So, when a request arrives for a bean, the container allocates a bean, and the Stateless session bean method returns the bean placed back into the pool. If no bean is available for a request, it is placed in a queue.

Set Up the Dependencies

In order to use the Java EE8 Enterprise Beans 3.2, we want to make sure we will add the latest version to the dependencies configuration section of the pom.xml file, which will ensure that all Java EE 8 APIs will be available during the compiling time:

```
<dependency>
  <groupId>javax</groupId>
  <artifactId>javaee-web-api</artifactId>
  <version>8.0</version>
  <scope>compile</scope>
  <optional>true</optional>
</dependency>
```

You can check the Maven Repository to find the latest Java EE 8 APi pom.xml file:

```
https://search.maven.org/remotecontent?filepath=javax/javaee-api/8.0/
javaee-api-8.0.pom
```

The Bean Class

A stateless session bean class is any standard Java class that has a class-level annotation of @Stateless. If deployment descriptors are used instead of annotations, then the bean class should be denoted as a stateless session bean in the ejb-jar.xml descriptor. If you use both annotations and deployment descriptors (mixed mode), then the @Stateless annotation must be specified if any other class-level or member-level annotations are specified in the bean class. If both annotations and deployment descriptors are used, then the settings or values in the deployment descriptor will override the annotations in the classes during the deployment process.

Note   Starting with EJB 3.1, a session bean class can be a subclass of another session bean class.

To illustrate the use of stateless session beans, we will create a SearchFacade session bean that provides various search facilities to client applications regarding available wines. The workflow is as follows:

1. Users of the application will type in or choose one or more search criteria, which will be submitted to the SearchFacade session bean.

2. The SearchFacade bean will access back-end databases to retrieve the requested information. To simplify the code examples in this chapter, we will actually retrieve the list of hard-coded values within the bean class. In later chapters, we will augment the SearchFacade bean to access the back-end database.

3. The bean returns to the client applications the information that satisfied the search criteria.

Listing 2-1 shows the definition of the SearchFacade bean. In the following sections of this chapter, we will build the code that will show the preceding workflow in action. SearchFacadeBean is a standard Java class with a class-level annotation of @Stateless.

Listing 2-1. SearchFacadeBean.java

```
package com.apress.ejb.chapter02;
import javax.ejb.Stateless;
@Stateless(name="SearchFacade")
public class SearchFacadeBean implements SearchFacade, SearchFacadeLocal {
    public SearchFacadeBean() {
    }
}
```

The Business Interface

A stateless session business interface is a standard Java interface with no other special requirements. This interface has a list of business method definitions that will be available for the client application. A session bean can have a business interface that is implemented by the bean class; generated at design time by tools such as JDeveloper, NetBeans, or Eclipse; or generated at deployment time by the EJB container.

Business interfaces can also use annotations, as described in the following list:

- The @Remote annotation can be used to denote the remote business interface.

- The @Local annotation can be used to denote the local business interface.

Note   Starting with EJB 3.1, session beans support the "no-interface local view." This is a variation of the local view that exposes public methods of a bean class without a separate business interface.

If no annotation is specified in the interface, then the public methods of the bean class itself become its own *de facto* local interface.

If your architecture has a requirement whereby the client application (web application or rich client) has to run on a different Java Virtual Machine (JVM) from the one that is used to run the session beans in an EJB container, then you need to use the remote interface. Make sure that the methods in the interface remote are really supposed to be remotely exposed. The separate JVMs can be on the same physical machine or on separate machines. If your application architecture is going to use the same JVM for both the client application and the session beans, then performance is improved by using a local interface (which can be the no-interface option).

It is possible that your application architecture requires both remote and local interfaces. For example, an enterprise might have an order entry application that is developed using session beans that have business methods for submitting new orders and also addressing administrative tasks, such as data entry for the products. Potentially, you could have two different client applications that access the back-end order entry application, as follows:

- A web client application (as shown in Figure 2-3) that can be run in the same JVM as the session bean and used to submit new orders

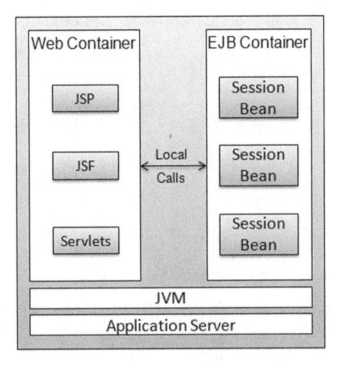

Figure 2-3. *A web client using local interfaces of session beans*

- A rich client application (as shown in Figure 2-4) that runs on an end-user desktop machine and is used by the administrator for data entry purposes

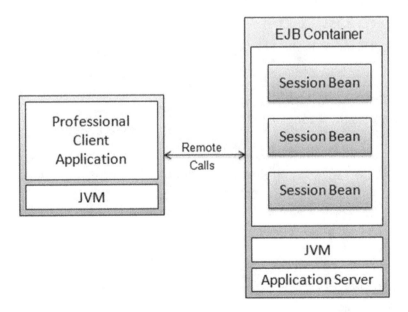

Figure 2-4. *A rich client using remote interfaces of session beans*

The SearchFacade session bean has both remote and local interfaces, as shown in Figure 2-5.

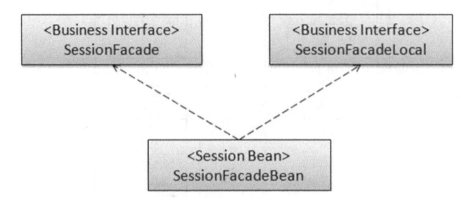

Figure 2-5. *The business interfaces of the SearchFacade session bean*

Listing 2-2 shows the code snippet for the SearchFacade remote business interface with an @Remote annotation and a wineSearch() method declaration. The wineSearch() method takes one parameter that represents the type of the wine, and it returns a list of wines that match the wine type criteria.

Listing 2-2. SearchFacade.java

```
package com.apress.ejb.chapter02;
import java.util.List;
import javax.ejb.Remote;

@Remote
public interface SearchFacade {
    List wineSearch(String wineType);
}
```

Listing 2-3 shows the code snippet for the SearchFacade local business interface with an @Local annotation and a wineSearch() method declaration.

Listing 2-3. SearchFacadeLocal.java

```
package com.apress.ejb.chapter02;
import java.util.List;
import javax.ejb.Local;
```

```
@Local
public interface SearchFacadeLocal {
    List wineSearch(String wineType);
}
```

Business Methods

The methods implemented in the bean class must correspond to the business methods declared in the remote or local business interfaces. They are matched up based on the convention that they have the same name and method signature. Other methods in the bean class that do not have the corresponding declaration in the business interfaces will be private to the bean class methods.

The SearchFacade bean implements one method, wineSearch(), which has been declared in both remote and local business interfaces. The wineSearch() method returns a static wines list based on the type of wine. Listing 2-4 shows the implementation for wineSearch().

Listing 2-4. SearchFacadeBean.java

```
package com.apress.ejb.chapter02;
import java.util.ArrayList;
import java.util.List;
import javax.ejb.Stateless;

@Stateless(name="SearchFacade")
public class SearchFacadeBean implements SearchFacade, SearchFacadeLocal {
    public SearchFacadeBean() {
    }

    public List wineSearch(String wineType) {
        List wineList = new ArrayList();
        if (wineType.equals("Red")) {
        wineList.add("Bordeaux");
        wineList.add("Merlot");
        wineList.add("Pinot Noir");
        }
```

```
        else if (wineType.equals("White")) {
        wineList.add("Chardonnay");
        }

        return wineList;
    }
}
```

Asynchronous Business Methods

Asynchronous methods immediately return to the caller without waiting for the method execution to complete. Asynchronous methods are typically used for processor-intensive or long-running, background tasks, such as printing a document or sending a large e-mail.

Starting with EJB 3.1, a session bean can declare that one or more of its methods can be executed asynchronously. When a session bean client invokes an asynchronous method, the container immediately returns the control to the client. This allows the client to perform tasks in parallel while the business method completes its execution on a separate thread. For example, clients can use this functionality to show the progress of a long-running task using a progress bar.

An asynchronous method is defined by annotating a business method with `javax.ejb.Asynchronous` annotation. An `@Asynchronous` annotation at the class level marks all the business methods of the session bean as asynchronous. An asynchronous method must return either `void` or an implementation of the `java.lang.concurrent.Future<V>` interface. Asynchronous methods that return `void` cannot throw application exceptions. Application exceptions can only be thrown by asynchronous methods that return `Future<V>`.

Asynchronous methods defined on a bean class should have the following signature:

```
public void <METHOD>(Object)
```

or

```
public java.util.concurrent.Future<V> <METHOD>(Object) throws <APPLICATION-EXCEPTION>
```

Session bean clients invoke asynchronous methods in the same way they invoke synchronous methods. If an asynchronous method has been defined to return a result, the client immediately receives an instance of Future<V> interface. A client can use this instance for any of the following operations:

- Retrieving the final result set using the get() method. Since this method call blocks synchronously until a result is returned or an exception is thrown, typically it is not called until isDone() returns true.

- Checking the status of the asynchronous method using the isDone() method.

- Cancelling the method invocation using cancel(boolean) method. Calling cancel() does not interrupt the thread, it simply sets a state flag that can be checked within the running method so that it may gracefully interrupt its execution and return.

- Checking if the method invocation was cancelled using isCancelled() method.

- Checking for exceptions.

Note   Session bean methods that are exposed as web services can't be asynchronous.

If an asynchronous method returns a result, it must return that result using the javax.ejb.AsyncResult<V> convenience wrapper object. Note that this object is not actually returned to the client but is intercepted by the EJB container and unwrapped to service method calls on the Future<V> object that was actually returned to the client when the client invoked the method.

Dependency Injection

In Chapter 1, we introduced the concept of dependency injection as a programming design pattern. In this section, we will take a cursory look into using dependency injection in stateless session beans. Dependency injection is discussed in detail in Chapter 10.

EJB containers provide the facilities to inject various types of resources into stateless session beans. Typically, in order to perform user tasks or process requests from client applications, the business methods in the session bean require one or more types of resources. These resources can be other session beans, data sources, or message queues. Managed beans can be injected into session beans using Contexts and Dependency Injection (CDI).

The resources that the stateless session bean is trying to use can be injected using annotations or deployment descriptors. Resources can be acquired by annotation of instance variables or annotation of the setter methods. Listing 2-5 shows an example of a setter and instance variable–based injection of myDb, which represents the data source.

Listing 2-5. Data Source Injection

```
@Resource
DataSource myDb;

// or
@Resource
public void setMyDb(DataSource myDb) {
    this.myDb = myDb;
}
```

You'll typically use the setter injections to preconfigure or initialize properties of the injected resource.

Lifecycle Callback Methods

There will be certain instances or use cases in which the application using session beans requires fine-grained control over lifecycle events like its own creation, removal, and so on. For example, the SearchFacade session bean might need to perform some database initialization when it is created or close some database connections when it is destroyed. The application can gain fine-grained control over the various stages of the bean life cycle via methods known as *callback methods*. A callback method can be any method in the session bean that has callback annotations. The EJB container calls these methods at the appropriate stages of the bean's life cycle (bean creation and destruction).

Following are two such callbacks for stateless session beans:

- PostConstruct: Denoted with the @PostConstruct annotation. Methods on the bean class that use a specific signature, as described below, can be marked with this annotation.

- PreDestroy: Denoted with the @PreDestroy annotation. Again, any method in the bean class with a specific signature, as described below, can be marked with this annotation.

Callback methods defined on a bean class should have the following signature:

```
void <METHOD>()
```

Callback methods can also be defined on a bean's listener class; these methods should have the following signature:

```
void <METHOD>(Object)
```

where Object may be declared as the actual bean type, which is the argument passed to the callback method at runtime. Lifecycle callback methods can have public, private, protected, or package-level access. A lifecycle callback method must not be declared as final or static.

PostConstruct callbacks happen after a bean instance is instantiated in the EJB container. If the bean is using any dependency injection mechanisms for acquiring references to resources or other objects in its environment, PostConstruct will occur after injection is performed and before the first business method in the bean class is called. In the case of the SearchFacade session bean, you could have a business method, wineSearchByCountry(), which would return the wine list for a particular country and have a PostConstruct callback method, initializeCountryWineList(), that would initialize the country's wine list whenever the bean gets instantiated. Ideally, you would load the list from a back-end datastore; but in this chapter, we will just use some hard-coded values that get populated into a HashMap, as shown in Listing 2-6.

Listing 2-6. The PostConstruct Method

```
@PostConstruct
public void initializeCountryWineList() {
    // countryMap is HashMap
    countryMap.put("Australia", "Sauvignon Blanc");
    countryMap.put("Australia", "Grenache");
```

```
    countryMap.put("France","Gewurztraminer");
    countryMap.put("France","Bordeaux");
}
```

The `PreDestroy` callback happens before the container destroys an unused or expired bean instance from its object pool. This callback can be used to close any connection pool that has been created with dependency injection and also to release any other resources.

In the case of the `SearchFacade` session bean, we could add a `PreDestroy` callback method (`destroyWineList()`) into the `SearchFacade` bean, which would clear the country wine list whenever the bean gets destroyed. Ideally, during `PreDestroy`, we would close any resources that have been created with dependency injection; but in this chapter, we will just clear the `HashMap` that has the countries and wine list. Listing 2-7 shows the `destroyWineList()` code.

Listing 2-7. The PreDestroy Method

```
@PreDestroy
public void destroyWineList() {
    countryMap.clear();
}
```

Interceptors

The EJB specification provides annotations called *interceptors*, which allow you to interpose on a business method invocation to add your own wrapper code before and/or after the method is called. An interceptor method can be defined for session and message-driven beans (MDBs). We will show you the usage of interceptors in the session bean context.

There are number of use cases for interceptors in a typical application in which you would find a need to perform a certain task before or after the business method is invoked. For example, you may wish to do one of the following:

- Perform additional security checks before a critical business method that transfers more than $100,000 dollars

- Do some performance analysis to compute the time it takes to perform the task

- Do additional logging before or after the method invocation

There are two ways to define an interceptor. You can either add an @AroundInvoke annotation on a particular method, or you can annotate the bean class to designate an interceptor class that will interpose on all (or an explicit subset of) methods on the bean class. An interceptor class is denoted by the @Interceptor annotation on the bean class with which it is associated. In the case of multiple interceptor classes, the @Interceptors annotation is used. Method specific interceptor is denoted by applying the @Interceptors annotation to the business method. Methods that are annotated with @AroundInvoke should have the following signature:

```
Object <METHOD>(InvocationContext) throws Exception
```

AroundInvoke methods can have public, private, protected, or package-level access. An AroundInvoke method must not be declared as final or static. The definition of InvocationContext is as follows:

```
package javax.ejb;
public interface InvocationContext {
    public Object getBean();
    public java.lang.reflect.Method getMethod();
    public Object[] getParameters();
    public void setParameters(Object[] params);
    public EJBContext getEJBContext();
    public java.util.Map getContextData();
    public Object proceed() throws Exception;
}
```

The following list describes the methods in the preceding code:

- getBean() returns the instance of the bean on which the method was called.

- getMethod() returns the method on the bean instance that was called.

- getParameters() returns the parameters for the method call.

- setParameters() modifies the parameters used for the method call.

- getEJBContext() gives the interceptor methods access to the bean's EJBContext.

- getContextData() allows values to be passed between interceptor methods in the same InvocationContext instance using the Map returned.

- proceed() invokes the next interceptor, if there is one, or invokes the target bean method.

In the SearchFacade session bean, we can add an interceptor that logs the time taken to execute each business method when invoked by the client applications. Listing 2-8 shows a time log method that will print out the time taken to execute a business method. InvocationContext is used to get the name of bean class and the invoked method name. Before invoking the business method, current system time is captured and deducted from the system time after the business method is executed. Finally, the details are printed out to the console log using System.out.println.

Listing 2-8. The Interceptor Method

```
@AroundInvoke
public Object TimerLog (InvocationContext ctx) throws Exception {
    String beanClassName = ctx.getClass().getName();
    String businessMethodName = ctx.getMethod().getName();
    String target = beanClassName + "." + businessMethodName ;
    long startTime = System.currentTimeMillis();
    System.out.println ("Invoking " + target);
    try {
        return ctx.proceed();
    }
    finally {
        System.out.println ("Exiting" + target);
        long totalTime = System.currentTimeMillis() - startTime;
        System.out.println ("Business method" + businessMethodName +
        "in" + beanClassName + "takes" + totalTime + "ms to execute");
    }
}
```

Stateful Session Beans

Similar to stateless session beans, stateful beans comprise a bean class and, optionally, one or more business interfaces.

The Bean Class

A stateful session bean class is any standard Java class that has a class-level annotation of @Stateful. If deployment descriptors are used instead of annotations, the bean class should be denoted as a stateful session bean. In the case of mixed mode, in which you are using annotations *and* deployment descriptors, the @Stateful annotation must be specified if any other class-level or member-level annotations are specified in the class.

To illustrate a stateful session bean, we will create a ShoppingCart session bean that will keep track of the items added to a user's shopping cart and their respective quantities. In this chapter, we will use hard-coded values for the shopping cart to illustrate the state and conversation maintenance between the client and stateful session bean. Listing 2-9 shows the definition of a ShoppingCart session bean.

Listing 2-9. ShoppingCartBean.java

```
package com.apress.ejb.chapter02;
import javax.ejb.Stateful;
@Stateful(name="ShoppingCart")
public class ShoppingCartBean implements ShoppingCart, ShoppingCartLocal {
    public ShoppingCartBean() {
    }
}
```

There will be certain use cases in which the application wants to be notified by the EJB container before or after transactions take place and then use these notifications to manage data and cache. A stateful session bean can receive this kind of notification by the EJB container when it implements the javax.ejb.SessionSynchronization interface. This is an optional feature. There are three different types of transaction notifications that the stateful session bean receives from the EJB container:

- `afterBegin`: Indicates that a new transaction has begun

- `beforeCompletion`: Indicates that the transaction is going to be committed

- `afterCompletion`: Indicates that a transaction has been completed

For example, the `ShoppingCart` session bean could implement the `javax.ejb.SessionSynchronization` interface to get an `afterCompletion` notification so that it can clear out the shopping cart cache.

The Business Interface

Business interfaces for stateful session beans are similar to those used for stateless session beans, and they are annotated in the same way, using `@Local` and `@Remote` annotations. Local views of stateful session beans can be accessed without a separate local business interface. The `ShoppingCart` session bean has both remote and local interfaces, as shown in Figure 2-6.

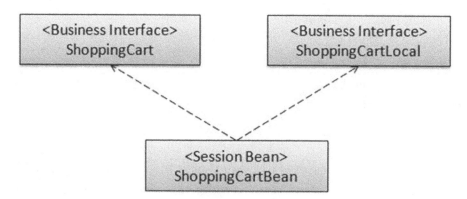

Figure 2-6. *Business interfaces for ShoppingCart*

We will primarily use the local interface from our web application. The remote interface is added to facilitate unit testing of the bean in this chapter.

Listings 2-10 and 2-11 show the remote and local `ShoppingCart` business interfaces, with `@Remote` and `@Local` annotations, respectively.

Listing 2-10. ShoppingCart.java

```
package com.apress.ejb.chapter02;
import javax.ejb.Remote;
@Remote
public interface ShoppingCart {
}
```

Listing 2-11. ShoppingCartLocal.java

```
package com.apress.ejb.chapter02;
import javax.ejb.Local;
@Local
public interface ShoppingCartLocal {
}
```

Alternatively, you can use the coding style shown in Listing 2-12, in which you can specify the @Local and @Remote annotations before specifying @Stateful or @Stateless with the name of the business interface.

Listing 2-12. ShoppingCartBean.java

```
package com.apress.ejb.chapter02;
import javax.ejb.Local;
import javax.ejb.Remote;
import javax.ejb.Stateful;

@Local({ShoppingCartLocal.class})
@Remote({ShoppingCart.class})
@Stateful(name="ShoppingCart")

public class ShoppingCartBean implements ShoppingCart, ShoppingCartLocal {
    public ShoppingCartBean() {
    }
}
```

Note   We will follow the earlier convention in this book, in which @Local and @Remote annotations are marked on the business interfaces.

Business Methods

Business methods in stateful session beans are similar to those in stateless session beans. We will augment the ShoppingCart bean by adding business methods that will add and remove wines from the shopping cart and return a list of cart items.

Listing 2-13 shows the ShoppingCart bean implementing the addWineItem(), removeWineItem(), and getCartItems() methods.

Listing 2-13. ShoppingCartBean.java

```java
package com.apress.ejb.chapter02;
import java.util.ArrayList;
import javax.ejb.Stateful;

@Stateful(name="ShoppingCart")
public class ShoppingCartBean implements ShoppingCart, ShoppingCartLocal {
    public ShoppingCartBean() {
    }
    public ArrayList cartItems;
    public void addWineItem(String wine) {
        cartItems.add(wine);
    }

    public void removeWineItem(String wine) {
        cartItems.remove(wine);
    }

    public void setCartItems(ArrayList cartItems) {
        this.cartItems = cartItems;
    }

    public ArrayList getCartItems() {
        return cartItems;
    }
}
```

Lifecycle Callback Methods

Stateful session beans support callback events for construction, destruction, activation, and passivation. Following are the callbacks that map to the preceding events:

- PostConstruct: Denoted with the @PostConstruct annotation.

- PreDestroy: Denoted with the @PreDestroy annotation.

- PreActivate: Denoted with the @PreActivate annotation.

- PrePassivate: Denoted with the @PrePassivate annotation.

The PostConstruct callback happens after a bean instance is instantiated in the EJB container. If the bean is using any dependency injection mechanism for acquiring references to resources or other objects in its environment, the PostConstruct event happens after injection is performed and before the first business method in the bean class is called.

In the case of the ShoppingCart session bean, we could have a business method called initialize() that initializes the cartItems list, as shown in Listing 2-14.

Listing 2-14. The PostConstruct Method

```
@PostConstruct
public void initialize() {
    cartItems = new ArrayList();
}
```

The PreDestroy callback happens after any method where an @Remove annotation has been completed. In the case of the ShoppingCart session bean, we could have a business method called exit() that writes the cartItems list into a database. In this chapter, we will just print out a message to the system console to illustrate the callback. Listing 2-15 shows the code for the exit() method, which has the @PreDestroy annotation.

Listing 2-15. The PreDestroy Method

```
@PreDestroy
public void exit() {
    // items list into the database.
    System.out.println("Saved items list into database");
}
```

The @Remove annotation is a useful lifecycle method for stateful session beans. When the method with the @Remove annotation is called, the container will remove the bean instance from the object pool after the method is executed. Listing 2-16 shows the code for the stopSession() method, which has the @Remove annotation.

Listing 2-16. The Remove Method

```
@Remove
public void stopSession() {
    // The method body can be empty.
    System.out.println("From stopSession method with @Remove annotation");
}
```

The PrePassivate callback kicks in when a stateful session bean instance is idle for too long. During this event, the container might passivate and store its state to a cache. The method tagged with @PrePassivate is called before the container passivates the bean instance.

The PostActivate event gets raised when the client application again uses a passivated stateful session bean. A new instance with restored state is created. The method with the @PostActivate annotation is called when the bean instance is ready.

Interceptors

There are some minor differences between interceptors for stateless and stateful session beans. AroundInvoke methods can be used with stateful session beans. For stateful session beans that implement SessionSynchronization, afterBegin occurs before any methods that have AroundInvoke annotations and before the beforeCompletion() callback method.

Exception Handling

The EJB specification outlines two types of exceptions:

- Application exceptions
- System exceptions

Application exceptions are exceptions related to execution of business logic that the client should handle. For example, an application exception might be raised if the client application passes an invalid argument, such as the wrong credit card number.

System exceptions, on the other hand, are caused by system-level faults, such as Java Naming and Directory Interface (JNDI) errors or failure to acquire a database connection. A system exception must be a subclass of a `java.rmi.RemoteException` or a subclass of a `java.lang.RuntimeException` that is not an application exception.

From the EJB application point of view, application exceptions are completed by writing application-specific exception classes that subclass the `java.lang.Exception` class.

In the case of a system exception, the application catches particular exceptions, such as a `NamingException` that results from a JNDI failure, and throws an `EJBException`. In this chapter, the examples aren't using any resources as such, but there are more examples of system exceptions in the later chapters.

Singleton Session Beans

Introduced in EJB 3.1, a *singleton session bean* is a session bean component that is instantiated only once per application. For an application, only one instance of a singleton session bean can ever exist. Once instantiated, a singleton session bean lives for the full duration of the application. The singleton session bean maintains its state between client invocations, but it cannot save that state after a container shutdown or crash. Similar to stateless and stateful session beans, the singleton session bean is comprised of a bean class and, optionally, one or more business interfaces.

The Bean Class

A singleton session bean class is any standard Java class that has a class-level annotation of `@Singleton`. If deployment descriptors are used instead of annotations, the bean class should be denoted as a singleton session bean. If you are using annotations and deployment descriptors (mixed mode), then the `@Singleton` annotation must be specified if any other class-level or member-level annotations are specified in the class.

Note   Singleton can be initialized when called for the first time or on deployment using the annotation "@Startup."

To illustrate a singleton session bean, we will create a ShopperCount session bean that will keep track of the number of users logged onto our shopping website. Listing 2-17 shows the definition of the ShopperCount session bean.

Listing 2-17. ShopperCountBean.java

```
package com.apress.ejb.chapter02;

import javax.ejb.Singleton;
import javax.ejb.Startup;
@Singleton (name = "ShopperCount")
@Startup
public class ShopperCountBean {
    private int shopperCounter;

    // Increment number of shopper counter
    public void incrementShopperCount() {
        shopperCounter++;
    }

    // Return number of shoppers
    public int getShopperCount() {
        return shopperCounter;
    }
}
```

A singleton session bean is instantiated at the discretion of the EJB container. However, you can annotate the bean class with @Startup to indicate that the container must initialize the singleton bean during the application startup sequence.

When multiple singleton session beans are used within an application, the application might require that they be initialized in a specific sequence. @DependsOn annotation declares the startup dependencies of a singleton session bean. Listing 2-18 shows the definition of the LogShopperCount session bean that is dependent on the ShopperCount session bean.

Listing 2-18. LogShopperCount.java

```
package com.apress.ejb.chapter02;

import javax.ejb.Singleton;
import javax.ejb.Startup;
import javax.ejb.DependsOn;
import java.util.logging.Logger;

@Singleton
@Startup
@DependsOn("ShopperCount")
public class LogShopperCount {
    private final Logger log = Logger.getLogger("LogShopperCount.class");

    public void logShopperCount() {
        // Log shopper count
    }
}
```

Unlike stateless and stateful session beans, a singleton session bean must not implement the `javax.ejb.SessionSynchronization` interface or use session synchronization annotations.

The Business Interface

Business interfaces for singleton session beans are similar to the interfaces for stateless and stateful session beans, and they are annotated in the same way using `@Local` and `@Remote` annotations. Singleton session beans support the no-interface local view, making the declaration of a business interface optional for a local view.

Business Methods

Business methods in singleton session beans are similar to the methods in stateless and stateful session beans. We will augment the `ShopperCount` bean by adding a business method that will reset the counter.

Listing 2-19 shows the ShopperCount bean implementing business methods.

Listing 2-19. ShopperCountBean.java

```java
package com.apress.ejb.chapter02;

import javax.ejb.Singleton;
import javax.ejb.Startup;

@Singleton(name = "ShopperCount")
@Startup
public class ShopperCountBean {
    private int shopperCounter = 0;

    // Increment number of shopper counter
    public void incrementShopperCount() {
        shopperCounter++;
    }

    // Return number of shoppers
    public int getShopperCount() {
        return shopperCounter;
    }

    // Reset counter
    public void resetCounter() {
        shopperCounter = 0;
    }
}
```

Lifecycle Callback Methods

Singleton life cycle goes so that we will create the singleton session bean instance and then after inject the container; it will be put the instance in a managed pool named "method-ready" waiting for a request.

Singleton session beans support callback events for construction and destruction. Following are the callbacks that map to the preceding events:

- PostConstruct: Denoted with the @PostConstruct annotation

- PreDestroy: Denoted with the @PreDestroy annotation.

PostConstruct callback happens after a bean instance is instantiated in the EJB container. If the bean is using any dependency injection mechanism for acquiring references to resources or other objects in its environment, the PostConstruct event happens after injection is performed and before the first business method in the bean class is called.

PreDestroy callback happens during application shutdown. The container considers the DependsOn relationship between singleton session beans and removes them in a sequence that is in the reverse order of the sequence in which they were created. For the ShopperCount example, LogShopperCount bean will be removed before the ShopperCount bean.

Listing 2-20 shows the code for the applicationStartup() method with the @PostConstruct annotation. This method resets the shopperCounter on startup. Listing 2-20 also shows the code for the applicationShutdown() method with the @PreDestroy annotation. This method prints a message on application shutdown.

Listing 2-20. ShopperCountBean.java

```java
package com.apress.ejb.chapter02;

import javax.annotation.PostConstruct;
import javax.annotation.PreDestroy;
import javax.ejb.Singleton;
import javax.ejb.Startup;

@Singleton(name = "ShopperCount")
@Startup
public class ShopperCountBean {
    private int shopperCounter;

    // Increment number of shopper counter
    public void incrementShopperCount() {
        shopperCounter++;
    }

    // Return number of shoppers
    public int getShopperCount() {
        return shopperCounter;
    }
```

```
// Reset counter
public void resetCounter() {
    shopperCounter = 0;
}

// Reset counter
@PostConstruct
public void applicationStartup() {
    System.out.println("From applicationStartup method.");
    resetCounter();
}

@PreDestroy
public void applicationShutdown() {
    System.out.println("From applicationShutdown method.");
}
}
```

Like a stateless session bean, a singleton session bean is never passivated, so the @PrePassivate and @PostActivate annotations should not be used to decorate methods on a singleton session bean.

Concurrency Management

A singleton session bean is instantiated only once per application, and hence it is designed to support concurrent access. Concurrent access means multiple clients can access the same instance of a singleton session bean at the same time. The management of concurrent access is transparent to the clients. A client needs only a reference to a singleton session bean, and it is unconcerned about other clients accessing the same instance of the singleton session bean.

Concurrency is managed in two ways:

- **Container-Managed concurrency:** The container controls concurrent access and allows fine-grained control of the state synchronization behavior by offering a fixed set of options. This is the default concurrency management type.

- **Bean-Managed concurrency:** The container allows full access to the concurrent bean instance, and the user is responsible for state synchronization.

The type of concurrency—container-managed or bean-managed—is specified by the javax.ejb.ConcurrencyManagement annotation specified on the singleton session bean class. For container-managed concurrency, the type attribute of @ConcurrencyManagement is set to javax.ejb.ConcurrencyManagementType.CONTAINER; for bean-managed concurrency, the type attribute of @ConcurrencyManagement is set to javax.ejb.ConcurrencyManagementType.BEAN.

Container-Managed Concurrency

For a singleton session bean using container-managed concurrency, the container manages concurrency by associating each business method with either a shared Read lock or an exclusive Write lock. A Read or Write lock is specified using the @Lock annotation.

Listing 2-21 demonstrates container-managed concurrency by using the Read lock on the getShopperCount method and Write lock on the incrementShopperCount method. With this change, multiple clients can get the value of shopperCounter concurrently, but access to incrementShopperCount is blocked for all other clients while one client is accessing it.

Listing 2-21. ShopperCountBean.java

```
package com.apress.ejb.chapter02;

import javax.annotation.PostConstruct;
import javax.annotation.PreDestroy;
import javax.ejb.ConcurrencyManagement;
import javax.ejb.ConcurrencyManagementType;
import javax.ejb.Lock;
import javax.ejb.LockType;
import javax.ejb.Singleton;
import javax.ejb.Startup;
```

```java
@Singleton(name = "ShopperCount")
@Startup
@ConcurrencyManagement(ConcurrencyManagementType.CONTAINER)
public class ShopperCountBean {
    private int shopperCounter;
    // Increment number of shopper counter
    @Lock(LockType.WRITE)
    public void incrementShopperCount() {
        shopperCounter++;
    }

    // Return number of shoppers
    @Lock(LockType.READ)
    public int getShopperCount() {
        return shopperCounter;
    }

    // Reset counter
    public void resetCounter() {
        shopperCounter = 0;
    }

    // Reset counter
    @PostConstruct
    public void applicationStartup() {
        resetCounter();
    }

    @PreDestroy
    public void applicationShutdown() {
        System.out.println("From applicationShutdown method.");
    }
}
```

For a singleton session bean, an @Lock annotation at the class level specifies that all business methods will use the specified lock type unless a different type is explicitly set at the method level. When the @Lock annotation is not explicitly present on the singleton session bean class, the default lock type, @Lock(LockType.WRITE), is applied to all business methods.

Bean-Managed Concurrency

In the case of bean-managed concurrency, the container allows full concurrent access to the singleton session bean instance, and the bean developer must provide protection to the bean's internal state against synchronization errors that result from concurrent access. You can use synchronization primitives like `synchronized` and `volatile` for this purpose.

Error Handling

Errors can occur during initialization of a singleton session bean. These errors are fatal and, as a result, the singleton session bean instance must be discarded. Attempted invocations on a singleton session bean instance that failed to initialize will result in the `javax.ejb.NoSuchEJBException`. Once a singleton session bean is instantiated successfully, it will not be destroyed if exceptions are thrown from either business methods or callbacks.

Timer Service

The *EJB Timer Service* is a container-managed service that allows callbacks to be scheduled for time-based events. Timer notifications can be scheduled to occur at a calendar-based schedule, at a specific time, after a specific time, or at specific recurring intervals.

Remember that Enterprise bean timers are either programmatic timers or automatic timers.

Use timers for application-level processes. Don't use timers for real-time events. Typical examples of using a timer include the following:

- A timer in an expense reporting application prints newly filed expenses every evening at 9 PM.

- A timer in a bug tracking application emails a list of open bugs to team members every morning at 6 AM.

- A timer in a human resources application emails a list of public holidays to all the employees on the 1st of January every year.

Note   The timer service of the enterprise bean can be used to enable scheduling timed notifications for all types of enterprise beans except for stateful session beans.

As we just said Enterprise bean timers are either programmatic timers or automatic timers. The programmatic timers can be set by explicitly calling one of the timer creation methods of the TimerService interface, while the automatic timers are created by deploying an enterprise bean that contains a method annotated with the javax.ejb. Schedule or javax.ejb.Schedules annotations.

Creating a timer is simplified in EJB 3.1 via introduction of @Schedule and @Schedules annotations that automatically create timers based on metadata specified on a method. In Listing 2-22, we augment our LogShopperCount by adding a recurring timer that will log the shopper count every two hours.

Listing 2-22. LogShopperCount.java

```
package com.apress.ejb.chapter02;

import javax.ejb.DependsOn;
import javax.ejb.Schedule;
import javax.ejb.Singleton;
import javax.ejb.Startup;

@Singleton
@Startup
@DependsOn("ShopperCountBean")
public class LogShopperCount {

        // Logs shopper count every 2 hours
        @Schedule(hour="*/2")
        public void logShopperCount() {
        // Log shopper count
        }
}
```

Pass the `Timer` object in methods annotated with `@Schedule` to get information about the timer. Listing 2-23 demonstrates the use of the `Timer` object to get information about the timer that just expired.

Listing 2-23. LogShopperCount.java

```java
package com.apress.ejb.chapter02;

import javax.ejb.DependsOn;
import javax.ejb.Schedule;
import javax.ejb.Singleton;
import javax.ejb.Startup;
import javax.ejb.Timer;

@Singleton
@Startup
@DependsOn("ShopperCount")
public class LogShopperCount {

// Logs shopper count every 2 hours
@Schedule(hour="*/2")
public void logShopperCount(Timer timer) {
// Log shopper count
String timerInfo = (String) timer.getInfo();
System.out.println(timerInfo);
}
}
```

Calendar-Based Time Expressions

The Timer Service is inspired by the UNIX cron utility. Table 2-1 lists the various attributes of a calendar-based time expression.

Table 2-1. Attributes of calendar-based time expression

Attribute	Description	Allowable Values	Default
second	One or more seconds within a minute	[0, 59]	0
minute	One or more minutes within an hour	[0, 59]	0
hour	One or more hours within a day	[0, 23]	0
dayOfMonth	One or more days within a month	[1, 31] or [−7, -1] or "Last" or {1st, 2nd, 3rd, 4th, 5th, "Last"} {"Sun", "Mon", "Tue", "Wed", "Thu", "Fri", "Sat"}	*
month	One or more months within a year	[1, 12] or {"Jan", "Feb", "Mar", "Apr", "May", "Jun", "Jul", "Aug", "Sep", "Oct", "Nov", "Dec"}	*
dayOfWeek	One or more days within a week	[0, 7] or {"Sun", "Mon", "Tue", "Wed", "Thu", "Fri", "Sat"}	*
year	A particular calendar year	4-digit calendar year	*

Note   For dayOfWeek, both 0 and 7 represent Sunday and a negative number (−7 to −1), which means the nth day or days before the end of the month. All string constants ("Sun", "Jan", "Last", "1st") are case insensitive. Increments are supported only by second, minute, and hour. Duplicate values within a list are ignored.

Examples of Calendar-Based Time Expressions

Let us see some examples that demonstrate the use of calendar-based time expressions.

- "Every second of every minute of every hour of everyday"

  - @Schedule(second="*", minute="*", hour="*")

- "Every fifteen minutes within the hour"

    - `@Schedule(minute="*/15", hour="*")`

    - `@Schedule(minute="0, 15, 30, 45", hour="*")`

- "Every Friday at midnight"

    - `@Schedule(dayOfWeek="Fri")`

- "Every six hours on weekends"

    - `@Schedule(hour="*/6", dayOfWeek="Sat, Sun")`

- "Every weekday morning at 7:30am U.S. Pacific Time"

    - `@Schedule(minute="30", hour="7", dayOfWeek="Mon-Fri", timezone="America/Los_Angeles")`

- "On 10th of January and September at 6am"

    - `@Schedule(month="Jan, Sep", dayOfMonth="10", hour="6")`

- "Last Friday of December at 6pm"

    - `@Schedule(month="Dec", dayOfMonth="Last Fri", hour="18")`

- "Second to last day (one day before the last day) of each month"

    - `@Schedule(dayOfMonth="-1")`

- "Every day only for year 2013"

    - `@Schedule(year="2013")`

Timer Persistence

Timers are persistent. A timer is persisted by the Timer Service by storing it in a database. The database used by the Timer Service can be changed by setting the Timer Service's Timer DataSource setting to a valid JDBC resource. Persistence helps timers survive application shutdown, container crashes, and container shutdowns.

Persistence can be disabled on a per-timer basis by setting the persistent attribute of the @Schedule annotation to false. A non-persistent timer's lifetime is associated with the JVM that created it. A non-persistent timer is considered cancelled in the event of application shutdown, container crash, or crash/shutdown of the JVM on which the timer was created.

Client View for Session Beans

A session bean can be seen as a logical extension of a client program or application, where much of the logic and data processing for that application happens. A client application typically accesses the session object through the session bean's client view interfaces. These are the business interfaces that were discussed in earlier sections.

A client application that accesses session beans can be one of three types:

- *Remote*: Remote clients run in a separate JVM from the session beans that they access, as shown in Figure 2-4. A remote client accesses a session bean through the bean's remote business interface. A remote client can be another EJB, a Java client program, or a Java servlet. Remote clients have location independence, meaning that they can use the same API as the clients running in the same JVM.

- *Local*: Local clients run in the same JVM, as shown in Figure 2-3, and access the session bean through the local business interface. A local client can be another EJB, or a web application using Java Servlets, JavaServer Pages (JSP), or JavaServer Faces (JSF). Local clients are location dependent. Remote and local clients are compared in Table 2-2.

Table 2-2. *Considerations for Choosing Between Local and Remote Clients*

Remote	Local
Loose coupling between the bean and the client	Lightweight access to a component
Location independence	Location dependence
Expensive remote calls	Must be collocated with the bean
Objects must be serialized	Not required
Objects are passed by value	Objects are passed by reference

- *Web Services*: You can publish stateless session beans as web services that can be invoked by Web Services clients. We will discuss Web Services and clients in Chapter 6.

In some cases, the session beans need to have both local and remote business interfaces to support different types of client applications. A client can obtain a session bean's business interface via dependency injection or JNDI lookup. Before invoking the methods in the session bean, the client needs to obtain a stub object of the bean via JNDI. Once the client has a handle to the stub object, it can call the business methods in the session bean. In the case of a stateless session bean, a new stub can be obtained on every invocation. In the case of a stateful session bean, the stub needs to be cached on the client side so that the container knows which instance of the bean to return on subsequent calls. Using dependency injection, we can obtain the business interface of the SearchFacade session bean with the following code:

```
@EJB SearchFacade searchFacade;
```

If the client accessing the session bean is remote, the client can use JNDI lookup once the context interface has been obtained with the right environment properties. Local clients can also use JNDI lookup, but dependency injection results in simpler code. Listing 2-24 shows the SearchFacadeTest client program's code that looks up the SearchFacade bean, invokes the wineSearch() business method, and prints out the returned list of wines. SearchFacadeClient also looks up the ShopperCount singleton bean and invokes the getShopperCount() business method to print the number of shoppers logged.

Note If the remote client is a Java application or command-line program, an application client container can be used to invoke the session beans. Application client containers support dependency injection for remote clients. We will discuss application client containers in Chapter 12, along with other types of client applications.

Listing 2-24. SearchFacadeClient.java

```
package com.apress.ejb.chapter02;
import java.io.IOException;
import java.io.PrintWriter;
import java.util.List;
import javax.ejb.EJB;
```

```
import javax.servlet.ServletException;
import javax.servlet.annotation.WebServlet;
import javax.servlet.http.HttpServlet;
import javax.servlet.http.HttpServletRequest;
import javax.servlet.http.HttpServletResponse;

@WebServlet(name = "SearchFacadeClient", urlPatterns = {
"/SearchFacadeClient"})
public class SearchFacadeClient extends HttpServlet {

    @EJB
    SearchFacadeBean searchFacade;

    @EJB
    ShopperCountBean shopperCount;
    protected void processRequest(HttpServletRequest request,
    HttpServletResponse response)
            throws ServletException, IOException {
        response.setContentType("text/html;charset=UTF-8");
        PrintWriter out = response.getWriter();
        try {

            out.println("<html>");
            out.println("<head>");
            out.println("<title>Servlet SearchFacadeClient</title>");
            out.println("</head>");
            out.println("<body>");
            out.println("<h1> Starting Search Facade test ... </h1>");

            out.println("<h1>SearchFacade Lookup</h1>");
            out.println("<h1>Searching wines</h1>");
            List winesList = searchFacade.wineSearch("Red");
            out.println("<h1>Printing wines list</h1>");
            for (String wine:(List<String>)winesList ){
                out.println("<h1>" + wine + "</h1>");
            }
```

```
            System.out.println("Printing Shopper Count after
            incrementing it ...");
            shopperCount.incrementShopperCount();
            out.println("<h1>" + shopperCount.getShopperCount() + "</h1>");

            out.println("</body>");
            out.println("</html>");
        } finally {
            out.close();
        }
    }

    @Override
    protected void doGet(HttpServletRequest request, HttpServletResponse
    response)
            throws ServletException, IOException {
        processRequest(request, response);
    }

    @Override
    protected void doPost(HttpServletRequest request, HttpServletResponse
    response)
            throws ServletException, IOException {
        processRequest(request, response);
    }

    @Override
    public String getServletInfo() {
        return "Short description";
    }
}
```

Listing 2-25 shows the ShoppingCartClient servlet, which looks up the stateful ShoppingCart session bean, calls the addWineItem() business method to add a wine to the shopping cart, calls the getCartItems() business method to get the items in the cart, and finally prints the list of wines in the shopping cart.

Listing 2-25. ShoppingCartClient.java

```java
package com.apress.ejb.chapter02;
import java.io.IOException;
import java.io.PrintWriter;
import java.util.ArrayList;
import java.util.List;
import javax.ejb.EJB;
import javax.servlet.ServletException;
import javax.servlet.annotation.WebServlet;
import javax.servlet.http.HttpServlet;
import javax.servlet.http.HttpServletRequest;
import javax.servlet.http.HttpServletResponse;

@WebServlet(name = "ShoppingCartClient", urlPatterns = {
"/ShoppingCartClient"})
public class ShoppingCartClient extends HttpServlet {

    @EJB
    ShoppingCartBean shoppingCart;
     protected void processRequest(HttpServletRequest request,
     HttpServletResponse response)
            throws ServletException, IOException {
        response.setContentType("text/html;charset=UTF-8");
        PrintWriter out = response.getWriter();
        try {
            out.println("<html>");
            out.println("<head>");
            out.println("<title>Servlet ShoppingCartClient</title>");
            out.println("</head>");
            out.println("<body>");
            out.println("<h1>Starting Shopping Cart test ... </h1>");

            out.println("<h1>ShoppingCart Lookup </h1>");
            out.println("<h1>Adding Wine Item </h1>");
            shoppingCart.addWineItem("Zinfandel");
            out.println("<h1>Printing Cart Items </h1>");
```

```java
            ArrayList cartItems = shoppingCart.getCartItems();
            for (String wine: (List<String>)cartItems) {
                out.println("<h1>" + wine + "</h1>");
            }

            out.println("</body>");
            out.println("</html>");
        } finally {
            out.close();
        }
    }

    @Override
    protected void doGet(HttpServletRequest request, HttpServletResponse
    response)
            throws ServletException, IOException {
        processRequest(request, response);
    }

    @Override
    protected void doPost(HttpServletRequest request, HttpServletResponse
    response)
            throws ServletException, IOException {
        processRequest(request, response);
    }

    @Override
    public String getServletInfo() {
        return "Short description";
    }
}
```

Listing 2-26 shows the ShopperCountClient servlet, which looks up the singleton ShopperCount session bean, calls the resetCounter() business method to reset the shopper count, calls the incrementShopperCount() business method to increment the shopper count, and finally prints the total number of shoppers counted. The value of shopper count will be visible across the application.

Listing 2-26. ShopperCountClient.java

```java
package com.apress.ejb.chapter02;
import java.io.IOException;
import java.io.PrintWriter;
import javax.ejb.EJB;
import javax.servlet.ServletException;
import javax.servlet.annotation.WebServlet;
import javax.servlet.http.HttpServlet;
import javax.servlet.http.HttpServletRequest;
import javax.servlet.http.HttpServletResponse;

@WebServlet(name = "ShopperCountClient", urlPatterns =
{"/ShopperCountClient"})
public class ShopperCountClient extends HttpServlet {
    @EJB
    ShopperCountBean shopperCount;
    protected void processRequest(HttpServletRequest request,
    HttpServletResponse response)
            throws ServletException, IOException {
        response.setContentType("text/html;charset=UTF-8");
        PrintWriter out = response.getWriter();
        try {
            /* TODO output your page here. You may use following sample
            code. */
            out.println("<html>");
            out.println("<head>");
            out.println("<title>Servlet ShopperCountClient</title>");
            out.println("</head>");
            out.println("<body>");

            out.println("<h1>Resetting Shopper Count ... </h1>");
            shopperCount.resetCounter();
            out.println("<h1>Incrementing Shopper Count ... </h1>");
            shopperCount.incrementShopperCount();
            out.println("<h1>Shopper Count: " + shopperCount.
            getShopperCount() + "</h1>");
```

```
            out.println("</body>");
            out.println("</html>");
        } finally {
            out.close();
        }
    }

    @Override
    protected void doGet(HttpServletRequest request, HttpServletResponse
    response)
            throws ServletException, IOException {
        processRequest(request, response);
    }

    @Override
    protected void doPost(HttpServletRequest request, HttpServletResponse
    response)
            throws ServletException, IOException {
        processRequest(request, response);
    }

    @Override
    public String getServletInfo() {
        return "Short description";
    }
}
```

Compiling, Deploying, and Testing the Session Beans

Session beans need to be packaged into EJB JAR (.jar) files before they are deployed into EJB containers. In the case of some EJB containers or application servers, packaged EJB archives need to be assembled into Enterprise Archive (EAR) files before deployment. EJB containers or application servers provide deployment utilities or Ant tasks to facilitate deployment of EJBs. Java IDEs (integrated development environments) like JDeveloper, NetBeans, and Eclipse also provide deployment features that allow developers to package, assemble, and deploy EJBs to application servers. Packaging, assembly, and deployment are covered in detail in Chapter 11.

So far in this chapter we have developed one stateless session bean (SearchFacade), one stateful session bean (ShoppingCart), and one singleton session bean (ShopperCount). The following sections will walk you through the steps necessary to compile, deploy, and test these session beans.

Prerequisites

Before performing any of the steps detailed in the next sections, complete the "Getting Started" section of Chapter 1. This section will walk you through the installation and environment setup required for the samples in this chapter.

Compiling the Session Beans and Their Clients

Copy the Chapter02-SessionSamples directory and its contents into a directory of your choice. Run the NetBeans IDE and open the Chapter02-SessionSamples project using the File ➤ Open Project menu. Make sure the Open Required Projects check box is checked, as shown in Figure 2-7.

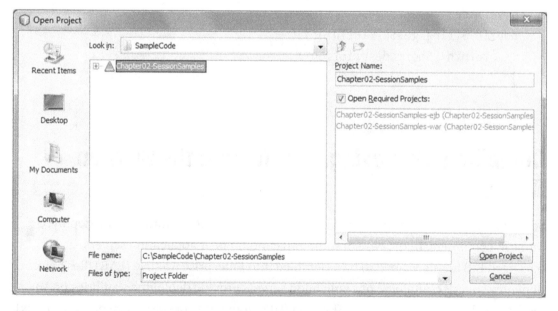

Figure 2-7. *Opening the Chapter02-SessionSamples project*

Expand the `Chapter02-SessionSamples-ejb` node and observe that the three session beans that we created appear in the `com.apress.ejb.chapter02` package. Similarly, the three client servlets appear under the `Chapter02-SessionSamples-war` node, as shown in Figure 2-8.

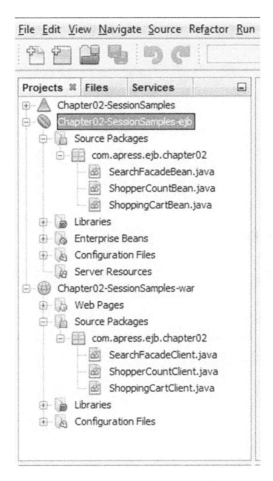

Figure 2-8. *Verifying that Session Beans and their clients are available in the project*

Invoke the context menu on `Chapter02-SessionSamples` node and build the application by selecting the `Clean` and `Build` menu option, as shown in Figure 2-9.

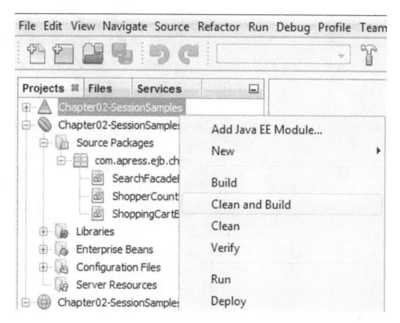

Figure 2-9. *Building the application*

Deploying the Session Beans and Their Clients

Once you have compiled the session beans and the servlet clients, you can deploy
the application to the GlassFish application server. Invoke the context menu on
Chapter02-SessionSamples node and deploy the application by selecting the Deploy
menu option, as shown in Figure 2-10.

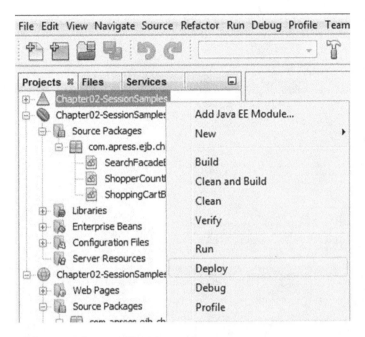

Figure 2-10. *Deploying the application*

NetBeans will start the integrated GlassFish application server and deploy the application to the server as shown in Figure 2-11.

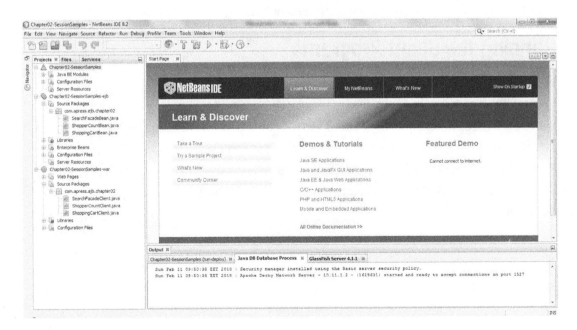

Figure 2-11. *Application deployment result*

The server's log window will log the deployment status of the application as shown in Figure 2-12.

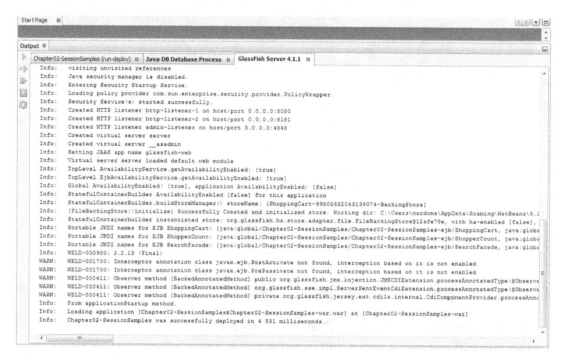

Figure 2-12. *Log showing successful deployment*

Running the Client Programs

Once the session beans and their client servlets are successfully deployed, we need to set the run target that we wish to execute. We have a choice of three run targets: `ShopperCountClient`, `SearchFacadeClient`, or `ShoppingCartClient`. To set the run target invoke the context menu on `Chapter02-SessionSamples` node and select the `Properties` menu option. Select the `Run` category and enter the run target in `Relative URL` text field and OK the dialog. Notice in Figure 2-13 that JDK 1.8 is used as library to build the Application.

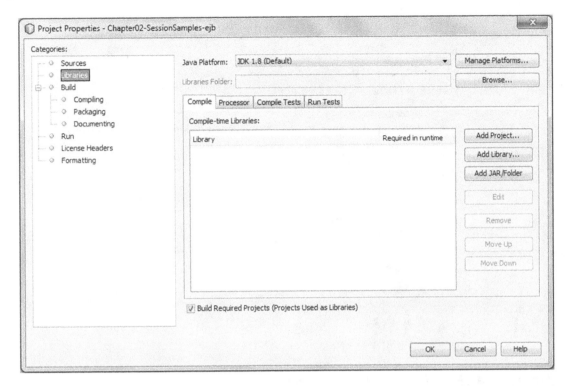

Figure 2-13. *JDK 1.8 as buiding Java libraries*

To run the client servlets, invoke the context menu on Chapter02-SessionSamples node and select the Run menu option as shown in Figure 2-14.

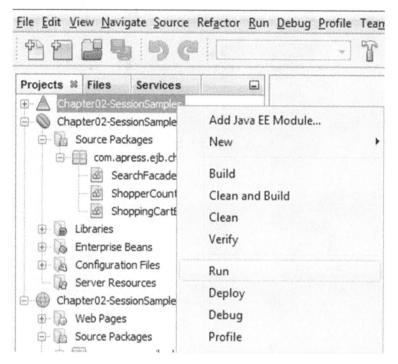

Figure 2-14. *Running the selected servlet*

NetBeans will open your default browser and execute the selected servlet. The output for the three client servlets is shown in Figures 2-15, 2-16 and 2-17.

Resetting Shopper Count ...

Incrementing Shopper Count ...

Shopper Count: 1

Figure 2-15. *Output of ShopperCountClient servlet*

Starting Search Facade test ...

SearchFacade Lookup

Searching wines

Printing wines list

Bordeaux

Merlot

Pinot Noir

2

Figure 2-16. *Output of SearchFacadeClient servlet*

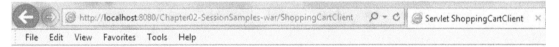

Starting Shopping Cart test ...

ShoppingCart Lookup

Adding Wine Item

Printing Cart Items

Zinfandel

Figure 2-17. *Output of ShoppingCartClient servlet*

Note   The application client container will be covered in detail in Chapter 12.

Summary

This chapter covered EJB session bean details using a specific set of examples. We looked at the simplified EJB model for developing session beans using standard Java language artifacts, such as Java classes and interfaces. We looked at session beans and some typical use cases in which session beans can be used for developing applications. We discussed three different types of session beans (stateless, stateful, and singleton), including the differences between them, and some general use cases for each. We covered session bean usage in 2-tier and 3-tier application architectures. We discussed the usage of dependency injection in stateless, stateful, and singleton beans. We considered ways to gain fine-grained control over application flow, including the use of lifecycle callback methods and interceptors in stateless and stateful beans, as well as the use of annotations like @PostConstruct and @PreDestroy. We looked at what is required to compile/build, package, and deploy session beans to the GlassFish application server. Finally, we looked at running the sample client programs using the GlassFish application client container.

In the next two chapters, we will drill down into the Java Persistence API (JPA) so that you can learn how to map POJOs to database tables and perform query and CRUD operations.

CHAPTER 3

Entities and the Java Persistence API (JPA)

Now that you have explored how EJB provides business services through session beans, we'll turn your attention to a different kind of component called *entities*, which are classes that represent tables in a database, and whose instances represent rows in those tables. Whereas session beans provide services to a client application, entities represent the business data. A common pattern is for a session bean to provide a convenient interface for manipulating entities in the context of transactional, security, access control, and other enterprise services. Methods to perform Create, Retrieve, Update, and Delete operations, also known as CRUD methods, are exposed on a session bean to the client to provide a "façade" pattern that we will use throughout the book.

The Java Persistence consists of four areas:

- The Java Persistence API

- The Java Persistence Criteria API

- The Query Language

- Object & Relational Mapping Metadata

Java Persistence API (JPA) was first introduced in Java EE 5, and it marked a departure from the previous persistence model of "entity beans" that were defined as part of the EJB specification. JPA is widely regarded as a tremendous improvement over the entity beans model defined in earlier versions of EJB. JPA borrows unabashedly from both proprietary and open source models such as TopLink, Hibernate, JDO, and Spring, which gained traction as popular alternatives to the often heavyweight and cumbersome entity bean model defined in earlier EJB revisions. Consequently, like session beans, entities are simple POJOs (plain old Java objects), and apart from a sliver of metadata indicating that they are an entity—captured in a Java annotation or in the

J. Wetherbee et al., *Beginning EJB in Java EE 8*, https://doi.org/10.1007/978-1-4842-3573-7_3

persistence XML descriptor—they are a very clean representation of the underlying database table. While JPA expanded the persistence model in reach and ability, entities themselves conveniently became largely decoupled from their supporting persistence framework, allowing them to be used as ordinary POJOs as well as objects managed by the persistence framework, both inside and outside a Java EE container.

JPA 1.0 was introduced in Java EE 5, JPA 2.0 accompanied Java EE 6, JPA 2.1 followed by Java EE 7, and JPA 2.2 was included in Java EE 8. The final version of JPa 2.2 will be part of Java EE 9.

Note   When using a JPA 1.0, JPA 2.0, or JPA 2.1 implementation, the schema will be `orm_1_0.xsd`, `orm_2_0.xsd` or `orm_2_1.xsd` respectively, located at `http://xmlns.jcp.org/xml/ns/persistence/`. When using the JPA 2.2 the schema will be instead named persistence_2_2.xsd and it will be also located as before at `http://xmlns.jcp.org/xml/ns/persistence/`

In this book we will utilize version 2.2 of the Java Persistence API as part of the Java EE 8.

Notice that in general JPA 2.2 is just a small release with a few new features added, while the rest of them will be still part of the JPA 2.1.

Maintenance release of JPA 2.2 started during 2017 under JSR 338 and was finally approved on June 19, 2017.

Here is the official Java Persistence 2.2 Maintenance release statement:

"The Java Persistence 2.2 specification enhances the Java Persistence API with support for repeating annotations; injection into attribute converters; support for mapping of the java.time.LocalDate, java.time.LocalTime, java.time.LocalDateTime, java.time.OffsetTime, and java.time.OffsetDateTime types; and methods to retrieve the results of Query and TypedQuery as streams."

The JPA 2.2. changelog file can be found here:

`https://jcp.org/aboutJava/communityprocess/maintenance/jsr338/ChangeLog-JPA-2.2-MR.txt`

In the spirit of this book, the two chapters on persistence will cover the most commonly used features included in JAP 2.2, describing their use through practical examples using our online wine store application. This chapter will get you started writing entity classes and using the key persistence features. The next chapter will explore more advanced persistence features. Through examples, these chapters explain the major areas of the persistence-programming model. They are not meant, however, to be a substitute for the expansive JPA specification. We encourage you to refer to the JPA spec when you're ready to explore details that go beyond the scope of this discussion.

Table 3-1 summarizes what we'll be covering in this chapter.

Table 3-1. *Key Topics in This Chapter*

Concept	Description
An entity example	We begin with a simple JavaBean and progressively add annotations required to transform it into a simple entity and then beyond.
Primary entity annotations	Further refining the requirements of an entity, the entity class must have a no-argument `public` or `protected` constructor and must not be `final`. Entities define their persistent structure through their JavaBeans property accessors or instance variables, and they may also include custom methods.
The `EntityManager`	The `EntityManager` object provides persistence services, including transaction management and query, merge, remove, find, and refresh operations. It is central to an understanding of the JPA persistence framework.
Entity life cycle	An entity instance may go through many formal states during its life as an in-memory Java object. Understanding these different states will help you know when the entity is in a consistent or inconsistent state with the back-end database and how to reconcile these differences within a transactional context.
Object/relational (O/R) mapping	JPA defines declarative markup through annotations and/or XML descriptors to map entity fields to table columns in a relational database management system (RDBMS).
Entity relationships	Entity classes may hold unary and collection references to themselves or to other entities. Note that, in JPA, relationship fields are not bidirectionally maintained by the container.
Java Persistence Query	JPA defines an SQL-like language—JPQL—that supports queries along with bulk update and Language (JPQL) delete operations. Queries may either be defined statically, as named queries, or dynamically. Queries may take bind parameters and return Java objects, including entity instances or Maps.

(continued)

Table 3-1. (*continued*)

Concept	Description
Persistence vs. Adaption	As a practical consideration when designing your entity classes, consider whether the entity class is the primary design object or whether the database schema is the source of truth. In the former case, the database serves mainly to persist the entity data; whereas in the latter case, the entity class serves to adapt the table into Java.
Example application	Finally, we give an example application consisting of three JPA entities, an EJB, and an HTTP servlet that demonstrates all of the concepts in this chapter in a simple, working model.

An Entity Example

Let's take a look at how you can transform a simple JavaBean into an entity and progressively customize it to add functionality and flexibility.

A Simple JavaBean: Customer.java

We begin with a simple JavaBean, as shown in Listing 3-1. This class has properties as defined by the JavaBeans standard. Each property on the JavaBean is represented to the world outside the bean through a pair of property accessor methods. For each property, a getter method retrieves its data, and a setter method assigns it. Internally, these property accessor methods read and write to a private, dedicated instance variable on the JavaBean class.

Listing 3-1. A Simple JavaBean

```
public class Customer {
  private long customerId;
  private String name;

  public long getCustomerId() { return customerId; }
  public void setCustomerId(long customerId) { this.customerId = customerId; }
  public String getName() { return name; }
  public void setName(String name) { this.name = name; }
}
```

A Simple Entity: Customer.java

Listing 3-2 shows our simple JavaBean after it has been transformed into an entity.

Listing 3-2. A Simple Entity

```
@Entity
public class Customer implements Serializable {
  @Id
  private long customerId;
  private String name;

  public long getCustomerId() { return customerId; }
  public void setCustomerId(long customerId) { this.customerId = customerId; }
  public String getName() { return name; }
  public void setName(String name) { this.name = name; }
}
```

The only changes required were to add the @Entity and @Id annotations. The @Id annotation identifies customerId as the primary key for the entity, which is required to express its unique identity. These are the minimum metadata requirements to transform this class into an entity. We also added the Serializable interface, as this is a good practice to ensure compatibility with remote clients.

The @Entity Annotation

The @Entity annotation is required to identify this class as an entity at the time the entity is deployed. When entities are deployed in a persistence archive (JAR file), they may be accompanied by non-entity classes. This annotation, or its equivalent declaration in the orm.xml file, tells the container to look for further annotations on the class and otherwise handle its O/R mappings, allow it to participate in queries and persistent relationships with other entities, and undergo byte weaving or other procedures when they are later instantiated by the persistence provider. All classes that are not marked as entities are ignored by the persistence provider during deployment.

The @Id Annotation

The @Id annotation indicates which field or fields—there may be several—is the entity's primary key, or identifier. The value in the identifier field (or fields) must be unique across all entity instances of the entity type Customer so that it can uniquely identify this entity. In the case that the primary key spans multiple columns in the table, a composite primary key is required, and the @Id fields may be replaced by a single field that is annotated @EmbeddedId. We will discuss how to specify composite keys later in the chapter.

Comparison with EJB 2.x

The fundamental JPA coding construct is the entity class. In EJB 2.x and earlier, an entity bean served as the primary persistence object and was comprised of a bean class and a local and/or remote component and home interface. Beginning with JPA, most of the trappings of the entity bean have been stripped away or simplified through strong use of defaults and annotations. What remains is simply the entity bean class, known now as the *entity class*, or more simply still, the *entity*. While it is equally valid to specify persistence metadata in an XML descriptor, for brevity, all examples in this chapter use Java annotations. As in the EJB 3 realm, each declarative construct specified by an annotation has a corresponding representation in the XML descriptor for the persistence unit (collection of collocated entities), and so may be equivalently specified in XML. The decision whether to use annotations or XML is entirely a matter of personal choice.

Configuration by Default

The previous two annotations were specified explicitly. Given the EJB 3 simplified development model that leverages configuration by default, you will not be surprised to find out that a lot of other metadata in this example is implied by default. Before exploring these default settings, it is worth considering why the @Entity and @Id annotations were chosen to be specified explicitly, rather than implied implicitly.

The @Entity annotations could have been the default settings for each class deployed through a persistence archive, and a hypothetical @NotEntity annotation could have been used to specify a non-entity class. However, following the pattern set by session- and message-driven beans, the explicit opt-in pattern was chosen instead.

Similarly, all fields could have been assumed to be part of the primary key, but in practice only a small subset (usually only one) of an entity's properties typically comprises an entity's primary key. The spec designers felt that it makes better sense in this case to use the opt-in pattern of explicitly specifying @Id on primary key fields, implying that all columns are not part of the primary key. This type of decision characterizes the configuration-by-default approach, in which annotations are not required for the more common cases and are only used when an override is needed.

The next section will examine some of the behavior that this Customer entity acquired by default, and it will show how you can override this default behavior.

An Entity with Defaults Exposed: Customer.java

Listing 3-3 shows the same entity with some of its defaults shown.

Listing 3-3. An Entity with Defaults Shown

```
@Entity(name="Customer")
@Table(name=" CUSTOMER")
public class Customer implements Serializable {
  @Id
  @Column(name="CUSTOMERID", table="CUSTOMER", unique=true,
          nullable=false, insertable=true, updatable=true)
  private long customerId;

  @Basic(fetch=FetchType.EAGER)
  @Column(name="NAME", table="CUSTOMER")
  private String name;

  // ...
}
```

Each entity has a name, and unless otherwise specified, this name defaults to the unqualified class name, which in this case is LiCustomer. This name is used when referring to the entity in query statements (Java Persistence Query Language, or JPQL, is covered in Chapter 4) and is typically specified when the unqualified class name is awkward or is a reserved name in JPQL.

The @Table Annotation

An entity instance typically represents a single row in a table, and it exposes each column value in that row through a corresponding property on the entity. Consequently, an entity must map to a table in a database, and that table is specified using the @Table annotation. Its name defaults to the entity name. Since not all databases support mixed-case table names, this translates to a table named CUSTOMER.

The @Column Annotation

Similarly, each field declared on the entity maps by default to a column with the same name, and so the customerId and name fields map to the CUSTOMERID and NAME columns in the CUSTOMER table. The @Column annotation may also be used to override default column-type information, as well as column-level constraints, such as those used to indicate that the column is optional, insertable, and/or updatable. Ordinarily, it is only necessary to specify this level of detail when you are relying on the container to create the table when an entity is deployed.

The @Basic Annotation

Entity fields that are of simple Java types, such as String or int (like the customerId and name fields), are automatically configured by the JPA to use the @Basic annotation. Arrays of simple types, and any other type that implements the Serializable interface, may also be marked @Basic.

The persistence framework provides automatic conversion of column data types to certain Java types, and JPA persistence providers will attempt to define a suitable default column type when generating tables for entity classes during deployment. Most numeric, string, and date types will be converted automatically.

Table 3-2 presents a list of Java types that can be annotated @Basic and mapped automatically.

Table 3-2. *Field/Property Types That Are Valid for Simple Mappings*

Java Type
Java primitive types (`int`, `long`, `char`, and so on)
Primitive wrapper types (`Integer`, `Long`, `Char`, and so on)
Java serializable types
User-defined serializable types
enums
`java.lang.String`
`java.math.BigInteger`
`java.math.BigDecimal`
`java.util.Date`
`java.util.Calendar`
`java.sql.Date`
`java.sql.Time`
`java.sql.Timestamp`
`byte[]`
`Byte[]`
`char[]`
`Character[]`

Additional Field Types

There are a number of other type specifiers that may be applied to different types of columns. For instance, an entity may also hold references to other entities, and these references are also represented by properties on the entity. We will look at some examples of how to specify these relationship properties later in this chapter.

An entity may have methods beyond its property access methods, but typically these are limited to support methods for managing add and remove operations from collection relationship properties.

Coding Requirements

In addition to the @Entity annotation and a primary key specifier, the minimal coding requirements for an entity are that it has a public or protected default (no-argument) constructor and that the class is not final. In this Customer example, a default constructor was implied since, in the absence of any non-default constructors on a public class, a default constructor is assumed by Java. Non-default constructors may also be specified on an entity, and they are often used for initializing the entity with its mandatory properties.

The java.io.Serializable Interface

Entities that will be passed by value, as when passed by remote session beans to Java SE clients that are external to the EJB container, must implement the java.io.Serializable marker (no method) interface. Implementing this interface indicates to the compiler that it must enforce all fields on the entity class to be serializable so that any instance can be serialized to a byte stream and passed using remote method invocation (RMI) over HTTP.

Placing Annotations on Instance Variables vs. JavaBean Property Accessors

When defining an entity class, you may choose to place member-level annotations on the entity instance variables or on the corresponding JavaBean property accessors for those instance variables. As with the decision between specifying metadata using annotations or XML, this is largely a matter of personal preference.

Note   Since JPA 2.0, Java developers are allowed to annotate both instance variables and property getters. Previously, all entities in an inheritance hierarchy had to choose a single approach to follow.

Regardless of where the member-level annotations are specified, the entity's instance variables must not be public, and clients of that entity, including related entities, must always access an entity's properties through accessor methods. It is up to the entity provider to decide which property accessors to make public, exposing them to clients; and which to make protected, making them available only to the persistence provider. When annotating instance variables, the entity need not define any property accessor methods, if desired.

By policy, only the persistence framework and the class methods themselves are allowed to access these fields directly. For both access types, clients must access field data through public accessor or other methods on the entity class.

There are several material consequences of choosing one approach over the other. These are discussed in the following sections.

Entity Data Access

When annotations are specified on the entity's instance variables, the persistence manager accesses the instance variables directly when reading and writing a persistent property to and from the entity. When annotating property accessors instead of instance variables, the persistence manager reads and writes property data through these property accessors.

Annotating the entity's instance variables directly avoids the overhead of method calls and provides a slight performance optimization, since the persistence manager talks directly to the fields. Annotating the property accessors provides a simple way for the entity developer to intercept and perform custom logic during all attempts to read and write property data.

This latter option affords the entity developer a chance lazily to derive persistent property values on demand, if desired. However, be aware that any validation or side-effect code on the property accessor methods will be called during entity state transitions. As you'll see in the next chapter, if the entity developer wishes to initialize transient data or refine persistent data at the time that the entity's persistent state is first loaded, or prior to saving changes out to persistent storage, it is preferable to perform these steps using entity lifecycle callback methods. Using the combination of field-level annotations and entity lifecycle callbacks has the benefit that validation and other code in the setter methods will only be called when a client calls the setter, and not when the entity is being instantiated from persistent storage by the framework.

Another consideration is how the entity behaves when it is involved in a query. This is a similar issue, since a query statement may both retrieve and update field data on an entity. Thus, it is important to be aware of any possible side effects of using property accessors.

Property Name

The second material impact of choosing whether to annotate instance variables or property accessors occurs when the property accessor expresses a default field name that is different from the instance variable name. When annotating property accessors, the logical property name is derived from the getter using the JavaBean property-naming convention, whereas if the instance variable is annotated, the logical property name becomes the instance variable's name.

Example: Annotating Instance Variables

The code snippet in Listing 3-4 demonstrates instance variable annotation, and it illustrates validation and side-effect code. In this example, which can also be found in the Source Code area for this chapter, the entity provider narrows the client interface to expose only the get/setZipCode() methods, but specifies both zipCodeInternal and zipCode properties to the persistence provider. Placing annotations on the instance variables provides a clean separation between the entity's client-side API and its persistence-side interface.

Listing 3-4. An Entity That Uses Instance Variable Annotations

```
@Entity
public class Address implements Serializable {
  @Id
  private long addressId;
  @Column(name = "ZIP")
  private int zipCodeInternal;
  @Transient
  private String zipCode;

  public long getAddressId() { return addressId; }
  public void setAddressId(long addressId) { this.addressId = addressId; }
```

```java
public String getZipCode() {
  if (zipCode == null && zipCodeInternal > 0) {
    zipCode = convertToStr(zipCodeInternal);
  }
  return zipCode;
}

public void setZipCode(String zipCode) throws IllegalArgumentException {
  // Validate the zipcode String, to make sure it reduces cleanly to
  // either a 5- or 9- digit integer, and assign it to the internal
  // persistent 'zipCodeInternal' class field
  // ... <validation code here>...
  this.zipCode = zipCode;
  zipCodeInternal = convertToInt(zipCode);
}

private int convertToInt(String zipCode) {
  return new Integer(zipCode).intValue();
}

private String convertToStr(int zipCode) {
  return new Integer(zipCode).toString();
}
}
```

The get/setZipCode() methods allow the entity to transform the internal data lazily into a client-friendly String representation, but only when requested. No property accessors are even specified for the zipCodeInternal instance variable.

The @Transient Annotation

You may not wish to make all fields or properties of an entity class persistent. Derived or transient fields may be annotated @Transient to indicate that they should be ignored by the persistence framework. The zipCode instance variable is marked @Transient, indicating that the persistence provider should not manage it. This instance variable serves only to adapt the internal int value into a client-friendly, derived String value.

Example: Annotating Property Accessors

Listing 3-5 demonstrates how an entity developer may use side-effect code when annotating an entity's property accessors.

Listing 3-5. An Entity That Uses Property Accessor Annotations

```
@Entity
public class Address implements Serializable {

  private BigDecimal addressId;
  private int zipCode;
  private String city;

  @Id
  public BigDecimal getAddressId() { return addressId; }
  public void setAddressId(BigDecimal addressId) { this.addressId =
  addressId; }

  public int getZipCode() { return zipCode; }
  public void setZipCode(int zipCode) {
    if (zipCode != this.zipCode)
    {
      city = null; // Force city to be lazily re-derived
      this.zipCode = zipCode;
    }
  }

  public String getCity() {
    //  Derive the city from the zipcode property, if available
    if (city == null && zipCode > 0) {
      city = deriveCityFromZip();
    }
    return city;
  }
  public void setCity(String city) {
    this.city = city;
  }
```

```
private String deriveCityFromZip() {
  /* Implementation here. . . */
  return null;
}
}
```

Placing the @Id annotation on the getAddressId() property accessor disambiguates the access policy, indicating that property accessors should be used by the persistence provider. Forcing the persistence provider to assign data through the property accessor affords the entity the opportunity to reset the city value when a new zip code is assigned. Also, knowing that the city field will be obtained by the persistence manager through its getter method allows the entity lazily to calculate its value only when requested through the getCity() accessor. Should the usage of this entity involve many calls to setZipCode() before the entity is persisted (or merged) out to the database, it is more efficient to defer deriving the city value until it is actually requested. Were this entity to use instance variable access, it would be necessary to update the city field eagerly each time the zipCode was assigned, since a request could come at any time to merge the entity changes into the database. As mentioned earlier, however, the use of entity lifecycle callback methods could avoid the overhead of eagerly deriving this value.

Access Type Summary

JPA offers two models for how the persistence provider accesses the field data on an entity, either directly through instance variables and indirectly through property accessors. In the general case, we have found that annotating an entity's instance variables is preferable to annotating its property accessors. You'll rarely have a need to validate data coming in from the persistent store, and any side-effect code in setter methods typically should be performed lazily, not eagerly at the time the entity is instantiated. Furthermore, field-level annotations allow you to decouple the public property types exposed through that field's get/set methods from the underlying column representation. For instance, you may want to expose the zipCode property as a String through the getZipcode()/setZipcode() methods, but convert it internally to an integer, using a field of type Integer, for persistence to an INTEGER column in the database. Finally, the use of entity lifecycle callback methods provides the opportunity for additional initialization or preparation, both after the entity data is loaded and before it is saved.

Declaring the Primary Key

An entity must declare its primary key. The primary key serves to identify an entity instance uniquely among all of the instances of the entity type. A primary key may be simple, represented by a single field of a basic Java class, like String or Long, as in the previous Customer example (Listing 3-2). Alternatively, a primary key may be complex, represented by a composite class comprised of multiple elementary fields or properties.

The underlying column or columns on the entity's table that are mapped to by the primary key field or fields may be formally bound by a database primary key constraint, but this is not a requirement. It is, however, required that the primary key column value or values for any entity instance resolve to a unique value across all instances of that entity. Database constraints are useful in enforcing this requirement, and in their absence, care should be taken to ensure that unique values are assigned by application.

Simple Primary Key

A simple primary key is declared by annotating a single basic-type field on the entity class with the @Id annotation (see Listing 3-6). A basic-type field is a basic Java type (a list of basic types is shown in Table 3-2).

Listing 3-6. An Entity with a Simple Primary Key

```
@Entity
public class Customer implements Serializable {
    @Id
    private Integer id;
    private String name;

    public Customer() {}
    public Customer(Integer id) { this.id = id; }

    public Integer getId() { return id; }
    public void setId(Integer id) { this.id = id; }

    public String getName() { return name; }
    public void setName(String name) { this.name = name; }
}
```

Note that we could eliminate the usefulness of an alternate constructor in our entity class by using a database sequence to populate the PK value automatically. Listing 3-7 shows how this might look, using an ID value generator provided by JPA.

Listing 3-7. An Entity with a Simple Primary Key That Is Populated Using @GeneratedValue

```
@Entity
@SequenceGenerator(name = " CustomerSequence",
                   sequenceName = " CUSTOMER_SEQ",
                   initialValue = 100, allocationSize = 20)
public class Customer implements Serializable {
    @Id
    @GeneratedValue(strategy = GenerationType.SEQUENCE,
                    generator = " CustomerSequence")
    private Integer id;
    private String name;

    public Integer getId() { return id; }
    public void setId(Integer id) { this.id = id; }

    public String getName() { return name; }
    public void setName(String name) { this.name = name;}
}
```

The @GeneratedValue Annotation

The @GeneratedValue annotation tells the persistence framework to auto-populate this column with the specified sequence generator, which must be defined on one of the entities in your persistence archive. (It is defined directly on the Customer entity.) A @SequenceGenerator annotation defines a sharable sequence generator, which can either define a new framework-generated sequence or refer to an existing sequence in your database. ID generators will be explored more fully in Chapter 4.

Composite Primary Key

If an entity's primary key maps to multiple database columns, it uses a complex, or composite, primary key. This may be represented in one of two ways on the entity class. The entity may declare each field in the composite key directly on the entity class (annotating each one with @Id), and specify a composite key class that provides these exact same fields in an @IdClass annotation. Alternatively, the entity may designate a single, complex field to represent its primary key by annotating that field with @EmbeddedId. The class type of the @EmbeddedId field is the entity's composite key class. This composite key class is annotated @Embeddable and must specify the mapping details for each of its fields. These fields will end up mapping to the base table on the entity. With either approach, the composite primary key class must override the hashCode() and equals(Object obj) methods on java.lang.Object.

Listing 3-8 shows how these options look.

Listing 3-8. An Entity with a Composite Primary Key Using @IdClass

```
@Entity
@IdClass(CustomerPK.class)
public class Customer implements Serializable {
    @Id
    private Integer customerId;
    @Id
    private String name;

    public Integer getCustomerId() { return customerId; }
    public void setCustomerId(Integer customerId) { this.customerId =
    customerId; }
    public void setName(String name) { this.name = name; }
    public String getName() { return name; }
}
```

The @IdClass Annotation

The @IdClass identifies an ordinary POJO (such as the example shown in Listing 3-9) that does not require any metadata. Any mapping details required for the primary key fields are specified on the fields on the entity.

Listing 3-9. A Simple POJO that Serves as a Composite Primary Key

```java
public class CustomerPK implements Serializable {

  private Integer id;
  private String name;

  public void setId(Integer id) { this.id = id; }
  public Integer getId() { return id; }

  public void setName(String name) { this.name = name; }
  public String getName() { return name; }

  @Override
  public int hashCode() { return 0; /* Implementation here */ }
  @Override
  public boolean equals(Object obj) { return false; /* Implementation here
*/ }
}
```

The composite primary key class must conform to the access type (annotated instance variables vs. property accessors) of the entity, and all its fields or properties must have matching fields or properties on the entity class. The corresponding fields on the entity must be annotated @Id.

The @EmbeddedId Annotation

Alternatively, the entity may designate one of its fields or properties to be its composite primary key by annotating it @EmbeddedId (see Listing 3-10).

Listing 3-10. An Entity Using an @EmbeddedId Annotation

```java
@Entity
public class Customer implements Serializable {
  @EmbeddedId
  private CustomerPK customerId;

  public CustomerPK getCustomerId() { return customerId; }
  public void setCustomerId(CustomerPK customerId) {
```

```
      this.customerId = customerId;
  }

  // . . .
}
```

The @Embeddable Annotation

Every @EmbeddedId must reference a class that is marked @Embeddable. Listing 3-11 shows the corresponding embeddable composite key class.

Listing 3-11. An @Embeddable Composite Key Class

```
@Embeddable
public class CustomerPK implements Serializable {
  Long id;
  String name;

  public void setId(Long id) { this.id = id; }
  public Long getId() { return id; }

  public void setName(String name) { this.name = name; }
  public String getName() { return name; }

  @Override
  public int hashCode() { return 0; /* Implementation here */ }
  @Override
  public boolean equals(Object obj) { return false; /* Implementation here
*/ }
}
```

The composite key class CustomerPK must be annotated @Embeddable. Unlike in the @IdClass case, its instance variables or property accessors may have @Column annotations to specify their mapping details.

Summary of Entity Examples

The basic @Entity and @Id annotations are sufficient to define an entity class, making the on-ramp to coding entities very straightforward. As you become more familiar with the annotations available to you, and as your requirements become more demanding, you can simply add annotations to your entities to achieve powerful persistence features.

We just covered the very basics in this section. We'll now turn our attention away from the entity class itself and toward the EntityManager and some other important services in the persistence framework. Later, we'll return to explore more annotations that satisfy more complex needs.

The Persistence Archive

Until now, we have referred to the persistence archive as the encapsulation of a group of collocated entities that are deployed as a JAR file. This archive defines the entities and related non-entity classes that are bundled together for deployment. Strictly speaking, a persistence archive does not need to live in its own dedicated .jar file. Persistence archives can be bundled inside .war files, EJB .jar files, and even exist as .class files and a META-INF/persistence.xml file on a Java application's class path.

Regardless of its surrounding context, we now take a closer look at the contents of this archive.

The persistence.xml File

A persistence archive requires a persistence.xml file in its META-INF directory. This file groups subsets of entities in the archive into what are known as *persistence units*. A persistence.xml file must define at least one persistence unit, and the same entity may be included in multiple persistence units within the same persistence.xml file.

The persistence.xml and orm.xml mapping files and schemas were updated in JPA 2.2 version.

The persistence.xml file defines a persistence unit, and it is located in the META-INF directory of the root of the persistence unit.

The orm.xml file, contained in the META-INF directory of the root of the persistence unit, includes the managed persistence classes used to take the form of annotations of the object-relational mapping information. The orm.xml mapping file or other mapping file will be loaded as a resource by the persistence provider.

Note   The JPA versions 2.1 and 2.2 request that the XML file mappings, such as persistence.xml and orm.xml, to be located in the Java class path.

The JPA 2.2 version says that:

"An object/relational mapping XML file named orm.xml may be specified in the META-INF directory in the root of the persistence unit or in the META-INF directory of any jar file referenced by the persistence.xml."

Notice that we can add more mapping files that may be present anywhere on the class path and the Classloader can load them as resources.

Listing 3-12 demonstrates an example of a persistence.xml file.

Listing 3-12. An Example of a persistence.xml File

```
<?xml version="1.0" encoding="UTF-8" ?>
<persistence xmlns="http://xmlns.jcp.org/xml/ns/persistence"
    xmlns:xsi="http://www.w3.org/2001/XMLSchema-instance"
    xsi:schemaLocation="http://xmlns.jcp.org/xml/ns/persistence
    http://xmlns.jcp.org/xml/ns/persistence/persistence_2_2.xsd"
    version="2.2">
  <persistence-unit name="Chapter03PersistenceUnit" transaction-type="JTA">
    <provider>org.eclipse.persistence.jpa.PersistenceProvider</provider>
    <jta-data-source>jdbc/wineapp</jta-data-source>
    <class>com.apress.ejb.chapter03.entities.Address</class>
    <class>com.apress.ejb.chapter03.entities.Customer</class>
    <class>com.apress.ejb.chapter03.entities.CustomerOrder</class>
    <exclude-unlisted-classes>false</exclude-unlisted-classes>
    <properties>
      <property name="eclipselink.ddl-generation" value="create-tables"/>
    </properties>
  </persistence-unit>
  <persistence-unit name="Chapter03PersistenceUnit-JSE" transaction-
  type="RESOURCE_LOCAL">
    <provider>org.eclipse.persistence.jpa.PersistenceProvider</provider>
    <class>com.apress.ejb.chapter03.entities.Customer</class>
    <properties>
```

```
    <property name="javax.persistence.jdbc.driver" value="oracle.jdbc.
    OracleDriver"/>
    <property name="javax.persistence.jdbc.url" value="jdbc:oracle:thin:
    @localhost:1521:XE"/>
    <property name="javax.persistence.jdbc.user" value="wineapp"/>
    <property name="javax.persistence.jdbc.password" value="221CE6B0A87AC
    61AE68FF3A13OF7F666"/>
    <property name="eclipselink.logging.level" value="FINER"/>
  </properties>
 </persistence-unit>
</persistence>
```

Notice the attribute version="2.2" that since JDK version 8 can be used as Ja PA version.

This `persistence.xml` file defines two persistence units, `Chapter03PersistenceUnit` and `Chapter03PersistenceUnit-JSE`. The `Customer` class is defined in both. The first persistence unit is used by Java EE clients (like session beans), whereas the second unit is configured for use by Java SE clients (like the `CustomerService.java` class shown in Listing 3-14). Specifying different configuration settings in the two persistence units allows you to insulate the client from the configuration details of the persistent units, and it makes an entity that is run in both Java SE and EE environments appear virtually the same in both cases.

The EntityManager

The `EntityManager` is the client's gateway to entity management services offered by the JPA persistence framework. Client sessions must obtain an `EntityManager` instance before interacting with persistent entity instances. The `EntityManager` provides support for querying, updating, refreshing, and removing existing entity instances, and for registering entity classes to create new persistent objects with identity.

Persistence Context

The `EntityManager` maintains a cache of instances within a transactional context called a *persistence context*. The persistence context allows the `EntityManager` to track modified, created, and removed entity instances, and to reconcile entity instances with changes that were committed by external transactions concurrent with the `EntityManagers` own transaction.

Entity instances queried through the `EntityManager` may be freely passed to clients both inside and outside the EJB container. Clients may access and update the entity data as they would an ordinary Java object. To apply changes back to the persistent store, the client calls the `merge()` method on the `EntityManager` within a transactional scope, and the `EntityManager` persists the state of the entity data into the back-end store.

Acquiring an EntityManager Instance

An `EntityManager` instance can be acquired both from within the EJB container (Java EE) and outside it (Java SE). This offers clients the flexibility to interact with persistent entity beans in a uniform way, without regard to whether the persistence code is running inside or outside the Java EE container.

A Session Bean Using Container Injection

Listing 3-13 provides an example of a session bean acquiring an `EntityManager` instance through container injection.

Listing 3-13. A Session Bean Injected with an EntityManager Instance

```
@Stateless
public class CustomerManager {

  @PersistenceContext(unitName="Chapter03PersistenceUnit")
  private EntityManager em;

  public void createCustomer() {
    final Customer cust = new Customer();
```

```
    cust.setName("Moneybags MgGee");
    em.persist(cust);
  }
}
```

In this example, we use container injection to obtain an `EntityManager` instance that is bound to the `Chapter03PersistenceUnit` persistence unit, which includes our `Customer` entity from Listing 3-7. We then use this `EntityManager` to persist a new `Customer` instance. Note that this example assumes that an ID generator or other service exists to auto-populate the primary key of the new instance.

A Java SE Service Client Using an EntityManagerFactory

There are times when container injection is not an option, or when more control over the life cycle of the `EntityManager` is desired by the application. In such cases, the client can obtain an `EntityManager` by first acquiring an `EntityManagerFactory`. The `javax.persistence.Persistence` class serves as a factory for acquiring an `EntityManagerFactory`, and it may be used from both a Java EE environment and a Java SE environment. Listing 3-14 shows how an ordinary Java SE service client would obtain an `EntityManager`.

Listing 3-14. A POJO that Serves as an Entity Façade

```
public class CustomerService {

  public static void main(String[] args) {
    final EntityManagerFactory emf =
      Persistence.createEntityManagerFactory("Chapter03PersistenceUnit-JSE");
    final EntityManager em = emf.createEntityManager();
    final Customer cust = new Customer();
    cust.setName("Best Customer Ever");
    em.persist(cust);
  }
}
```

Here we create an EntityManagerFactory that is again bound to the Chapter03PersistenceUnit-JSE persistence unit, which includes our Customer entity from Listing 3-7. We then create an EntityManager instance from that factory and use it to persist a new Customer instance.

Looking Up the EntityManager Through JNDI

A third option, available also through both Java SE and EE environments, is to look up the EntityManagerFactory, or the EntityManager itself, through Java Naming and Directory Interface (JNDI). Listing 3-15 shows an example of how this is done from within a session bean.

Listing 3-15. EntityManager Lookup Through JNDI

```
@Stateless
@PersistenceContext(unitName="Chapter03PersistenceUnit")
public class CustomerServiceBean {
    @Resource
    SessionContext ctx;

    public void performService() {
        EntityManager em = (EntityManager)ctx.lookup("Chapter03Persistence
        Unit");
        // ...
    }
}
```

The injected SessionContext resource provides a JNDI namespace for acquiring other resources at runtime.

Transaction Support

The EntityManager also exposes methods to begin, commit, and roll back transactions for use with resource-local (non-JTA) transactions. This topic is covered in depth in Chapter 8.

The Entity Life Cycle

An entity instance may go through many formal states during its life as an in-memory Java object. Understanding these different states will help you know when the entity is in a consistent or inconsistent state with the back-end database, and how to reconcile these differences within a transactional context.

An entity instance will typically go through many states of persistence during its lifetime as a Java object. Since EJB 3, entity classes are completely transparent. They are created using ordinary constructors instead of the Home and LocalHome factory interfaces of earlier EJB versions. They may be freely passed to and from the EJB container and between clients, and they may be updated by a client without the overhead of a callback to the EJB container.

The Life Cycle of a New Entity Instance

Let's take a look at the life cycle of a newly created persistent entity instance. In its life, the entity may visit the new, managed, detached, and removed states.

New Entity Instance

A client creates a new entity instance by using one of the entity's Java constructors. This is a significant simplification over earlier EJB specifications, which required that users define create() factory methods on the entity bean's Home and/or LocalHome interfaces. The default (no argument) constructor is required of all entity classes, but additional constructors may also be defined. The client may live outside or within an EJB container. At the point of construction, it is in the new state and does not yet have persistent identity because it has not been associated with an EntityManagers persistence context. The client is free to call any of its methods and assign data values, and all updates to the entity are kept local to the entity class.

Managed Entity Instance

To turn this entity class into a persistent object, the client acquires an EntityManager instance and calls the EntityManager.persist() method. Listing 3-16 shows a code snippet from a session bean that acquires the EntityManager through injection and then persists the entity instance passed as a parameter to the persistEntity() method.

Listing 3-16. Example Showing How an Entity Instance Is Made Persistent

```java
@Stateless
public class MySessionEJB {

  @PersistenceContext(unitName = "Chapter03PersistenceUnit")
  private EntityManager em;

  public void persistEntity(Object entity) {
    em.persist(entity);
  }
}
```

When the entity is made persistent, it is added to a persistence context as a managed instance. Being managed affords the entity the following advantages:

- By default, all fields on the entity are designated to be lazily loaded by the persistence provider. While a lazy designation is really only a hint (see the "Lazy vs. Eager Field Bindings" section later in the chapter), lazy field binding can be seamlessly performed only on managed instances.

- When an entity is managed, changes made to it may be tracked by the persistence manager to optimize subsequent `EntityManager.merge()` operations. For instance, change tracking may be handled directly on the entity instance using byte weaving provided by the persistence provider when the entity was instantiated. This is particularly important when managing a network of related entities, so that a minimum of effort is required to calculate the change set when the network of entities is merged back to the persistence context.

In general, there is no guarantee that a call to `EntityManager.persist()` will cause an SQL INSERT statement to be performed immediately. It is up to the persistence manager to decide whether to perform this step immediately or at a later time but prior to committing the transaction. In this example, however, the default behavior of a method on a Stateless session bean is to create a new transaction and commit the work each time one of its methods is called, so the entity was not only inserted but committed as well.

Sequence values may have been assigned to the entity instance, and other side-effect code may also have been executed during this step.

Detached Entity Instance

The entity remains in a managed state for the life of the persistence context in which it is contained, or until it is removed from the database. If one of these events occurs, or if the instance is passed by value to a client, it becomes a detached entity instance and is no longer associated with a persistence context. Detached entities do not undergo change tracking or other internal optimizations. In particular, the persistence provider is not available to bind fields lazily that were not already bound at the time the entity became detached, and attempting to access a detached entity's field that has not yet been bound will throw a runtime exception. To merge its state back into the persistence context and make it a managed instance once again, you need to pass a detached entity to the `EntityManager.merge()` method.

While an entity instance returned from an `EntityManager.merge()` call is managed, changes are not propagated immediately to the persistent storage; they merely update the entity itself. Suppose the client modifies the entity:

```
entity = mySession.persistEntity(entity);
entity.setName("foo");
```

After the second statement above, the name change has been applied only to the entity instance, and no changes have been propagated to the persistence context or to the database. To apply these changes to the persistence context, you would call the `EntityManager.merge()` operation, as follows:

```
// Assumes the EntityManager em was obtained, possibly through injection
em.merge(entity);
```

This updates the persistence context cache, and possibly updates the row in the underlying database as well, depending on the transactional settings in effect.

Removed Entity Instance

An entity becomes a removed instance when its `remove()` method is called. The row (or rows, if this entity maps to multiple tables) that represents its persistent state will be removed when the context transaction is committed.

O/R Mapping

We have examined a number of annotations that define the general behavior of an entity. Let us now explore the annotations involved in the O/R mapping of persistent fields or properties on the entity to table columns in the database.

The heart of an entity class is the list of fields or properties that define its persistent structure. These fields or properties that define its persistent state must map to columns in a database table. It is the job of the persistence framework to load this state from the database into an entity instance before it is handed out to a client and to copy this state back out to the rows of the table when it is persisted. Whereas in earlier versions of EJB, this O/R mapping information was specific to the various container-managed persistence (CMP) providers, in JPA, this mapping markup is now part of the specification. Like nearly every part of EJB since version 3.0, users have the choice of specifying this information through annotations or using XML in the orm.xml file.

The @Table Annotation (Revisited)

The @Table annotation lets you specify details about the base table to which an entity is mapped. Listing 3-17 shows the @Table annotation definition.

Listing 3-17. The @Table Annotation

```
@Target({ElementType.TYPE})
@Retention(RetentionPolicy.RUNTIME)
public @interface Table {
    String name() default "";
    String catalog() default "";
    String schema() default "";
    UniqueConstraint[] uniqueConstraints() default {};
}
```

Each entity identifies a database table that will hold its persistent data as follows:

```
@Entity
@Table(name="ADDRESSES")
public class Address implements Serializable {
    . . .
}
```

Here, the @Table annotation is used to override the default table name for the Address entity. In the absence of an @Table annotation, the default table name is the same name as the entity class itself. (It would default to "ADDRESS" in this example.) The @Table annotation also allows you to specify database schema and constraint information for use when the table is generated during deployment. An entity may also map to more than one table by specifying the @SecondaryTable annotation.

Note   The predefined annotation types @Target and @Retention may be specified on an annotation definition to provide information to the compiler about the annotation. The @Target annotation identifies the program element (in our example, a part of a class) that can accept the annotation. The @Retention annotation is used to indicate whether the annotation should be available only in the Java source file or also in the compiled class file. When @Retention(SOURCE) is specified, the annotation is useful as documentation, and it may be used by a design-time tool like an integrated development environment (IDE), but the annotation usage is not compiled into the .class file. When @Retention(RUNTIME) is specified, the information is also compiled into the .class file, and so it may be obtained through Java reflection for use by deployment or runtime tools like the EJB container.

The @Column Annotation (Revisited)

Entity class fields or properties are mapped to database columns using the @Column annotation. Again, if no @Column annotation is defined for a field through its instance variable or property accessor, the mapped column name gets its name from the field.

Listing 3-18 gives the definition of the @Column annotation.

Listing 3-18. The @Column Annotation

```
@Target({ElementType.METHOD, ElementType.FIELD})
@Retention(RetentionPolicy.RUNTIME)
public @interface Column {
    String name() default "";
    boolean unique() default false;
```

```
    boolean nullable() default true;
    boolean insertable() default true;
    boolean updatable() default true;
    String columnDefinition() default "";
    String table() default "";
    int length() default 255;
    int precision() default 0; // decimal precision
    int scale() default 0; // decimal scale
}
```

As you can see, it is possible to specify a column's attributes fully if desired. This is useful when you want to give deploy-time directives to generate custom column definitions. Most typically, you will use the name attribute to decouple the column name from the field or property name, as when the column name is too utilitarian or cryptic.

Here, the field identifier is told to map to a column called ID, releasing the naming dependency that binds them by default:

```
@Entity
@Table(name="ADDRESSES")
public class Address implements Serializable {
    ...
    @Column(name="ID")
    String identifier;
    ...
}
```

Complex Mappings

More complex mappings, including those involving multiple tables per entity, complex data types, embedded classes, and inheritance hierarchies will be covered in the next chapter. For now, let us examine how relationships between entities are mapped.

Entity Relationships

Entities may hold single-value and collection references to themselves or to other entities. Additionally, relationships may be exposed as relationship fields on either one or both entities involved in the relationship. For those of you familiar with EJB 2.x, be aware that in JPA, relationship fields are no longer bidirectionally maintained by the container. Updating the field at one end of a bidirectional relationship no longer causes the field at the other end to be updated automatically as well. When mapping a relationship field, its primary key always represents the target entity. The source, or owning end of the relationship, may be mapped to a foreign key on the source entity's table, but there is no requirement that an actual database foreign key constraint be specified on the underlying columns.

Let's take a look at how JPA lets you define relationships.

@OneToOne

Following is the definition of the @OneToOne relationship annotation:

```
@Target({ElementType.METHOD, ElementType.FIELD})
@Retention(RetentionPolicy.RUNTIME)
public @interface OneToOne {
    Class targetEntity() default void.class;
    CascadeType[] cascade() default {};
    FetchType fetch() default EAGER;
    boolean optional() default true;
    String mappedBy() default "";
}
```

The @OneToOne relationship is represented by a single-value entity reference at one or both ends of the relationship. One relationship field will map to columns on its table that reference the primary key columns on the table at the other end of the relationship.

Here is an example in which `Customer` uses `Address`, but `Address` knows nothing about its usage by `Customer`, and so it does not have a relationship field in its class:

```
@Entity
public class Customer implements Serializable {
    . . .
    @OneToOne
    @JoinColumn(name="MAILING_ADDRESS_REF",
                referencedColumnName="ADDRESS_PK")
    protected Address address;
    . . .
}
```

To make this a bidirectional relationship, simply add a relationship field to `Address` that points back to `Customer`:

```
@Entity
public class Address implements Serializable {
    . . .
    @OneToOne(mappedBy="address")
    protected Customer customer;
    . . .
}
```

Note that by using the (`mappedBy="address"`) attribute, there is no need to specify the @JoinColumn information on the `Address.customer` field redundantly. Also, the entity type at the other end of the relationship is derived from the `customer` field type.

If you were then to make the relationship unidirectional but in the opposite direction, you would just move the @JoinColumn annotation from `Customer.address` onto `Address.customer` and then remove the `Customer.address` field.

@OneToMany and @ManyToOne

Similarly, here are the definitions of the @OneToMany and @ManyToOne annotations:

@OneToMany:

```
@Target(value = {ElementType.METHOD, ElementType.FIELD})
@Retention(value = RetentionPolicy.RUNTIME)
public @interface OneToMany {

  public Class targetEntity() default void.class;
  public CascadeType[] cascade() default {};
  public FetchType fetch() default FetchType.LAZY;
  public String mappedBy() default "";
  public boolean orphanRemoval() default false;
}
```

@ManyToOne:

```
@Target(value = {ElementType.METHOD, ElementType.FIELD})
@Retention(value = RetentionPolicy.RUNTIME)
public @interface ManyToOne {

  public Class targetEntity() default void.class;
  public CascadeType[] cascade() default {};
  public FetchType fetch() default FetchType.EAGER;
  public boolean optional() default true;
}
```

The @OneToMany relationship annotation is added to a Collection relationship field where the entity at the other end either does not have a relationship field, or where it has a single-value relationship field pointing back to this entity. If there is a field on the entity at the other end of the relationship, it will be annotated @ManyToOne, indicating that it is an entity that is part of a Collection and that it knows the entity type that owns the Collection. As with an @OneToOne relationship field, specifying a mappedBy attribute on an @OneToMany relationship is enough to identify the mapping used for both relationship fields.

```
@Entity
public class Orders implements Serializable {
    . . .
    @OneToMany(mappedBy="orders")
```

```
    protected Collection<OrderItems> orderItemsCollection;
    . . .
}

@Entity
public class OrderItems implements Serializable {
    . . .
    @ManyToOne
    @JoinColumn(name="SELECTION_REF", referencedColumnName="SELECTION_PK")
    protected Orders orders;
    . . .
}
```

Note that by using generic collection types (Collection<OrderItems>), the persistence framework is able to determine the entity type at the other end of the relationship. With that, all that is needed to resolve the mapping for the @OneToMany side is the field or property name on that entity, which in this case is orders.

@ManyToMany

Following is the definition of the @ManyToMany relationship annotation:

```
@Target(value = {ElementType.METHOD, ElementType.FIELD})
@Retention(value = RetentionPolicy.RUNTIME)
public @interface ManyToMany {
  public Class targetEntity() default void.class;
  public CascadeType[] cascade() default {};
  public FetchType fetch() default FetchType.LAZY;
  public String mappedBy() default "";
}
```

The @ManyToMany annotation is assigned to a Collection relationship field to indicate that the target entity also has a Collection of the source entity type. This type of mapping requires an @JoinTable, commonly known as an *intersection table*. The join table holds references back to the primary keys of the entities at either end of the relationship. In the example that follows, the intersection table EJB_PROJ has two columns: EMP_ID is a reference column back to the ID primary key column on the EMPLOYEE table, and PROJ_ID is a reference column pointing to the ID primary key column on the PROJECT table.

```
@Entity
public class Employee implements Serializable {
    . . .
    @ManyToMany(mappedBy="employees", cascade=CascadeType.PERSIST)
    @JoinTable(name="EMP_PROJ",
                joinColumns={@JoinColumn(name="EMP_ID",
                                        referencedColumnName="ID")},
                inverseJoinColumns={@JoinColumn(name="PROJ_ID",
                                        referencedColumnName="ID")})
    protected Collection<Project> projects;
    . . .
}

@Entity
public class Project implements Serializable {
    . . .
    @ManyToMany(mappedBy="projects")
    protected Set<Employee> employees;
    . . .
}
```

Use of the (mappedBy="projects") attribute on @ManyToMany allows the mapping information contained in the @JoinTable annotation to be shared by both relationship fields.

Lazy vs. Eager Field Bindings

By default, and for performance reasons, all field values are designated to be fetched lazily, due to the fact that the implied fetch attribute found on each of the field mappings (@Basic, @OneToMany, and so on) holds a default value of FetchType.LAZY. This default FetchType.LAZY value is, in fact, only a hint, and the persistence manager is not bound to honor the request. For many fields, including nearly all simple values, it would be a significant burden to lazily fault in the fields of an entity, as they are actually required, so the persistence manager generally ignores the `FetchType.LAZY` directive and loads them eagerly anyhow.

When the non-default value `FetchType.EAGER` is specified on a field mapping, however, this is not an optional request. When a field is so decorated, the persistence manager is obliged to bind its value eagerly when the entity is instantiated. This is particularly relevant when dealing with relationship fields. A relationship field may be annotated with the `fetch=FetchType.EAGER` attribute to ensure that, should the entity become detached, it will still be possible for clients to traverse that relationship field to access the related entity instances.

When an entity is managed, relationship values will be bound at the time they are first requested. However, when an entity is instantiated and then detached, as when it is serialized and passed to a remote client, it may be desirable to prebind all of its relationship fields eagerly. In this case, you can override the default `fetch` values and set `(fetch=FetchType.EAGER)` on the relationship fields. Be aware of the consequences of this action, however, since this may cause a storm of cascaded loading if the eagerly loaded collections in turn eagerly load their referenced objects, and so on.

Cascading Operations

Entities that are related to other entities may cascade certain lifecycle operations across references. This allows an operation on one entity to propagate to certain other related entities. The cascade options are defined through annotations on the individual relationship fields so that you can precisely control the cascading behavior. Here are the cascade options:

```
public enum CascadeType {
    ALL,
    PERSIST,
    MERGE,
    REMOVE,
    REFRESH
}
```

For example, a `Customer` entity that holds a reference to an exclusively owned `Address` entity may wish to have all operations on the `Customer` propagated to the `Address` instance.

```
@Entity
public class Customer implements Serializable {

    . . .

    @OneToOne(cascade=CascadeType.ALL)
    protected Address address;

    . . .

}
```

When an `EntityManager` operation like `persist()` or `remove()` is called on the `Customer` entity, the operation will also be called on the `Address` instance held in the `address` field and on any cascading fields of that `Address` instance, and so on.

Use of these `cascade` annotation attributes allows the entity developers to specify cascading behavior declaratively and succinctly, and it saves the client from having to keep track of the network of instances that need to be manipulated when a `persist()`, `merge()`, `remove()`, or `refresh()` lifecycle operation is performed on a top-level instance.

Java Persistence Query Language (JPQL)

The Java Persistence API provides two methods for querying entities such as the Java Persistence query language (JPQL) and the Criteria API.

Let's compare a bit JPQL and Criteria APIs. JPQL queries are generally more concise and readable than Criteria queries. JPQL is easy to learn for programmers with previous SQL knowledge.

JPQL queries are not typesafe, which means that they require a cast when retrieving the query result from the entity manager. Because of that the type-casting errors may not be caught at compiling time.

Also, JPQL queries do not support open-ended parameters. Criteria API queries are typesafe and therefore don't require casting. Remember that when comparing performance between JPQL and Criteria API, Criteria API queries provide better performance because JPQL dynamic queries must be parsed each time they are called.

One of the common Criteria API disadvantages is that they are typically more verbose than JPQL queries. This means that they will require the programmers to create many objects and perform operations on those objects before submitting the Criteria API query to the entity manager.

JPA defines its own query language to support entity-based queries along with bulk update and delete operations. JPQL shares much in common with SQL, with the main difference being that the primary structures are entities and fields instead of tables and columns. Like SQL, JPQL queries may be defined either statically, through declared @NamedQuery annotations, or as dynamic statements submitted to the EntityManager and processed at runtime. Queries may take bind parameters, and their returned results may be entities or ordinary Java objects.

By expressing queries in terms of entities and their fields, JPQL statements become independent of the underlying schema. Thus, a JPQL query need not change when an entity's mappings are modified.

JPQL queries are executed by the EntityManager on the persistence context, so query results will include uncommitted data that is pending in the context transaction.

@NamedQuery and @NamedQueries

```
@Target({TYPE}) @Retention(RUNTIME)
public @interface NamedQuery {
    String name();
    String query ();
    LockModeType lockMode() default LockModeType.NONE;
    QueryHint[] hints() default {};
}
@Target({TYPE}) @Retention(RUNTIME)
public @interface NamedQueries {
    NamedQuery [] value ();
}
```

An entity may declare named JPQL statements inside @NamedQuery annotations to define reusable queries. A @NamedQuery consists simply of a name and a query containing the JPQL text. @NamedQuery names must be unique across the persistence unit.

```
@Entity
@NamedQueries({
  @NamedQuery(name="Inventory.findAll",
              query="select o from Inventory o"),
  @NamedQuery(name="Inventory.findByYear",
```

```
            query="select o from Inventory o where o.year=:year"),
  @NamedQuery(name="Inventory.findByRegion",
            query="select o from Inventory o where o.region=?1 ")
})
public class Inventory implements Serializable {
    . . .
}
```

Binding Query Parameters

Queries may take bind parameters, either as named parameters or indexed parameters. To invoke the queries from the previous section, client code, such as a session bean, might issue the following calls:

```
@Stateless
public class InventoryManagerBean implements InventoryManager,
                                             InventoryManagerLocal {
    . . .
    /** <code>select o from Inventory o</code> */
    public List<Inventory> findAllInventory() {
        return em.createNamedQuery("Inventory.findAll", Inventory.class).
        getResultList();
    }
    /** <code>select o from Inventory o where o.year=:year</code> */
    public List<Inventory> findInventoryByYear(Object year) {
        return em.createNamedQuery("Inventory.findByYear", Inventory.
        class).setParameter("year",year).getResultList();
    }

    /** <code>select object(o) from Inventory o where o.region=?1 </code> */
    public List<Inventory> findInventoryByRegion(Object p1) {
        return em.createNamedQuery("findInventoryByRegion", Inventory.
        class).setParameter(0,p1).getResultList();
    }
    . . .
}
```

Note that the findInventoryByYear query takes a named parameter, :year, whereas findInventoryByRegion uses an indexed parameter, ?1. These approaches are equivalent but require different setParameter() calls when binding the parameters prior to query execution time, as shown in the previous sample code.

Dynamic Queries

So far, we have shown example queries that are defined through the @NamedQuery annotation on an entity class. It is also possible to execute queries dynamically by passing query strings that may be constructed on the fly at runtime.

Listing 3-19 shows an example of how this is done.

Listing 3-19. Example of Dynamic JPQL Usage

```
@Stateless
public class CustomerManagerBean {

  @PersistenceContext(unitName = "Chapter03PersistenceUnit")
  private EntityManager em;

  /** <code>select object(o) from Customer o</code> */
  public List<Customer> findAllCustomers() {
    return em.createQuery("select o from Customer o", Customer.class).
    getResultList();
  }

  // ...
}
```

Bulk Update and Delete Operations

JPQL may also be used to perform bulk update and delete operations across multiple instances of a specific entity class, including subclass instances. These JPQL statements may also take parameters and return the number of entity instances affected by the operation. An example of a bulk delete operation is shown in Listing 3-20.

Listing 3-20. Example of a Bulk Delete Statement in JPQL

```
@Stateless
public class CustomerManagerBean {

  @PersistenceContext(unitName = "Chapter03PersistenceUnit")
  private EntityManager em;

  /**
   * Perform a bulk delete of fulfilled CustomerOrder items
   */
  public int bulkDeleteFulfilledOrders() {
    return em.createQuery("delete from CustomerOrder o where o.status =
    'FULFILLED'").executeUpdate();
  }

  // ...
}
```

Bulk delete and update statements are executed through the EntityManagers query engine using the EntityManager.createQuery() call. They may also be specified either declaratively, through @NamedQuery elements, or dynamically, as shown above in Listing 3-20.

Caution   Care should be taken when performing bulk update and delete operations, since they bypass the PersistenceContext and can lead to cache inconsistency. They are essentially translated straight into SQL and executed without observing optimistic locking checks or following cascade rules specified on relationship fields. As a rule of thumb, bulk operations should be performed in their own transaction context, or else at the beginning of a transaction. If a PersistenceContext whose type is PersistenceContextType.EXTENDED is used, make sure you call EntityManager.flush() after performing a bulk operation. That way, no entities will exist in the cache following the bulk operation that might be out of date or removed.

Complex Queries

We will cover more advanced areas of JPQL in the next chapter, including queries that return ordinary, non-entity Java objects; and native queries written in SQL, which may return results that are converted into entity instances.

Note   One of the most important changes in JPA 2.2 is the ability to stream the result of a query execution using the method Stream getResultStream() added to Query and TypedQuery interface. This can be very usable when we need to process a huge result set.

Persistence vs. Adaption

One of the decisions an application designer has to make when approaching JPA entity classes is whether to design them top down or bottom up: that is, whether first to create the entities and let the database schema follow, or whether to create the database schema first. It is, of course, possible to build both entities and tables in parallel, but in many cases one or the other of these objects is fixed, and the other must be built to match.

Forward Generation—Persistence

In the top-down model, the entity class serves as the source of truth, and the database schema is created to provide persistence for the entity class data. The underlying table(s) can be generated as a side effect of deploying the entity class; you may wish to specify metadata in @Table, @Column, and related annotations to guide the deployment tool in generating the structure of the schema.

Reverse Engineering—Adaption

In the bottom-up approach, the database schema is the source of truth: the schema is fixed, and the Java objects—entity classes—exist to adapt the database objects into the Java world. This process, typically provided through an IDE using an EJB reverse engineering tool, generates a default entity class for each table and a default field for each column.

Which One Is Right for Your Project?

Both approaches are equally common in real-world development projects. Your needs will dictate which tools you will want to use to glue the database to the entity beans. You may think of the issue as one of persistence vs. adaption: does the database schema exist solely to provide persistence for the entity beans, or are you adapting the database schema into the Java space? Consider this question when you begin to create your entity beans.

Example Application: CustomerOrderManager

In the CustomerOrderManager example, we show how a session bean may serve as a façade for a handful of interrelated JPA entities. Our `CustomerOrderManager` session bean exposes CRUD (create, retrieve, update, delete) operations as service methods, allowing clients to access and manipulate `Customer`, `CustomerOrder`, and `Address` entities. These service methods on the session façade provide transaction, access control, and other enterprise-level services, and they allow the persistence framework to handle the interface between the JPA entities and the underlying RDBMS.

Customer.java

The `Customer.java` class, shown in Listing 3-21, hosts a pair of named queries and has a simple primary key. It holds two unidirectional `@OneToOne` relationships with the `Address` entity implemented through the `billingAddress` and `shippingAddress` fields. It also has a bidirectional `@OneToMany` relationship with `CustomerOrder`, exposed through the `customerOrders` field. Note that the property accessors for the `customerOrders` field are complemented by `addCustomerOrder()` and `removeCustomerOrder()` methods. These methods should be used by clients when adding or removing a `CustomerOrder` from a `Customer` to ensure that the relationship fields on both entity classes involved are properly updated with the correct relationship information.

Listing 3-21. Customer.java

```
@Entity
@NamedQueries({
  @NamedQuery(name = "Customer.findAll",
              query = "select o from Customer o"),
```

```java
  @NamedQuery(name = "Customer.findByEmail",
                query = "select o from Customer o where o.email = :email")})
@Table(name = "CH03_CUSTOMER")
@TableGenerator(name = "Customer_ID_Generator",
                table = "CUSTOMER_ID_GENERATOR",
                pkColumnName = "PRIMARY_KEY_NAME",
                pkColumnValue = "Customer.id",
                valueColumnName = "NEXT_ID_VALUE")
public class Customer implements Serializable {

  @Id
  @Column(nullable = false)
  @GeneratedValue(strategy = GenerationType.TABLE,
                generator = "Customer_ID_Generator")
  private BigDecimal id;
  @Version
  private int version;
  @Column(length = 4000)
  private String email;
  @OneToMany(mappedBy = "customer", cascade = {CascadeType.ALL})
  private List<CustomerOrder> customerOrders;
  @OneToOne(cascade = {CascadeType.ALL})
  @JoinColumn(name = "BILLING_ADDRESS")
  private Address billingAddress;
  @OneToOne(cascade = {CascadeType.ALL})
  @JoinColumn(name = "SHIPPING_ADDRESS")
  private Address shippingAddress;

  public BigDecimal getId() { return id; }
  public void setId(BigDecimal id) { this.id = id; }

  public int getVersion() { return version; }
  public void setVersion(int version) { this.version = version; }

  public String getEmail() { return email; }
  public void setEmail(String email) { this.email = email; }
```

```java
public List<CustomerOrder> getCustomerOrders() { return customerOrders; }
public void setCustomerOrders(List<CustomerOrder> customerOrders) {
  this.customerOrders = customerOrders;
}

public CustomerOrder addCustomerOrder(CustomerOrder customerOrder) {
  if (customerOrders == null) {
    customerOrders = new ArrayList<CustomerOrder>();
  }
  customerOrders.add(customerOrder);
  customerOrder.setCustomer(this);
  return customerOrder;
}

public CustomerOrder removeCustomerOrder(CustomerOrder customerOrder) {
  getCustomerOrders().remove(customerOrder);
  customerOrder.setCustomer(null);
  return customerOrder;
}

public Address getBillingAddress() { return billingAddress; }
public void setBillingAddress(Address billingAddress) {
  this.billingAddress = billingAddress;
}

public Address getShippingAddress() { return shippingAddress; }
public void setShippingAddress(Address shippingAddress) {
  this.shippingAddress = shippingAddress;
}
}
```

An instance of the CustomerOrder entity, shown in Listing 3-22, represents an order placed by a customer. For this example, we have eliminated the related OrderItem entities for brevity. The full-blown Apress Wines Online application, which includes a number of other entities as well, is explored in Chapter 7.

Listing 3-22. CustomerOrder.java

```
@Entity
@NamedQueries({
  @NamedQuery(name = "CustomerOrder.findAll",
              query = "select o from CustomerOrder o")})
@Table(name = "CH03_CUSTOMER_ORDER")
@TableGenerator(name = "CustomerOrder_ID_Generator",
                table = "CUSTOMERORDER_ID_GENERATOR",
pkColumnName = "PRIMARY_KEY_NAME", pkColumnValue = "CustomerOrder.id",
valueColumnName = "NEXT_ID_VALUE")
public class CustomerOrder implements Serializable {

  @Id
  @Column(nullable = false)
  @GeneratedValue(strategy = GenerationType.TABLE,
                  generator = "CustomerOrder_ID_Generator")
  private BigDecimal id;
  @Version
  private int version;
  @Temporal(TemporalType.DATE)
  @Column(name = "CREATION_DATE")
  private Date creationDate;
  private String status;
  @ManyToOne
  @JoinColumn(name = "CUSTOMER_ID")
  private Customer customer;

  public Date getCreationDate() { return creationDate; }
  public void setCreationDate(Date creationDate) {
    this.creationDate = creationDate;
  }

  public BigDecimal getId() { return id; }
  public void setId(BigDecimal id) { this.id = id; }
```

```java
public String getStatus() { return status; }
public void setStatus(String status) { this.status = status; }

public int getVersion() { return version; }
public void setVersion(int version) { this.version = version; }

public Customer getCustomer() { return customer; }
public void setCustomer(Customer customer) { this.customer = customer; }
}
```

The final entity in this example is Address, shown in Listing 3-23. The Address entity is referenced by the Customer entity but holds no relationship field of its own, making the references from Customer unidirectional.

Listing 3-23. Address.java

```java
@Entity
@NamedQueries({
  @NamedQuery(name = "Address.findAll",
              query = "select o from Address o")})
@Table(name = "CH03_ADDRESS")
@TableGenerator(name = "Address_ID_Generator",
                table = "CH03_ADDRESS_ID_GEN",
                pkColumnName = "PRIMARY_KEY_NAME",
                pkColumnValue = "Address.id",
                valueColumnName = "NEXT_ID_VALUE")
public class Address implements Serializable {

  @Column(length = 4000)
  private String city;
  @Id
  @Column(nullable = false)
  @GeneratedValue(strategy = GenerationType.TABLE,
                  generator = "Address_ID_Generator")
  private BigDecimal id;
  private String state;
  @Column(length = 4000)
  private String street1;
```

```
@Column(length = 4000)
private String street2;
@Version
private Integer version;
@Column(name = "ZIP_CODE")
private int zipCode;

public String getCity() { return city; }
public void setCity(String city) { this.city = city; }

public BigDecimal getId() { return id; }
public void setId(BigDecimal id) { this.id = id; }

public String getState() { return state; }
public void setState(String state) { this.state = state; }

public String getStreet1() { return street1; }
public void setStreet1(String street1) { this.street1 = street1; }

public String getStreet2() { return street2; }
public void setStreet2(String street2) { this.street2 = street2; }

public Integer getVersion() { return version; }
public void setVersion(Integer version) { this.version = version; }

public int getZipCode() { return zipCode; }
public void setZipCode(int zipCode) { this.zipCode = zipCode; }
}
```

The CustomerOrderManager Stateless session bean serves as a façade for the three entities shown previously, and it offers an interface to the persist(), merge(), and remove() methods on EntityManager. It is shown in Listing 3-24.

Listing 3-24. CustomerOrderManager.java

```
@Stateless
public class CustomerOrderManager {

  @PersistenceContext(unitName = "Chapter03PersistenceUnit")
  private EntityManager em;
```

```java
public CustomerOrderManager() {
}

public <T> T persistEntity(T entity) {
  em.persist(entity);
  return entity;
}

public <T> T mergeEntity(T entity) {
  return em.merge(entity);
}

public void removeCustomer(Customer customer) {
  customer = em.find(Customer.class, customer.getId());
  em.remove(customer);
}

/** <code>select o from Customer o</code> */
public List<Customer> getCustomerFindAll() {
  return em.createNamedQuery("Customer.findAll", Customer.class).
  getResultList();
}

public void removeAddress(Address address) {
  address = em.find(Address.class, address.getId());
  em.remove(address);
}

/** <code>select o from Address o</code> */
public List<Address> getAddressFindAll() {
  return em.createNamedQuery("Address.findAll", Address.class).
  getResultList();
}

public void removeCustomerOrder(CustomerOrder customerOrder) {
  customerOrder = em.find(CustomerOrder.class, customerOrder.getId());
  em.remove(customerOrder);
}
```

```
/** <code>select o from CustomerOrder o</code> */
public List<CustomerOrder> getCustomerOrderFindAll() {
  return em
    .createNamedQuery("CustomerOrder.findAll", CustomerOrder.class)
    .getResultList();
}

/** <code>select o from CustomerOrder o where o.email = :email</code> */
public List<CustomerOrder> getCustomerOrderFindByEmail(String email) {
  return em
    .createNamedQuery("CustomerOrder.findByEmail", CustomerOrder.class)
    .setParameter("email", email)
    .getResultList();
  }
}
```

To deploy this example, you will need a persistence.xml file that declares a named persistence unit that can be referenced by the session bean (see Listing 3-25).

Listing 3-25. persistence.xml

```
<?xml version="1.0" encoding="UTF-8"?>
<persistence xmlns="http://xmlns.jcp.org/xml/ns/
persistence" xmlns:xsi="http://www.w3.org/2001/XMLSchema-
instance"   xsi:schemaLocation="http://xmlns.jcp.org/xml/ns/persistence
http://xmlns.jcp.org/xml/ns/persistence/persistence_2_2.xsd" version="2.2">
<persistence-unit name="Chapter03PersistenceUnit" transaction-type="JTA">
    <provider>org.eclipse.persistence.jpa.PersistenceProvider</provider>
    <jta-data-source>jdbc/wineapp</jta-data-source>
    <class>com.apress.ejb.chapter03.entities.Address</class>
    <class>com.apress.ejb.chapter03.entities.CustomerOrder</class>
    <class>com.apress.ejb.chapter03.entities.Customer</class>
    <exclude-unlisted-classes>true</exclude-unlisted-classes>
    <properties>
```

```
        <property name="eclipselink.ddl-generation" value="create-tables"/>
    </properties>
  </persistence-unit>
</persistence>
```

Compiling, Deploying, and Testing the JPA Entities

Prerequisites

Before performing any of the steps detailed in the next sections, complete the "Getting Started" section of Chapter 1. This section will walk you through the installation and environment setup required for the samples in this chapter.

Opening the Sample Application

Copy the Chapter03-PersistenceSamples directory and its contents into a directory of your choice. Run the NetBeans IDE, and open the Chapter03-PersistenceSamples project using the File ➤ Open Project menu. Make sure the 'Open Required Projects' check box is checked. See Figure 3-1.

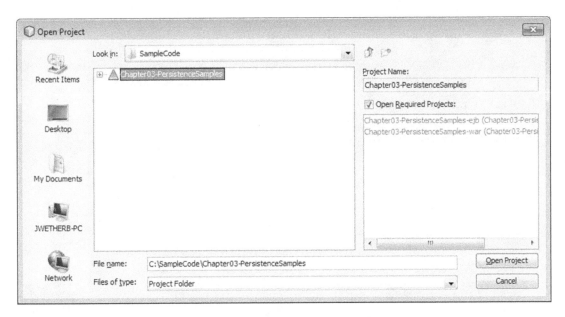

Figure 3-1. *Opening the Chapter03-PersistenceSamples project*

Expand the `Chapter03-PersistenceSamples-ejb` node and observe the packages containing the EJB façade and the JPA entities for this sample application, and the sources for the chapter listings. The `persistence.xml` file can be found in the `Configuration Files` folder, and the JDBC data-sources that specify the database connection are found in the `glassfish-resources.xml` file under `Server Resources`. As described in "The Persistence Archive" section above, a JPA persistence archive may be packaged in various ways within the application. In this example, we are bundling the persistence archive together with the EJB façade, in the EJB .jar file.

The client HTTP servlet, `CustomerOrderManagerClient.java`, lives in the `Chapter03-PersistenceSamples-war` project. See Figure 3-2.

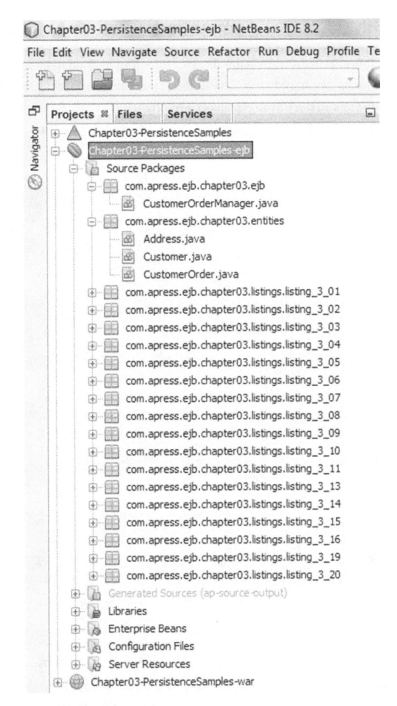

Figure 3-2. *Verifying that the EJB and the JPA artifacts are available in the project*

Creating the Database Connection and Sample Schema

The samples in this chapter require a database connection and a database schema populated with tables that map to the JPA entities. To create the database itself, click on the Services tab, expand the Databases icon, and invoke "Create Database. . ." on the Java DB node. Create a database named "WineApp," with username and password wineapp/wineapp as shown in Figure 3-3.

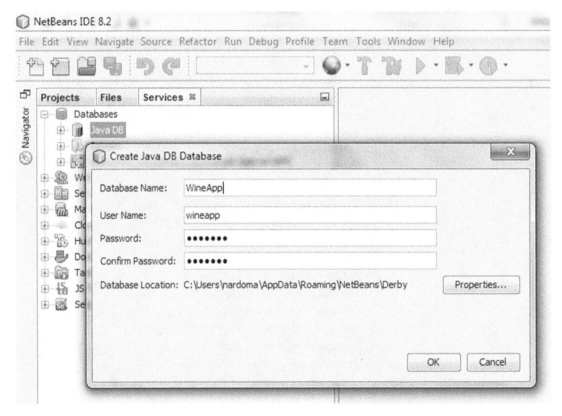

Figure 3-3. *Creating the WineApp database and connection*

This last step created a database connection, which can now be used to create the database schema. To do this, switch to the Files tab, expand the Chapter03-PersistenceSamples folder and then the database folder, right-click on the Chapte03-WineAppSchema.sql file, and choose "Run File." In the dialog, be sure to select the new WineApp connection created in the previous step. You can safely ignore errors that are raised in the Chapter03-WineAppSchema.sql script caused by an attempt to clean out objects that don't yet exist. See Figure 3-4.

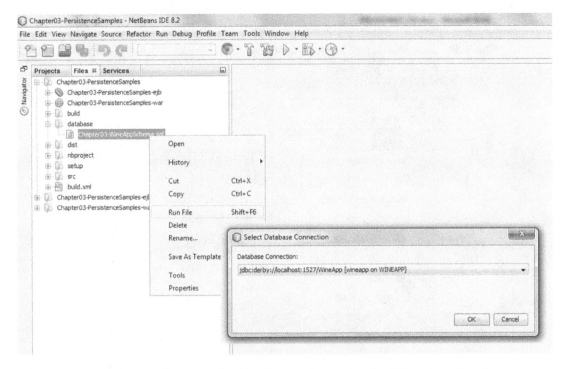

Figure 3-4. *Creating the sample database schema in the WineApp database*

Compiling the Entities, EJBs, and the Client

Invoke the context menu on Chapter03-PersistenceSamples node and build the application by selecting the Clean and Build menu option. See Figure 3-5.

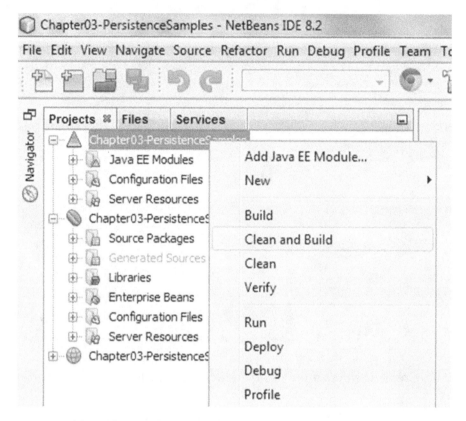

Figure 3-5. *Building the application*

Deploying the JPA Persistence Unit, the EJB Module, and the Servlet

Once you have compiled the application, you can deploy it to the GlassFish application server. Invoke the context menu on Chapter03-PersistenceSamples node and deploy the application by selecting the Deploy menu option. See Figure 3-6.

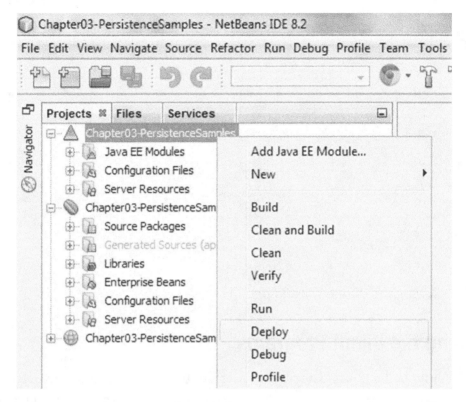

Figure 3-6. *Deploying the application*

NetBeans will start the integrated GlassFish application server and deploy the application to the server. The server's log window will log the deployment status of the application. See Figure 3-7.

Figure 3-7. *Log showing successful deployment*

Running the Client Programs

Once the entities, the EJB, and its client servlet are successfully deployed, we need to set the run target that we wish to execute. To set the run target, invoke the context menu on Chapter03-PersistenceSamples node and select the Properties menu option. Select the Run category, enter the run target "CustomerOrderManagerClient" in the Relative URL text field, and OK the dialog.

To run the client HTTP servlet, invoke the context menu on Chapter03-PersistenceSamples node and select the Run menu option, as shown in Figure 3-8.

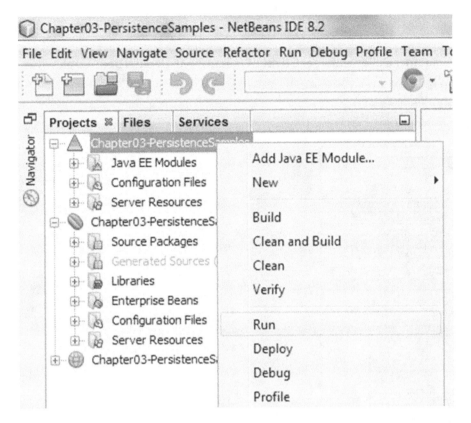

Figure 3-8. *Running the selected servlet*

NetBeans will open your default browser and execute the selected servlet. Any existing conflicting data is deleted, new test data is created, and then it is queried and rendered in tabular format. To avoid circular dependencies, an entity's properties are displayed only the first time it is encountered; any subsequent reference to that entity is shown as [<entity> <PK> already printed]. Referenced objects, including lists of referenced objects, are show in nested table cells. Here is the output for the client servlet, showing the log of the servlet's actions. See Figure 3-9.

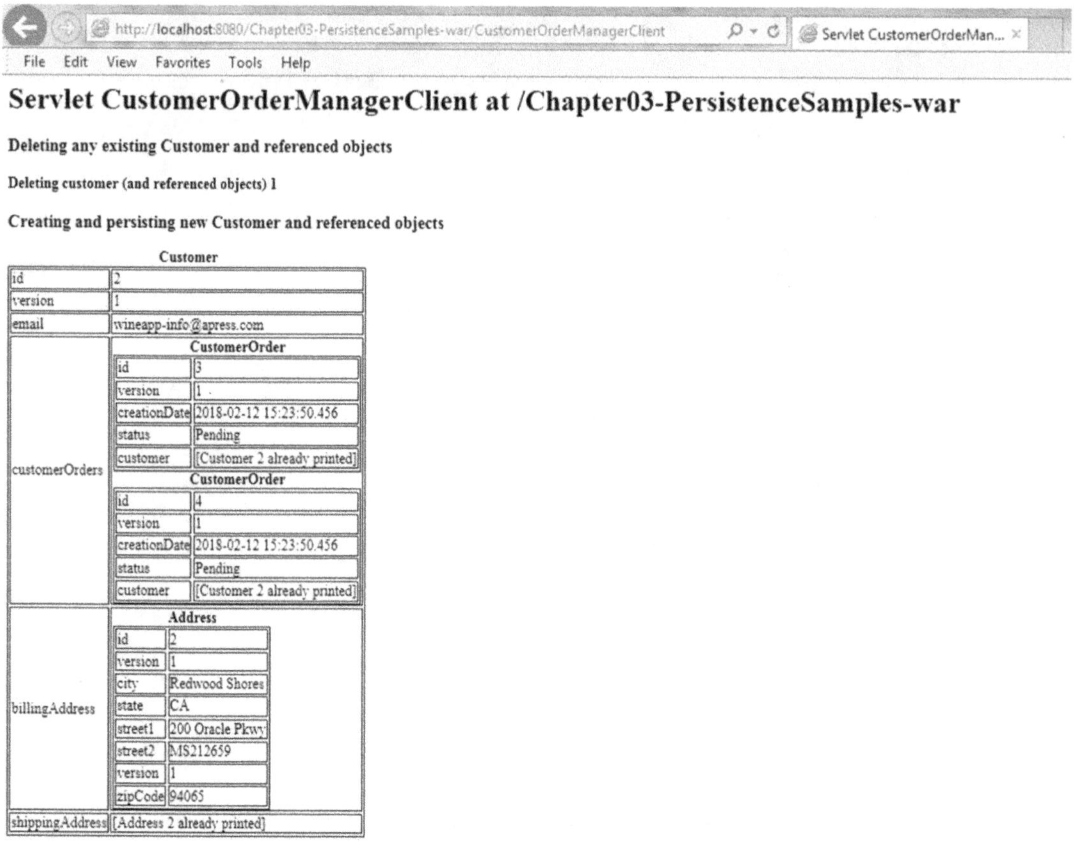

Figure 3-9. *Output of CustomerOrderManagerClient servlet*

Take a look at the code in `CustomerOrderManagerClient.java`. Feel free to experiment by creating additional entities, testing the `mergeEntity()` and other service methods on the EJB session bean, and observing the resulting behavior. To reset the test schema back to its original state, you can always re-execute the step depicted in Figure 3-4.

Summary

This chapter introduced the Java Persistence API 2.2 introduced with Java EE 8 and a few of the essential services it offers. We examined how a simple JavaBean can be transformed into a JPA entity simply by adding a couple of annotations. We then extended this example to illustrate how you can further refine your entities to add greater flexibility by declaratively specifying additional annotations on the entity class.

We explored these essential components of JPA: the persistence archive, the persistence unit, the persistence context, and the `EntityManager`. We walked through the entity life cycle to examine an entity's behavior as it transitions between the following states: new, managed, detached, and removed.

The section on O/R mapping explored how entities map to their underlying tables, and how you can control the basic mapping to allow a field to map to a column with a different name.

We discussed the role of an entity's primary key, explored both simple and composite primary keys, and how to define each. We showed how to configure an ID generator to have JPA auto-assign an entity's PK at the time it is persisted.

We then delved into entity relationships and discussed the relationship field types supported by JPA: `@OneToOne`, `@OneToMany`, `@ManyToOne`, and `@ManyToMany`.

A discussion of JPQL ensued with examples of how to declare and execute named queries and how to use dynamic and bulk update and delete queries.

We concluded with a sample application that illustrated how related entities interact and how they can be manipulated through a session façade that is in turn called from an HTTP servlet.

CHAPTER 4

Advanced Persistence Features

We have organized the persistence sections of this book into three main chapters. The previous chapter introduced the Java Persistence API (JPA), and it gave you a starting point for creating entities, wiring up object/relational (O/R) mappings, and writing queries that retrieve them. With an understanding of these concepts, you can create and build applications with powerful, persistent entities that run both inside and outside an EJB container.

In this chapter, we build upon this knowledge and explore areas of the Java Persistence API (JPA) that offer greater flexibility and power to your applications, including the following:

- How to define and work with entity inheritance hierarchies

- How to work with abstract entities, mapped superclasses, and non-entity classes

- How to build queries with Java Persistence Query Language (JPQL), native SQL, and the query criteria API

- How to configure ID generators to auto-populate primary key fields

- How to specify entity lifecycle callbacks

- How to configure optimistic locking

The third main area of the Persistence API, which will be covered in Chapter 8, involves EJB support for transaction management when working with JPA entities. The EJB container provides you with options for session beans to manage the life cycle of the `EntityManager`, control the longevity of your persistence context, and use either Java Transaction API (JTA) or resource-local transactions. With good knowledge of the way EJB and JPA support transactions and how you can apply this technology, you will have the tools to build full-scale, persistent enterprise applications.

157

© Jonathan Wetherbee, Massimo Nardone, Chirag Rathod, and Raghu Kodali 2018
J. Wetherbee et al., *Beginning EJB in Java EE 8*, https://doi.org/10.1007/978-1-4842-3573-7_4

As with the rest of this book, this chapter covers many of the concepts defined in the specification, but it is not intended to supplant it. Indeed, readers are strongly encouraged to consult the spec as a reference document and a resource for exploring these concepts in even greater depth, and to discover others that go beyond the scope of this introductory text. Here we focus on translating some of the fundamental features from spec into their applied use, providing examples of how the new persistence features can be used to accomplish your real-world goals of building component-based enterprise Java applications.

Each of the major concepts in this chapter is captured in a separate, runnable example. The steps required to run the examples are covered at the end of the chapter in the section entitled "Compiling, Deploying, and Testing the JPA Entities." The general structure is that we provide a stand-alone NetBeans project for each example and supply each with its own JPA persistence unit, entities, and Java test service classes. You can run and test the examples from a Java client in a pure Java SE environment without running Glassfish, or you can execute the servlets that accompany each of these projects to run the sample in a Java EE Web environment.

Note   As discussed in the previous chapter, entities may designate their persistent state to be defined by either their instance variables or bean property accessors. To improve readability in this chapter, we use the term *field* to refer generically to the persistent members of an entity, leaving open the detail of how the entity declares its persistent properties.

Mapping Entity Inheritance Hierarchies

Java has supported single class inheritance—in which a non-interface class may extend a single other class—since its inception. While it has been a common practice to exploit the code reuse and polymorphism benefits of inheritance in many areas of the business domain, data inheritance was not supported in the EJB persistence domain until the introduction of JPA. This had been a major shortcoming since, in the real world, data is often hierarchical; and the lack of standard, built-in support for inheritance of data objects has required countless workarounds and headaches. Leveraging the ease of use of JDK annotations, JPA delivers declarative support for defining and mapping entity inheritance hierarchies, including abstract entities and polymorphic relationships and queries.

Note   An *abstract entity* is an entity class that contains the `abstract` modifier and therefore cannot be instantiated in its own right. An abstract entity must be an intermediate class in an entity inheritance hierarchy; it may not itself be a leaf entity since it may only be instantiated through one of its subentities. Correspondingly, all leaf entities in an entity inheritance hierarchy must be concrete and therefore instantiable. An abstract entity exists to provide a common data structure for its subentities and to represent its subentities through polymorphic relationships with other entities.

Much of the entity inheritance support in JPA is borne of the work of designers and tool developers who have, over the years, come up with ways to roll their own O/R mappings, and JPA has conveniently adopted several alternative inheritance mapping approaches that derive from these efforts.

Within a given entity inheritance hierarchy, a single inheritance strategy applies to all entities in the hierarchy. Additionally, all entities in a hierarchy must use the same primary key type, regardless of the inheritance strategy. This makes it reasonable for the container to support polymorphic relationships, regardless of the mapping strategy employed for the class hierarchy.

Also, should your database have the restriction that a table be limited to 256 columns, note that entities are free to distribute their field mappings across joined rows in multiple tables.

Getting Started

All of the code snippets in this chapter exist in runnable form that you can download and execute directly in your local environment together with SQL scripts for creating the corresponding tables and other database artifacts in your local database. The steps for running the samples are described at the end of the chapter. Since these examples deal only with entities, we can leverage the pure Java SE (outside-the-container) support offered in JPA and skip the step of deploying these entities into a Java EE container. You will see that a simple Java class is sufficient to create an `EntityManager` that can interact with these entities and drive example tests. Seeing these concepts in action will help clear up questions left unanswered here, and the samples should also provide a useful launch pad for testing out your own ideas.

Entity Inheritance Mapping Strategies

JPA provides declarative support for three main implementation strategies that dictate how the entities in a hierarchy map to underlying tables. We will examine each strategy by applying it to a sample entity hierarchy and explore the strengths and weaknesses of each approach. This comparison is intended to help you decide how to map each of the entity hierarchies in your own application.

Sample Entity Hierarchy

To illustrate how these three strategies are manifested in code, Figure 4-1 shows a sample entity hierarchy that demonstrates both inheritance and polymorphic relationships.

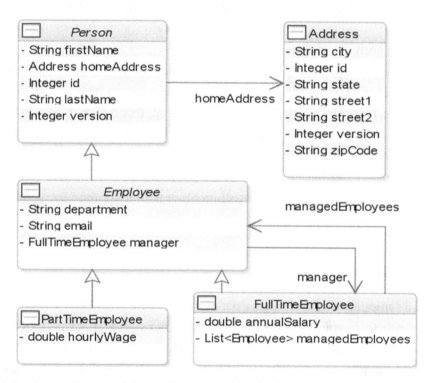

Figure 4-1. *An entity type hierarchy, rooted in the base entity Person, showing relationships between entities both inside and outside the hierarchy*

In this example, the Person entity serves as the root class in an entity hierarchy, and it is extended by the Employee entity. Employee is further specialized to produce two other entities: FullTimeEmployee and PartTimeEmployee. Inheritance relationships are expressed in the figure through unnamed white arrowheads, and ordinary entity relationships are expressed with named open arrowheads.

The root Person entity and the intermediate Employee entity are both abstract in our example. Only the leaf entities FullTimeEmployee and PartTimeEmployee, and the stand-alone entity Address, are concrete and instantiable. Note that even abstract entities may be involved in relationships with other entities and, as you will see from the code that follows, abstract entities may also be used in JPQL statements. Whenever a non-leaf entity is referenced, that reference implicitly assumes that the actual concrete implementation being referenced may be that entity or any of its subclass entities. Non-leaf entities may also be concrete, though, and had we chosen to do this in our example, we could have made these base classes concrete.

The root Person entity also holds a single-value reference to an Address instance, represented by the homeAddress field on Person. This relationship is inherited by all subclasses of Person; so all instances of Employee (FullTimeEmployee and PartTimeEmployee) can also refer to their homeAddress field. Note that there is no corresponding field on Address referencing Person, so this is a unidirectional relationship. From our coverage of entity relationships in the previous chapter, you will recall that this is a one-to-one relationship.

Note   A relationship between two entities that is exposed through a field on only one of the entities is known as a *unidirectional relationship*. A relationship exposed through fields on both entities involved is known as a *bidirectional relationship*.

In addition, we have defined a one-to-many, bidirectional relationship between a FullTimeEmployee (a manager) and a collection of Employees (its managedEmployees). Because this relationship is exposed through fields at both ends of the relationship (in this case, the two entities involved are actually the same entity, Employee), this is a bidirectional, one-to-many relationship.

As you look at each example, you will see how the Java source files are essentially constant across the three inheritance mapping strategies. Only the class-level annotations for declaring the inheritance strategies, and some details, like the table names, separate the entities in one example from another. This is a key benefit—the chosen inheritance strategy can be replaced without impacting the entities' Java API. In the three sections that follow, we will illustrate how each mapping strategy can be applied to this hierarchy.

In these inheritance examples, we included a separate table for the Address entity alongside the tables mapped to each inheritance hierarchy, as depicted in the database schema diagrams. It is not strictly necessary to replace the ADDRESS table for each entity hierarchy, since whatever table is associated with the Person entity could hold its own foreign key reference to a common ADDRESS table. However, we took this approach to help isolate each inheritance example.

Object/Relational Inheritance Mapping Strategies

Note   Unless otherwise specified, you can assume that all JPA classes mentioned in this chapter are in the `javax.persistence.*` package.

Now that we have defined our entity hierarchy, let's look at how each of the three O/R strategies supported natively by JPA can be used to map this Person entity hierarchy, and the associated Address entity, to a relational schema. Here is a summary of each strategy defined by the InheritanceType enum:

```
public enum InheritanceType
{ SINGLE_TABLE, JOINED, TABLE_PER_CLASS };
```

- SINGLE_TABLE: Single-table-per-class inheritance hierarchy. This is the default strategy. The entity hierarchy is essentially flattened into the sum of its fields, and these fields are mapped down to a single table.

- JOINED: Common base table with joined subclass tables. In this approach, each entity in the hierarchy maps to its own dedicated table that maps only the fields declared on that entity. The root entity in the hierarchy is mapped to the base table, and the tables for all other entities in the hierarchy reference this base table.

- TABLE_PER_CLASS: Single-table-per-outermost concrete entity class. The third inheritance mapping option is also not required of JPA containers for compliance with the final draft of the JPA 2.1 spec, so portable applications should avoid it until it is officially mandated or at least widely supported. This strategy maps each leaf (that is, outermost, concrete) entity to its own dedicated table. Each such leaf entity branch is flattened, combining its declared fields with the declared fields on all of its superentities, and the sum of these fields is mapped onto its table.

The @GeneratedValue Annotation

In each of the inheritance strategy examples, we use the @GeneratedValue annotation to auto-populate the entity's primary key for both the Person entity hierarchy and the stand-alone Address entity. In our examples, we designate a field named id as the primary key, simply for consistency. Specifying an ID generator in metadata allows the persistence provider to assign an entity its ID value before the entity is actually saved as a row in the database. Declarative specification of the @GeneratedValue annotation is certainly easier than assigning the ID in application code, and it is also an optimization over the alternative of auto-populating the ID value using a database trigger. Since the ID value is used when persisting relationship mappings, this saves the persistence manager the trouble of querying the row back again from the database to retrieve the trigger-populated value. Details on how to customize sequence- or table-based ID generators are provided later in the chapter.

We will now explore each strategy, discussing its strengths and weaknesses, and illustrating its use through examples.

Note   Java source files for the examples shown in the listings below can all be found in the Source Code area for this chapter.

Single-Table-per-Class Inheritance Hierarchy (InheritanceType.SINGLE_TABLE)

The default inheritance mapping strategy is SINGLE_TABLE, in which all the entities in the class hierarchy map onto a single table. A dedicated discriminator column on this table identifies the specific entity type associated with each row, and each entity in the hierarchy is given a unique value to store in this column. By default, the discriminator value for an entity is its entity name, although an entity may override this value using the @DiscriminatorValue annotation. This approach performs well for querying, since only a single table is involved, and if your type of hierarchy can abide by the practical limitations, this is probably the best approach to use.

Figure 4-2 shows a diagram of a schema that maps our example entities using the SINGLE_TABLE strategy. We have chosen to prefix these tables with CH04_ST_ to avoid conflicts with the PERSON and ADDRESS tables in our example schema that are used by the full Enterprise Wines Online application.

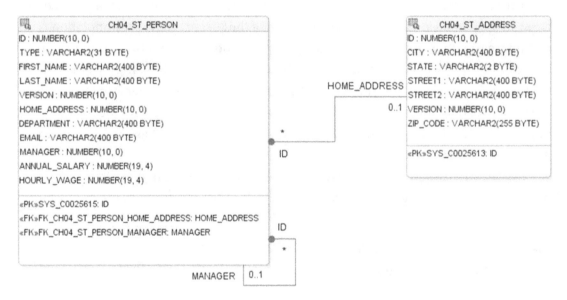

Figure 4-2. *The CH04_ST_PERSON table holds all entity instances in the entity hierarchy rooted by Person. The CH04_ST_ADDRESS table holds the associated Address instances.*

All of the properties across the entity hierarchy rooted by the Person entity map to columns on a single table, CH04_ST_PERSON. This table holds a foreign key reference, bound to the HOME_ADDRESS column, to CH04_ST_ADDRESS, which is mapped to the Address entity. It also holds a foreign key reference, using the MANAGER column, back to itself. This foreign key is not constrained to be unique, indicating that multiple rows may hold the same value in their MANAGER column.

Example Entity Classes

Listings 4-1 through 4-4 show how the entities in the Person hierarchy are mapped using the SINGLE_TABLE inheritance strategy. The inheritance strategy is declared on the root entity in the hierarchy, and it also applies to all subentities in the hierarchy. Annotations introduced in the example entities that have not yet been covered are explained in the sections that follow.

Listing 4-1. Person.java, an Abstract Root Entity in a SINGLE_TABLE Inheritance Hierarchy

```
/*
 * Person: An abstract entity, and the root of an inheritance hierarchy
 *
 * To create ID generator table "CH04_ST_PERSON_ID_GEN":
 * CREATE TABLE "CH04_ST_PERSON_ID_GEN" ("PRIMARY_KEY_NAME" VARCHAR2(4000)
   PRIMARY KEY,     "NEXT_ID_VALUE" NUMBER(38));
 *
 * To initialize this table with data for this entity's ID generator
   'Person.id' (starting with     value '0'):
 * INSERT INTO "CH04_ST_PERSON_ID_GEN" VALUES ('Person.id', 0);
 */
@Entity
@NamedQueries({ @NamedQuery(name = "Person.findAll", query = "select o from
Person o") })
@Table(name = "CH04_ST_PERSON")
@TableGenerator(name = "Person_ID_Generator", table = "CH04_ST_PERSON_ID_
GEN", pkColumnName = "PRIMARY_KEY_NAME",
                pkColumnValue = "Person.id", valueColumnName = "NEXT_ID_VALUE")
@Inheritance(strategy = InheritanceType.SINGLE_TABLE)
```

```
@DiscriminatorColumn(name="TYPE")
public abstract class Person
  implements Serializable
{
  @SuppressWarnings("compatibility:-7074714881275658754")
  private static final long serialVersionUID = 5291172566067954515L;

  @Id
  @Column(nullable = false)
  @GeneratedValue(strategy = GenerationType.TABLE, generator = "Person_ID_
  Generator")
  private Integer id;
  @Column(name = "FIRST_NAME", length = 400)
  private String firstName;
  @Column(name = "LAST_NAME", length = 400)
  private String lastName;
  @OneToOne(cascade=CascadeType.ALL)
  @JoinColumn(name = "HOME_ADDRESS")
  private Address homeAddress;
  @Version
  private Integer version;
  public Person() {
  }

  /* get/set methods... */
}
```

Listing 4-2. Employee.java, an Abstract Intermediate Entity in a SINGLE_TABLE
Inheritance Hierarchy

```
/*
 * Employee: An abstract entity that extends Person
 */
@Entity
@NamedQueries({
  @NamedQuery(name = "Employee.findAll", query = "select o from Employee o")})
@Table(name = "CH04_ST_EMPLOYEE")
```

```
public abstract class Employee extends Person implements Serializable {
  @SuppressWarnings("compatibility:276774077273820023")
  private static final long serialVersionUID = -8529011412038476148L;
  @Column(length = 400)
  private String department;
  @Column(length = 400)
  private String email;
  @ManyToOne
  @JoinColumn(name = "MANAGER")
  private FullTimeEmployee manager;

  public Employee() {
  }

  /* get/set methods... */
}
```

Listing 4-3. FullTimeEmployee.java, a Concrete Leaf Entity in a SINGLE_TABLE
Inheritance Hierarchy

```
/*
 * FullTimeEmployee: A concrete leaf entity
 */
@Entity
@NamedQueries({
  @NamedQuery(name = "FullTimeEmployee.findAll", query = "select o from
  FullTimeEmployee o")})
@Table(name = "CH04_ST_FT_EMPLOYEE")
public class FullTimeEmployee
        extends Employee
        implements Serializable {
  @SuppressWarnings("compatibility:9058152191575937294")
  private static final long serialVersionUID = -73016811208098048021L;
  @Column(name = "ANNUAL_SALARY")
  private double annualSalary;
  @OneToMany(mappedBy = "manager", cascade = {CascadeType.PERSIST,
  CascadeType.MERGE})
```

```
  private List<Employee> managedEmployees;

  public FullTimeEmployee() {
  }

  /* get/set methods... */
}
```

Listing 4-4. PartTimeEmployee.java, a Concrete Leaf Entity in a SINGLE_TABLE Inheritance Hierarchy

```
/*
 * PartTimeEmployee: A concrete leaf entity
 */
@Entity
@NamedQueries({
  @NamedQuery(name = "PartTimeEmployee.findAll", query = "select o from
  PartTimeEmployee o")})
@Table(name = "CH04_ST_PT_EMPLOYEE")
public class PartTimeEmployee extends Employee implements Serializable {
  @SuppressWarnings("compatibility:-4882346458268010846")
  private static final long serialVersionUID = 40179992391598782091L;
  @Column(name = "HOURLY_WAGE")
  private double hourlyWage;

  public PartTimeEmployee() {
  }

  /* get/set methods... */
}
```

Outside of this entity hierarchy lives the Address entity, shown in Listing 4-5. This entity is the target of a unidirectional @OneToOne relationship with the root (and abstract) Person entity shown previously.

Listing 4-5. Address.java, a Concrete Stand-Alone Entity

```
/*
 * Address: A standalone entity
 *
 * To create ID generator table "CH04_ST_ADDRESS_ID_GEN": CREATE TABLE
   "CH04_ST_ADDRESS_ID_GEN"
 * ("PRIMARY_KEY_NAME" VARCHAR2(4000) PRIMARY KEY, "NEXT_ID_VALUE" NUMBER(38));
 *
 * To initialize this table with data for this entity's ID generator
   'Address.id' (starting with
 * value '0'): INSERT INTO "CH04_ST_ADDRESS_ID_GEN" VALUES ('Address.id', 0);
 */
@Entity
@NamedQueries({
  @NamedQuery(name = "Address.findAll", query = "select o from Address o")})
@Table(name = "CH04_ST_ADDRESS")
@TableGenerator(name = "Address_ID_Generator", table = "CH04_ST_ADDRESS_ID_
GEN", pkColumnName = "PRIMARY_KEY_NAME",
                pkColumnValue = "Address.id", valueColumnName = "NEXT_ID_VALUE")
public class Address
        implements Serializable {
  @SuppressWarnings("compatibility:-5340972441524875330")
  private static final long serialVersionUID = -5279408726470732092L;
  @Id
  @Column(nullable = false)
  @GeneratedValue(strategy = GenerationType.TABLE, generator = "Address_ID_
  Generator")
  private Integer id;
  @Column(length = 400)
  private String city;
  @Column(length = 2)
  private String state;
  @Column(length = 400)
  private String street1;
  @Column(length = 400)
```

```
    private String street2;
    @Version
    private Integer version;
    @Column(name = "ZIP_CODE")
    private String zipCode;

    public Address() {
    }

    /* get/set methods... */
}
```

Let's take a look at some of the annotations that were introduced in this example.

The @JoinColumn Annotation

An Employee entity has a manager field of type FullTypeEmployee, and it is mapped this way:

```
@ManyToOne
@JoinColumn(name = "MANAGER")
private FullTimeEmployee manager;
```

The manager field is of type FullTimeEmployee and maps to the to the MANAGER column, identified by the name = "MANAGER" attribute on the @JoinColumn annotation. The MANAGER column happens to be a foreign key reference to the table mapped by the FullTypeEmployee entity, which in this case is the same CH04_ST_PERSON table. Defining a foreign key for such columns is not strictly necessary, but it is generally considered good database design. Because the manager field maps to the foreign key column, it is considered the *owning* end of the relationship.

The entity at the other end of this bidirectional relationship, FullTimeEmployee, holds the managedEmployees field.

```
@OneToMany(mappedBy = "manager", cascade = {CascadeType.PERSIST,
CascadeType.MERGE})
private List<Employee> managedEmployees;
```

Since we have already specified the mapping on the owning end, this field can simply refer to that manager field, using the mappedBy = "manager" attribute. In this way, both relationship fields are mapped to the same foreign key, and a join table is not required.

Note   JPA lets you map a @OneToMany field to a foreign key on the target entity's table even when the target entity doesn't expose a corresponding @ManyToOne relationship field. To do this you use a @JoinColumn on the @OneToMany field that identifies the remote foreign key, instead of using the mappedBy attribute.

This managedEmployees field contains a list of Employee instances, which in practice will be concrete FullTimeEmployee and/or PartTimeEmployee instances.

The cascade = { CascadeType.PERSIST, CascadeType.MERGE } attribute indicates that any merge or persist operation performed on this entity, Employee, must also be applied to any FullTimeEmployee instances referenced by this relationship field. For example, if a new Employee instance is created and assigned a FullTimeEmployee as its manager, the act of persisting the Employee instance through EntityManager.persist() will also cause any referenced FullTimeEmployee instances to be persisted as well, if they have not already been persisted.

The Person entity has a relationship with Address through the homeAddress field.

```
@OneToOne(cascade=CascadeType.ALL)
@JoinColumn(name = "HOME_ADDRESS")
private Address homeAddress;
```

Because there is no corresponding field on Address that references Person, this is a unidirectional relationship. The cascade property on @OneToOne indicates which operations should be propagated to the referenced object. Because we have specified a cascade rule of CascadeType.ALL, all events–DETACH, MERGE, PERSIST, REFRESH, and REMOVE–applied to a Person are automatically applied to its homeAddress object.

The @DiscriminatorColumn Annotation

Whenever we map multiple entity classes to a single table, as we do with the InheritanceType.SINGLE_TABLE strategy, there must be some way to identify the concrete entity type of any given row in the table. To determine the entity type, the persistence manager looks for a column named DTYPE in the root entity's table to obtain this information. If your schema requires a different column name to capture this information, you may use the @DiscriminatorColumn annotation to identify which column JPA should use; in Listing 4-1, the Person.java entity specifies a discriminator column named TYPE, through the @DiscriminatorColumn(name = "TYPE") annotation. Were we to use a column named DTYPE, as we do for the remaining examples, we could have skipped this annotation altogether and accepted the default value.

The @DiscriminatorValue Annotation

The value that gets stored in the discriminator column is known as a discriminator value. Each concrete entity declares, either explicitly or by tacitly accepting the default, a unique discriminator value that serves to identify the concrete entity type associated with each row in the table. The discriminator value defaults to the entity name, and in this example, we have accepted this default value for each of the entities in the hierarchy. When adapting legacy tables and data into JPA, and you wish to map preexisting discriminator values to entities with dissimilar names, you can use the @DiscriminatorValue annotation to specify the discriminator value to use for each entity in the hierarchy that requires an override.

Pros and Cons of the SINGLE_TABLE Strategy

We consider each inheritance hierarchy from a design time and performance perspective, weighing strengths and weaknesses. We start with the SINGLE_TABLE strategy.

Design-Time Considerations

The SINGLE_TABLE mapping approach works well when the type hierarchy is fairly simple and stable. Adding a new type to the hierarchy and adding fields to existing supertypes simply involves adding new columns to the table. In particularly large deployments, however, this may have an adverse impact on the index and column layout inside the database. If your hierarchy will possibly outgrow the column limitations of a single table, which is typically 256 columns, or if for some reason you need to map more than one very large field to inline LOB (Large OBject) columns, you may have to introduce an @SecondaryTable mapping. In this case, it might be wiser to adopt one of the approaches that follow. In addition, NOT NULL constraints may not be used on columns that are not shared by all types in the hierarchy.

172

Performance Impact

The SINGLE_TABLE strategy is very efficient for querying across all types in the hierarchy, or for specific types. No table joins are required by the internal persistence framework—only a WHERE clause listing the type identifiers is necessary. In particular, relationships involving types that employ this mapping strategy perform well.

Sample Client Code

As we mentioned in the "Getting Started" section of this chapter, we have put together sample client code to test the inheritance examples, along with the other examples that appear later in this chapter. In the Sample Code provided for this chapter, we offer both a Java client and an HTTP servlet for each of the inheritance examples. Listing 4-6 shows a simple Java class that serves as a façade, like an EJB Session bean façade, for instantiating an EntityManager for the Chapter04-PersistenceIISamples-SingleTable persistence unit and exposing the CRUD methods for manipulating the JPA entities in that unit. Listing 4-7 shows a Java client for this service that exercises these CRUD methods and prints out the results. We could have used an actual EJB Session façade for this purpose as well, but we wanted to demonstrate how an ordinary Java class can interact with JPA entities in a non-JavaEE environment.

In the Sample Code area, we offer a similar Java service façade and accompanying Java clients for the other inheritance strategies. They are identical across each inheritance strategy except for the persistence unit used by each, and the entity classes that are annotated with the specific inheritance strategy details.

Similarly, we provide a simple HTTP servlet client for each inheritance strategy, demonstrating JPA entity use in a JavaEE Web environment. These servlets replace the Java client, and they interact directly with the same Java service façade.

Listing 4-6. JavaServiceFacade.java, a Java Class that Serves as a Façade for the Entities Defined in Figure 4-1

```
/*
 * Java service façade that obtains an EntityManager running outside of a
 * Java EE container, and illustrates CRUD operations on a handful of entities.
 * Employs auto-commit behavior, emulating the default transaction behavior of
 * a Stateless Session bean.
 */
```

```java
public class JavaServiceFacade {
  private final EntityManager em;

  public JavaServiceFacade() {
    //  To support an non-JavaEE environment, we avoid injection and create
        an EntityManagerFactory
    //  for the desired persistence unit. From this factory we then create
        the EntityManager.
    final EntityManagerFactory emf = Persistence.createEntityManagerFactory
("Chapter04-PersistenceIISamples-SingleTable");
    em = emf.createEntityManager();
  }

  /**
   * All changes that have been made to the managed entities in the
     persistence context are
   * applied to the database and committed.
   */
  private void commitTransaction() {
    final EntityTransaction entityTransaction = em.getTransaction();
    if (!entityTransaction.isActive()) {
      entityTransaction.begin();
    }
    entityTransaction.commit();
  }

  public Object queryByRange(String jpqlStmt, int firstResult, int maxResults) {
    Query query = em.createQuery(jpqlStmt);
    if (firstResult > 0) {
      query = query.setFirstResult(firstResult);
    }
    if (maxResults > 0) {
      query = query.setMaxResults(maxResults);
    }
    return query.getResultList();
  }
```

```java
public <T> T persistEntity(T entity) {
  em.persist(entity);
  commitTransaction();
  return entity;
}
public <T> T mergeEntity(T entity) {
  entity = em.merge(entity);
  commitTransaction();
  return entity;
}

public void removeEmployee(Employee employee) {
  employee = em.find(Employee.class, employee.getId());
  em.remove(employee);
  commitTransaction();
}

/**
 * <code>select o from Employee o</code>
 */
public List<Employee> getEmployeeFindAll() {
  return em.createNamedQuery("Employee.findAll", Employee.class).
  getResultList();
}

public void removeFullTimeEmployee(FullTimeEmployee fullTimeEmployee) {
  fullTimeEmployee = em.find(FullTimeEmployee.class, fullTimeEmployee.
  getId());
  em.remove(fullTimeEmployee);
  commitTransaction();
}

/**
 * <code>select o from FullTimeEmployee o</code>
 */
```

```java
public List<FullTimeEmployee> getFullTimeEmployeeFindAll() {
  return em.createNamedQuery("FullTimeEmployee.findAll",
  FullTimeEmployee.class).getResultList();
}

public void removePartTimeEmployee(PartTimeEmployee partTimeEmployee) {
  partTimeEmployee = em.find(PartTimeEmployee.class, partTimeEmployee.getId());
  em.remove(partTimeEmployee);
  commitTransaction();
}

/**
 * <code>select o from PartTimeEmployee o</code>
 */
public List<PartTimeEmployee> getPartTimeEmployeeFindAll() {
  return em.createNamedQuery("PartTimeEmployee.findAll",
  PartTimeEmployee.class).getResultList();
}

public void removePerson(Person person) {
  person = em.find(Person.class, person.getId());
  em.remove(person);
  commitTransaction();
}

/**
 * <code>select o from Person o</code>
 */
public List<Person> getPersonFindAll() {
  return em.createNamedQuery("Person.findAll", Person.class).getResultList();
}

public void removeAddress(Address address) {
  address = em.find(Address.class, address.getId());
  em.remove(address);
  commitTransaction();
}
```

```
/**
 * <code>select o from Address o</code>
 */
public List<Address> getAddressFindAll() {
  return em.createNamedQuery("Address.findAll", Address.class).getResultList();
}
}
```

Listing 4-7. JavaServiceFacadeClient.java, a Java Client to the JavaServiceFacade
that Illustrates Removing, Creating, and Retrieving the Entities Defined in Figure 4-1

```
/*
 * Java client for a Java service façade
 */
public class JavaServiceFacadeClient {
  public static void main(String[] args) {
    try {
      final JavaServiceFacade javaServiceFacade = new JavaServiceFacade();

      //------------------------------------------------------------------------
      // Clear out any previous test data. Due to "cascade" settings on the
      // "Person.homeAddress" relationship field, removing a Person will
         remove its
      // Address as well.
      //------------------------------------------------------------------------
      for (PartTimeEmployee parttimeemployee : (List<PartTimeEmployee>)
        javaServiceFacade.getPartTimeEmployeeFindAll()) {
          javaServiceFacade.removePartTimeEmployee(parttimeemployee);
      }
      for (FullTimeEmployee fulltimeemployee : (List<FullTimeEmployee>)
        javaServiceFacade.getFullTimeEmployeeFindAll()) {
        javaServiceFacade.removeFullTimeEmployee(fulltimeemployee);
      }
```

```
//-------------------------------------------------------------------------
// Create FullTimeEmployee and PartTimeEmployee instances, along
   with their Address
// objects, and persist them in the database.
//-------------------------------------------------------------------------
Address add = new Address();
add.setCity("San Mateo");
add.setState("CA");
add.setStreet1("1301 Ashwood Ct");
add.setZipCode("94402");
javaServiceFacade.persistEntity(add);

FullTimeEmployee ft = new FullTimeEmployee();
ft.setAnnualSalary(1000D);
ft.setDepartment("HQ");
ft.setEmail("x@y.com");
ft.setFirstName("Brian");
ft.setLastName("Jones");
ft.setHomeAddress(add);
ft = javaServiceFacade.persistEntity(ft);
add = new Address();
add.setCity("San Francisco");
add.setState("CA");
add.setStreet1("53 Surrey St");
add.setZipCode("94131");
javaServiceFacade.persistEntity(add);

final PartTimeEmployee pt = new PartTimeEmployee();
pt.setHourlyWage(100D);
pt.setDepartment("SALES");
pt.setEmail("a@b.com");
pt.setFirstName("David");
pt.setLastName("Holmes");
pt.setHomeAddress(add);
pt.setManager(ft);
javaServiceFacade.persistEntity(pt);
```

```
    //----------------------------------------------------------------
    //   Retrieve the entities through their type-specific JPQL queries
         and print them out
    //----------------------------------------------------------------
    System.out.println("\nPersons:\n");
    for (Person person : (List<Person>) javaServiceFacade.getPersonFindAll()) {
      printPerson(person);
    }
    System.out.println("\nEmployees:\n");
    for (Employee employee : (List<Employee>) javaServiceFacade.
    getEmployeeFindAll()) {
      printEmployee(employee);
    }
    System.out.println("\nPartTimeEmployees:\n");
    for (PartTimeEmployee parttimeemployee : (List<PartTimeEmployee>)
      javaServiceFacade.getPartTimeEmployeeFindAll()) {
      printPartTimeEmployee(parttimeemployee);
    }
    System.out.println("\nFullTimeEmployees:\n");

for (FullTimeEmployee fulltimeemployee : (List<FullTimeEmployee>)
javaServiceFacade.getFullTimeEmployeeFindAll()) {
        printFullTimeEmployee(fulltimeemployee);
    }
    System.out.println("\nAddresses:\n");
    for (Address address : (List<Address>) javaServiceFacade.
    getAddressFindAll()) {
      printAddress(address);
    }
  } catch (Exception ex) {
    ex.printStackTrace();
  }
}
```

```java
    private static void printEmployee(Employee employee) {
      System.out.println("dept = " + employee.getDepartment());
      System.out.println("email = " + employee.getEmail());
      System.out.println("manager = " + employee.getManager());
      System.out.println("firstName = " + employee.getFirstName());
      System.out.println("id = " + employee.getId());
      System.out.println("lastName = " + employee.getLastName());
      System.out.println("version = " + employee.getVersion());
      System.out.println("homeAddress = " + employee.getHomeAddress());
    }
    private static void printFullTimeEmployee(FullTimeEmployee fulltimeemployee) {
      System.out.println("annualSalary = " + fulltimeemployee.getAnnualSalary());
      System.out.println("managedEmployees = " + fulltimeemployee.
                                            getManagedEmployees());
      System.out.println("dept = " + fulltimeemployee.getDepartment());
      System.out.println("email = " + fulltimeemployee.getEmail());
      System.out.println("manager = " + fulltimeemployee.getManager());
      System.out.println("firstName = " + fulltimeemployee.getFirstName());
      System.out.println("id = " + fulltimeemployee.getId());
      System.out.println("lastName = " + fulltimeemployee.getLastName());
      System.out.println("version = " + fulltimeemployee.getVersion());
      System.out.println("homeAddress = " + fulltimeemployee.getHomeAddress());
    }

    private static void printPartTimeEmployee(PartTimeEmployee parttimeemployee) {
      System.out.println("hourlyWage = " + parttimeemployee.getHourlyWage());
      System.out.println("dept = " + parttimeemployee.getDepartment());
      System.out.println("email = " + parttimeemployee.getEmail());
      System.out.println("manager = " + parttimeemployee.getManager());
      System.out.println("firstName = " + parttimeemployee.getFirstName());
      System.out.println("id = " + parttimeemployee.getId());
      System.out.println("lastName = " + parttimeemployee.getLastName());
      System.out.println("version = " + parttimeemployee.getVersion());
      System.out.println("homeAddress = " + parttimeemployee.getHomeAddress());
    }
```

```
  private static void printPerson(Person person) {
    System.out.println("firstName = " + person.getFirstName());
    System.out.println("id = " + person.getId());
    System.out.println("lastName = " + person.getLastName());
    System.out.println("version = " + person.getVersion());
    System.out.println("homeAddress = " + person.getHomeAddress());
  }

  private static void printAddress(Address address) {
    System.out.println("city = " + address.getCity());
    System.out.println("id = " + address.getId());
    System.out.println("state = " + address.getState());
    System.out.println("street1 = " + address.getStreet1());
    System.out.println("street2 = " + address.getStreet2());
    System.out.println("version = " + address.getVersion());
    System.out.println("zipCode = " + address.getZipCode());
  }
}
```

Common Base Table with Joined Subclass Tables (InheritanceType.JOINED)

In the JOINED strategy, each entity in the hierarchy introduces its own table, but only to map fields that are declared on that entity type. The root entity in the hierarchy maps to a root table that defines the primary key structure to be used by all tables in the entity hierarchy, as well as the discriminator column and optionally a version column. Each of the other tables in the hierarchy defines a primary key that matches the root table's primary key, and they optionally add a foreign key constraint from their ID column(s) to the root table's ID column(s). The non-root tables do not hold discriminator type or version columns. Since each entity instance in the hierarchy is represented by a virtual row that spans its own table as well as the tables for all of its superentities, it eventually joins with a row in the root table that captures this discriminator type and version information. Querying all the fields of any type requires a join across all of the tables within the supertype hierarchy.

Figure 4-3 illustrates the schema that maps our entities using the JOINED inheritance strategy. As in the previous example, we have prefixed the tables with the strategy indicator, in this case CH04_JOIN_, so that all of the tables in these examples can be loaded into a single test schema without danger of name collision.

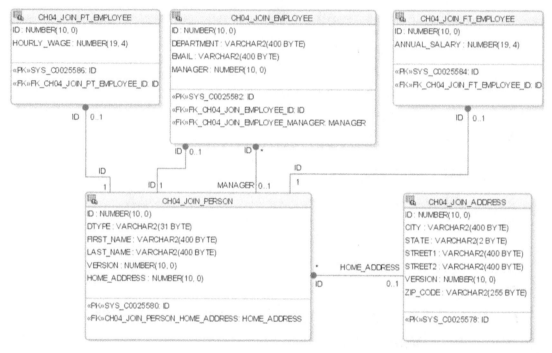

Figure 4-3. *A schema that maps our example entities using the JOINED strategy. Each entity in the hierarchy has its own table to persist its declared fields. The table CH04_JOIN_ADDRESS holds associated Address instances.*

Example Entity Classes

Let's now take a look at the entity classes that map to the previous schema. We have omitted the class bodies for each of these entities, since the only differences between these entities and the ones shown in the previous SINGLE_TABLE strategy example lie in the entity's class-level annotations. Listings 4-8 through 4-11 show the entities in the Person hierarchy, while Listing 4-12 shows the Address entity.

Listing 4-8. Person.java, an Abstract Root Entity in a JOINED Inheritance
Hierarchy

```
/*
 * Person: An abstract entity, and the root of an inheritance hierarchy
 */
@Entity
@NamedQueries({
  @NamedQuery(name = "Person.findAll", query = "select o from Person o")})
@Table(name = "CH04_JOIN_PERSON")
@TableGenerator(name = "Person_ID_Generator", table = "CH04_JOIN_PERSON_ID_GEN",
                pkColumnName = "PRIMARY_KEY_NAME", pkColumnValue = "Person.id",
                valueColumnName = "NEXT_ID_VALUE")
@Inheritance(strategy = InheritanceType.JOINED)
public abstract class Person implements Serializable {
  /* The class body is identical across all inheritance strategies */
}
```

Listing 4-9. Employee.java, an Abstract Intermediate Entity in a JOINED
Inheritance Hierarchy

```
/*
 * Employee: An abstract entity that extends Person
 */
@Entity
@NamedQueries({
  @NamedQuery(name = "Employee.findAll", query = "select o from Employee o")})
@Table(name = "CH04_JOIN_EMPLOYEE")
public abstract class Employee extends Person implements Serializable {
  /* The class body is identical across all inheritance strategies */
}
```

Listing 4-10. FullTimeEmployee.java, a Concrete Leaf Entity in a JOINED Inheritance Hierarchy

```
/*
 * FullTimeEmployee: A concrete leaf entity
 */
@Entity
@NamedQueries({
  @NamedQuery(name = "FullTimeEmployee.findAll", query = "select o from
  FullTimeEmployee o")})
@Table(name = "CH04_JOIN_FT_EMPLOYEE")
public class FullTimeEmployee extends Employee implements Serializable
{  /* The class body is identical across all inheritance strategies */
}
```

Listing 4-11. PartTimeEmployee.java, a Concrete Leaf Entity in a JOINED Inheritance Hierarchy

```
/*
 * PartTimeEmployee: A concrete leaf entity
 */
@Entity
@NamedQueries({
  @NamedQuery(name = "PartTimeEmployee.findAll", query = "select o from
  PartTimeEmployee o")})
@Table(name = "CH04_JOIN_PT_EMPLOYEE")
public class PartTimeEmployee extends Employee implements Serializable {
  /* The class body is identical across all inheritance strategies */
}
```

Listing 4-12. Address.java, a Concrete Stand-Alone Entity

```
/**
 * Address: A standalone entity
 */
@Entity
@NamedQueries({
```

```
@NamedQuery(name = "Address.findAll", query = "select o from Address o")})
@Table(name = "CH04_JOIN_ADDRESS")
@TableGenerator(name = "Address_ID_Generator", table = "CH04_JOIN_ADDRESS_ID_GEN",
               pkColumnName = "PRIMARY_KEY_NAME",pkColumnValue = "Address.id",
               valueColumnName = "NEXT_ID_VALUE")
public class Address implements Serializable {
  /* The class body is identical across all inheritance strategies */
}
```

You can see from the highlighted differences that they are very minimal. Ignoring table name differences, which are thrown in simply out of our desire to avoid name collisions with the tables in the other examples, only the @Inheritance annotation has changed on the root entity Person. Aside from its table and sequence names, the Address entity is identical to Listing 4-5, the previous example of the SINGLE_TABLE strategy.

Pros and Cons of the JOINED Strategy

Design-Time Considerations

With the JOINED strategy, introducing a new type to the hierarchy, at any level, simply involves interjecting a new table into the schema. Subtypes of that type will automatically join with that new type at runtime. Similarly, modifying any entity type in the hierarchy by adding, modifying, or removing fields affects only the immediate table mapped to that type. This option provides the greatest flexibility at design time, since changes to any type are always limited to that type's dedicated table.

Performance Impact

The JOINED approach does not suffer from the use of UNION operations, but inherently requires multiple JOIN operations to perform just about any query. Querying across all instances initially involves only a single query of the topmost base entity's table to retrieve a list of all of the primary keys of instances in the hierarchy. Due to the presence of the discriminator column in the base entity's table, resolution of these instances into entity classes can be efficient, depending on the lazy loading strategies employed by the persistence manager implementation.

Single-Table-per-Outermost Concrete Entity Class (InheritanceType.TABLE_PER_CLASS)

Support for the final inheritance mapping strategy is optional for persistence providers. It is not required for compliance with the JPA spec, so portable applications should avoid it until it is officially mandated or at least widely supported. This inheritance mapping option maps each outermost concrete entity to its own, dedicated table. Each table maps all of the fields in that entity's entire type hierarchy; since there is no shared table, no columns are shared. The only table structure requirement is that all tables must share a common primary key structure, meaning that the name(s) and type(s) of the primary key column(s) must match across all tables in the hierarchy.

For good measure, Figure 4-4 illustrates our third type of hierarchy using the TABLE_PER_CLASS inheritance strategy, which demonstrates the use of the single-table-per-entity subclass approach. The tables are required to share nothing in common except the structure of their primary key; and since the table implicitly identifies the entity type, no discriminator column is required. Note that while tables are shown for the abstract entities Person and Employee, they are not actually used. Future versions of EclipseLink (the reference implementation of JPA) will probably be amended to suppress generation of these tables when using the TABLE_PER_CLASS inheritance strategy. Annotating these classes @MappedSuperclass instead of @Entity would prevent classes from being generated in this case but would also prevent these classes from participating in Entity relationships or JPQL statements.

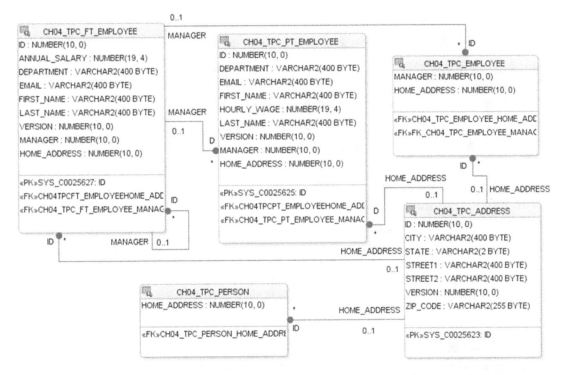

Figure 4-4. *A schema that maps our example entities using the TABLE_PER_ CLASS strategy. Concrete leaf entities are mapped to dedicated tables that contain columns that map all of their declared and inherited fields.*

Example Entity Classes

Listings 4-13 through 4-16 show how the entities mapped to these tables are annotated. Since only the class-level annotations are different from the previous strategy, the method bodies are stripped out.

Listing 4-13. Person.java, an Abstract Root Entity in a TABLE_PER_CLASS Inheritance Hierarchy

```
/**
 * Person: An abstract entity, and the root of an inheritance hierarchy
 */
@Entity
@NamedQueries({
  @NamedQuery(name = "Person.findAll", query = "select o from Person o")})
```

```
@Table(name = "CH04_TPC_PERSON")
@TableGenerator(name = "Person_ID_Generator", table = "CH04_TPC_PERSON_ID_GEN",
                pkColumnName = "PRIMARY_KEY_NAME", pkColumnValue = "Person.id",
                valueColumnName = "NEXT_ID_VALUE")
@Inheritance(strategy = InheritanceType.TABLE_PER_CLASS)
public abstract class Person implements Serializable {
  /* The class body is identical across all inheritance strategies */
}
```

Listing 4-14. Employee.java, an Abstract Intermediate Entity in a TABLE_PER_
CLASS Inheritance Hierarchy

```
/*
 * Employee: An abstract entity that extends Person
 */
@Entity
@NamedQueries({
  @NamedQuery(name = "Employee.findAll", query = "select o from Employee o")})
@Table(name = "CH04_TPC_EMPLOYEE")
public abstract class Employee extends Person implements Serializable {
  /* The class body is identical across all inheritance strategies */
}
```

Listing 4-15. FullTimeEmployee.java, a Concrete Leaf Entity in a TABLE_PER_
CLASS Inheritance Hierarchy

```
/*
 * FullTimeEmployee: A concrete leaf entity
 */
@Entity
@NamedQueries({
  @NamedQuery(name = "FullTimeEmployee.findAll", query = "select o from
  FullTimeEmployee o")})
@Table(name = "CH04_TPC_FT_EMPLOYEE")
public class FullTimeEmployee extends Employee implements Serializable {
  /* The class body is identical across all inheritance strategies */
}
```

Listing 4-16. PartTimeEmployee.java, a Concrete Leaf Entity in a TABLE_PER_CLASS Inheritance Hierarchy

```
/*
 * PartTimeEmployee: A concrete leaf entity
 */
@Entity
@NamedQueries({
  @NamedQuery(name = "PartTimeEmployee.findAll", query = "select o from
  PartTimeEmployee o")})
@Table(name = "CH04_TPC_PT_EMPLOYEE")
public class PartTimeEmployee extends Employee implements Serializable {
  /* The class body is identical across all inheritance strategies */
}
```

Again, the `Address` class in the `TABLE_PER_CLASS` example is identical to the previous examples, aside from the table and sequence names we have chosen.

Pros and Cons of the TABLE_PER_CLASS Strategy

Design-Time Considerations

With the TABLE_PER_CLASS strategy, as new outermost concrete types are introduced into the hierarchy, new tables are added. This is nice because neither existing tables nor their data are affected in any way. However, since each type also maps all of its supertype fields, introducing a new field on a base class, or a new base entity itself, requires modifying the tables for all affected subtypes across the hierarchy to map any newly introduced fields.

Performance Impact

With the TABLE_PER_CLASS approach, querying across multiple types requires a UNION select statement, which may not perform well, but querying a single type is very efficient, since only one table is involved in the query. Polymorphic relationships (which involve supertypes) in this hierarchy should be avoided since they will necessarily require this UNION operation to resolve to concrete subtype instances.

Comparison of O/R Implementation Approaches

Now that we have explored the three inheritance mapping implementations, let's look at some of the characteristics of a class inheritance hierarchy that should be considered when choosing which implementation approach to use for your type hierarchies. The following list contains subjective questions about your own entity hierarchies. They do not have precise answers; rather, they are meant to stimulate design considerations when building your application.

- Class hierarchies can be static, with a fixed number of subtypes, or they can be dynamic, with varying numbers of subtypes. How often will you need to incorporate new subtypes into your hierarchy?

- Hierarchies can be deep, with lots of subclasses, or they can be shallow, with only a few. How granular is your hierarchy?

- The types in a hierarchy may diverge greatly, with very different sets of properties on the subclasses than on the base class, or with very little difference in properties. How much do the persistent property sets of your entities diverge from one another?

- Will other entities define relationships with classes in this type hierarchy; and, if so, will the base classes frequently be the referenced type?

- Will types in this hierarchy be frequently queried, updated, or deleted? How will the presence or absence of SQL JOIN or UNION operations impact your application's performance?

- During the life of your application, how frequently will you be updating the structure of the type hierarchy itself? The impact of this type of change varies for each inheritance strategy with considerations that include the following:

  - Adding or removing new types to the hierarchy (as when refactoring classes).

  - Adding, removing, or modifying fields on an entity in the hierarchy.

- Adding, removing, or modifying relationships involving types in this hierarchy.

Note   A comparison of the performance of these three inheritance strategies, along with details on how to set up your own performance comparison tests, is explored in Chapter 9. Check out the results of our performance tests; and test your own entity hierarchies as you build them, to help you decide which strategy makes the best sense in the context of your application.

Using Abstract Entities, Mapped Superclasses, and Non-Entity Classes in an Inheritance Hierarchy

Within an entity class hierarchy, JPA allows both non-entity classes and abstract classes to be intermixed. Using the JOINED example above, let's look at how we map these classes.

Abstract Entity Class

As shown in the previous section on inheritance hierarchies, JPA entities may be either concrete or abstract. An abstract entity is simply an entity that cannot be instantiated on its own—it can still be involved in entity relationships and queries, and its fields are persisted following the mapping strategy for its type hierarchy. Listing 4-17 is an example of one of our abstract entities.

Listing 4-17. Person.java, an Abstract Root Entity in a JOINED Inheritance Hierarchy

```
/**
 * Person: An abstract entity, and the root of an inheritance hierarchy
 */
@Entity
@NamedQueries({
  @NamedQuery(name = "Person.findAll", query = "select o from Person o")})
@Table(name = "CH04_JOIN_PERSON")
@TableGenerator(name = "Person_ID_Generator", table = "CH04_JOIN_PERSON_ID_GEN",
                pkColumnName = "PRIMARY_KEY_NAME", pkColumnValue = "Person.id",
                valueColumnName = "NEXT_ID_VALUE")
@Inheritance(strategy = InheritanceType.JOINED)
```

```
public abstract class Person implements Serializable {
    ...
    @OneToOne(cascade=CascadeType.ALL)
    @JoinColumn(name = "HOME_ADDRESS")
    private Address homeAddress;
    ...
}
```

Not only is the abstract Person entity queryable (here we have defined a "Person.
findAll" named query), it also holds an association with the Address entity that
is shared by all of its subclasses. Although Person is abstract, it can specify its own
mappings and its own table. It just won't have its own discriminator value, since there
will never be a concrete entity instance of the base class Person.

Mapped Superclass (@MappedSuperclass)

A mapped superclass is a non-entity class that is nonetheless recognized by the
persistence manager, and which declares persistent fields and their mappings. Since
it is not an entity, it may not be the target of persistent entity relationships, nor may
it be used in JPQL queries. It may, however, provide persistent properties common
to any entities that extend it, whether directly or indirectly. Starting with the previous
inheritance example, let us transform the root entity, Person, into a mapped superclass.
Listings 4-18 and 4-19 show the transformed classes.

Listing 4-18. Person.java, an Abstract Mapped Superclass (Non-Entity)

```
/**
 * Person: A Mapped Superclass, and the base class (but not the root entity)
 * of an inheritance hierarchy
 *
 * To create ID generator table "CH04_MS_PERSON_ID_GEN": CREATE TABLE
 * "CH04_MS_PERSON_ID_GEN" ("PRIMARY_KEY_NAME" VARCHAR2(4000) PRIMARY KEY,
 * "NEXT_ID_VALUE" NUMBER(38));
 *
```

```
 * To initialize this table with data for this entity's ID generator
   'Person.id'
 * (starting with value '0'): INSERT INTO "CH04_MS_PERSON_ID_GEN" VALUES
 * ('Person.id', 0);
 */
@MappedSuperclass
@TableGenerator(name = "Person_ID_Generator", table = "CH04_MS_PERSON_ID_GEN",
                pkColumnName = "PRIMARY_KEY_NAME", pkColumnValue = "Person.id",
                valueColumnName = "NEXT_ID_VALUE")
public abstract class Person implements Serializable {
  @SuppressWarnings("compatibility:-7074714881275658754")
  private static final long serialVersionUID = 5291172566067954515L;
  @Id
  @Column(nullable = false)
  @GeneratedValue(strategy = GenerationType.TABLE, generator = "Person_ID_
  Generator")
  private Integer id;
  @Column(name = "FIRST_NAME", length = 400)
  private String firstName;
  @Column(name = "LAST_NAME", length = 400)
  private String lastName;
  @OneToOne(cascade=CascadeType.ALL)
  @JoinColumn(name = "HOME_ADDRESS")
  private Address homeAddress;
  @Version
  private Integer version;

  public Person() {
  }

  /* get/set methods */
}
```

Listing 4-19. Employee.java, an Abstract Root Entity in a JOINED Entity
Inheritance Hierarchy, and a Subclass of a Mapped Superclass

```
/*
 * Employee: The root of an inheritance hierarchy. Extends Person, a Mapped
   Superclass.
 */
@Entity
@NamedQueries({
  @NamedQuery(name = "Employee.findAll", query = "select o from Employee o")})
@Table(name = "CH04_MS_EMPLOYEE")
@Inheritance(strategy = InheritanceType.JOINED)
public abstract class Employee extends Person implements Serializable {
  @SuppressWarnings("compatibility:276774077273820023")
  private static final long serialVersionUID = -8529011412038476148L;
  @Column(length = 400)
  private String department;
  @Column(length = 400)
  private String email;
  @ManyToOne
  @JoinColumn(name = "MANAGER")
  private FullTimeEmployee manager;

  public Employee() {
  }

  /* get/set methods */
}
```

The Person class becomes a mapped superclass (@MappedSuperclass), and it is
stripped of its @NamedQuery, @Table, and @Inheritance annotations. @Inheritance is
moved onto Employee, which becomes the new root entity in the hierarchy.

While a mapped superclass may not be referenced as the target of a persistence
relationship field, it may have persistence relationship fields of its own, so the
homeAddress field that references the Address entity is perfectly legal.

Also note that we can continue to define the @Id and @Version fields on the mapped superclass, and we can even continue to specify an ID generator for the id field. Entities that extend this mapped superclass map these fields, along with all other fields defined on the mapped superclass, onto their own tables.

Non-Entity Class

Entities may also make use of non-entity classes within their type hierarchies. An entity may subclass a non-entity class, or a non-entity class may extend it. Such classes may be concrete or abstract, and so they may be instantiable, but their fields will not be persistable or maintained by the JPA persistence framework. They also may not participate at all in persistent entity relationships or JPQL queries. If a class in a type hierarchy serves only as an organizing construct for its subclasses, and it is not involved in entity relationships (and there is no other reason to mark it as an entity), then it is best left as an ordinary class. It can always be turned into an entity later by annotating it or designating it an entity in the XML descriptor.

Non-Entity Single-Value and Collection Fields

Finally, an entity may embed a non-entity class, or a collection of non-entity classes, for its own private use. Such embedded references may be to single objects or to collections of objects. Single-object fields are typically of the type of which we are already familiar: Basic object types, like String, int, or Long, which are implicitly marked @Basic. Single-object fields may also have complex types, and we are familiar with these already as entity references, using fields marked @OneToOne or @ManyToOne. When fields reference complex non-entity types, they are marked @Embedded and the target class must be annotated @Embeddable. Collection references to non-entity objects are marked @ElementCollection, and they may be collections of either @Basic or @Embeddable class types. Let's take a closer look at these non-entity field references.

@Embedded and @Embeddable

An entity or mapped superclass may contain fields marked @Embedded, and their type must be a class that is correspondingly marked @Embeddable. Like a mapped superclass, an embeddable class may hold mapping metadata for its persistent fields. When used in this way, the field that references an embeddable object is marked @Embedded and the

195

fields on the embeddable class map to the owning entity's table. Embeddable classes are wholly owned by the class that embeds them and are persisted, merged, queried, and removed in concert with their owning object. Instances of embeddable classes have no persistent identity of their own, and they may not be passed around among entities. They are generally used for their convenience as a field organization tool, allowing a set of persistent fields to be encapsulated as a single field on the owning entity.

As an example, let us transform our Address entity (Listing 4-20) into an embeddable class and embed it as a field on the Person entity (Listing 4-21). Figure 4-5 shows the underlying schema configured like our JOINED hierarchy, with the exception that the data columns on CH04_JOIN_ADDRESS have been folded into the CH04_EMB_PERSON table.

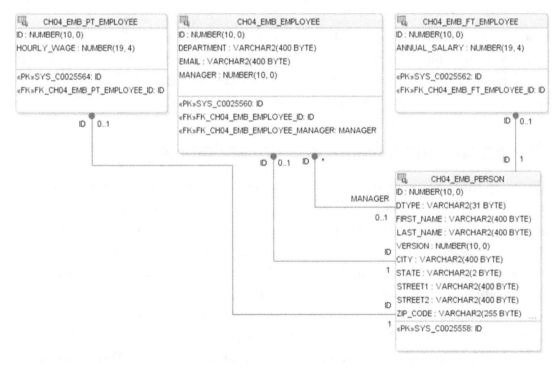

Figure 4-5. *Table CH04_EMB_PERSON holds columns for all fields in the Person entity, as well as fields from an embedded Address*

The transformation of Address.java into an @Embeddable, non-entity class is shown in Listing 4-20. The @Id and @Version fields are now gone, since an Address no longer has identity on its own. The Employee, FullTimeEmployee, and PartTimeEmployee entities are unchanged from the JOINED hierarchy configuration.

Listing 4-20. Address.java, an Embeddable Non-Entity Class

```java
/**
 * Address: An embeddable non-entity class
 */
@Embeddable
public class Address implements Serializable {
  @SuppressWarnings("compatibility:-5340972441524875330")
  private static final long serialVersionUID = -5279408726470732092L;
  @Column(length = 400)
  private String city;
  @Column(length = 2)
  private String state;
  @Column(length = 400)
  private String street1;
  @Column(length = 400)
  private String street2;
  @Column(name = "ZIP_CODE")
  private String zipCode;

  public Address() {
  }

  /* get/set methods */
}
```

Listing 4-21. Person.java, an Entity that Holds an @Embedded homeAddress Field

```java
/**
 * Person: An abstract entity, and the root of an inheritance hierarchy
 *
 * To create ID generator table "CH04_EMB_PERSON_ID_GEN": CREATE TABLE
   "CH04_EMB_PERSON_ID_GEN"
 * ("PRIMARY_KEY_NAME" VARCHAR2(4000) PRIMARY KEY, "NEXT_ID_VALUE" NUMBER(38));
 *
```

```
 * To initialize this table with data for this entity's ID generator
   'Person.id' (starting with
 * value '0'): INSERT INTO "CH04_EMB_PERSON_ID_GEN" VALUES ('Person.id', 0);
 */
@Entity
@NamedQueries({
  @NamedQuery(name = "Person.findAll", query = "select o from Person o")})
@Table(name = "CH04_EMB_PERSON")
@TableGenerator(name = "Person_ID_Generator", table = "CH04_EMB_PERSON_ID_GEN",
                pkColumnName = "PRIMARY_KEY_NAME", pkColumnValue = "Person.id",
                valueColumnName = "NEXT_ID_VALUE")
@Inheritance(strategy = InheritanceType.JOINED)
public abstract class Person implements Serializable {
  @SuppressWarnings("compatibility:-7074714881275658754")
  private static final long serialVersionUID = 5291172566067954515L;
  @Id
  @Column(nullable = false)
  @GeneratedValue(strategy = GenerationType.TABLE, generator = "Person_ID_
  Generator")
  private Integer id;
  @Column(name = "FIRST_NAME", length = 400)
  private String firstName;
  @Column(name = "LAST_NAME", length = 400)
  private String lastName;
  @Embedded
  private Address homeAddress;
  @Version
  private Integer version;

  public Person() {
  }

  /* get/set methods */
}
```

When a Person instance is persisted, the values of fields on its homeAddress instance are saved into columns on the CH04_EMB_PERSON table.

@ElementCollection

A useful mapping feature introduced since JPA 2.0 is the ability to embed collections of non-entity objects within an entity or mapped superclass and to make them wholly owned by the embedding class. The @ElementCollection is the collection analog to using @Embeddable and @Basic fields; only the instances in the collection are always stored in a separate table from the owning entity or mapped superclass. Similarly, it is the non-entity analog to the entity relationship types @OneToMany. Listing 4-22 shows our Employee entity holding two element collections: one of @Embeddable instances and one of @Basic instances.

Listing 4-22. Person.java, an Entity that Holds two @ElementCollection fields

```
@Entity
public abstract class Person implements Serializable {
  ...
  @ElementCollection(fetch=FetchType.LAZY)
  private List<Address> addresses;

  @ElementCollection
  Private Collection<String> favoriteCities;

  public Person() {
  }

  /* get/set methods */
}
```

This code snippet demonstrates some of the simplest forms of @ElementCollection usage, largely assuming default mappings. By using more advanced mappings, you can customize the way the collection mapping table is wired up to the root table for Person, whether lookup should be eager or lazy, column and table names, how to specify an element collection as a Map, and many other details.

Polymorphic Relationships

As shown in the previous examples, entity relationships can be specified between both concrete and abstract entities in a hierarchy. You can define a relationship with any entity in an inheritance hierarchy, and it will implicitly involve subtypes of that entity as well. Even persistent entity relationship fields declared on mapped superclasses are polymorphic. A relationship that implicitly includes subtypes in this way is known as a *polymorphic relationship*.

In JPA, relationships may be defined against any other entity class, including abstract supertype entities in a hierarchy. This support for polymorphic relationships complements JPA's support for mapping class hierarchies, and it provides a powerful construct for querying entities at any level across an entity type hierarchy. In the previous example of entity hierarchy, the `FullTimeEmployee.manager`-to-`Employee.managedEmployees` relationship illustrates a one-to-many, bidirectional relationship between the concrete `FullTimeEmployee` (manager) and its collection of abstract `Employee` (managedEmployee) instances. This example shows a relationship between entities within the same hierarchy, but it could just as easily be defined between entities in separate entity hierarchies.

Relationship Mapping

Mapping polymorphic relationships requires no special knowledge about the inheritance table mapping strategy for either entity in the relationship. This is evident from the fact that the relationship field mappings remained identical across our sample entity classes as we applied each of the three inheritance mapping strategies. All relationships map to the primary key of the target class, a mapping assumption made possible because of the spec requirement that all classes in a class hierarchy share a common primary key structure, even if each subclass maps to its own table. The mapping information defined for each entity is sufficient for the JPA persistence framework to resolve base type references onto the actual subclass instances. Relationship fields are derived automatically using `JOIN` and `UNION` statements, and these queries are further constrained by the use of `WHERE` clauses, which refer to discriminator column values.

Polymorphic JPQL Queries

Similarly, JPQL and criteria API queries can select or join entities of a supertype class, and any instances of subtypes matching the query criteria will be returned in the query result list. What's more, queries may use internal JOIN clauses to bind references to types anywhere along a supertype hierarchy, with the only restriction being that the left and right side of the JOIN clause resolve to a common base type.

In the previous inheritance hierarchy, the "Person.findAll" and "Employee.findAll" named queries defined on the abstract Person and Employee entities are examples of polymorphic queries. Instances returned from these queries are all concrete entities—either FullTimeEmployee or PartTimeEmployee.

By way of example, let us look at some code from our sample client. Listing 4-23 queries all Employee instances whose home address is somewhere in San Mateo. The query is issued on the abstract Employee entity, and it traverses through the homeAddress relationship field defined on the root Person entity. Any entities that are returned from this will be concrete, either FullTimeEmployee or PartTimeEmployee.

Listing 4-23. Code Listing that Demonstrates Polymorphic Relationship Usage in JPQL

```
// Ad-hoc JPQL to demonstrate polymorphic relationship usage
final String stmt =
  "select o from Employee o where o.homeAddress.city = 'San Mateo'";
final List<Employee> emps = em.createQuery(stmt).getResultList();
for (Employee emp : emps)
{
  System.out.println(emp.getFirstName());
  System.out.println(emp.getLastName());
}
```

Using Native SQL Queries

JPQL offers the ability to reference entity fields by name and join with other entities through relationships, without regard to the underlying mapping details. This offers a fair degree of independence between the database schema definer and the query definer roles. There are times, however, when you'll want to take control of the query to leverage specific indexes, return sparse data sets, or otherwise issue a query that is more conveniently expressed in SQL. JPA lets you do this easily, and it even offers support for mapping the query results back to entities if you desire.

As an example, you may wish to use a native SQL query to return just the name and primary key column data from a table that happens to map to one of your entities. The queried name values could then be presented to the user through a combo box, and only when the user chooses a name would you go out to the `EntityManager` and bind that name's corresponding primary key value to an entity instance using the `EntityManager.find(Object primaryKey)` call. Had you used JPQL to return a collection of fully loaded entities, instead of just the sparse key and name data set, you would have queried more data fields than necessary, causing more resources to be consumed than were actually needed.

The example in Listing 4-24 shows how to define a named native SQL query that returns instances of entity type `Address`. Executing this named native query is the same to the client as executing the equivalent JPQL named query.

Listing 4-24. Code Listing that Demonstrates Native SQL Support

```
@NamedNativeQueries({
  @NamedNativeQuery(name = "Address.findAllNative",
    query = "select id, city, state, street1, street2, zip_code from ch04_
    join_address",
    resultClass=Address.class)})
```

The Query Criteria API

JPA, since version 2.0, introduced an alternative to JPQL for defining and executing queries, using strongly typed components. Using only Java, the criteria API allows you to dynamically construct arbitrarily complex queries and execute them to return the same results that could be achieved through JPQL, but with compile-time type checking. Since the same underlying query engine is used for both the JPQL and criteria API, they are equivalent in strength, and there is an analogous criteria API call for each feature that can be expressed in JPQL. For situations where a query is also dynamically defined through a query builder, for instance, the criteria API can be more manageable than dynamically constructing an equivalent JPQL statement. We discussed in Chapter 3 which changes were introduced in JPA 2.2 as part of Java EE 8.

While the full criteria API, like the full feature set of the JPQL language, goes beyond the scope of this book, we show an example of how it can be used in Listing 4-25.

Listing 4-25. Code Listing that Demonstrates use of the query criteria API

```
/**
 *  Criteria API equivalent to the following JPQL query:
 *
 *     select o from Address o where o.city = :city
 */
public List<Address> getAddressFindByCity(String city) {
  // Define a query to return objects of type Address
  CriteriaBuilder cb = em.getCriteriaBuilder();
  CriteriaQuery<Address> c = cb.createQuery(Address.class);
  Root<Address> addr = c.from(Address.class);

  // Add the SELECT clause
  c.select(addr);

  // Define a predicate in the WHERE clause to compare the city
  // property with a parameter value
  ParameterExpression<String> p = cb.parameter(String.class, "city");
  c.where(cb.equal(addr.get("city"), p));

  // Bind the 'city' parameter
  TypedQuery<Address> q = em.createQuery(c);
  q.setParameter("city", city);

  // Return the query results as a List<Address>
  return q.getResultList();
}
```

The criteria API is a more formal approach but can be extremely useful in the right application situation.

Composite Primary Keys and Nested Foreign Keys

When mapping entities to a new schema, it is good practice to designate a single, dedicated column to be the primary key column, as we have done in the previous examples. An entity's primary key value cannot be updated once it has been assigned. Also, dedicating a column to hold the primary key instead of using a name or other column that holds meaningful property data eliminates potential conflicts that might arise should a user wish to modify a semantically significant field that happens to be part of the primary key. It is also desirable to follow a single approach that is common to all of your entities, and use of a single dedicated column for the primary key is a simple pattern that we have found to work well.

There are cases, however, in which the schema has already been defined and is being adapted into Java as JPA entities, and cases in which, for other reasons, a composite primary key is required. A legacy case that we run into a lot occurs when a composite primary key includes columns, such as foreign key columns, that are also involved in relationships with other entities. On top of this, these relationships are necessarily mandatory (since all primary key columns must be NOT NULL), so you will need to be careful about how you persist your entity graphs when you need to persist such related entities in order to avoid NOT NULL constraints when the row data is inserted during the EntityManager.persist() call.

There are two ways you can use a composite primary key to implement your entity's identity. They are described in the following sections.

Using an Embedded Composite Key (@EmbeddedId)

If the fields of the composite key do not represent useful property data that you consider to be part of the entity definition, you can designate a single entity field to be the primary key field and set its type to be the composite key class type. This composite key class is marked @Embedded. Its fields will be mapped as if they were part of the entity itself, but they will only be accessible to clients through the composite field.

The embedded composite key field myId on the entity is annotated @EmbeddedId. In Listing 4-26, we introduce the @Embeddable class MyIdClass, containing the field's firstName and lastName fields that were previously on Person.

Listing 4-26. MyIdClass.java, an @Embeddable class suitable for use as an
@EmbeddedId

```java
@Embeddable
public class MyIdClass {
  @Column(name = "FIRST_NAME", length = 400)
  private String firstName;
  @Column(name = "LAST_NAME", length = 400)
  private String lastName;

  @Override
  public boolean equals(Object obj) {
    return (obj instanceof MyIdClass &&
            firstName.equals(((MyIdClass) obj).getFirstName()) &&
            lastName.equals(((MyIdClass) obj).getLastName()));
  }

  @Override
  public int hashCode() {
    return System.identityHashCode(this);
  }

  /* get/set methods */
}
```

Listing 4-27 shows this new class being used as an @EmbeddedId on the Person class.

Listing 4-27. Person.java, Illustrating Usage of a Composite Primary Key Using
an @EmbeddedId Annotation

```java
@Entity
@NamedQueries({
  @NamedQuery(name = "Person.findAll", query = "select o from Person o")})
@Table(name = "CH04_EMBID_PERSON")
public class Person implements Serializable {
  @SuppressWarnings("compatibility:-7074714881275658754")
  private static final long serialVersionUID = 5291172566067954515L;
  @EmbeddedId
```

```
    private MyIdClass myId = new MyIdClass();
    @Version
    private Integer version;

    public Person() {
    }

    /* get/set methods */
}
```

To transform the Person class to use an embedded ID, we replaced the @Id Integer id field with the @EmbeddedId myIdClass myId field. To fit this entity back into our sample JOINED entity hierarchy, the manager relationship field on Person's Employee subentity and the PK fields on all subentities would need to be modified to map to all of the columns in the new primary key.

Exposing Composite Key Class Fields Directly on the Entity Class (@IdClass)

An alternative approach to mapping a composite primary key is to declare fields explicitly on the entity class for each field in the primary key class, but annotate each of them @Id, as shown in Listing 4-28. If any of the fields on the primary key double as useful properties on your entity, you will probably want to take this approach. You then define a new composite key class that declares each of these @Id fields, taking care that they exactly match the key class fields in name and type.

Starting with the classes from the previous example that used an @EmbeddedId, we can modify MyIdClass to remove the @Embedded annotation, as shown in Listing 4-28.

Listing 4-28. MyIdClass.java, a Serializable Java class suitable for Use as an @IdClass

```
public class MyIdClass implements Serializable {
    @Column(name = "FIRST_NAME", length = 400)
    private String firstName;
    @Column(name = "LAST_NAME", length = 400)
    private String lastName;
```

```
public MyIdClass() {
}

public MyIdClass(String firstName, String lastName) {
  this.firstName = firstName;
  this.lastName = lastName;
}

@Override
public boolean equals(Object obj) {
  return obj instanceof MyIdClass && firstName.equals(((MyIdClass) obj).
getFirstName()) && lastName.equals(((MyIdClass) obj).getLastName());
}

@Override
public int hashCode() {
  return System.identityHashCode(this);
}
/* get/set methods */
}
```

This composite key class requires no special annotations. It is primarily used when looking up a Person instance through its primary key, using the EntityManager.find() method.

On Person, both the firstName and lastName fields are now marked @Id. We have added an @IdClass annotation that identifies MyIdClass as the composite primary key class, as shown in Listing 4-29.

Listing 4-29. Person.java, an Entity Employing an @IdClass as a Composite Primary Key

```
@Entity
@NamedQueries({
  @NamedQuery(name = "Person.findAll", query = "select o from Person o")})
@Table(name = "CH04_IDCLASS_PERSON")
@IdClass(MyIdClass.class)
```

```
public class Person implements Serializable {
  @SuppressWarnings("compatibility:-7074714881275658754")
  private static final long serialVersionUID = 5291172566067954515L;
  @Id
  @Column(name = "FIRST_NAME", length = 400)
  private String firstName;
  @Id
  @Column(name = "LAST_NAME", length = 400)
  private String lastName;
  @Embedded
  private Address homeAddress;
  @Version
  private Integer version;

  public Person() {
  }

  /* get/set methods */
}
```

Mapping Relationships That Use Composite Keys

When defining a relationship in which the target entity uses a composite primary key, the owning entity must map its relationship field to columns of the corresponding type. This requires use of the @JoinColumns annotation (or equivalent XML metadata). If these columns happen to be nested in the owning entity's primary key, or if they are otherwise NOT NULL constrained, then the relationship must be bound at the time the EntityManager.persist() operation is called to persist this entity into the persistence context, or at least by the time EntityManager.flush() is called to issue the database INSERT call.

In the following example, the PersonPK composite primary key class contains two fields—id and addressId—that are mandatory (NOT NULL) since they are part of the primary key. Since the addressId and the relationship field homeAddress both map to the same ADDRESS_ID column, and only one of these fields may be insertable and updatable, we must mark one of the fields to be read-only. In Listing 4-30, the relationship field homeAddress is marked as read-only by assigning the insertable=false and updatable=false attributes on the @JoinColumn annotation.

Listing 4-30. Person.java, with a Composite Primary Key that Maps to a Column that Is Shared by Both an Ordinary @Id Field and a Relationship Field

```
/*
 * Person: An abstract entity, and the root of a SINGLE_TABLE hierarchy,
 * demonstrating use of a composite key that contains a field whose mapped
 * column is also mapped to a relationship field.
 */
@Entity
@Inheritance(strategy = InheritanceType.SINGLE_TABLE)
@NamedQueries({
  @NamedQuery(name = "Person.findAll", query = "select o from Person o")})
@TableGenerator(name = "Person_ID_Generator", table =
"CH04_FKINPK_PERSON_ID_GEN",
                pkColumnName = "PRIMARY_KEY_NAME", pkColumnValue = "Person.id",
                valueColumnName = "NEXT_ID_VALUE")
@Table(name = "CH04_FKINPK_PERSON")
@IdClass (PersonPK.class)
public abstract class Person
  implements Serializable
{
  @Id
  @Column(name = "ADDRESS_ID")
  private Integer addressId;
  @Id
  @Column(nullable = false)
  @GeneratedValue(strategy = GenerationType.TABLE, generator = "Person_ID_
  Generator")
  private Integer id;
  @Column(name = "FIRST_NAME")
  private String firstName;
  @Column(name = "LAST_NAME")
  private String lastName;
  @Version
  private Integer version;
  @OneToOne(cascade = { CascadeType.ALL })
```

```
@JoinColumn(name = "HOME_ADDRESS")
private Address homeAddress;

public Person() {
}

/* get/set methods */
}
```

When using this `Person` class, you may retrieve data through the `homeAddress` relationship field, but you may not update this field. Its value must be populated at the time the entity is persisted, and since it is part of the entity's primary key, it may not subsequently be modified.

Support for Optimistic Locking (@Version)

As shown in the previous examples, you can use the `@Version` annotation to designate a field to be used by the `EntityManager` to perform optimistic locking for merge operations and concurrency management. *Optimistic locking* is a useful performance optimization that offloads work that would otherwise be required of the database. Databases typically offer a *pessimistic locking* service that allows the database client (in our case, the JPA `EntityManager`) to lock a row in a table to prevent another client from updating it while the `EntityManager` is applying some changes. This is an effective mechanism to ensure that two clients do not modify the same row at the same time, but it requires expensive, low-level access checks inside the database. An alternative to pessimistic locking is to move concurrency control into a database client like the `EntityManager` and employ an optimistic locking strategy. Using a dedicated `@Version` column, the `EntityManager` follows a couple of simple rules. Whenever it sends a modified entity out to the database, as during a commit or flush operation, it looks at the current value of the entity instance's `@Version` field, queries the current state of that entity's row from the database, and compares the version values. If they are the same, it increments the entity instance's `@Version` field (or whatever field is annotated `@Version`), and it sends the change out to the database, causing an `UPDATE` statement to be executed. If the version values are different, this means that some other client modified the row between the time the row was last queried by the `EntityManager` and loaded into an entity instance and the time that instance was flushed back out to the database. When such a difference is detected, we call it a *concurrency exception*, and the EntityManager throws an exception and marks the transaction for rollback. The client of the EntityManager needs to anticipate that a concurrency exception might occur, and it must be prepared to resolve the conflict, typically by notifying the user of the conflict so that the entity can be refreshed before proceeding.

The use of a dedicated @Version column on an entity allows the EntityManager to perform optimistic locking simply by comparing the value of the @Version field stored in the entity instance with the value of the VERSION column in the database. If you don't specify an @Version field, the EntityManager has to walk through each field in the entity instance and compare its value to its corresponding, mapped column in the database, which is far more laborious. A declared @Version field will be auto-populated by the persistence framework and should not be updated by application code.

The bottom line is that it's not a requirement to use an @Version field, but it's good practice to define an @Version field on your entities to allow the EntityManager to take advantage of this optimization.

Support for Autogenerated Primary Key Values (@GeneratedValue)

In addition to built-in optimistic locking support through the @Version column, JPA provides several convenient ways to auto-populate primary key columns when an entity is persisted. You can declare that a field's value should be populated using the following:

- An automatic mechanism maintained by the persistence framework (strategy=GenerationType.AUTO)

- A custom database sequence (strategy=GenerationType.SEQUENCE or GenerationType.IDENTITY)

- A custom database table, emulating a pseudo-sequence (strategy=GenerationType.TABLE)

We have found the auto-populated PK feature to be very high on the convenience scale, saving us from coding this up for each entity in our application. Using schema generation settings on the persistence unit in persistence.xml allows you to have JPA auto-create the required artifacts (sequence or table) in the database and even configure them with the settings specified through JPA metadata using annotations or XML. Once installed, the AUTO case generates unique identifiers for any @Id field that is annotated @GeneratedValue or @GeneratedValue(strategy=GenerationType.AUTO), and at least it leaves the entity class a little less cluttered. Since not all databases support sequence objects, you may wish to use a table generator, as shown in the examples throughout this chapter.

Listing 4-31 demonstrates usage of the default ID generation feature.

Listing 4-31. Person.java, Employing a Default ID Generator

```
@Entity
@Inheritance(strategy = InheritanceType.JOINED)
@DiscriminatorColumn(name = "TYPE")
@Table(name = "CH04_JOIN_PERSON")
@NamedQuery(name = "findAllPerson", query = "select object(o) from Person
o")
public abstract class Person implements Serializable {
    @Id
    @GeneratedValue
    private Long id;
    /* ... */
}
```

SQL scripts to generate all the tables and sequences for the examples in this chapter are available in the Sample Code area. In addition, JPA providers generate DDL objects, and even some DML that it requires, to support any entities that are deployed; so pre-creating a schema is not strictly necessary. However, while JPA will take guidance about what table and column names to use, for example, there is currently no way to specify the names of constraints or other artifacts that are created automatically for you. Thus, if you need to control the names and other details of the mapped objects, it is best to pre-create the schema before you first deploy your persistence unit.

To illustrate how to pre-create the tables and sequences required for ID generation, Listings 4-31 and 4-32 show the DDL required to create the ID generator tables and sequences used in these examples.

Listing 4-32. Usage of @GeneratedValue with a @SequenceGenerator

```
/**
 * To create ID generator sequence "CH04_SEQID_PERSON_ID_GEN":
 * CREATE SEQUENCE "CH04_SEQID_PERSON_ID_GEN" INCREMENT BY 50 START WITH 50;
 */
@Entity
@Table(name = "CH04_JOIN_PERSON")
@SequenceGenerator(name = "Person_ID_Generator", sequenceName = "CH04_JOIN_
PERSON_ID_GEN",
                   allocationSize = 50, initialValue=1)
@Inheritance(strategy = InheritanceType.JOINED)
public abstract class Person implements Serializable {
  ...
  @Id
  @Column(nullable = false)
  @GeneratedValue(strategy = GenerationType.SEQUENCE, generator = "Person_
  ID_Generator")
  private Integer id;
  ...
}
```

Listing 4-33 provides an example of a table-based ID generator declaration, along with an INSERT statement for creating a named row for the pseudo-sequence.

Listing 4-33. Usage of @GeneratedValue with a @TableGenerator

```
/**
 * To create ID generator table "CH04_JOIN_PERSON_ID_GEN": CREATE TABLE
 * "CH04_JOIN_PERSON_ID_GEN" ("PRIMARY_KEY_NAME" VARCHAR2(4000) PRIMARY KEY,
 * "NEXT_ID_VALUE" NUMBER(38));
 *
 * To initialize this table with data for this entity's ID generator 'Person.id'
 * (starting with value '0'): INSERT INTO "CH04_JOIN_PERSON_ID_GEN" VALUES
 * ('Person.id', 0);
 */
```

```
@Entity
@Table(name = "CH04_JOIN_PERSON")
@TableGenerator(name = "Person_ID_Generator", table = "CH04_JOIN_PERSON_ID_GEN",
                pkColumnName = "PRIMARY_KEY_NAME", pkColumnValue = "Person.id",
                valueColumnName = "NEXT_ID_VALUE")
@Inheritance(strategy = InheritanceType.JOINED)
public abstract class Person implements Serializable {
  ...
  @Id
  @Column(nullable = false)
  @GeneratedValue(strategy = GenerationType.TABLE, generator = "Person_ID_
  Generator")
  private Integer id;
  ...
}
```

Interceptors: Entity Callback Methods

JPA provides support for a number of callback methods, or *interceptors*, that allow you to add your own custom code when certain lifecycle events occur on an entity or a mapped superclass. You can register interceptors to be invoked when certain lifecycle events occur on specific entity types, or broadly whenever a lifecycle event occurs on any entity. The latter case is one of the few times when you must use XML to specify metadata, since the effect is applied globally across all entities in the persistence unit.

The following annotations may be applied to methods to indicate that they are entity callback methods:

- @PrePersist

- @PostPersist

- @PreRemove

- @PostRemove

- @PreUpdate

- @PostUpdate

- @PostLoad

To use a callback method, you write a method to perform the behavior you desire and then simply annotate it using one of the above lifecycle callback annotations (for instance, @PrePersist). Callback methods may have any name you choose, but must not take any parameters and must return void. A single method may be annotated with multiple entity callback annotations, if desired.

Alternatively, callback classes may be registered for an entity (or a mapped superclass) to intercept one or more lifecycle events on one or more entity types. Multiple interceptor methods may be registered for any given entity lifecycle event, and they are executed in the order in which they are specified.

Entity callback methods can be used to validate an entity's contents prior to the entity being persisted, and to populate transient, derived fields following instantiation. Listing 4-34 shows how you might plug an @PreUpdate interceptor into the FullTimeEmployee entity in your company's payroll system to give all employees from a certain ZIP code an automatic raise whenever that employee instance is updated for any reason. (Wishful thinking!)

Listing 4-34. FullTimeEmployee.java, Employing an Illicit Entity Callback to Finally Stick It to the Man!

```
@Entity
@Inheritance
public class FullTimeEmployee extends Employee {
  ...
  @PreUpdate
  public void wishfulThinking() {
    if (getHomeAddress().getZipCode() == 94402) {
      setSalary(getSalary() + 10000);
    }
  }
  ...
}
```

Compiling, Deploying, and Testing the JPA Entities

For each of the seven major features described in this chapter, we provide a stand-alone NetBeans project to test the feature from a pure Java SE context. In addition, each of these projects is accompanied by a dedicated HTTP servlet that will test the same code through a Java EE Web application. You are encouraged to explore these samples from both client environments, edit the JPA entities and test code, and observe the results.

Prerequisites

Before performing any of the steps detailed in the next sections, complete the "Getting Started" section of Chapter 1. This section will walk you through the installation and environment setup required for the samples in this chapter.

Opening the Sample Application

Copy the Chapter04-PersistenceIISamples directory and its contents into a directory of your choice. Run the NetBeans IDE, and open the Chapter04-PersistenceIISamples project using the File ➤ Open Project menu. Make sure that the "Open Required Projects" check box is checked. See Figure 4-6.

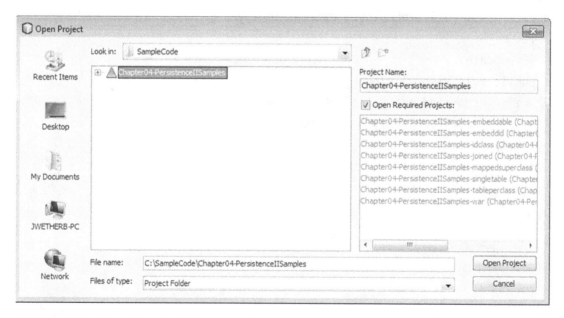

Figure 4-6. *Opening the Chapter04-PersistenceIISamples project*

No EJB Session beans are used in these examples, although they could easily have been used instead of the Java service façade classes. The Java facades emulate the default transactional behavior of a Stateless Session bean by auto-committing the results whenever they perform a persist, merge, or remove operation. The principle difference is that EJBs execute in an EJB container, which offers enterprise services that are not required for these JPA examples.

The samples for this chapter consist of seven Java class libraries and one Web application containing a servlet for each of the seven Java libraries. Expand the first Java class library—Chapter04-PersistenceIISamples-embeddable, and observe the general structure common to each project as shown in Figure 4-7.

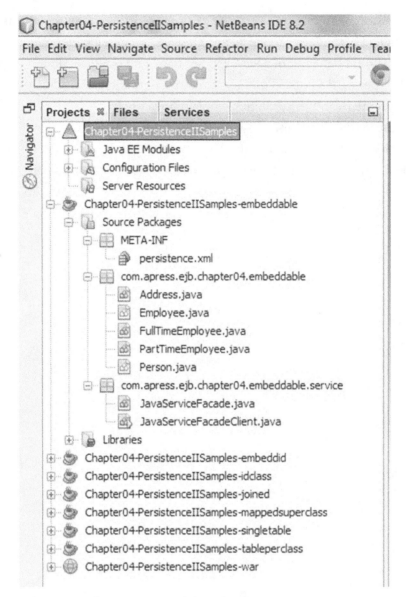

Figure 4-7. *Observing the structure of the Chapter04-PersistenceIISamples-joined project*

Each Java class library contains the following:

- A single JPA persistence unit consisting of some number of JPA entities or other mapped classes along with a META-INF/ persistence.xml file

- A Java service façade–JavaServiceFacade.java–a wrapper class that provides CRUD methods for manipulating the JPA entities in the context persistence unit

- A Java client–JavaServiceFacadeClient.java–for the service façade that executes the test case for that persistence unit

Creating the Database Connection

The samples in this chapter require a database connection, and for these tests we will use the Derby database that is bundled with NetBeans and Glassfish. If you have not already created the WineApp database, also used for the Chapter 3 examples, click on the Services tab, expand the Databases icon, and invoke "Create Database..." on the Java DB node. Create a database named "WineApp" with username and password wineapp/wineapp as shown in Figure 4-8.

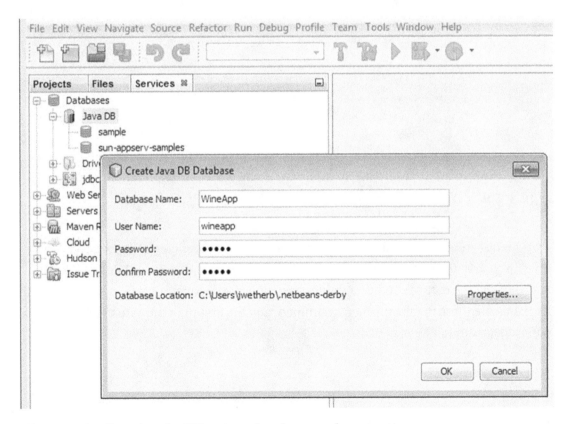

Figure 4-8. *Creating the WineApp database and connection*

In case you did create the WineApp database in Chapter 3, then you should find it underneath the Java DB section as shown in Figure 4-9.

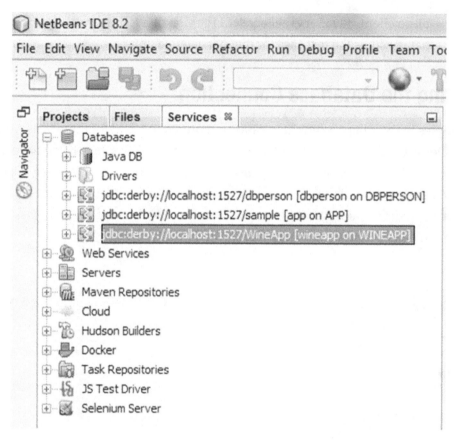

Figure 4-9. *"WineApp" Java DB*

This last step created a database connection and is referenced from the persistence units in each of the persistence.xml files found in the JPA projects. While it is possible to pre-create the database objects (tables, sequences, key constraints, and so on), we will let JPA create these database objects automatically the first time they are needed by each persistence unit.

Compiling the Sources

Invoke the context menu on Chapter04-PersistenceIISamples node, and build the application by selecting the Clean and Build menu option as shown in Figure 4-10.

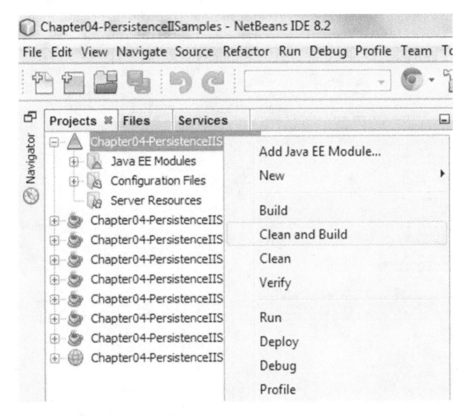

Figure 4-10. *Building the application*

CHAPTER 4   ADVANCED PERSISTENCE FEATURES

Running the Client Programs

After the WineApp database has been created and you have built the projects, you can run
the sample clients. Open the Chapter04-PersistenceIISamples-singletable project,
and expand the com.apress.ejb.chapter04.singletable.service package. You will
see the Java service façade (JavaServiceFacade.java) and its client class. Right-click
on JavaServiceFacadeClient.java, and choose "Run File." The test will run within
NetBeans, and the output is sent to a log window. See Figure 4-11.

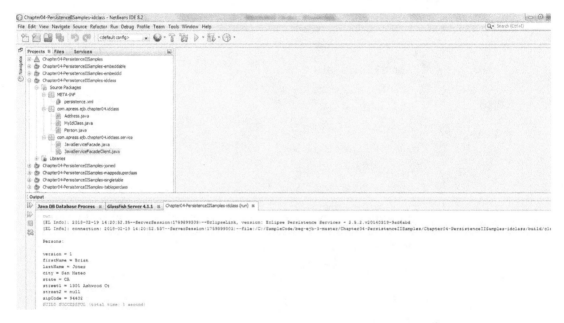

Figure 4-11. *Executing the SINGLE_TABLE inheritance example in a Java SE
environment*

Next run the HTTP servlet client by opening the Chapter04-PersistenceIISamples-war
project and expanding the package com.apress.ejb.chapter04.client. Open
the browser that is used by NetBeans to run servlets. (If you're not sure, open the
NetBeans preferences by going to Tools ➤ Options ➤ General.) Right-click on
SingleTableInheritanceClient.java servlet, and choose "Run File" to run the test as
a Web application as shown in Figure 4-12.

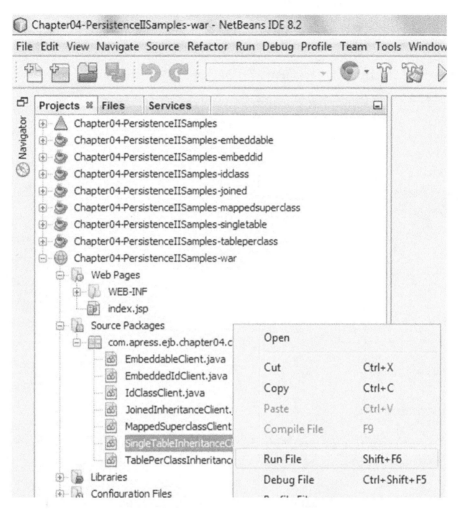

Figure 4-12. *Executing the* `com.apress.ejb.chapter04.client` *Servlet*

NetBeans will execute the servlet in the default browser as shown in Figure 4-13. During execution of the test, any existing conflicting data is deleted, new test data is created, and then it is queried and rendered in tabular format. Referenced objects, including lists of referenced objects, are shown in nested table cells. Here in Figure 4-13 is the output for this client servlet, showing the log of the servlet's actions.

Servlet SingleTableInheritanceClient at /Chapter04-PersistenceIISamples-war

Deleting any existing Address and Person hierarchy data

Deleting parttimeemployee (and related objects) 2

Deleting fulltimeemployee (and related objects) 1

Creating and persisting new Address for FullTimeEmployee

Creating and persisting new FullTimeEmployee

Creating and persisting new Address for PartTimeEmployee

Creating and persisting new PartTimeEmployee

Persons:

FullTimeEmployee

firstName	Brian
id	51
lastName	Jones
version	1

	Address	
	id	51
	version	1
	city	San Mateo
homeAddress	state	CA
	street1	1301 Ashwood C:
	street2	null
	version	1
	zipCode	94400

PartTimeEmployee

Figure 4-13. *Executing the SINGLE_TABLE inheritance example in a Java EE Web environment*

Take a look at the code in `SingleTableInheritanceClient.java`. Feel free to experiment by creating additional entities, testing the query and other service methods on the Java service façade, and observing the resulting behavior. To reset the test schema back to its original state, you can always delete the WineApp test database and then re-execute the step depicted in Figure 4-8.

Testing the Other Persistence Examples

The remaining six projects each test a different feature covered in this chapter and identified on the project name. You are encouraged to use these projects as a reference for how to configure the various inheritance hierarchies, mapped superclasses, embedded classes, and complex primary keys.

Since each project in this chapter shares the same structure, and a dedicated HTTP servlet tester accompanies each, the above steps can guide you through executing each example in the same way.

Summary

We have covered a fair bit of ground in this chapter, and with this information in hand, you should be ready to go out and build some powerful entities that are configured to best suit your application domain. Below is a summary of the key concepts we covered in this chapter.

Mapping Entity Inheritance Hierarchies

JPA provides built-in support for three common O/R mapping strategies for entity class inheritance hierarchies: SINGLE_TABLE, JOINED, and TABLE_PER_CLASS. We examined the strengths and weaknesses of each approach, and we offered examples of common use cases that map best to each strategy.

Using Abstract Entities, Mapped Superclasses, and Non-Entity Classes in an Inheritance Hierarchy

JPA offers flexible solutions when it comes to mixing entities with abstract and non-entity classes in a type hierarchy. Entities may be either concrete or abstract. Only entity classes may be queried or serve as the targets of mapped entity relationships, but entities may still make use of non-entity classes, both by embedding them using @Embedded and @ElementCollection and by extending them or being extended by them. We showed some examples that mix these options together to illustrate their use.

Polymorphic Relationships

Relationships can be specified between entities, including abstract supertype entities in a hierarchy. This lets you define a relationship with entities anywhere along an inheritance hierarchy that will implicitly involve subtypes of that entity as well.

Polymorphic JPQL Queries

Similarly, JPQL queries can select or join entities of a supertype class, and any instances of subtypes matching the query criteria will be returned in the query result. We looked at how to use JPQL to build reusable @NamedQuery objects as well as the QueryCriteria API introduced since JPA 2.0.

Using Native SQL Queries

The EntityManager lets you issue native SQL queries as an overture to experienced SQL developers and as an optimization to avoid the overhead of querying across all of an entity's fields when only a few are actually needed. We provided an example of how to define a named native SQL query that returns entity instances so that the results could be seamlessly integrated into an application.

Using the Query Criteria API

As a type-safe alternative to JPQL, the criteria API introduced since JPA 2.0 allows you to construct queries by dynamically assembling the constituent clauses and predicates into a CriteriaQuery object that can be invoked to retrieve entity or other results. Figure 4-14 shows how the persistence.xml file looks in the NetBeans IDE 8.2.

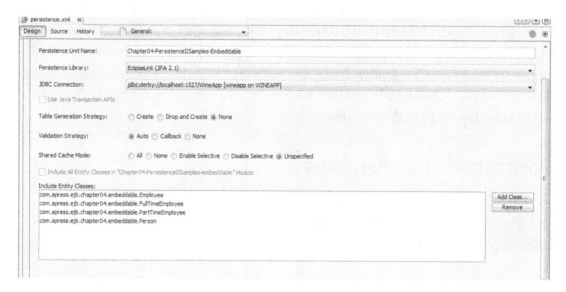

Figure 4-14. *Persistence.xml file*

Composite Primary Keys and Nested Foreign Keys

We explored the different types of composite primary key usage, showing how to use an @EmbeddedId field and multiple @Id fields. When an entity's primary key maps to columns that are also involved in relationships to other entities (as when the primary key contains one or more columns that are also part of a foreign key), things can get a little bit dicey. We provided some examples of how to deal with this situation.

Support for Optimistic Locking

Using the @Version annotation, you can designate a field (one that is common to all entities in your inheritance hierarchy) to be used by the EntityManager to perform optimistic locking when managing concurrency, such as during merge operations. This field will be auto-populated by the persistence framework and should not be updated by application code.

Support for Autogenerated Primary Automatic Key Values

JPA offers declarative support for the population of @Id fields with unique values. We provided examples of how to declare both database sequence-based and table-based ID generators.

Interceptors: Entity Callback Methods

You can designate methods on your entity class, or on the helper class of your choosing, to handle entity lifecycle callbacks. We listed the callback methods available to you and explained how to use them to register your own custom methods that will be called during lifecycle events.

CHAPTER 5

EJB Message-Driven Beans

This chapter discusses the need for message-oriented architecture. It introduces Java Message Service (JMS), the typical architecture for messaging applications, and it details the concepts behind EJB message-driven beans (MDBs). The chapter also covers annotations, dependency injection, and interceptors in relation to MDBs.

Message-Oriented Architecture

Today's IT organizations have dozens of applications and services that perform such well-defined tasks as inventory, billing, expense reporting, and order entry. With the evolution of the Internet and e-business, enterprises have started to think about how different applications can work independently but still be a part of an information workflow process at the same time.

This new demand brings us to the concept of integrating existing applications, as well as building new applications that work coherently with existing applications. Integrating existing applications with new applications is a very complex task: first due to the large number of applications used by most enterprises, and second because of their complex business workflow.

Messaging is one of the most viable solutions for integrating existing and new applications in an asynchronous communication and loosely coupled transaction model. Asynchronous messaging allows applications to communicate by exchanging messages independently without them having to be hardwired to each other. An application or business process sending a message does not have to wait for the receiver as long as both sender and receiver understand and agree upon a message format and an intermediate destination.

© Jonathan Wetherbee, Massimo Nardone, Chirag Rathod, and Raghu Kodali 2018
J. Wetherbee et al., *Beginning EJB in Java EE 8*, https://doi.org/10.1007/978-1-4842-3573-7_5

Here are the MDBs messaging concepts:

- Process of sending a loosely coupled, asynchronous message.

- The sender doesn't know when the message is received.

- The sender can guarantee that the message will not be lost en route.

- The MOM (message-oriented middleware) service acts like a voicemail when the receiver is AFK.

What Is JMS?

JMS is a Java Message-Oriented Middleware (MOM) API that allows applications to send and receive messages asynchronously. JMS is part of the standard Java EE API as defined by JSR 914. JMS is analogous to JDBC (Java Database Connectivity), which provides a standard API to connect to several types of databases (Oracle, DB2, MySQL). Likewise, JMS provides a standard API to connect to several types of messaging systems (IBM MQ, SonicMQ).

Note   MOM stores the Message in a Location specified by the sender and later collected by the consumer.

JMS architecture consists of the following:

- **JMS provider:** A messaging system (as shown in Figure 5-1) that handles the routing and delivery of messages. A JMS provider can be a messaging component of an application server (such as Oracle WebLogic Server, IBM WebSphere, Oracle GlassFish Server). JMS providers are also known as *JMS servers*.

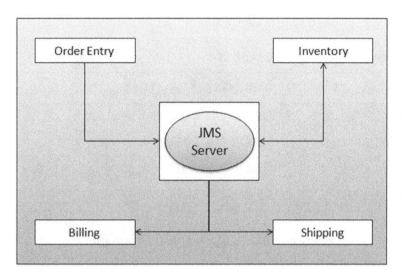

Figure 5-1. *A JMS messaging system*

- **JMS client:** Any Java application or Java EE component that uses the JMS API either to consume or produce a JMS message.

- **JMS consumer:** A JMS client application that consumes JMS messages. The inventory, billing, and shipping applications shown in Figure 5-1 are JMS message consumers.

- **JMS producer:** A JMS client that generates the message. The order entry application shown in Figure 5-1 is a JMS message producer.

- **JMS message:** A message consisting of a header, properties, and a body. The header identifies the message and contains a standard information just like JMSTimestamp. MOM sets this header to the current time when the message is sent. The properties provide additional attributes that are specific to the application and provider. The property is explicitly created by the application Message. setBooleanProperty("",true); and it can be Boolean, byte, double, float, int, long, short, String, Object, etc. The body contains the content of the message and it can be ObjectMessage, ByteMessage, MapMessage, StreamMessage, and TestMessage. The JMS specification provides support to send and receive different types of messages. Table 5-1 shows the message types and descriptions.

Table 5-1. *JMS Message Types*

Message Type	Description
ByteMessage	Consists of a series of bytes
MapMessage	Consists of a set of name/value pairs
ObjectMessage	Consists of a serialized Java object
StreamMessage	Consists of a sequence of primitive data types
TextMessage	Consists of strings

JMS has two types of resources: JMSContext and Destination.

JMS application will retrieve the JMSContext using DI with the CDI @Inject and configure the JMSContext to connect to a connection factory with @JMSConnectionFactory.

Messaging Application Architecture

Generally, two different classes of messaging applications exist:

- The point-to-point (P2P) model: only one consumer will process a given message, PTP message destinations are called queues, A writes to the queue and B reads from the queue.

- The publish-subscribe (pub-sub) model: each subscriber receives a copy of the message.

The P2P model is based on message queues, where a queue holds the JMS messages sent by the JMS client application. Message producers and consumers decide upon a common queue to exchange messages.

The P2P model is used if there is one and only one message consumer for each message. For example, the order entry system shown in Figure 5-2 sends a new order into the message queue, which is picked up by the inventory system. Similarly, the message sent by the inventory system is consumed by the shipping system, and the message from the shipping system is consumed by the billing system.

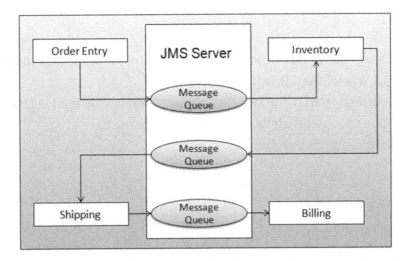

Figure 5-2. *A JMS messaging system using queues*

The pub-sub model is based on topics, where the topic is the destination address of the message. Multiple recipients or JMS consumers can retrieve each message. In this model, publishers are not always aware of possible subscribers. The pub-sub model is used for broadcast-type applications, as shown in Figure 5-3, in which a message is delivered for more than one JMS client. Topics, each having a unique name, are defined in the messaging server. Each message, with its associated subject, gets published and delivered to all subscribers.

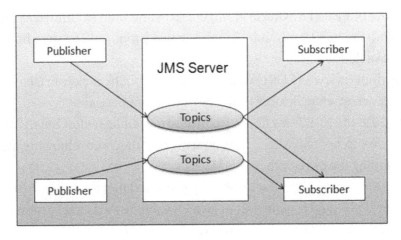

Figure 5-3. *A JMS messaging system using topics*

JMS 2.0

JMS 2.0 was released in April 2013, and it was the first update to the JMS specification since version 1.1 was released in 2002.

JMS 2.0 is currently part of the Java EE 7 platform and can be used in Java EE Web or EJB applications or as a stand-alone in a Java SE environment.

The JMS 2.0 main goals include:

- – API modernization

- – Java EE Alignment

- – EJB3/MDB Alignment

- – Minor Corrections and Clarifications since version 1.1

- – New API for sending and receiving messages

- – New API also supports resource injection

The JMS 2.0's biggest change was the introduction of a new API for sending and receiving messages, helping the programmer to reduce the amount of code to write.

JMS 2.1

JMS 2.1 was first proposed by Oracle in August 2014 and then submitted as JSR 368 in accordance with the Java Community Process. It was proposed and then finally approved to be part of Java EE 8.

The early draft review 1 (EDR1) was published for public review in October 2015, including a new chapter on flexible JMS message-driven beans.

In March 2016 the EDR2 was finally published for public review but then Oracle stopped the development of JMS 2.1, announcing that they were changing the Java EE 8 priorities including the development of JMS 2.1.

Finally, in November 2016 Oracle formally proposed that the JSR be withdrawn and confirmed that JMS would remain part of Java EE 8, but the existing version JMS 2.0 would be used rather than a new version 2.1.

The JMS 2.1 specification can be found in this web page:

`https://jcp.org/en/jsr/detail?id=368`

Here are the most important changes in JMS 2.1:

- Alignment with Java SE 8

- Flexible MDBs (EE)

- Change in the asynchronous messaging, including how MDB implements any MessageListener interface to any CDI bean

- CDI Beans as Listeners

- Batch delivery including Acknowledgment Modes, the setMessageListener (EE), etc.

- Repeatable Annotations including the redelivery configuration (EE)

Using MDBs

An *MDB* is an asynchronous message consumer that processes messages delivered via JMS. While MDBs do the job of processing the messages, the EJB container in which the MDBs run take care of the services (transactions, security, resources, concurrency, message acknowledgment), letting the bean developer focus on the business logic of processing messages. Traditional JMS applications would have to custom write some of these services. MDBs are stateless in nature, which means that EJB containers can have numerous instances of MDBs execute concurrently to process hundreds of JMS messages coming in from various applications or JMS producers and also provide quality of service (QoS), such as high availability and reliability for enterprise applications.

EJB client applications cannot access MDBs directly as they can with session beans and entities. The only way to communicate with an MDB would be by sending a JMS message to the destination to which the MDB is listening. Any Java application or Java EE component using the JMS API can be the message provider for the MDB by sending messages to queues or topics.

When Do You Use MDBs?

Earlier in the chapter, we discussed the need for asynchrony in enterprises. Asynchronous messaging provides loose coupling between applications, systems, and services, thus providing greater flexibility and change management for applications and systems. MDBs provide a standard messaging component model that achieves the goal of asynchronous and message-oriented architecture in enterprises.

Figure 5-4 shows a message-oriented application that has order entry, inventory, billing, and shipping systems that communicate asynchronously to handle a workflow that starts with a new purchase order and ends when the order gets shipped to the customer. An order entry system captures a new order from a customer, processes the order, and sends it into a designated message queue (in Figure 5-4, this is the New Order queue). The inventory system picks up the message from the queue and checks whether or not the inventory is available. If not, it sends a message to the Suppliers queue; if the order can be shipped, then it puts a message into the Order Ready queue. This new message is picked up by the billing system, which processes the billing for the customer and puts a message back into the Shipping queue. Finally, the shipping application picks up the message, gets the order shipped to the customer, and sends an e-mail to the customer with tracking information.

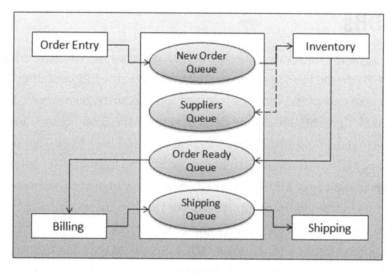

Figure 5-4. *An order-to-shipping JMS messaging system*

MDB Classes

Unlike a session bean, an MDB doesn't have any business interfaces. It has only the following:

- A message-driven class

- An optional callback listener class

- An optional interceptor class

An *MDB class* is any standard Java class that has a class-level annotation @MessageDriven. If deployment descriptors are used instead of annotations, the bean class should be denoted as an MDB class. In the case of mixed mode, in which you are using annotations and deployment descriptors, the @MessageDriven annotation must be specified if any other class-level or member-level annotations are specified in the bean class. The @MessageDriven annotation parameters can be used to specify the JMS queues or topics to which the bean is listening. Table 5-2 details the parameters.

Table 5-2. *Parameter details for the @MessageDriven Annotation*

Parameter	Description
ActivationConfigProperty	The set of properties used to specify the destination name and type
description	A description of the bean class
mappedName	The physical Java Naming and Directory Interface (JNDI) name of the topic or queue to which the MDB is listening
messageListener	The interface name of the interface class that the MDB is extending
name	The name of the MDB, if it has to be a different name than the bean class

To illustrate the use of an MDB, we will create the use case shown in Figure 5-5. We will have an application client, which will be a Java command-line program that invokes a business method in the OrderProcessing session bean. The OrderProcessing session bean will create and send a JMS message to a topic registered/configured in the GlassFish application server. An MDB, StatusMailer, will listen to the topic and process the incoming message. The message received will contain details for the customer, and it will be used to send an e-mail notification to the customer regarding his or her order status. This simple use case will allow us to demonstrate how MDBs work and how to inject different types of resources in session beans and MDBs.

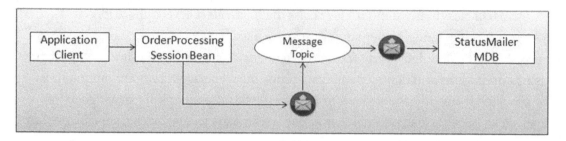

Figure 5-5. *A sample MDB use case*

Listing 5-1 shows the definition of a StatusMailer MDB. We have marked the StatusMailerBean class with the @MessageDriven annotation.

Listing 5-1. StatusMailerBean.java

```
package com.apress.ejb.chapter05;
import javax.ejb.MessageDriven;
@MessageDriven
public class StatusMailerBean {
}
```

An MDB class has one method, onMessage(), which gets invoked by the EJB container on the arrival of a message in the queue/topic to which the MDB is listening. The onMessage() method contains the business logic on how to process the incoming message. The onMessage() method contains one parameter, which is the JMS message. In the case of the StatusMailer bean, the onMessage() method checks whether the message is of MapMessage type, and then it gets the customer information from the message, creates an e-mail message about the order status, and then sends an e-mail to the customer. Listing 5-2 shows the onMessage() method code. In a try block, we start by checking whether the message received is of type MapMessage, as we are expecting. If it is, then we use getStringProperty() to retrieve the values of the from, to, subject, and content attributes in the message.

Listing 5-2. The onMessage Method Code

```
package com.apress.ejb.chapter05;
import javax.ejb.MessageDriven;
@MessageDriven
public class StatusMailerBean {
    public void onMessage(Message message){
```

```
    try {
        if (message instanceof MapMessage) {
            MapMessage orderMessage = (MapMessage)message;
            String from = orderMessage.getStringProperty("from");
            String to = orderMessage.getStringProperty("to");
            String subject = orderMessage.getStringProperty("subject");
            String content = orderMessage.getStringProperty("content");
        }
        else {
            System.out.println("Invalid message ");
        }
    } catch (Exception ex) {
        ex.printStackTrace();
    }
    }
}
```

In addition to marking the standard Java class with the @MessageDriven annotation, the following requirements apply to an MDB class:

- The MDB class must implement the message listener interface. In the case of JMS, this will be javax.jms.MessageListener.

- The class cannot be final or abstract.

- The class should have a no-argument public constructor that is used by the EJB container to create instances of the bean class.

If both annotations and deployment descriptors are used, the settings or values in the deployment descriptor will override the annotations in the classes during the deployment process.

Configuration Properties

Bean developers can provide configuration properties along with MDB classes, which get used at deployment time. The EJB container uses these properties to configure the bean and link it to the appropriate JMS provider. These configuration properties can be set using the @ActivationConfigProperty annotation. This annotation can be provided as one of the parameters for the @MessageDriven annotation. Listing 5-3 shows the @MessageDriven annotation with properties for the StatusMailer MDB. We have defined two ActivationConfigProperty annotations that specify the logical destination name and the destination type.

Listing 5-3. The @MessageDriven Annotation with Properties for the StatusMailer MDB

```
@MessageDriven(activationConfig= {
@ActivationConfigProperty(propertyName="destinationName", ↵
propertyValue="StatusMessageTopic"), ↵
@ActivationConfigProperty(propertyName="destinationType", ↵
propertyValue="javax.jms.Topic")
}, mappedName="StatusMessageTopic")

public class StatusMailerBean implements javax.jms.MessageListener {

}
```

Standard configuration properties available for MDBs in EJB version 3.0 and 3.1 correspond to the configuration properties in JMS version 1.1. Standard configuration properties for MDBs in EJB version 3.2 have been extended to correspond to the configuration properties in JMS version 2.0. Table 5-3 shows the correspondence between the EJB version and JMS version.

Table 5-3. *Mapping of EJB MDB version to JMS version*

EJB Version	JMS Version
EJB 3.0	JMS 1.1
EJB 3.1	JMS 1.1
EJB 3.2	JMS 2.0
EJB 3.2	JMS 2.1

In the following sections, we will show what configuration properties can be set for MDBs.

Message Acknowledgment

The EJB container provides a message acknowledgment service. There are two message acknowledgment modes:

- Auto-acknowledge
- Dups-ok-acknowledge

In the case of Auto-acknowledge, the message delivery acknowledgment happens after the onMessage() method. This property is useful for applications that require no duplicate messages. For example, a new order should be received by the inventory system once and only once. In the case of Dups-ok-acknowledge, the acknowledgment is done lazily, which means that there might be duplicate delivery of messages, but it reduces the overhead for the session in terms of immediate acknowledgment. For example, an e-mail message that gets sent out during the order process can possibly allow duplicate messages. We can use the @ActivationConfigProperty annotation to specify the message acknowledgment property. Listing 5-4 shows the property set to allow duplicates.

Listing 5-4. The @ActivationConfigProperty Annotation

```
@MessageDriven(
activationConfig= {
@ActivationConfigProperty(propertyName="acknowledgeMode", ↵
propertyValue="Dups-ok-acknowledge")}
)
```

The Message Selector

The message selector allows filtering of incoming messages based on the selection criteria provided by the bean developer using the @ActivationConfigProperty annotation. This property is useful for restricting the messages that the bean receives. For example, the MDB that processes the incoming orders might only process orders pertaining to red and white wines. The property name used to specify is messageSelector.

Message Destination

The message destination describes whether the MDB listens on a queue or topic. Bean developers can provide the description in the bean using the @ActivationConfigProperty annotation. The value of the property must be either javax.jms.Queue or javax.jms.Topic. For example, a new order may need to be processed by an inventory system as a next step in the workflow; in this case, the order entry system doesn't have to broadcast the new order message. Both the order entry and inventory system can agree on a particular destination. Listing 5-3 shows the code to specify destination name and type.

Subscription Durability

If the bean is designed to listen to a topic, then the bean developer can further specify the durability of the message. The topic can be either Durable or Non-Durable. Usage of Durable topics ensures reliability for the applications. They ensure that messages are not missed, even if the EJB container is temporarily offline. For example, we may need to make sure that the new purchase orders received from client applications are not lost if the EJB container goes down. All purchase orders have to be reliably processed by the MDBs. We can use the @ActivationConfigProperty annotation to specify the durability using the subscriptionDurability property. Listing 5-5 shows the code to set the property to Durable. If this property is not set, the container will assume the default of Non-Durable.

Listing 5-5. The Code to Set the Property to Durable

```
@MessageDriven(
activationConfig= {
@ActivationConfigProperty(propertyName="subscriptionDurability",
propertyValue="Durable")}
)
```

In the StatusMailer MDB, we will create properties using the @ActivationConfigProperty annotation. The message's destinationName is set to StatusMessageTopic, and destinationType is set to javax.jms.Topic. We will use the mappedName parameter to specify the physical destination name of the topic. In our case, it is the same as destinationName. Listing 5-6 shows the StatusMailer MDB in its current state of completion.

Listing 5-6. StatusMailerBean.java

```java
package com.apress.ejb.chapter05;
import javax.ejb.ActivationConfigProperty;
import javax.jms.Message;
import javax.ejb.MessageDriven;
import javax.jms.MapMessage;

@MessageDriven(activationConfig= {
@ActivationConfigProperty(propertyName="destinationName", propertyValue=
"StatusMessageTopic"),
@ActivationConfigProperty(propertyName="destinationType",
propertyValue="javax.jms.Topic")
}, mappedName="StatusMessageTopic")
public class StatusMailerBean implements javax.jms.MessageListener{
    public void onMessage(Message message){
        try  {
            if (message instanceof MapMessage) {
                MapMessage orderMessage = (MapMessage)message;
                String from = orderMessage.getStringProperty("from");
                String to = orderMessage.getStringProperty("to");
                String subject = orderMessage.getStringProperty("subject");
                String content = orderMessage.getStringProperty("content");
             }
            else {
                System.out.println("Invalid message ");
                }
        } catch (Exception ex)  {
            ex.printStackTrace();
        }
    }
}
```

Dependency Injection in MDBs

MDBs can use dependency injection to acquire references to resources such as JavaMail, EJBs, or other objects. The resources that an MDB tries to acquire and use must be available in the container context or environment context.

In the sample use case from Figure 5-5, we talked about creating an e-mail after the message is processed and sending the order status to the customer via e-mail. In order to do this in the StatusMailer message bean, we need to acquire a JavaMail session so that we can create an e-mail and send it. *JavaMail* is an API that provides a platform-independent framework for building mail applications. The JavaMail API is available with the Java EE platform.

We can acquire a JavaMail session in an MDB using dependency injection. Listing 5-7 shows the completed StatusMailer MDB using dependency injection and the JavaMail API. The @Resource annotation is used to inject a JavaMail session with the name mail/wineappMail, which has been registered as a mail resource in the GlassFish application server. The injected mail session is used to create javax.mail.Message, and the setter methods are used to create the headers and content of the mail message. Finally, the send() method in the javax.mail.Transport class is used to send the created message.

Listing 5-7. The Completed StatusMailer MDB Using Dependency Injection and the JavaMail API

```
package com.apress.ejb.chapter05;
import javax.annotation.Resource;
import javax.ejb.ActivationConfigProperty;
import javax.jms.Message;
import javax.ejb.MessageDriven;
import javax.jms.MapMessage;
import javax.mail.Transport;
import javax.mail.internet.InternetAddress;
import javax.mail.internet.MimeMessage;

@MessageDriven(activationConfig= {
@ActivationConfigProperty(propertyName="destinationName", ↵
propertyValue="StatusMessageTopic"), ↵
```

```java
@ActivationConfigProperty(propertyName="destinationType", ↵
propertyValue="javax.jms.Topic")
}, mappedName="StatusMessageTopic")

public class StatusMailerBean implements javax.jms.MessageListener{
@Resource(name="mail/wineappMail" )
private javax.mail.Session ms;

    public void onMessage(Message message){
        try  {
            if (message instanceof MapMessage) {
                MapMessage orderMessage = (MapMessage)message;
                String from = orderMessage.getStringProperty("from");
                String to = orderMessage.getStringProperty("to");
                String subject = orderMessage.getStringProperty("subject");
                String content = orderMessage.getStringProperty("content");
                javax.mail.Message msg = new MimeMessage(ms);
                msg.setFrom(new InternetAddress(from));
                InternetAddress[] address = {new InternetAddress(to)};
                msg.setRecipients(javax.mail.Message.RecipientType.TO,
                address);
                msg.setSubject(subject);
                msg.setSentDate(new java.util.Date());
                msg.setContent(content, "text/html");
                System.out.println("MDB: Sending Message...");
                Transport.send(msg);
                System.out.println("MDB: Message Sent");
             }
            else {
                System.out.println("Invalid message ");
                }

        } catch (Exception ex)  {
            ex.printStackTrace();
        }

    }
}
```

Lifecycle Callback Methods

There will be certain instances in which an application that uses MDBs requires fine-grained control. Two lifecycle event callbacks are supported for MDBs:

- `PostConstruct`

- `PreDestroy`

The `PostConstruct` callback occurs before the first message listener method invocation on the bean and after the container has performed the dependency injection. The `PreDestroy` callback occurs when the MDB is removed from the pool or destroyed.

For example, a `PostConstruct` callback can be used to initialize some attributes or resources, and a `PreDestroy` callback can be used to clean up or release the acquired resources.

Callback methods defined on an MDB class should have the following signature:

```
public void <METHOD> ()
```

Callback methods can also be defined on a bean's listener class, in which case the methods should have the following signature:

```
public void <METHOD>(Object)
```

where `Object` may be declared as the actual bean type, which is the argument passed to the callback method at run time.

Callback methods can be any methods in the MDB that have callback annotations. The following rules apply to these methods:

- The method should be public.

- The method cannot be final or static.

- The return type should be `void`.

The methods can take either zero or one argument, as shown previously. A callback listener class is denoted by the `@CallbackListener` annotation on the MDB class with which it is associated.

Interceptors

The EJB specification provides annotations called *interceptors*, which allow you to intercept a business method invocation. Interceptor methods can be defined for MDBs.

You can add either an @AroundInvoke annotation or an <around-invoke-method> element in the deployment descriptor for a particular method, or you can define an interceptor class whose methods are invoked before the onMessage() method is invoked in the MDB class. An interceptor class is denoted using the @Interceptor annotation on the MDB class with which it is associated. In the case of multiple interceptor classes, the @Interceptors annotation is used. Only one AroundInvoke method may be present on the bean class or on any given interceptor class. An AroundInvoke method cannot be an onMessage() method of the MDB class.

AroundInvoke methods should have the following signature:

```
public Object <METHOD>(InvocationContext) throws Exception
```

The definition of InvocationContext is as follows:

```
package javax.ejb;
public interface InvocationContext {
    public Object getBean();
    public java.lang.reflect.Method getMethod();
    public Object[] getParameters();
    public void setParameters(Object[] params);
    public EJBContext getEJBContext();
    public java.util.Map getContextData();
    public Object proceed() throws Exception;
}
```

The following list describes each of the methods:

- getBean(): Returns the instance of the bean on which the method was called

- getMethod(): Returns the method on the bean instance that was called

- getParameters(): Returns the parameters for the method call

- `setParameters()`: Allows modification of the parameters for the method call

- `getEJBContext()`: Gives the interceptor methods access to the bean's `EJBContext`

- `getContextData()`: Allows values to be passed between interceptor methods in the same `InvocationContext` instance using the `Map` returned

- `proceed()`: Invokes the next interceptor if there is one, or invokes the target bean method

Exception Handling

The EJB spec outlines two types of exceptions: application exceptions and system exceptions. For more general information on these exceptions, see the "Exception Handling" section of Chapter 2. In the case of an MDB, the listener method must not throw a `java.rmi.RemoteException` or, in general, a runtime exception. The client assumes that the message consumer continues to exist even though a runtime exception has occurred. If the client sends a message after a runtime exception is thrown, then the EJB container delegates the messages to a different MDB instance. Also, if you allow an exception to "escape" an MDB, the message isn't considered to be consumed, and it goes back on the queue/topic. Then the offending message gets redelivered. This is known as the "poison message" problem.

Callback methods can throw runtime exceptions. A runtime exception thrown by a callback method that executes within a transaction causes that transaction to be rolled back. Callback methods must not throw application exceptions.

Client View

To a client application, an MDB is simply a message consumer. A client application can be any Java client of a Java EE component that is using the JMS API to send a message. From the perspective of the client application, the existence of an MDB is completely hidden behind the destination or endpoint for which the MDB is the message listener.

A client's JNDI namespace may be configured to include the destinations or endpoints of MDBs installed in multiple EJB containers located on multiple machines on a network. The actual locations of an enterprise bean and EJB container are, in general, transparent to the client using the enterprise bean.

References to message destinations can be injected via the @Resource annotation (which is in the javax.annotation package) or via JNDI lookup in cases in which the resource has been defined in the deployment descriptor.

Note   Starting with EJB 3.2, a JMS resource adapter can construct a subscription name by looking up an MDB using its standard name.

In the use case discussed earlier and shown in Figure 5-5, we have a session bean that is acting as an intermediary between the client application and the message topic. The client application invokes a business method in the session bean, and the session becomes the client or JMS message producer that is creating and sending the message. To illustrate this, we will create a stateless session bean, OrderProcessing, with one business method, SendOrderStatus(). Listing 5-8 shows the code for the OrderProcessing session bean. We are using the @Resource annotation to inject the TopicConnectionFactory and Topic to which the StatusMailer MDB is listening. We will use some hard-coded values in the session bean to simulate the customer e-mail address and the content for the e-mail. In the try block, we create a connection to the statusMessageTopicConnectionFactory and start the connection. Using the created session, we create a topic session and topic producer with the createSession() and createProducer() methods. Finally, we create a MapMessage object; populate the message with the e-mail address, subject, and content; and send the message to the Topic using the send() method.

Listing 5-8. OrderProcessingBean.java

```
package com.apress.ejb.chapter05;
import javax.annotation.Resource;
import javax.ejb.Stateless;
import javax.jms.Connection;
import javax.jms.JMSException;
import javax.jms.MapMessage;
import javax.jms.MessageProducer;
import javax.jms.Session;
import javax.jms.Topic;
import javax.jms.TopicConnectionFactory;
```

```java
@Stateless(name = "OrderProcessing")
public class OrderProcessingBean
{
    public OrderProcessingBean() {
    }

    @Resource(mappedName = "StatusMessageTopicConnectionFactory")
    private TopicConnectionFactory statusMessageTopicCF;

    @Resource(mappedName = "StatusMessageTopic")
    private Topic statusTopic;

    public String SendOrderStatus() {
        String from = "chirag.rathod@oracle.com";
        String to = "chirag.rathod@oracle.com";
        String content =
        "Your order has been processed " + "If you have questions" +
        " call EJB Application with order id # " + "1234567890";

        try {
        System.out.println("Before status TopicCF connection");
        Connection connection = statusMessageTopicCF.createConnection();
        System.out.println("Created connection");
        connection.start();
        System.out.println("statted connection");
        System.out.println("Starting Topic Session");
        Session topicSession =
            connection.createSession(false, Session.AUTO_ACKNOWLEDGE);
        MessageProducer publisher = topicSession.
        createProducer(statusTopic);
        System.out.println("created producer");
        MapMessage message = topicSession.createMapMessage();
        message.setStringProperty("from", from);
        message.setStringProperty("to", to);
        message.setStringProperty("subject", "Status of your wine order");
        message.setStringProperty("content", content);
        System.out.println("before send");
```

```
        publisher.send(message);
        System.out.println("after send");
        }
        catch (JMSException e) {
            e.printStackTrace();
        }

        return "Created a MapMessage and sent it to StatusTopic";
    }
}
```

Note   In Listing 5-8, update the value of "from" and "to" fields to your e-mail ID.

One last thing we need to do to complete the use case discussed in Figure 5-5 is to come up with the client application that will look up the OrderProcessing session bean and invoke the SendOrderStatus() message. Listing 5-9 shows the code for the client application. In the try block, we are doing a JNDI lookup of the OrderProcessing session bean and calling the SendOrderStatus() business method.

Listing 5-9. StatusMailerClient.java

```
package com.apress.ejb.chapter05;
import java.io.IOException;
import java.io.PrintWriter;
import javax.ejb.EJB;
import javax.servlet.ServletException;
import javax.servlet.annotation.WebServlet;
import javax.servlet.http.HttpServlet;
import javax.servlet.http.HttpServletRequest;
import javax.servlet.http.HttpServletResponse;

@WebServlet(name = "StatusMailerClient", urlPatterns =
{"/StatusMailerClient"})
public class StatusMailerClient extends HttpServlet {
    @EJB
    OrderProcessingBean orderProcessing;
```

```
    protected void processRequest(HttpServletRequest request,
HttpServletResponse response)
            throws ServletException, IOException {
        response.setContentType("text/html;charset=UTF-8");
        PrintWriter out = response.getWriter();
        try {
            out.println("<html>");
            out.println("<head>");
            out.println("<title>Servlet StatusMailerClient</title>");
            out.println("</head>");
            out.println("<body>");

            out.println("<h1>OrderProcessing session bean lookup to be
            done</h1>");
            out.println("<h1>Invoking SendOrderStatus() business method
            now</h1>");
            out.println("<h1>" + orderProcessing.SendOrderStatus() +
            "</h1>");
            out.println("<h1>Done !!!</h1>");
            out.println("</body>");
            out.println("</html>");
        } finally {
            out.close();
        }
    }

    @Override
    protected void doGet(HttpServletRequest request, HttpServletResponse
    response)
            throws ServletException, IOException {
        processRequest(request, response);
    }

    @Override
    protected void doPost(HttpServletRequest request, HttpServletResponse
    response)
```

```
            throws ServletException, IOException {
        processRequest(request, response);
    }

    @Override
    public String getServletInfo() {
        return "Short description";
    }
}
```

In the next section, we will look at compiling, deploying, and running the use case on which we have worked.

Compiling, Deploying, and Testing MDBs

MDBs need to be packaged into EJB JAR (Java Archive) files before they can be deployed into EJB containers. These EJB archives can then be deployed. (For some EJB containers or application servers, they need to be assembled into EAR [Enterprise Archive] files). Most EJB containers or application servers provide deployment utilities or Ant tasks to facilitate deployment of EJBs to their containers. Java-integrated development environments (IDEs) like JDeveloper, NetBeans, and Eclipse also provide deployment features that allow developers to package, assemble, and deploy EJBs to application servers. Packaging, assembly, and deployment aspects are covered in detail in Chapter 11.

In this chapter, we have developed one stateless session bean (OrderProcessing) and one MDB (StatusMailer). JMS providers have to be configured with queues and topics that will be used by the client application and MDB accordingly before the MDBs are deployed.

The following sections describe the steps to compile, deploy, and test these MDBs and session beans.

Prerequisites

Before performing any of the steps detailed in the next sections, complete the "Getting Started" section of Chapter 1, which will walk you through the installation and environment setup required for the samples in this chapter.

Compiling the Session Beans and MDBs

Copy the Chapter05-MDBSamples directory and its contents into a directory of your choice. Run the NetBeans IDE, and open the Chapter05-MDBSamples project using the File ➤ Open Project menu. Make sure that the 'Open Required Projects' check box is checked. See Figure 5-6.

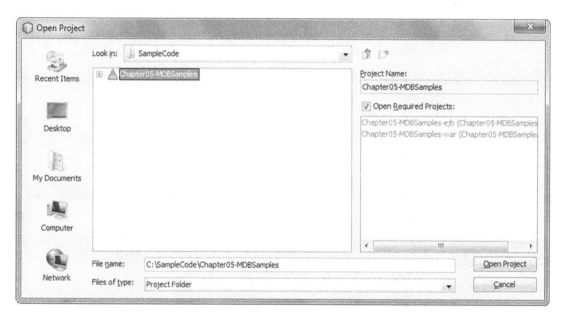

Figure 5-6. *Opening the Chapter05-MDBSamples project*

Expand the Chapter05-MDBSamples-ejb node, and observe that the MDB and the session bean that we created appear in the com.apress.ejb.chapter05 package. Similarly, the two client servlets appear under the Chapter05-MDBSamples-war node as shown in Figure 5-7.

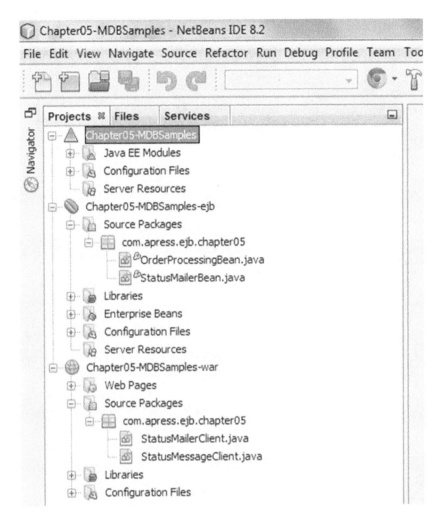

Figure 5-7. *Verifying that the MDB, Session Bean, and their clients are available in the project*

Invoke the context menu on `Chapter05-MDBSamples` node, and build the application by selecting the `Clean and Build` menu option as shown in Figure 5-8.

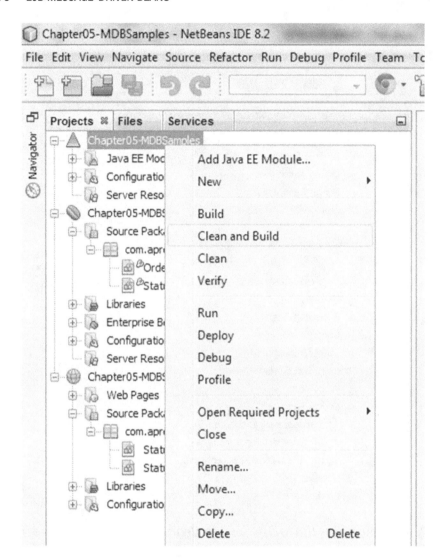

Figure 5-8. *Building the application*

Creating the JMS and JavaMail Resources

The StatusMailer MDB makes use of JMS and JavaMail resources. Before the Chapter05-MDBSamples application can be deployed to GlassFish, these resources have to be preconfigured. First we will start the GlassFish application server and then configure the JMS and JavaMail resources by using the web-based administrator console. c

Click the 'Services' tab available in the application navigator of NetBeans. 'GlassFish Server 3+' is listed under the 'Servers' node. Invoke the context menu on 'GlassFish Server 3+', and start the server by selecting the Start menu option. See Figure 5-9.

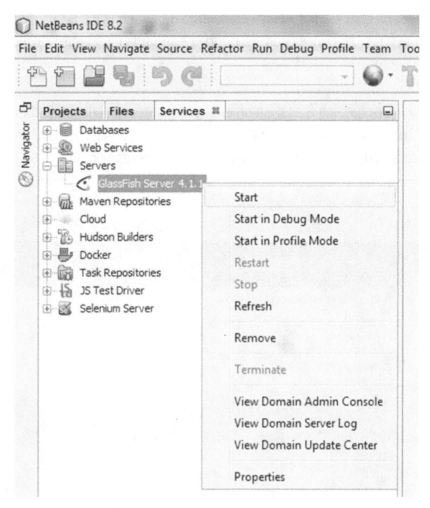

Figure 5-9. *Starting the GlassFish application server*

The GlassFish Server 4.1.1 starting log file is shown in Figure 5-10.

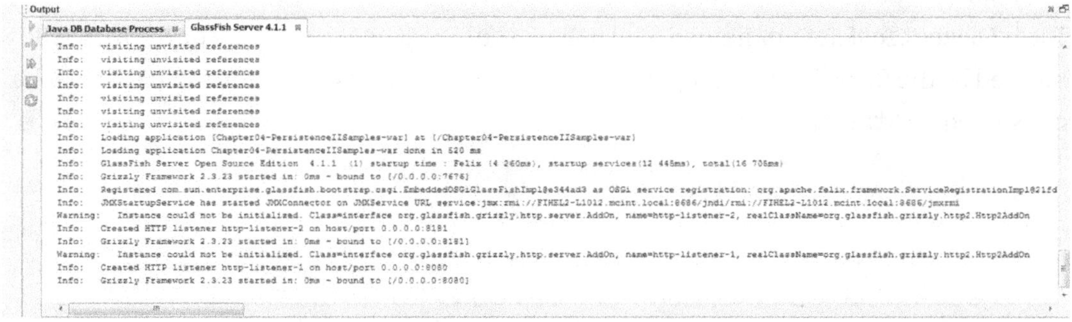

Figure 5-10. *GlassFish application server starting log file*

After the server has started, open your favorite browser and navigate to `http://localhost:4848/`. GlassFish version 4.1.1. server's administrator console will be loaded as shown in Figure 5-11.

Note   If you are running GlassFish on a different machine, substitute that machine name for `localhost` in the command-line arguments. Similarly, if you are running on a different port, substitute the port number you are running for 4848.

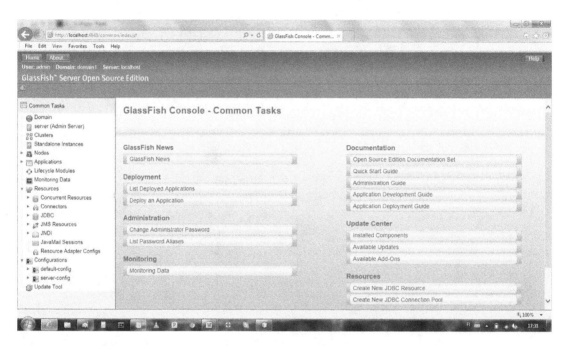

Figure 5-11. *GlassFish 4.1.1. server's administrator console*

Using the administrator console, as shown in Figure 5-12, create a JMS `TopicConnectionFactory` named `StatusMessageTopicConnectionFactory`, which will be used by the `OrderProcessing` session bean to send a message to the topic that will be consumed by `StatusMailer` MDB.

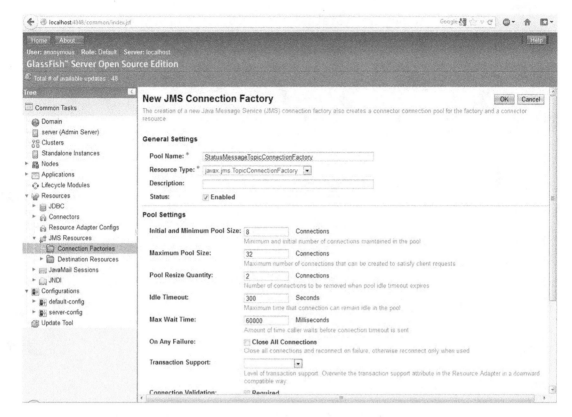

Figure 5-12. *Creating a TopicConnectionFactory*

Then create a JMS topic named StatusMessageTopic as shown in Figure 5-13.

Figure 5-13. *Creating the JMS topic*

Create a JavaMail resource named mail/wineappMail that will be used by the StatusMailer MDB to send out an e-mail as shown in Figure 5-14.

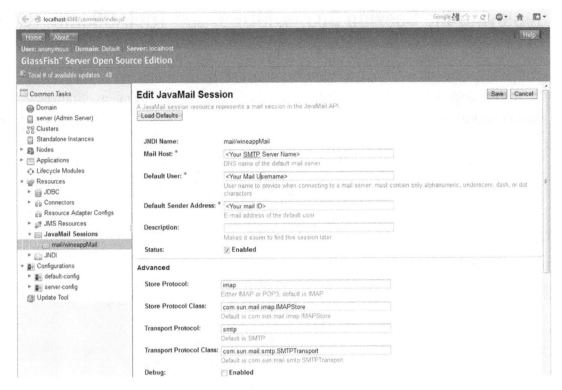

Figure 5-14. *Creating the JavaMail resource*

If the SMTP server requires authentication, then set the 'Additional Properties' as shown in Figure 5-15.

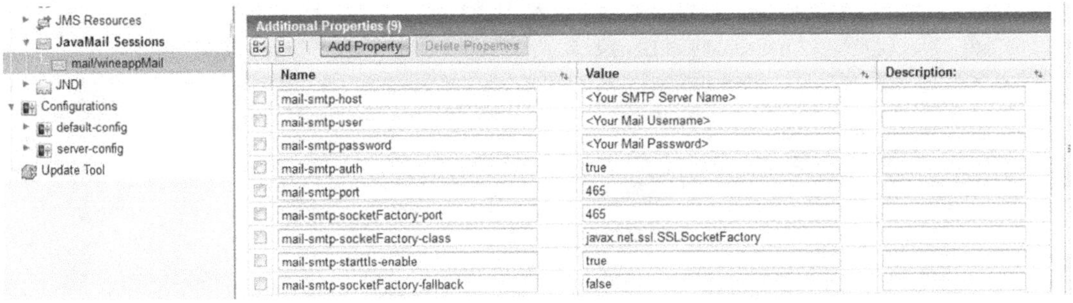

Figure 5-15. *Setting the Additional Properties for Authenticated SMTP Servers*

Deploying the Session Beans, MDBs, and Their Clients

Once you have configured the JMS and JavaMail resources, you can deploy the
application to the GlassFish application server. Invoke the context menu on Chapter05-
MDBSamples node, and deploy the application by selecting the Deploy menu option as
shown in Figure 5-16.

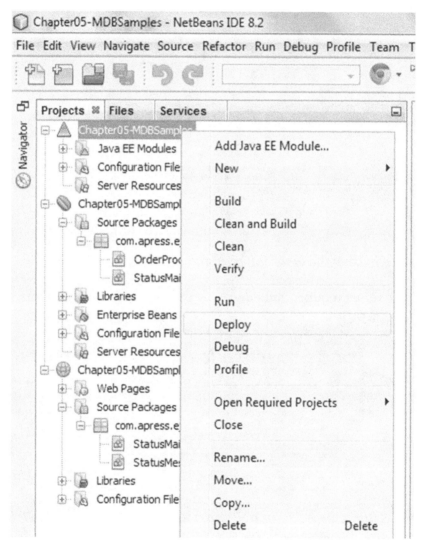

Figure 5-16. *Deploying the MDB, session bean and their clients*

Running the Client Programs

Once the MDB, session bean, and their client servlets are successfully deployed, we need to set the run target that we wish to execute. We have a choice of two run targets: StatusMailerClient or StatusMessageClient. To set the run target, invoke the context menu on Chapter05-MDBSamples node, and select the Properties menu option.

To run the client servlets, invoke the context menu on Chapter05-MDBSamples node, and select the Run menu option as shown in Figure 5-17.

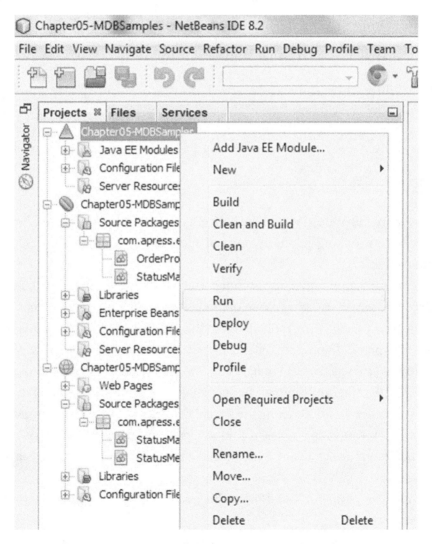

Figure 5-17. *Running the StatusMailerClient application target*

Once the StatusMailerClient runs successfully, NetBeans will open your default browser and execute the selected servlet. Here is the output from StatusMailerClient servlet. You should also be able to see an e-mail in the inbox where the message was sent as shown in Figure 5-18.

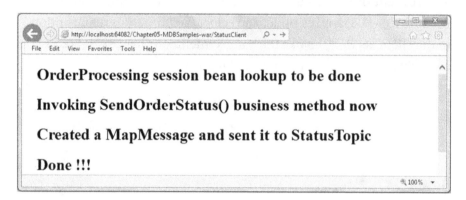

Figure 5-18. *Output of StatusMailerClient servlet*

Summary

In this chapter, we introduced you to the concept of message-oriented middleware and why enterprises are looking at loosely coupled applications that can converse in an asynchronous fashion.

We covered message application architecture with the P2P and pub-sub models, and we discussed why messaging is one of the best ways to implement asynchronous applications. We looked at JMS in detail, including different JMS components such as providers, consumers, clients, and different types of messages. We looked at MDBs and the different artifacts that can make them. We covered the different configuration properties of MDBs and how they can be set using annotations. We explained dependency injection in MDBs using the specific example of injecting a JavaMail resource. We discussed what it takes to compile, package, deploy, and test MDBs, along with information on how you can create different types of resources in the GlassFish application server. Finally, we covered running sample client programs using the application client container in GlassFish and viewing the output and receiving e-mail messages sent by MDBs.

In the next chapter, we will drill down into web services, including how you can publish session beans as web services and how to invoke web services from EJB applications.

EJB, Web Services, and Microservices

This chapter will explain Java EE 8Web Services and Microservices and their differences. We will introduce the core Web Services standards (SOAP, WSDL, UDDI, XML), and discuss the evolution of Web Services and Microservices support in the Java EE platform. We will also drill down into how you can publish EJB stateless session beans as Web services as well as how to invoke the published Web service from a command-line Java client program and a stateless session bean. Finally, we will show a short example about Microservices using the Spring Boot project.

What Are Web Services?

Web services fundamentally constitute a kind of business logic or functionality available in an application or module and are exposed via a service interface to a client application (commonly known as *service consumer*). The consumer of the Web service doesn't have to know any implementation details of the Web service—the client is able to access or invoke the Web service with the information provided in the service interface. This architecture fundamentally provides a loosely coupled model in which the consumer doesn't have to be aware of technology or infrastructure details particular to the implementation of the business logic exposed as a Web service.

© Jonathan Wetherbee, Massimo Nardone, Chirag Rathod, and Raghu Kodali 2018
J. Wetherbee et al., *Beginning EJB in Java EE 8*, https://doi.org/10.1007/978-1-4842-3573-7_6

The Web Services Architecture Working Group of the W3C (World Wide Web Consortium) provides the following definition for a Web service:

A Web service is a software system designed to support interoperable machine-to-machine interaction over a network. It has an interface described in a machine-processable format (specifically WSDL). Other systems interact with the Web service in a manner prescribed by its description using SOAP messages, typically conveyed using HTTP with an XML serialization in conjunction with other Web-related standards.

While the concept of abstracting out details to an interface has been used in several languages and distributed architectures (for example, EJB and CORBA), the key difference in Web services is the usage of standards to describe the abstraction, invocation, and registration of services.

Web services architecture goes by the find-bind-execute model in which you find the required service in a registry (UDDI), get the description of the service, bind it to the service (create the message that will be sent to the service based on the description), and finally execute or invoke the service. Figure 6-1 shows the find-bind-execute model. UDDI, WSDL, and SOAP are the standards that make this find-bind-execute model ubiquitous and different from earlier computing models.

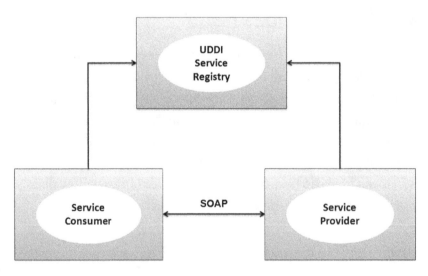

Figure 6-1. *Web services architecture*

UDDI

Universal Description, Discovery, and Integration (UDDI) provides a standards-based approach to locating a Web service and information on invoking that service. It also provides additional metadata about the service. UDDI helps you dynamically bind Web services instead of having to hardwire them to an external interface, and it also helps to provide taxonomy. Businesses or service providers can provide basic contact information (including identification), categorization for the service, information that describes its behavior, and the actual location of the Web service.

UDDI, which is currently in version 3, has evolved over the last few years. Version 1 focused on providing a registry for services, while version 2 focused on aligning the specification with other Web services specifications and flexible taxonomies. The current version focuses on delivering support for secure interaction of private or public implementations of the services. Several companies, including Oracle, SAP, Microsoft, IBM, Cisco, Computer Associates, and Systinet are members of the UDDI technical committee for the Organization for the Advancement of Structured Information Standards (OASIS). Most of the application server vendors (such as Oracle and IBM) either provide a UDDI registry as a standard component that comes with their application server, or an OEM UDDI registry (from Systinet or other registry providers) as part of their middleware platform.

WSDL

Web Services Description Language (WSDL), currently v 2.0, is a technology that is used to describe the interface of a service using XML. WSDL is a standard developed by the W3C to which several vendors and individuals have contributed over the last few years. WSDL describes what a service does, how to invoke its operations, and where to find it.

WSDL details can be split into two categories: service interface definition details and service implementation definition details. The service interface definition is an abstract or reusable service definition that can be instantiated and referenced by multiple service implementation definitions. It contains the following WSDL elements, which comprise the reusable portion of the service description. We will use a credit check Web service as an example to introduce the service interface definition elements listed here:

```
<definitions>
<types>
<message>
<portType>
<binding>
```

The <definitions> Element

The <definitions> element allows you to specify global declarations of namespaces that are visible through the WSDL document. It acts as a container for service descriptions. Listing 6-1 shows an example <definitions> element that defines a target namespace and other namespaces that are referred to by a credit service.

Listing 6-1. The <definitions> Element in CreditService.wsdl

```
<?xml version="1.0" encoding="UTF-8" standalone="yes"?>
<definitions targetNamespace="http://www.apress.com/ejb3/credit" ↵
name="CreditService" xmlns:tns="http://www.apress.com/ejb3/credit" ↵
xmlns:xsd="http://www.w3.org/2001/XMLSchema" ↵
xmlns:soap="http://schemas.xmlsoap.org/wsdl/soap/" ↵
xmlns=http://schemas.xmlsoap.org/wsdl/ />
```

The <types> Element

The <types> element is used to define the data types for the <message> element. XML schema definitions (XSDs) are most commonly used to specify the data types. Listing 6-2 shows an example <types> element that provides the schema location for the credit service.

Listing 6-2. The <types> Element in CreditService.wsdl

```
<types>
  <xsd:schema>
<xsd:import namespace="http://www.apress.com/ejb3/credit"↩
    schemaLocation="CreditServiceBeanService_schema1.xsd"/>
  </xsd:schema>
</types>
```

The <message> Element

The <message> element is used to define the format of data exchanged between a Web service consumer and a Web service provider. Listing 6-3 shows an example of two <message> elements: CreditCheck and CreditCheckResponse.

Listing 6-3. The <message> Element in CreditService.wsdl

```
<message name="CreditCheck">
  <part name="parameters" element="tns:CreditCheck"/>
</message>
<message name="CreditCheckResponse">
  <part name="parameters" element="tns:CreditCheckResponse"/>
</message>
```

The <portType> Element

The <portType> element is used to specify the operations of the Web service. Listing 6-4 shows the <portType> element for the credit service with the CreditCheck operation.

Listing 6-4. The <portType> Element in CreditService.wsdl

```
<portType name="CreditCheckEndpointBean">
  <operation name="CreditCheck">
    <input message="tns:CreditCheck"/>
    <output message="tns:CreditCheckResponse"/>
  </operation>
</portType>
```

The <binding> Element

The <binding> element describes the protocol, data format, and security for a
<portType> element. The standard bindings are HTTP or SOAP; or you can create one of
your own.

The "bindings" part of the WSDL specification is flexible—it allows you to provide
your own bindings environment instead of the default SOAP-over-HTTP model.
This flexibility of the specification has been widely exploited by WSIF (Web Services
Invocation Framework), which is an Apache open source project. WSIF provides a
nice way to expose existing Java, EJB, JMS (Java Message Service), and JCA-based
components as Web services with native bindings, which provide better performance
and that support native transactions. Listing 6-5 shows the <binding> element for the
credit service, using SOAP-over-HTTP.

Listing 6-5.   The <binding> Element in CreditService.wsdl

```
<binding name="CreditCheckEndpointBeanPortBinding" ↵
type="tns:CreditCheckEndpointBean"> ↵
   <soap:binding transport="http://schemas.xmlsoap.org/soap/http" ↵
style="document"/>
   <operation name="CreditCheck">
     <soap:operation soapAction=""/>
     <input>
       <soap:body use="literal"/>
     </input>
     <output>
       <soap:body use="literal"/>
     </output>
   </operation>
  </binding>
```

The service implementation definition part of the WSDL document identifies a Web
service. It contains the following elements:

```
<service>
<port>
```

The <service> Element

The <service> element contains a collection of <port> elements where each port is associated with an endpoint (a network address location or URL). Listing 6-6 shows an example of a <service> element for the credit service.

Listing 6-6. The <service> Element in CreditService.wsdl

```
<service name="CreditService">
  <port name="CreditCheckEndpointBeanPort" ↵
binding="tns:CreditCheckEndpointBeanPortBinding">
    <soap:address location="http://localhost:64082/CreditService/
    CreditCheckEndpointBean"/>
  </port>
</service>
```

Listing 6-7 shows the complete WSDL document for the credit service that we are going to develop later in the chapter.

Listing 6-7. The Complete WSDL Document for CreditService.wsdl

```
<?xml version='1.0' encoding='UTF-8'?>
<definitions xmlns:soap="http://schemas.xmlsoap.org/wsdl/soap/"
xmlns:tns="http://www.apress.com/ejb/credit" xmlns:xsd="http://www.
w3.org/2001/XMLSchema" xmlns="http://schemas.xmlsoap.org/wsdl/"
targetNamespace="http://www.apress.com/ejb/credit" name="CreditService">
  <types>
  <xsd:schema>
    <xsd:import namespace="http://www.apress.com/ejb3/credit" ↵
      schemaLocation="CreditServiceBeanService_schema1.xsd"/>
  </xsd:schema>
  </types>
  <message name="CreditCheck">
    <part name="parameters" element="tns:CreditCheck"/>
  </message>
```

```xml
  <message name="CreditCheckResponse">
    <part name="parameters" element="tns:CreditCheckResponse"/>
  </message>
  <portType name="CreditCheckEndpointBean">
    <operation name="CreditCheck">
      <input message="tns:CreditCheck"/>
      <output message="tns:CreditCheckResponse"/>
    </operation>
  </portType>
  <binding name="CreditCheckEndpointBeanPortBinding" type="tns:CreditCheck
EndpointBean">
    <soap:binding transport="http://schemas.xmlsoap.org/soap/http"
    style="document"/>
    <operation name="CreditCheck">
      <soap:operation soapAction=""/>
      <input>
        <soap:body use="literal"/>
      </input>
      <output>
        <soap:body use="literal"/>
      </output>
    </operation>
  </binding>
  <service name="CreditService">
    <port name="CreditCheckEndpointBeanPort"
    binding="tns:CreditCheckEndpointBeanPortBinding">
      <soap:address location="http://localhost:64082/CreditService/
      CreditCheckEndpointBean"/>
    </port>
  </service>
</definitions>
```

SOAP

Simple Object Access Protocol (SOAP), currently v 1.2, is an XML-based protocol used for exchanging information in a decentralized and distributed environment using XML. SOAP is a standard developed by the W3C. Fundamentally, SOAP is the default transport layer for the Web services.

A SOAP message is an ordinary XML document containing the following elements:

- The required `Envelope` element identifies the XML document as a SOAP message. `Envelope` is the top-level element in the document. The envelope is required, and it basically marks the start and end of the SOAP message (although messages can contain links to objects outside the envelope). The envelope contains the `Header` and the `Body` elements.

- The optional `Header` element contains header information. When the SOAP protocol is used over HTTP, the HTTP headers provide information about the content type, content length, and recipient of the message. A header is included to add features to a SOAP message without prior agreement between the communicating parties.

- The required `Body` element contains call-and-response information. `Body` is a mandatory element that contains the information for the recipient of the message.

- The optional `Fault` element provides information about errors that occur while the message is processed. The `Body` element can contain an optional `Fault` element to report errors.

Figure 6-2 illustrates the elements of a SOAP message.

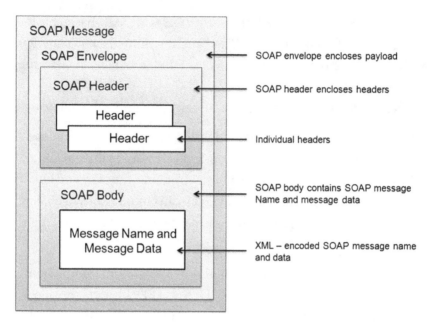

Figure 6-2. *A SOAP Message*

REST

REST (REpresentational State Transfer) is a software architecture pattern that uses HTTP (Hyper Text Transfer Protocol) to discover, query, and manipulate resources in a decentralized and distributed environment. In recent times, REST has gained popularity compared to WSDL-SOAP-based implementation because of its simplicity.

Using REST, the client accesses a resource on the server, using the URI (Universal Resource Identifier) and the standard set of HTTP methods (GET, POST, PUT, and DELETE). In response, the server returns a *representation* of the resource, which is nothing but a document that contains the current or intended state of the resource. After each access invocation and a corresponding new resource representation response, the client is said to *transfer state*, hence the name *Representational State Transfer*. The REST architectural pattern mandates the following six constraints:

1. *Client–server Architecture*: Clients and servers should be separate and can only interact via a uniform interface. This separation means that clients are not concerned with the data-storage internals of the server, and the server is not concerned with the user interface of the clients.

2. *Stateless Interaction*: Clients and server can only interact using a stateless protocol like HTTP. A server cannot store a client context between requests. All requests must contain all of the information required for those requests.

3. *Cacheable*: Server responses must identify themselves as cacheable or non-cacheable. This can be used to prevent clients from using stale data, and it can also help in improving the performance and scalability.

4. *Layered System*: Clients should be able to connect to an intermediary system seamlessly rather than directly to the end server. Intermediary systems provide facilities like load balancing and shared caching that improve scalability of the system.

5. *Named Resources*: Clients must be able to identify individual server resources in each request using URIs.

6. *Uniform Interface*: A uniform interface between clients and servers allow them to evolve independently.

RESTful Web Services

RESTful Web services are services that are built based on the above-mentioned REST principles. RESTful Web services use HTTP and implement operations that map to common HTTP methods as shown in Table 6-1.

Table 6-1. *HTTP Method to CRUD operation mapping*

HTTP Method	CRUD Operation
POST	create
GET	retrieve
PUT	update
DELETE	delete

Listing 6-8 shows a simple RESTful Web service named CreditCheck that takes a credit card number as an input and returns true or false based on its validity. For simplicity's sake, our method always returns true.

Listing 6-8. CreditCheck.java

```java
package com.apress.ejb.chapter06.services;
import javax.ws.rs.Consumes;
import javax.ws.rs.PUT;
import javax.ws.rs.Path;
import javax.ws.rs.PathParam;
import javax.ws.rs.Produces;

@Path("creditCheck")
public class CreditCheck {
    @PUT
    @Consumes("text/plain")
    @Produces("text/plain")
    @Path("isValid")
    public boolean isValid(@PathParam("cardNumber")String ccNumber) {
        return true;
    }
}
```

Users can invoke the isValid method in CreditCheck as follows, and ccNumber will be assigned the value 12345.

```
http://<host>:<port>/<resource>/creditCheck/isValid/12345
```

RESTful vs. SOAP-Based Web Services

Table 6-2 lists the important difference and similarities between RESTful Web service and SOAP-based Web service.

Table 6-2. *RESTful vs. SOAP-Based Web Services*

Criteria	SOAP	RESTful
Specification	JAX-WS	JAX-RS
Simple/Complex	Complex	Simple
Message Size	Large (XML markup)	Small (no extra XML markup)
Standards Based	Yes	No
Transport	HTTP, SMTP, JMS	HTTP
Caching	No	GET operations can be cached
Protocols	JMS, SMTP, HTTP	HTTP
Human Readable Payload	No	Yes
Language and Platform	Independent	Independent

When Do You Use Web Services?

Web services provide a standard way to expose existing or new applications and data to external parties—including customers, suppliers, and partners—or across departments in an enterprise, using industry standards. Web services can also be used to integrate heterogeneous applications and data.

While many enterprises use Web services internally, there are numerous examples of external Web services that are available. Some of the popular ones are package-tracking services (provided by shippers like FedEx, UPS, and USPS). E-commerce websites, like www.amazon.com, www.yahoo.com, www.ebay.com, and www.google.com expose their core functionality using Web services. Developers can subscribe and use the Web services provided by these e-commerce providers to develop applications that add value to, or provide seamless integration with, back-end systems.

Java EE 8 and Web Services

The Java EE platform has evolved over the last few years to become a mature, stable, reliable, and available platform for enterprise applications. While technologies like JDBC (Java Database Connectivity), JMS, and EJB have been in the Java EE platform right from the start, however, only in J2EE 1.4 has the development and deployment

of Web services assumed better shape as they've been standardized to make the
Web services in the Java EE platform more portable across application servers and
interoperable with .NET Web Services. The common goal for the Java EE specifications
was to provide ease of development and deployment for applications and services. Some
of the key specifications in Java EE that are related to Web services are JAX-WS, JAXB,
JAXR, SAAJ, and the JSR 224 annotations. In the following sections, we will show what
these specifications are and how they can be used with EJB. Figure 6-3 shows how EJB
interacts with different Web service-related specifications under the Java EE platform.

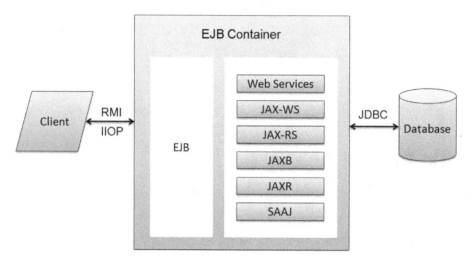

Figure 6-3. *EJB and Web Services*

JAX-WS

JAX-WS (Java API for XML Web Services) defines Java APIs and annotations for accessing
Web services from Java applications and Java EE components like EJBs. JAX-WS
provides mapping facilities between WSDL and Java interfaces, or from Java interfaces
to WSDL. WSDL-mapped interfaces are called *service endpoint interfaces.* JAX-WS
also provides the client-side and server-side APIs and annotations to send and receive
Web service requests via SOAP. The JAX-WS specification in Java EE depends on other
relevant specifications of the Java EE platform224 and JAXB. The current version of
JAX-WS is 2.3 (JSR 224). It also provides support for the latest Web services standards
like SOAP 1.2 and WSDL 2.0. Figure 6-4 shows a simplified diagram of a Web service
invocation.

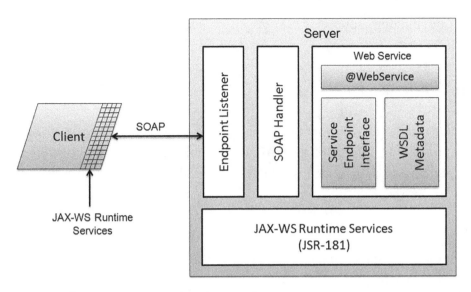

Figure 6-4. *Web service invocation internals*

JAX-RS

JAX-RS (JAX-RS: Java API for RESTful Web Services) defines Java APIs and annotations for creating Web services based on the REST architectural pattern. JAX-RS version 1.1 became an integral part of Java EE 6 through JSR-311. JAX-RS provides annotations like @PATH, @GET, @PUT, @POST, @DELETE, @HEAD, @PRODUCES, @CONSUMES, and so forth that help in mapping a POJO (plain old java objects) as a Web resource. The current version of JAX-RS is 2.1 (JSR 370).

JAXB

Web services consumers and providers use XML messages to send requests and responses. These messages can be something like a purchase order that has an XSD, which allows the parties involved (provider and consumer) to understand the purchase order. Working with XML documents using low-level language APIs can be time consuming and can involve complex code. The *JAXB (Java Architecture for XML Binding)* specification, in context of Java EE, provides standard APIs for representing XML documents as Java artifacts so that developers can work off Java objects that represent the XML documents based on schemas (XSD). The JAXB specification facilitates unmarshalling XML documents into sets of Java objects and marshalling sets of Java objects back into XML documents. The JAXB specification provides full support for XML schemas and binding support for JAX-WS, and it leverages other Java EE specifications, such as JSR 175.

JAXR

UDDI is the standard for Web services registry. The *JAXR (Java API for XML Registries)* specification defines a standard set of APIs that allows Java clients to access the registry. These APIs can also be used against XML registries other than UDDI ones.

SAAJ

Similar to the attachments that you can use in e-mail messages, you can send attachments to the SOAP messages that invoke Web services. *SAAJ (SOAP with Attachments API for Java) Java API for XML Registries* define a standard set of APIs that allow Java SE or EE components to construct SOAP messages with attachments.

JSR 224

JSR 224 (Web Services Metadata for the Java Platform) defines a standard set of annotations that can be used to simplify Web services development. These annotations can be used with Java classes or EJB session beans that can be JAX-WS components. JSR 224 supplements the old JSR-181 annotations.

EJB Stateless Session Beans as Web Services

Web services endpoints that are described using WSDL are stateless in nature. Stateless session beans also share the same statelessness and are well suited for developing Web services. The EJB specification relies on other Web services specifications in the Java EE platform, including JAX-WS, JAXB, and JSR 224, either to consume Web services or publish stateless session beans as Web services.

A *service endpoint interface (SEI)* is one that is mapped to a Web service. JAX-WS provides this mapping layer. In order to develop a new Web service, you can take either the bottom-up or top-down approach, both of which are described below.

In the case of the bottom-up approach, you start with an SEI and an implementation that can be published as a Web service. In this process, Web service artifacts like WSDL documents are generated at deployment time or by the administrative tools or utilities provided by Java EE application servers.

In the top-down case, you start with a WSDL document and generate an SEI using tools that implement JAX-WS. Once you have an SEI, you can add the implementation behind it. In the case of EJB stateless session beans, you need to use the annotations provided in the JAX-WS and JSR 224 specifications to mark the business interfaces and/or bean classes so that the right set of Web services artifacts will be generated at deployment time. Java EE specifications require that the annotations added to components be processed at deployment time to generate the right set of artifacts. EJB stateless session beans with Web services annotations are no different; they are also processed at deployment time by the deployment utilities provided by the application servers. There will be one stateless session bean for each SEI.

Developing a New Web Service

Stateless session beans are implemented using the programming model described in Chapter 2. In case you want to make a stateless session bean as a Web service, you will need the following classes:

- A bean class (implementation)

- A Web service endpoint interface (optional)

- Additional business interfaces if the bean class has local or remote clients

Creating a Bean Class

A *stateless session bean class* is any standard Java class that has a class-level annotation of `@Stateless`. Starting with version 3, the EJB specification doesn't mandate the requirement of SEIs. Providing an SEI along with a bean class is optional. In the use case in which the bean class will be published as a Web service without any service endpoint interface, the bean class will have the additional class-level annotation `@WebService` (JSR 224). The `@WebService` annotation is in the `javax.jws` package, and it marks the bean class as an implementation for a SOAP-based Web service.

The @WebService annotation takes the parameters described in Table 6-3.

Table 6-3. *The @WebService Annotation*

Parameter	Description	Additional Info
name	The name of the Web service that gets mapped to wsdl:portType.	If not specified, the name of the Java class is taken.
targetNamespace	The XML namespace used for the Web service.	If not specified, the name of the Java class is taken.
serviceName	The name of the Web service that gets mapped to wsdl:service.	If not specified, the name of the Java class is taken.
wsdlLocation	The location of the WSDL document, which comes in handy when the bean class is implementing existing Web service.	

To illustrate a stateless session bean that gets published as a Web service, we will create a CreditServiceEndpointBean that will be published as CreditService.

In Listing 6-9, we have a Java class, CreditCheckEndpointBean, which has two class-level annotations: @Stateless and @WebService. The @Stateless annotation provides an additional parameter to mark the bean as CreditCheckEndpointBean. If the same class is exposed to remote or local clients, those clients will access the stateless session bean with that name. The @WebService annotation provides two additional parameters: one to mark the service name as CreditService and the other to specify the target namespace (instead of using the default Java package structure).

Listing 6-9. CreditCheckEndpointBean.java

```java
package com.apress.ejb.chapter06.services;
import javax.ejb.Stateless;
import javax.jws.WebMethod;
import javax.jws.WebService;

@Stateless(name = "CreditCheckEndpointBean")
@WebService(serviceName = "CreditService", targetNamespace = "http://www.apress.com/ejb/credit")
```

```
public class CreditCheckEndpointBean  {
    public CreditCheckEndpointBean() {
    }

}
```

The @WebMethod annotation defined in JSR 224 allows you to customize the method that is exposed as a Web service operation. If no @WebMethod annotations are specified in the bean class that has the @WebService annotation, then all public methods are exposed as Web service operations.

The @WebMethod annotation takes the parameters described in Table 6-4.

Table 6-4. *The @WebMethod Annotation*

Parameter	Description	Additional Info
operationName	The name of the wsdl:operation that matches this method.	By default, this is the name of the Java method.
action	The action for this operation. In the case of SOAP bindings, it will be the value of the SOAP action header.	By default, this is the name of the Java method.

In Listing 6-10, we have added the following method into the CreditCheckEndpointBean class, which will be exposed as a Web service operation. The operation name is customized as CreditCheck using @WebMethod parameters. The method takes a java.lang.String parameter (which is the credit card number) and returns a java.lang.boolean value of true or false, depending on whether the credit card is valid. For simplicity's sake, we will always return true.

Listing 6-10. The validateCC Method in CreditCheckEndpointBean.java

```
@WebMethod(operationName="CreditCheck")
public boolean validateCC(String cc){
return true;
}
```

Web Service Endpoint Interface

JAX-WS doesn't mandate the requirement of an SEI to implement a Web service endpoint. You can use the annotations provided in JSR 224 to mark the bean class as a Web service and one or more business methods as Web service operations. In the use case in which an SEI is defined for a stateless session bean, the following should be observed:

- The SEI must have a `javax.jws.WebService` annotation.

- One or more methods can have a `javax.jws.WebMethod` annotation.

- All method parameters and return types should be compatible with the JAXB XML schema mapping definition.

- Arguments and return types of methods must be valid JAX-RPC value types, which include Java primitives (`int`, `long`, and so on), Java classes (`String`, `Date`, and so forth), Java Beans, and arrays.

- `Throw` clauses must include a `java.rmi.RemoteException` in addition to any other application exceptions.

Note   Support for JAX-RPC has been made optional since Java EE 7. Since Java EE 7, the specification encourages new applications to use the facilities provided by JAX-WS that simplify Web service development. The current version of JAX-RPC is 1.1.

In our examples, we are adding annotations to the bean class itself, as shown in Listings 6-9 and 6-10.

Listing 6-11 illustrates a service endpoint interface for the use case in which an SEI is provided, and Listing 6-12 shows the `CreditCheckEndpointBean` class implementing the SEI.

Listing 6-11. A Service Endpoint Interface for the Use Case

```
@WebService(serviceName="CreditService",targetNamespace="http://www.apress.
com/ejb/credit")
public interface CreditCheckEndpoint {
```

```
@WebMethod(operationName="CreditCheck")
   public boolean validateCC(String cc);
}
```

Listing 6-12. The CreditCheckEndpointBean Class Implementing the SEI

```
@Stateless
public class CreditCheckEndpointBean implements CreditCheckEndpoint {
    public CreditCheckEndpointBean() {
    }
    //implementation goes here
}
```

Packaging, Deploying, and Testing Web Services

Stateless session beans that have Web service annotations need to be packaged into *EJB Java Archive (JAR)* files before they are deployed into EJB containers. For some EJB containers or application servers, they first need to be assembled into EAR [Enterprise Archive] files). Most EJB containers or application servers provide deployment utilities or Ant tasks to facilitate deployment of EJBs to their containers. Java-integrated development environments (IDEs) like JDeveloper, NetBeans, and Eclipse also provide deployment features that allow developers to package, assemble, and deploy EJBs to application servers. Packaging, assembly, and deployment aspects are covered in detail in Chapter 11.

In this chapter, we have developed one stateless session bean (CreditCheckEndpointBean) with Web service annotations. We will perform the following steps to compile, deploy, and test the stateless session bean to be published as a Web service.

Prerequisites

Before performing any of the steps detailed in the next sections, complete the "Getting Started" section of Chapter 1, which walks you through the installation and environment setup required for the samples in this chapter.

Compiling the Session Bean

Copy the Chapter06-WebServiceSamples directory and its contents into a directory of your choice. Run the NetBeans IDE, and open the Chapter06-WebServiceSamples project using the File ➤ Open Project menu. Make sure that the 'Open Required Projects' check box is checked, as shown in Figure 6-5.

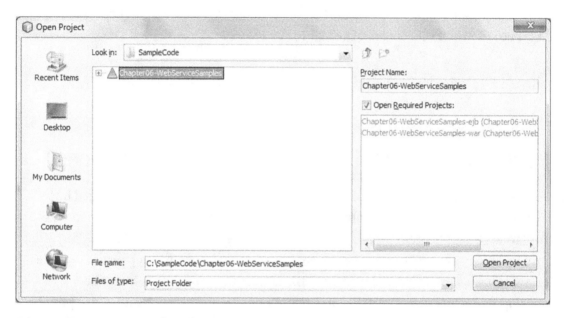

Figure 6-5. *Opening the Chapter06-WebServiceSamples project*

Expand the Chapter06-WebServiceSamples-ejb node as shown in Figures 6-6 and 6-7, and observe that the session bean-based Web service that we created appears in the com.apress.ejb.chapter06.services package. Similarly, the client servlet also appears under the Chapter06-WebServiceSamples-war node.

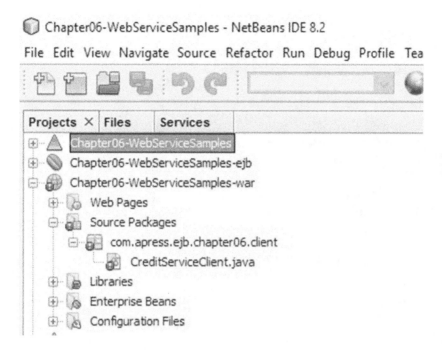

Figure 6-6. *Verifying that the Session Bean and its clients are available in the project*

Invoke the context menu on Chapter06-WebServiceSamples node, and build the application by selecting the Clean and Build menu option. The session bean-based Web service will compile without any errors, but the client in Chapter06-WebServiceSamples-war node will show compilation errors. We will ignore these errors in the client for now.

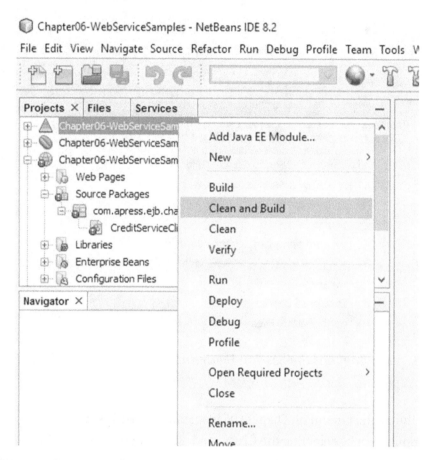

Figure 6-7. *Building the application*

Deploying the Session Bean-Based Web Service

Once we have compiled the session bean, we can deploy it to the GlassFish application server. Invoke the context menu on Chapter06-WebServiceSamples-ejb node, and deploy the application by selecting the Deploy menu option, as shown in Figure 6-8.

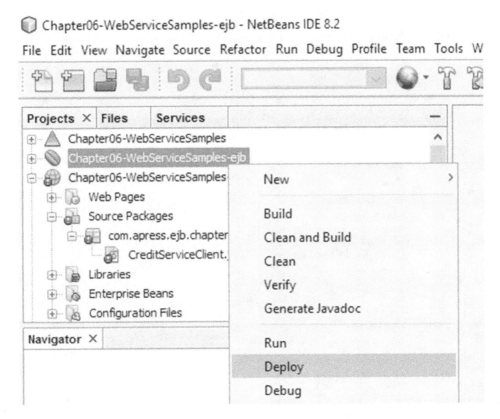

Figure 6-8. *Deploying CreditService*

Testing the Credit Service

After successful deployment, we can use the test harness to see if CreditService can be invoked properly or not. To invoke the test harness, expand the Web Services node under Chapter06-WebServiceSamples-ejb to expose the CreditCheckEndpointBean node, and select the Test Web Service menu option, as shown in Figure 6-9.

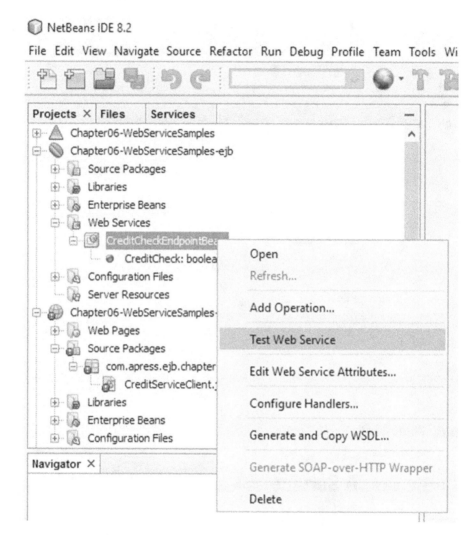

Figure 6-9. *Testing CreditService*

In the generated test harness page (shown in Figure 6-10), enter **12345** as the credit card number, and click the creditCheck button. You can also click on the WSDL File link to check its contents. Bookmark the WSDL File URL, as it will be used for creating a Web service client in the later sections.

http://localhost:8080/CreditService/CreditCheckEndpointBean?Tester

CreditService Web Service Tester

This form will allow you to test your web service implementation (WSDL File)

To invoke an operation, fill the method parameter(s) input boxes and click on the button labeled with the method name.

Methods :

public abstract boolean com.apress.ejb.credit.CreditCheckEndpointBean.creditCheck(java.lang.String)

| creditCheck | (| 12345 | × |) |

Figure 6-10.   *The Web service test harness*

In the generated page, you can test the results with a SOAP request and response, as shown in Figure 6-11.

Figure 6-11.   *SOAP request and response messages*

So far, we have seen how to test the deployed Web services using the test harness. In the next section, we will discuss Web Services clients and how you can develop and run programs that can invoke Web services. In our case, we will be testing against the deployed credit service.

Web Service Client View

A stateless session bean that is published as a Web service can be accessed using the client view described by the WSDL document that gets generated during deployment (as shown in Listing 6-7). Since the stateless session bean is published as a Web service using standards such as WSDL, any type of client application that can send and receive SOAP messages (irrespective of technology or language) can invoke it. The client application can be written using .NET or Java EE, or scripting languages such as PHP, Python, or Ruby. From the client point of view, what it sees as a contract is a WSDL document. In order to access the Web service, programmatic interfaces should be generated from the WSDL document.

Web services are location independent, and they can be accessed remotely. If the client application invoking a Web service is a Java client or other Java EE component, such as an EJB, it uses JAX-WS client APIs or annotations to invoke the Web service via SOAP and HTTP.

Developing a Java Client That Accesses the Web Service

In order to access a Web service via a WSDL service contract, the client program needs programmatic interfaces (commonly known as *stubs* or *proxies*) generated from the WSDL document. Once the stubs have been generated from the WSDL document, we can use the JAX-WS annotations to get a reference to the Web service and invoke it.

Generating Web Service Proxy Classes

We will start by generating stubs for the CreditService WSDL document using the Web Service Client wizard provided by the NetBeans IDE. Invoke the Web Service Client wizard from the context menu of Chapter06-WebServiceSamples-ejb node, as shown in Figure 6-12.

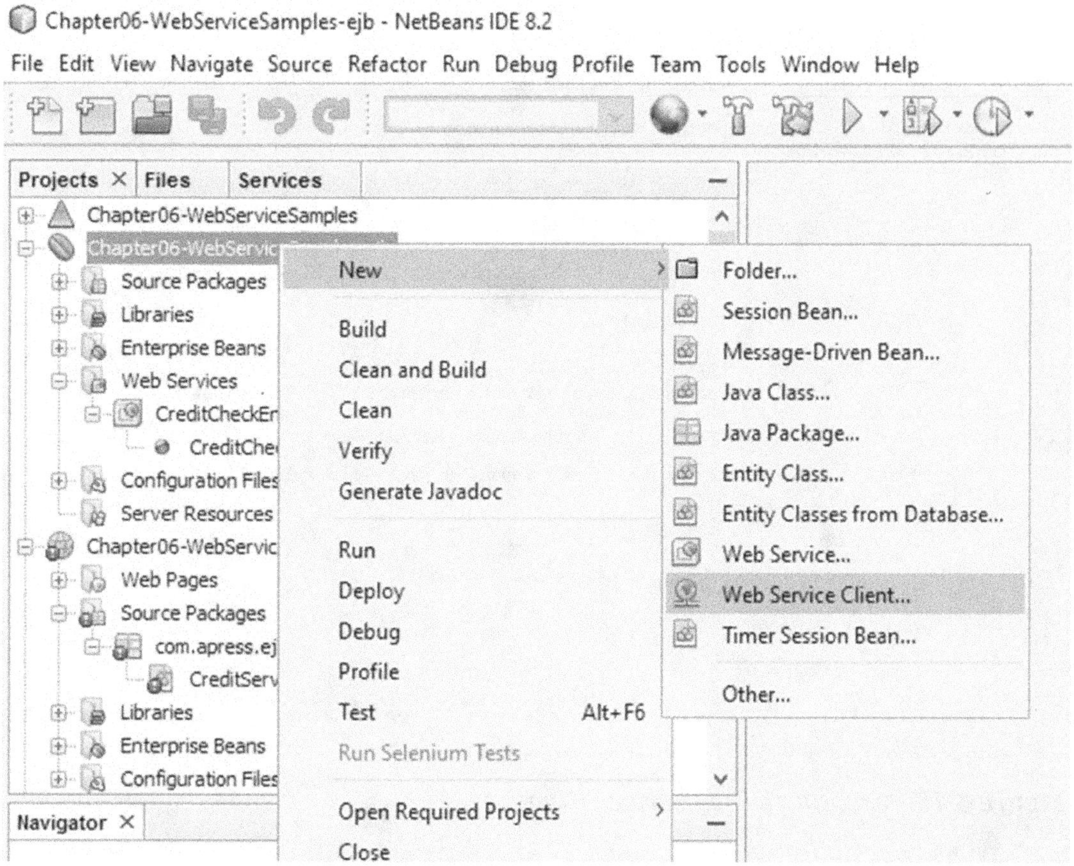

Figure 6-12. Invoking the Web Service Client wizard

In the Web Service Client wizard, select the WSDL URL radio button, and enter the WSDL File URL that you had bookmarked in the earlier section (see Figure 6-10). We also need to specify the package where the client Java artifacts will be generated. We will generate these artifacts in the com.apress.ejb.chapter06.services.client package. Enter these details, as shown in Figure 6-13, and finish the wizard.

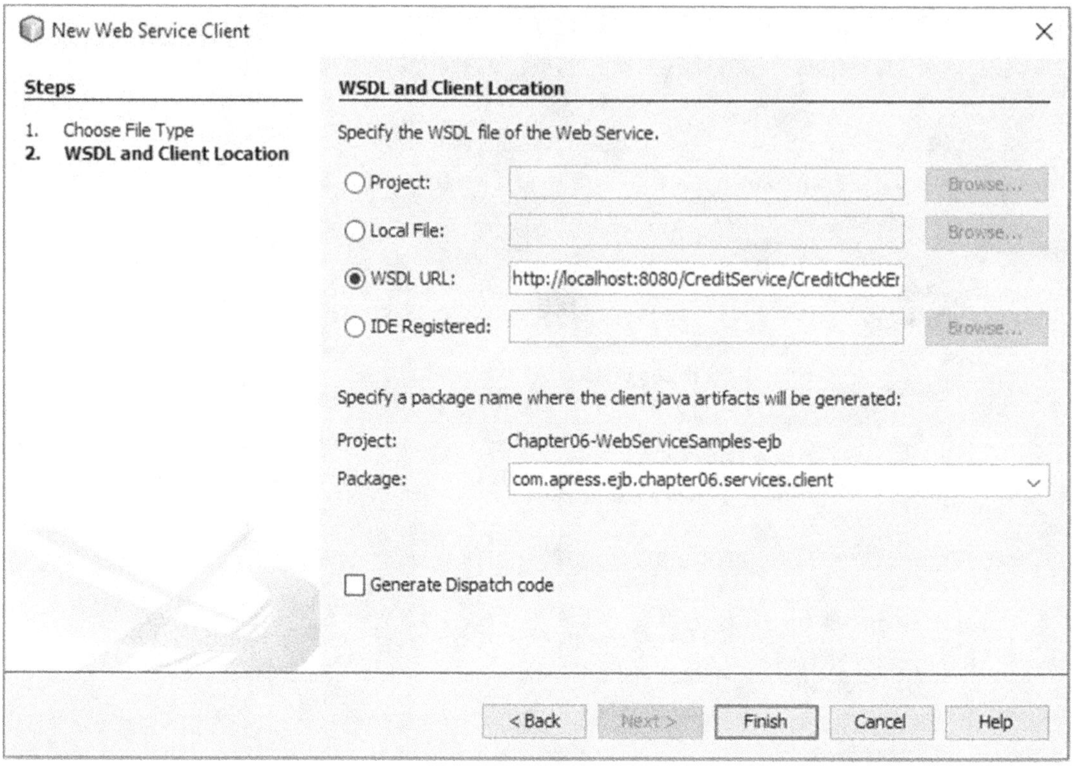

Figure 6-13. *Creating a Web Service Client*

Once the stubs are generated and compiled, we can see artifacts under Generated
Sources (jax-ws) node, as shown in Figure 6-14.

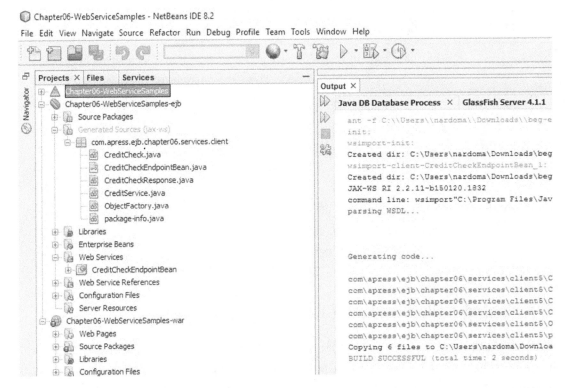

Figure 6-14. *Verifying the generated stub sources*

Note   GlassFish also provides the command-line utility wsimport.bat, which
can generate Web service stubs given a valid WSDL document. In case you are
deploying the Web service to other Java EE compatible servers, these servers
might also provide some tools or utilities to generate the stubs for the Web service.

Once the stubs are generated and compiled, the next step is to create a client that will
consume CreditService.

The JAX-WS specification provides the @WebServiceRef annotations that can be used
to declare a reference to a Web service, which in our case is CreditService.

The @WebServiceRef annotation can take the parameters described in Table 6-5.

Table 6-5. *The @WebServiceRef Annotation*

Parameter	Description	Additional Info
name	The name that identifies the Web service reference	The name that is local to the application component using the resource
wsdlLocation	The URL pointing to the location of the WSDL document	
type	The resource type	
value	The service type	
mappedName	The physical name of the resource used to map the resource to a vendor-specific container	

Developing a Web Service Client Program

The @WebServiceRef annotation either provides a reference to the SEI generated by the container, or a reference to the SEI provided by the application developer. Listing 6-13 shows a servlet class that is going to be a Web service client. In this servlet class, CreditServiceClient, we are using dependency injection to inject the credit service that we have deployed earlier as a Web service. The @WebServiceRef annotation is used to inject the CreditService that has been generated as the proxy class. Once we have injected the available resource, we use that proxy class to get the Web service port using the getCreditCheckEndpointBeanPort() method. After successfully getting the port, we can invoke the operations that are available on the port. In our case, we have defined only one operation, creditCheck. You can see that this is being invoked with a credit card number of 12345678.

Listing 6-13. CreditServiceClient.java

```
package com.apress.ejb.chapter06.client;
import com.apress.ejb.chapter06.services.client.CreditCheckEndpointBean;
import com.apress.ejb.chapter06.services.client.CreditService;
import java.io.IOException;
```

```java
import java.io.PrintWriter;
import javax.servlet.ServletException;
import javax.servlet.annotation.WebServlet;
import javax.servlet.http.HttpServlet;
import javax.servlet.http.HttpServletRequest;
import javax.servlet.http.HttpServletResponse;
import javax.xml.ws.WebServiceRef;

@WebServlet(name = "CreditServiceClient", urlPatterns = {"/CreditServiceClient"})
public class CreditServiceClient extends HttpServlet {
    @WebServiceRef(wsdlLocation = "http://localhost:64082/CreditService/
    CreditCheckEndpointBean?WSDL")
    CreditService service;
    protected void processRequest(HttpServletRequest request,
    HttpServletResponse response)
            throws ServletException, IOException {
        response.setContentType("text/html;charset=UTF-8");
        PrintWriter out = response.getWriter();
        try {
            out.println("<html>");
            out.println("<head>");
            out.println("<title>Servlet CreditServiceClient</title>");
            out.println("</head>");
            out.println("<body>");
            CreditCheckEndpointBean creditService = service.
            getCreditCheckEndpointBeanPort();
            out.println("<h1>Credit Check returned: " + creditService.
            creditCheck("12345678") + "</h1>");
            out.println("</body>");
            out.println("</html>");
        } finally {
            out.close();
        }
    }
```

```java
    @Override
    protected void doGet(HttpServletRequest request, HttpServletResponse
    response)
            throws ServletException, IOException {
        processRequest(request, response);
    }

    @Override
    protected void doPost(HttpServletRequest request, HttpServletResponse
    response)
            throws ServletException, IOException {
        processRequest(request, response);
    }

    @Override
    public String getServletInfo() {
        return "Short description";
    }
}
```

Compiling the Client Class

Invoke the context menu on the Chapter06-WebServiceSamples-war node, and build the client by selecting the Clean and Build menu option, as shown in Figure 6-15.

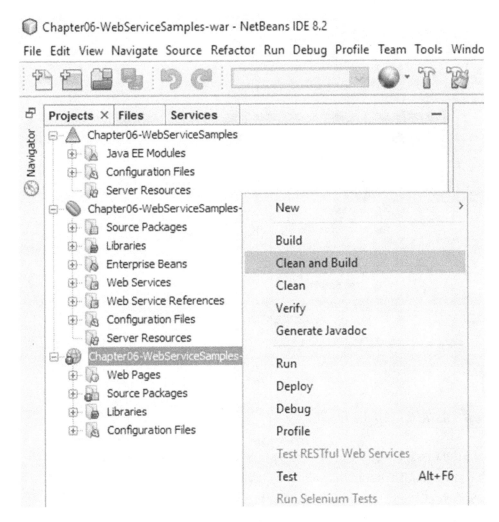

Figure 6-15. *Compiling the Web service client*

Running the Web Service Client

Once we have compiled the client, we need to run it.

To run the client servlet, invoke the context menu on the
Chapter06-WebServiceSamples node, and select the Run menu option, as shown in
Figure 6-16.

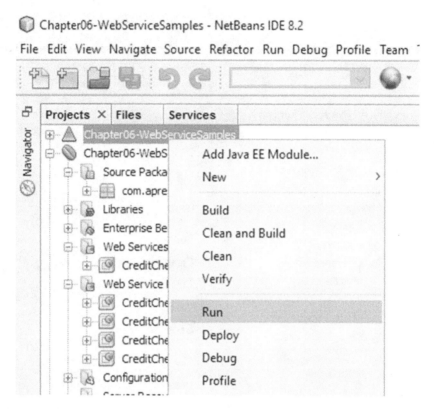

Figure 6-16. *Running the client*

Once the CreditServiceClient runs successfully, NetBeans will open your default browser and execute the selected servlet. Here is the output from the CreditServiceClient servlet as shown in Figure 6-17.

Credit Check returned: true

Figure 6-17. *Checking the servlet output*

Session Beans as Web Service Clients

A session bean can also be a client to a Web service. In the sample application that we will build in Chapter 7, the OrderProcessing session bean, which coordinates the workflow, can invoke the credit service to check the validity of the credit card before starting to process the order. To act as a client to a Web service, the OrderProcessing session bean would make use of the @WebServiceRef annotation, similar to what we have shown in the previous client sample.

Listing 6-14 shows the stateless session bean OrderProcessFacadeBean, which implements both local and remote business interfaces. The @WebServiceRef annotation is used to inject a reference to the CreditService WSDL document. The PerformCheckCredit() method in the OrderProcessFacadeBean session bean uses the injected reference to get the port in the CreditService and invokes the creditCheck operation. As you can see, the process of injecting the Web service, getting the port, and calling the operations from a session bean is similar to what we have done with the client that acted as a Web service client.

Listing 6-14. OrderProcessFacadeBean.java

```java
@Stateless(name="OrderProcessFacade")
public class OrderProcessFacadeBean implements OrderProcessFacade,
                                               OrderProcessFacadeLocal {
    @WebServiceRef(type=CreditService.class)
    CreditService service;
    public OrderProcessFacadeBean() {
    }

    private boolean PerformCreditCheck(Individual customer){
            String ccnum  = customer.getCcNum().toString();
            CreditCheckEndpointBean creditService =
                service.getCreditCheckEndpointBeanPort();
            return creditService.creditCheck(ccnum);
        }
}
```

What Are Microservices?

Microservices are a variant of the service-oriented architecture (SOA) architectural style.

Microservices define a new architectural structure model so that a simple application is developed as a set of multiple single and lightweight services.

Compared to previous architectural approaches, Microservices defined clearly a new trend in the software development industry.

A major benefit of Microservice is that each of them is independently deployable and scalable as well as that it can be written in different programming languages.

Microservices are commonly directly invoked by HTTP REST API calls. Standards like RAML (Restful API Modelling Language) allow for the formal definition of REST APIs.

The development of Microservices is a combination of direct calls through HTTP and indirect calls through a message broker.

We will see the main differences between monolithic and Microservices as well as provide an example of Microservice development.

Here are some of the most important advantages and disadvantages of Microservices:

Advantages:

- Better software practices
- Fault tolerance
- Evolutionary design
- Easy to deploy
- Reduce Coupling
- Right Tool for the Job
- Continuous Delivery
- Smaller codebases are easier to reason about
- Easy to replace old services
- Efficient Scaling
- Easier to develop, understand, and maintain
- Starts faster than a monolith
- Local changes can be easily deployed

- Improves fault isolation

- Not tech driven but business focused

Disadvantages:

- Tooling overhead

- Debugging

- Distributed transactions

- Latency

- Dependency

- Additional complexity of distributed systems

- Significant operational complexity, needs high level of automation.

- Rollout plan to coordinate deployments

Microservices Technology Stack might include:

- Java

- Spring

- Hibernate

- NodeJS

- PostgreSQL

- Redis

- Bootstrap

- AngularJS

- Amazon Web Services

- Docker

- RabbitMQ

- Hystrix

Figure 6-18 shows the Microservices concept.

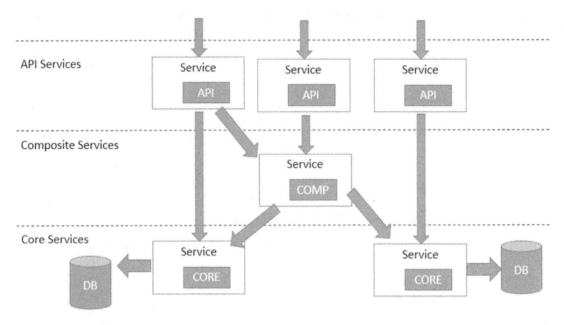

Figure 6-18. *Microservices concept*

Figure 6-19 shows the main differences between Monolith and Microservices.

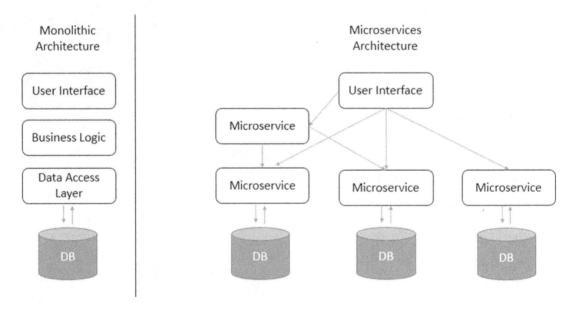

Figure 6-19. *Monolith vs Microservices*

In general, traditional software development processes result in relatively large teams working on a single, monolithic deployment artifact while Microservices are a fundamental shift in how IT approaches software development.

Figure 6-20 shows the Microservices general architecture.

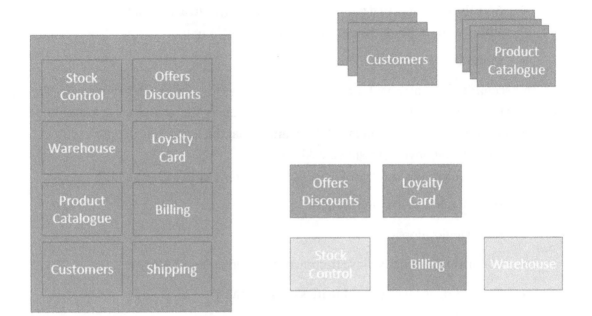

Figure 6-20. *Microservice Architecture*

Java EE 8 and Microservices

The Java EE platform can be used, of course, to develop Microservices.

In general, the Java EE set of specifications allows the Java developer to create easily monolithic applications since they don't need to worry about handling technical concerns like scaling, security, network handling, transaction management, etc. When developing monolithic applications, Java EE developers only have to focus on business concerns instead.

But the problem when developing a monolithic application is that the application will be structured as an EAR file with multiple modules including the following:

- An EJB-module that handles integration aspects like SOAP web services, Message handling, etc.

- An EJB-module with a common persistence layer to access data stores with traditional means like JPA, JDBC, JCA, etc.

- Multiple WAR modules

This scenario very easily will turn to be very complex to develop while with tools like Maven or OSGi, modularizing a Java EE application such as Microservices, has simplified the development of monoliths on Java EE, meaning that the Java EE developer's entire application can be deployed in a single WAR file.

Here are the major advantages of developing Microservices with Java EE:

- Java EE is incredibly lightweight

- Rapid to develop

- Majority of alternative Java frameworks based on Java EE APIs

- Concentrates on building business functionality

- Produces small skinny wars

- Versioned runtime – aids operations

Microservices development platforms in Java include:

- Java EE

- Microprofile

- OSGI

- Vertx

- Akka

- Dropwizard

- etc.

Java EE Microservice building tools include:

- Maven

- Gradle

Microservice creates the following artifacts types:

- jar, war, ear, rar, etc.

- Java EE server RT configuration

Next we will show an example of Java EE 8 Microservices.

Microservices Example Using Spring Boot and NetBeans

We will now show how to develop a Java EE 8 microservice application using Spring Boot and NetBeans IDE v8.2.

Spring Boot is an innovative project that can help the Java developer to create simple stand-alone, production-grade Spring based Applications, etc. Spring Boot can be found at `https://projects.spring.io/spring-boot/`

Prerequisites

Prerequisites for this example are the following:

- NetBeans IDE 8.2

- JDK 8 recommended

- Spring Boot plug-in: NB-SpringBoot created by Alex Falappa at `https://github.com/AlexFalappa/nb-springboot`

The first thing is that we must download and import the NB-SpringBoot plug-in into NetBeans IDE 8.2.

Once imported, the Figure 6-21 shows the NB-SpringBoot plug-in installed into NetBeans.

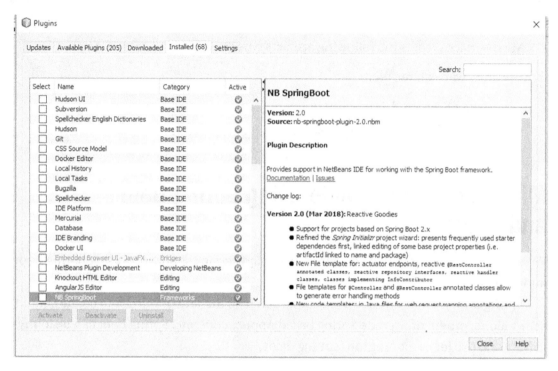

Figure 6-21. *NB-SpringBoot installed plug-in*

Now we can create our Microservice using Spring Boot.

Let's create a new project using the Spring Initializer directly from NetBeans as shown in Figure 6-22.

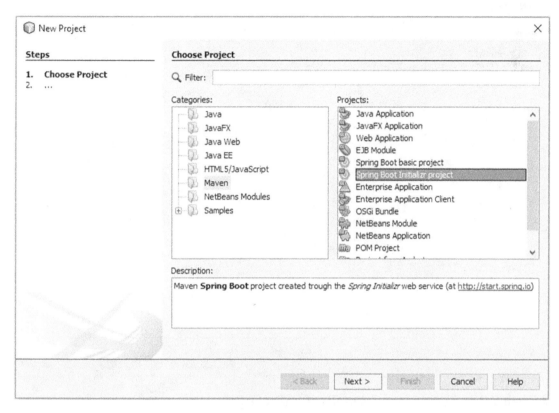

Figure 6-22. *New Maven SpringBoot project*

Add some project info: as shown in Figures 6-23, 6-24, and 6-25.

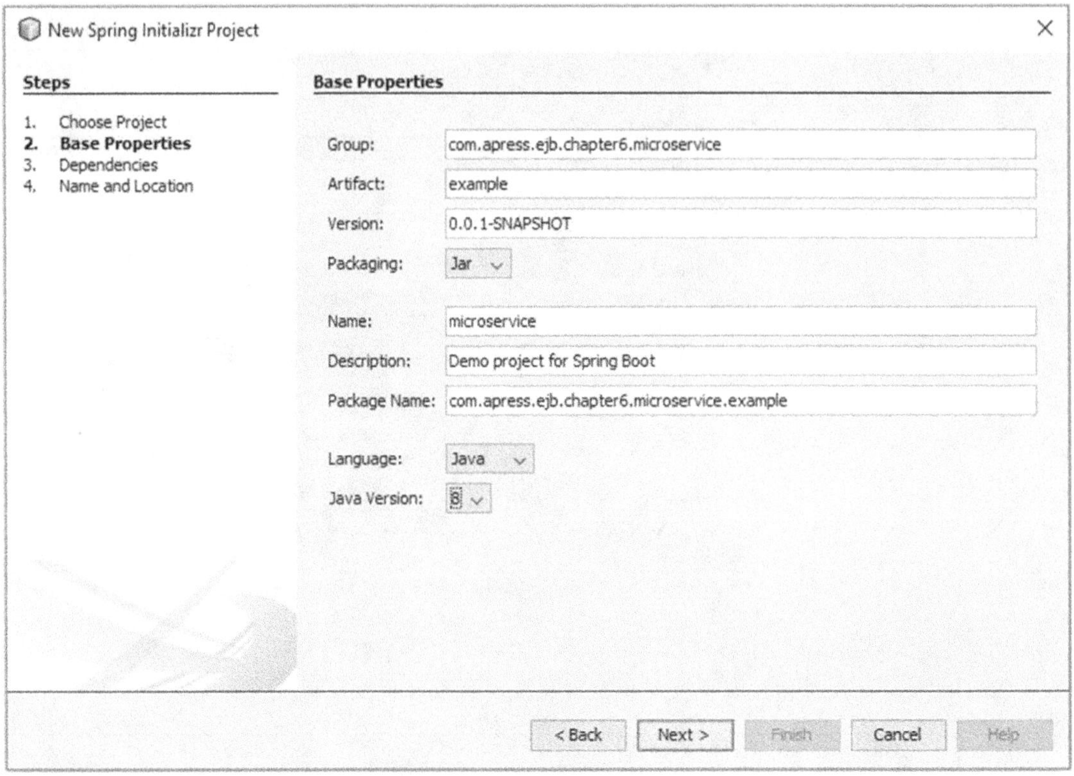

Figure 6-23. *New Maven SpringBoot project Info*

Add Spring Boot version and the needed dependencies like Web:

Figure 6-24. *New Maven SpringBoot project dependences*

Next, add the project name as "nb-springboot":

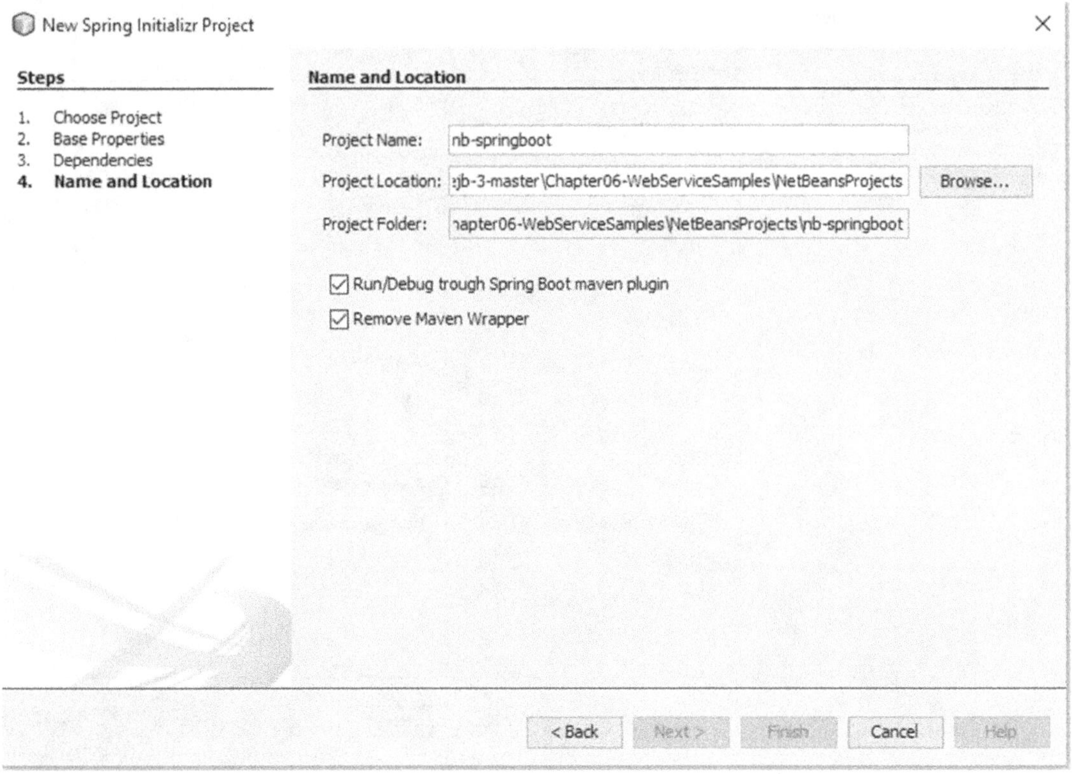

Figure 6-25. *New Maven SpringBoot project name*

Press Finish to create the project as show in Figure 6-26.

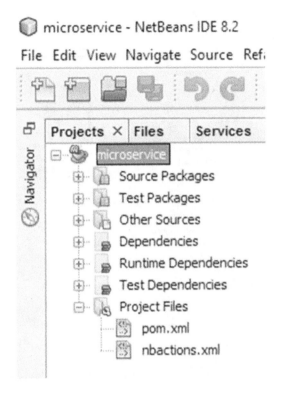

Figure 6-26. *New Maven SpringBoot project Microservice*

Now we need to create a new RestController Class file as shown in Figure 6-27.

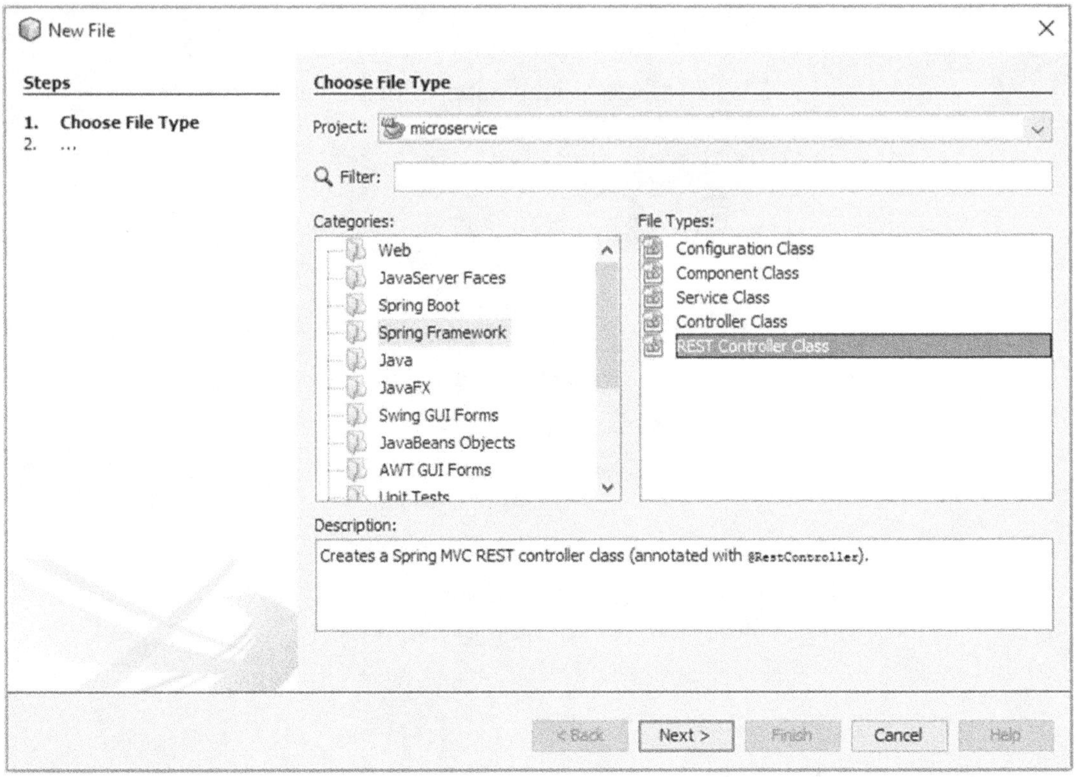

Figure 6-27. *New RestController file*

Add some info to the file and then press finish to create the file as shown in Figure 6-28.

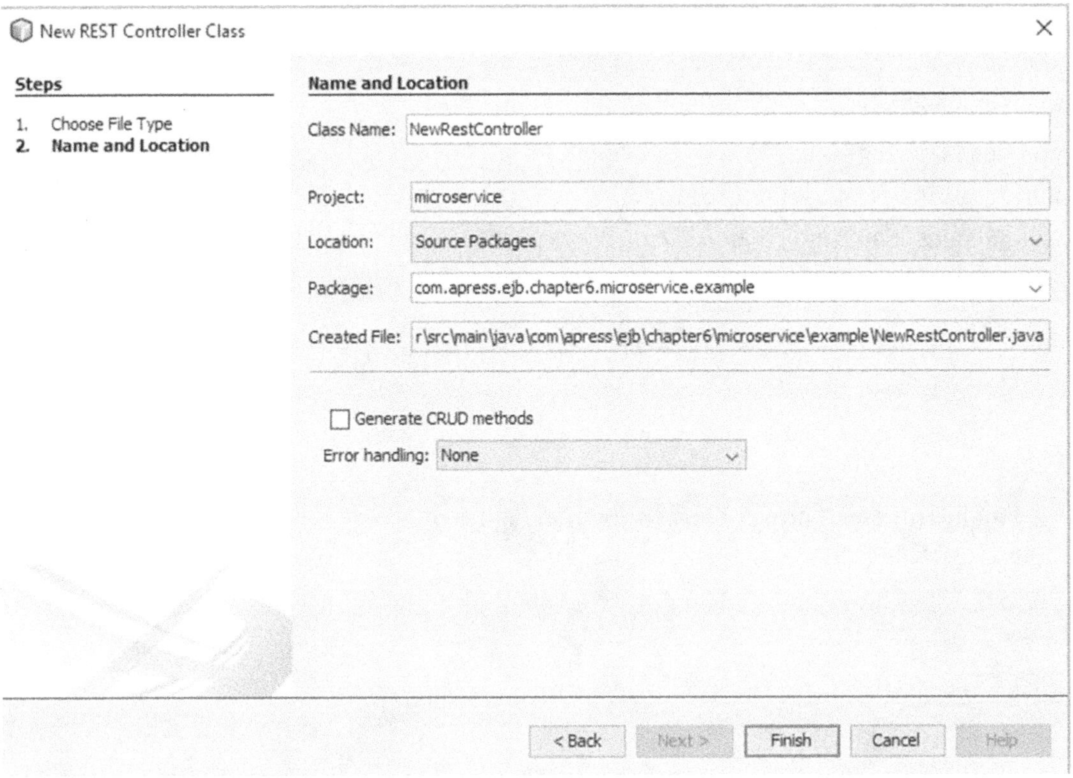

Figure 6-28. *Complete RestController file info*

Add some code to test our new Microservice NewRestController.java. See Listing 6-15.

Listing 6-15. NewRestController.java

```
/*
 * To change this license header, choose License Headers in Project Properties.
 * To change this template file, choose Tools | Templates
 * and open the template in the editor.
 */
package com.apress.ejb.chapter6.microservice.example;

import org.springframework.web.bind.annotation.RestController;
import org.springframework.web.bind.annotation.RequestMapping;
import static org.springframework.web.bind.annotation.RequestMethod.GET;
```

```
/**
 *
 * @author Massimo Nardone
 */
@RestController
@RequestMapping("/url")
public class NewRestController {
    @RequestMapping(path = "/microservice", method = GET)

    public String sayMicroService(){
        return "My first Java EE 8 microservice!";
    }

}
```

Finally run the Microservice as shown in Figure 6-29.

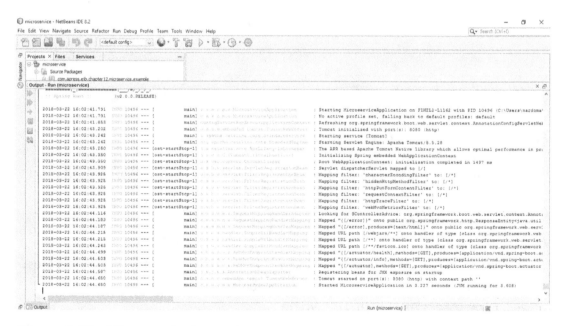

Figure 6-29. *Microservice is running*

Now our Java EE 8 Microservice is running and can be tested by typing
http://localhost:8080/microservice as seen in the result in Figure 6-30.

My first Java EE 8 microservice!

Figure 6-30. *Testing the new Microservice*

Summary

In this chapter, we introduced you to Web Services and Microservices as part of Java EE 8. We explained the Web Service architecture that goes by the find-bind-execute model—and how standards like UDDI, WSDL, and SOAP have made Web services ubiquitous as compared to earlier distributed computing models in terms of standardization and interoperability. We also briefly discussed the REST architectural pattern and RESTful Web services, which have simplified creation and use of Web services.

We looked into the details of the UDDI, SOAP, and WSDL standards, and we demonstrated how WSDL documents and SOAP messages are constructed with a simple credit service example.

We discussed some use cases for which Web services can be used, and we discussed how they fit into intranet and Internet models, including some examples of existing e-commerce sites that provide Web services.

We then dived into the Java EE platform and looked at different standards (JAX-WS, JAX-RS, JAXB, JAXR, SAAJ, and JSR 224) that are enabling developers to create Web services that are portable and interoperable within the .NET platform.

Then we looked at how to publish EJB stateless session beans as Web services using simple Web Services Metadata annotations. We developed a credit service that can be invoked from Web service clients.

Next we looked at compiling, deploying, and testing Web services using the GlassFish application server and servlet clients, and we also looked at how this programming model is similar to invoking Web services with EJBs.

Finally, we introduced the Java EE Microservices as part of the new Java Platform and how to build a simple Microservice example using Boot Spring project.

So far, we have discussed the individual components of the EJB specifications: session beans, JPA entities, MDBs, and Web services. In the next chapter, we will discuss how you can integrate all of these components to build an enterprise application.

CHAPTER 7

Integrating Session Beans, Entities, Message-Driven Beans, and Web Services

Introduction

Previous chapters in this book covered the individual components of EJB and related technologies. These included session beans, message-driven beans (MDBs), stateless session beans as Web services, and JPA entities. In this chapter, we will show you how to integrate these components into a complete Java EE 8 application using a fictitious wine store application as an example.

Application Overview

The sample application that we are going to develop in this chapter is the Wines Online application, which provides customers (either individuals or distributors) with a variety of search criteria with which they can browse, select wines, add them to a shopping cart, and process their order. Customers need to register with the Wines Online application before they can submit orders. Once an order is submitted, the customer's credit card is validated, and this triggers an order processing message and an e-mail notification to the customer on the status of the order.

Screens used by the customer to search, navigate, and submit orders are part of a simple JavaServer Faces (JSF) Web application that interacts with back-end services and components developed using EJBs. In this chapter, our focus will be on developing the back-end part of the application, which can be tested with both a servlet and a simple Java client. In Chapter 12, we will develop a JSF client for these back-end services.

319

© Jonathan Wetherbee, Massimo Nardone, Chirag Rathod, and Raghu Kodali 2018
J. Wetherbee et al., *Beginning EJB in Java EE 8*, https://doi.org/10.1007/978-1-4842-3573-7_7

As shown in Figure 7-1, the Wines Online application consists of several back-end components that are used by the client application, and these back-end components in turn make use of different types of services to perform CRUD (create, retrieve, update, delete) operations, send e-mail notifications to the customer about order status, process the incoming orders, and verify the credit card status of the customer. We will discuss the behavior and functionality of these components in the next section.

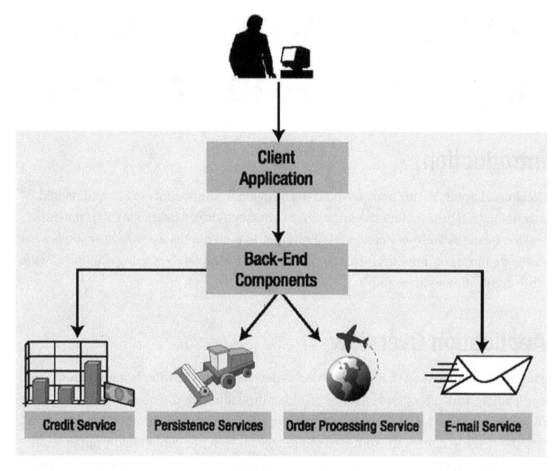

Figure 7-1. *The Wines Online application architecture*

Application Components and Services

The back-end wine store application consists of different types of EJBs that are created as components and services. The key components and services are described in the following sections.

The Shopping Cart Component

The shopping cart component manages the cart items for a registered customer who has logged into the application. This component is a stateful session bean, and it keeps track of cart items (wines and quantity) that are added to and removed from the shopping cart. Finally, the shopping cart component transfers the order information to the order processing component.

The Search Façade Component

The search façade component allows the customer to retrieve all wines or search for wines using criteria such as year, country, and varietal. This component is a stateless session bean, and it returns a list of wines based on executed search criteria.

The Customer Façade Component

The customer façade component allows customers to register themselves as members of the wine application and also retrieve customer information based on their e-mail addresses. This component is a stateless session bean.

The Order Processing Façade Component

The order processing façade component acts as a coordinator between the credit service and the order processing service. This component processes the cart items and creates a purchase order (PO) that can be consumed by the order processing service. This component is a stateless session bean.

Persistence Services

Persistence services comprise a packaged persistence unit that consists of a set of entities that are mapped to the wine store database schema. All other components and services in the back-end part of the application use this common persistence unit to perform CRUD operations.

The E-Mail Service

The e-mail service is an MDB that sends out an e-mail to the customer about the status of the order submitted. This service is essentially the same MDB that we built in Chapter 5, and it requires the same JMS and Java Mail Session resources.

The Credit Service

The credit service is a Web service that is consumed by the application. This service takes credit card information as an input message and returns the status of the credit for a particular customer. We will use the credit service developed in Chapter 6.

The Order Processing Service

The order processing service is an MDB that does the bulk of the order processing after a purchase order has been received.

The Wines Online Application Business Process

Figure 7-2 illustrates the process flow for the wine application. Once the shopping cart service submits the customer and cart item information to the order processing façade, it verifies that the customer credit card information is accurate and the card is valid before proceeding to process the order. After approval is received from the credit service, it creates a purchase order that contains the customer and order information and submits it to the order processing service. If a negative response is received from the credit service, the order is cancelled, and the e-mail service sends a notification to the customer. Once a purchase order is received by the order processing service, it proceeds to fulfill the order, which entails updating the inventory and sending an e-mail notification on the status of the order to the customer using the e-mail service.

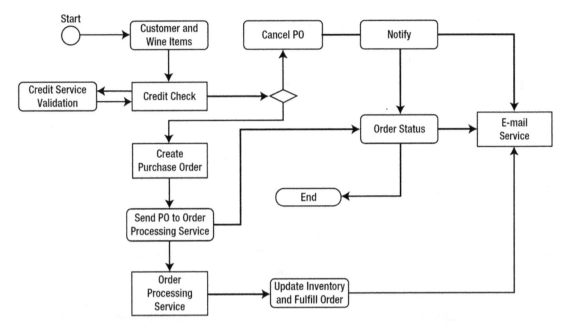

Figure 7-2. *The Wines Online application business process*

Figure 7-3 illustrates the interactions that occur among the components and services of the wine application. A step-by-step explanation of these interactions follows the diagram.

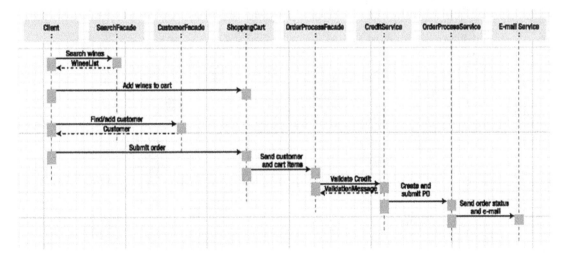

Figure 7-3. *The Wines Online application component and service interactions*

In-Depth Component/Service Walkthrough

In the following sections, we will walk through the code for each individual component to explain its interaction with the other components and services. Each of the listings contains code that is included in the Chapter07-IntegratedServices sample application. At the end of the chapter, you will find step-by-step instructions on how to configure, build, deploy, and execute this application.

Persistence Services

Persistence services present a domain model to the application in the form of a JPA persistence unit. This persistence unit is comprised of JPA entities along with an EntityManager for performing CRUD operations on the entities and for managing the persistent state of those entities in a transactional context.

Figure 7-4 illustrates the entities, the inheritance models, and the relationships between them. The Customer entity is inherited by the Individual and Distributor entities. InventoryItem, CartItem, and OrderItem entities inherit the WineItem entity. The BusinessContact entity is inherited by the Supplier entity. The wine store persistence unit also contains different types of relationships between these entities (including one-to-one, one-to-many, and many-to-many), which will be accessed from the application code. The mappings used in these entities were covered in Chapter 3 and Chapter 4. We will focus on the code that is used in other components of this application to integrate this persistence unit.

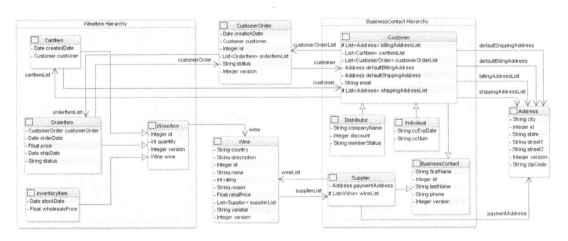

Figure 7-4. *The Wines Online domain model*

The Customer Façade Component

CustomerFacadeBean is a stateless session bean. It provides business methods to allow the client application either to query the customer based on its e-mail address or perform CRUD operations on the Customer entity and its subclasses. This façade is injected with an EntityManager via the @PersistenceContext annotation that it uses to perform CRUD operations on Customer entities. Listing 7-1 shows the getCustomerFindByEmail method in CustomerFacadeBean. This method calls the named query Customer.findByEmail defined in the Customer entity of the wine store persistence unit using the createNamedQuery() method in the EntityManager.

Note   createNamedQuery() is a method in the javax.persistence. EntityManager interface. This method creates an instance of javax.persistence.Query for executing a named query specified in JPQL (Java Persistence Query Language) or native SQL.

Listing 7-1. The getCustomerFindByEmail Method

```
public Customer getCustomerFindByEmail(String email) {
  return em.createNamedQuery("Customer.findByEmail", Customer.class).
  setParameter("email", email).
  getSingleResult();
}
```

Listing 7-2 shows the complete code for CustomerFacadeBean, which has the business methods to perform CRUD operations using the EntityManager. This bean class does not implement Local or Remote interfaces, and so the EJB container calls the bean class directly in Local mode.

Note   In Chapter 2, we provided the details on the differences between remote and client view architectures for session beans with a summary of advantages and disadvantages along with a discussion of the no-interface mode introduced in EJB 3.1. Chapter 3 provided the details on the methods that are available on the EntityManager to perform the CRUD operations.

Listing 7-2. CustomerFacadeBean.java

```java
@Stateless(name = "CustomerFacade", mappedName = "Chapter07-
IntegratedSamples-Chapter07-ServiceIntegration-ejb-CustomerFacade")
public class CustomerFacadeBean {
  @PersistenceContext(unitName = "Chapter07-WineAppUnit-JTA")
  private EntityManager em;

  public <T> T persistEntity(T entity) {
    em.persist(entity);
    return entity;
  }

  public <T> T mergeEntity(T entity) {
    return em.merge(entity);
  }

  public void removeCustomer(Customer customer) {
    customer = em.find(Customer.class, customer.getId());
    em.remove(customer);
  }

  /**
   * <code>select o from Customer o</code>
   */
  public List<Customer> getCustomerFindAll() {
    return em.createNamedQuery("Customer.findAll", Customer.class).
    getResultList();
  }

  public Customer getCustomerFindById(Integer id) {
    return em.find(Customer.class, id);
  }

  /**
   * <code>select o from Customer o where o.email = :email</code>
   */
  public Customer getCustomerFindByEmail(String email) {
```

```
    return em.createNamedQuery("Customer.findByEmail", Customer.class).
    setParameter("email", email).
    getSingleResult();
  }

  public Customer registerCustomer(Customer customer) {
    return persistEntity(customer);
  }
}
```

The Search Façade Component

SearchFacadeBean is a stateless session bean. This bean provides business methods
that allow the client application to query the Wine entity in the persistence unit based on
the year, country, and varietal of the wine. The persistence unit in SearchFacadeBean is
injected via the @PersistenceContext annotation. Listing 7-3 shows the complete code
for SearchFacadeBean, which has the business methods to perform search operations
using the EntityManager. This bean class has a business interface, SearchFacadeLocal,
which supports local client access. The methods getWineFindAll(),
getWineFindByYear(), getWineFindByCountry(), and getWineFindByVarietal() call
the respectively named queries defined in the Wine entity of the wine store persistence
unit using the createNamedQuery() method in the EntityManager, and return zero or
more Wine objects in java.util.List.

Listing 7-3. SearchFacadeBean.java

```
@Stateless(name = "SearchFacade", mappedName = "Chapter07-
IntegratedSamples-Chapter07-ServiceIntegration-ejb-SearchFacade")
public class SearchFacadeBean implements SearchFacadeLocal {
  @PersistenceContext(unitName = "Chapter07-WineAppUnit-JTA")
  private EntityManager em;

  public Object queryByRange(String jpqlStmt, int firstResult, int
  maxResults) {
    Query query = em.createQuery(jpqlStmt);
    if (firstResult > 0) {
      query = query.setFirstResult(firstResult);
    }
```

```java
  if (maxResults > 0) {
    query = query.setMaxResults(maxResults);
  }
  return query.getResultList();
}

public <T> T persistEntity(T entity) {
  em.persist(entity);
  return entity;
}

public <T> T mergeEntity(T entity) {
  return em.merge(entity);
}

public void removeWine(Wine wine) {
  wine = em.find(Wine.class, wine.getId());
  em.remove(wine);
}

/**
 * <code>select object(o) from Wine o</code>
 */
public List<Wine> getWineFindAll() {
  return em.createNamedQuery("Wine.findAll", Wine.class).getResultList();
}

/**
 * <code>select object(wine) from Wine wine where wine.year = :year</code>
 */
public List<Wine> getWineFindByYear(Integer year) {
  return em.createNamedQuery("Wine.findByYear", Wine.class).
  setParameter("year", year).
  getResultList();
}
```

```
/**
 * <code>select object(wine) from Wine wine where wine.country =
   :country</code>
 */
public List<Wine> getWineFindByCountry(String country) {
  return em.createNamedQuery("Wine.findByCountry", Wine.class).
  setParameter("country", country).
  getResultList();
}
/**
 * <code>select object(wine) from Wine wine where wine.varietal =
   :varietal</code>
 */
public List<Wine> getWineFindByVarietal(String varietal) {
  return em.createNamedQuery("Wine.findByVarietal", Wine.class).setParame
  ter("varietal",varietal).getResultList();
}
}
```

The Shopping Cart Component

ShoppingCartBean is a stateful session bean and uses an extended persistence context. This bean preserves the state of a customer who is logged into the system and is currently either adding or removing wine items from the shopping cart. Once the customer submits an order, ShoppingCartBean sends the customer information to the order processing façade, which takes care of processing the order. We have decided to use a stateful session bean for this use case for the following reasons:

- There is more than one type of client application that accesses the back-end application (Web, Swing, and command-line client).

- We want to show the usage of EJB stateful session beans in a typical application.

> **Note**   In general, there is a common belief that stateful session beans are a bit
> heavyweight to store the state (as compared to storing the state on the client using
> an HTTP session for Web clients). There is evidence that there isn't a drastic cost in
> terms of either performance or transactions associated with stateful session beans.
> (See *J2EE Performance Testing with BEA WebLogic Server,* by Peter Zadrozny
> [Apress, 2003], for thorough coverage of this topic.)

ShoppingCartBean has the business methods described in the following subsections.

Finding Customers

Listing 7-4 shows the findCustomer() method in ShoppingCartBean. This method
uses the injected CustomerFacadeBean and calls the findCustomerByEmail() method
to get an instance, which in our case happens to be an Individual subentity. Once a
Customer is retrieved, it is assigned to a class-level attribute so that it can be referenced
subsequently through other methods on this stateful session bean. Because we are using
an extended persistence context, this instance will remain managed throughout the
life of the bean, through transaction boundaries, unless it is actively removed from the
persistence context.

Listing 7-4. The findCustomer Business Method

```
public Customer findCustomer(String email) {
  customer = customerFacade.getCustomerFindByEmail(email);
  return customer;
}
```

Adding Wine Items

Listing 7-5 shows the addWineItem() method in ShoppingCartBean. This business
method is called by the client application to add a particular wine item to the shopping
cart along with the quantity. The code creates a new instance of the CartItem entity and
sets the quantity, wine, and time of creation using the setter methods in CartItem.

Note   A quick refresher on the three states of an entity instance: managed, detached, and new. A managed instance is one that is actively referenced by a persistence context, and all changes made to that instance are tracked by the persistence context. When the persistence context is synchronized with the database, all pending changes found in managed instances are flushed to the database through SQL statements. A detached entity instance is one that is no longer referenced by a persistence context, and so its changes are not being tracked. If a client modifies a detached instance, the client needs to ensure that those changes are merged into a managed instance (for instance, through an EntityManager.merge() call), or else the changes will never be synchronized with the database. A new entity instance is like a detached instance, only it has not yet been persisted in the database.

The addWineItem() method creates a new CartItem with the specified properties and adds it to the Customer instance. Because we queried the Customer instance and cached it in a class-level variable on our stateful session bean, we can count on it being in a managed state. ShoppingCartBean uses container-managed transactions, and the addWineItem() method defaults to using TransactionAttributeType.REQUIRED, so a transaction will be started and committed during the course of this method. When the commit is performed, the persistence context will be synchronized with the database, and any changes pending in our managed customer instance will be pushed out to the database. Because of the cascade rule on Customer's cartItemList property, any referenced CartItem instances will also be persisted. The result of this method call, then, will be a new row in CartItem's table with a foreign key reference to the Customer table (or Individual table, depending on how the entity inheritance hierarchy is mapped).

Listing 7-5. The addWineItem Business Method

```
public void addWineItem(Wine wine, int quantity) {
  CartItem cartItem = new CartItem(quantity, wine);
  customer.addCartItem(cartItem);
}
```

Removing Wine Items

Listing 7-6 shows the removeWineItem() method in ShoppingCartBean. This method lets the client applications remove the items from the shopping cart when requested by the end user (via the user interface). Again, because the customer attribute is a managed instance, any changes applied to it will be persisted at the conclusion of this method when the CMT transaction created at the outset of this method is committed.

Listing 7-6. The removeWineItem Business Method

```
public void removeWineItem(CartItem cartItem) {
  customer.removeCartItem(cartItem);
}
```

Submitting Orders to the Order Processing Façade

Listing 7-7 shows the sendOrderToOPC() method in ShoppingCartBean. This method is called by the client applications to submit the order when the end user finally decides to buy one or more wines. This method uses the injected OrderProcessFacadeBean and calls the processOrder() method to submit the order by passing the customer object.

Note   The rationale behind the naming of the sendOrderToOPC() method was that OrderProcess ➤ FacadeBean, which receives the purchase orders, in effect acts as an "order processing center." With this in mind, we decided to abbreviate "order processing center" to OPC so as to avoid an extremely long method name.

Listing 7-7. The sendOrderToOPC Business Method

```
public String sendOrderToOPC() {
  String result = null;
  try {
    orderProcessFacade.processOrder(customer);
    result = "Your Order has been submitted - you will be notified about
    the status via email";
  } catch (Exception ex) {
```

```
    ex.printStackTrace();
    result = "An error occurred while processing your order. Please contact
    Customer Service.";
  }

  return result;
}
```

Retrieving the Customer's Cart Items

Listing 7-8 shows the getCartItems() method in ShoppingCartBean. This method retrieves the current list of cart items from the customer field (which may be either an Individual or a Distributor entity type). This method will be useful when we build a JSF application in which we can show all of the cart items in the user interface before the customer submits the order.

Listing 7-8. The getCartItems Business Method

```
public List<CartItem> getCartItems() {
  return customer.getCartItemList();
}
```

The complete code for ShoppingCartBean is shown in Listing 7-9.

Listing 7-9. ShoppingCartBean.java

```
@Stateful(name = "ShoppingCart", mappedName = "Chapter07-IntegratedSamples-
Chapter07-ServiceIntegration-ejb-ShoppingCart")
public class ShoppingCartBean implements ShoppingCartLocal {
  @PersistenceContext(unitName = "Chapter07-WineAppUnit-JTA",
  type = PersistenceContextType.
  EXTENDED)
  private EntityManager em;
  private Customer customer;
  @EJB
  private CustomerFacadeBean customerFacade;
  @EJB
  private OrderProcessFacadeBean orderProcessFacade;
```

```java
public Customer getCustomer() {
  return customer;
}

public void addWineItem(Wine wine, int quantity) {
  CartItem cartItem = new CartItem(quantity, wine);
  customer.addCartItem(cartItem);
}

public void addWineItem(Wine wine) {
  CartItem cartItem = new CartItem();
  cartItem.setQuantity(20);
  wine = em.find(Wine.class, wine.getId());
  cartItem.setWine(wine);
  cartItem.setCreatedDate(new Timestamp(System.currentTimeMillis()));
  customer.addCartItem(cartItem);
}

public void removeWineItem(CartItem cartItem) {
  customer.removeCartItem(cartItem);
}

public void addCartItemsTemporarily() {
  List<Wine> wines = em.createNamedQuery("findAllWine").getResultList();
  for (Wine wine : wines) {
    final CartItem cartItem = new CartItem();
    cartItem.setCreatedDate(new Timestamp(System.currentTimeMillis()));
    cartItem.setQuantity(20);
    cartItem.setWine(wine);
    customer.addCartItem(cartItem);
  }
}

public Customer findCustomer(String email) {
  customer = customerFacade.getCustomerFindByEmail(email);
  return customer;
}
```

```java
public String sendOrderToOPC() {
  String result = null;
  try {
    orderProcessFacade.processOrder(customer);
    result = "Your Order has been submitted - you will be notified about
    the status via email";
  } catch (Exception ex) {
    ex.printStackTrace();
    result = "An error occurred while processing your order. Please
    contact Customer Service.";
  }

  return result;
}

public <T> T persistEntity(T entity) {
  em.persist(entity);
  return entity;
}

public <T> T mergeEntity(T entity) {
  return em.merge(entity);
}

public void removeCartItem(CartItem cartItem) {
  cartItem = em.find(CartItem.class, cartItem.getId());
  em.remove(cartItem);
}

public List<CartItem> getCartItems() {
  return customer.getCartItemList();
}

public void removeWine(Wine wine) {
  wine = em.find(Wine.class, wine.getId());
  em.remove(wine);
}
```

```java
  /**
   * <code>select object(o) from Wine o</code>
   */
  public List<Wine> getWineFindAll() {
    return em.createNamedQuery("Wine.findAll", Wine.class).getResultList();
  }

  /**
   * <code>select object(wine) from Wine wine where wine.year = :year</code>
   */
  public List<Wine> getWineFindByYear(Integer year) {
    return em.createNamedQuery("Wine.findByYear", Wine.class).
    setParameter("year", year).
    getResultList();
  }

  /**
   * <code>select object(wine) from Wine wine where wine.country =
     :country</code>
   */
  public List<Wine> getWineFindByCountry(String country) {
    return em.createNamedQuery("Wine.findByCountry", Wine.class).
    setParameter("country", country).
    getResultList();
  }

  /**
   * <code>select object(wine) from Wine wine where wine.varietal =
     :varietal</code>
   */
  public List<Wine> getWineFindByVarietal(String varietal) {
    return em.createNamedQuery("Wine.findByVarietal", Wine.class).
    setParameter("varietal",
    varietal).getResultList();
  }
}
```

The Order Processing Façade Component

OrderProcessFacadeBean is a stateless session bean. This bean provides business methods that are invoked by ShoppingCartBean to submit an order and other methods that interact with the credit and order processing services. OrderProcessFacadeBean has the business methods described in the following subsections.

Credit Check

Listing 7-10 shows the performCreditCheck() method in OrderProcessFacadeBean. This method uses a CreditService that was injected using the @WebServiceRef annotation to get the port of the Web service. Once the port is available, the code can call the creditCheck Web service operation, which takes a credit card number and returns a message on the validity of the card in true or false terms. We are using the credit service that we developed in Chapter 6.

Listing 7-10. The performCreditCheck Business Method

```
private boolean performCreditCheck(Individual individual) {
   String ccnum = individual.getCcNum().toString();
   CreditCheckEndpointBean creditService = service.getCreditCheckEndpointBeanPort();
   return creditService.creditCheck(ccnum);
}
```

Creating a Purchase Order

Listing 7-11 shows the processOrder() method in OrderProcessFacadeBean. ShoppingCartBean calls this business method when an order is submitted by the client application. This method has one parameter, which is of Customer entity type. The customer's shopping cart is contained in its cartItems list, each member of which references a wine and a quantity added to the cart by the customer while shopping.

To start with, the method checks whether the received entity is managed. If not, a call to the merge() method of the EntityManager is made to retrieve a managed Customer object.

Note   It is worth noting that when we run this application (following the steps at the end of this chapter), the customer parameter will be found in the persistence context, and so the merge step will not be performed. This is because `processOrder()` is called from an existing transactional context—the transaction that was created when its calling method, `ShoppingCartBean.sendOrderToOPC()` was invoked. A single persistence context is always bound to a given transaction, and in this case the extended persistence context from `ShoppingCartBean` is the one associated with this transaction. When `sendOrderToOPC()` is invoked, an existing context transaction is found and used. When `em.contains(customer)` is called inside `processOrder`, the EntityManager for `OrderProcessFacadeBean` observes that a persistence context is already associated with this transaction, and it uses this persistence context, which is the same extended persistence context associated with `ShoppingCartBean`. This is why the customer instance is already determined to be managed.

Once the managed customer entity is obtained, it checks whether the customer is an `Individual` or a `Distributor`. For individuals, a call to the `performCreditCheck()` method is made to verify the credit card. If the credit card is found to be invalid, the message "Invalid Credit Card" is sent back to the client application via `ShoppingCartBean`. For distributors, the `memberStatus` property is checked, and any value other than "APPROVED" is rejected.

If the customer is approved, then processing continues, and a new order of type `CustomerOrder` is created. This new order is populated with the collection of `CartItem` objects associated with the `Customer` and found in its `cartItems` property. For each cart item, an `OrderItem` object is created to capture the quantity of each wine and the total price for the wine in that cart item. The price for each order item is calculated using the available retail price information for each `Wine` entity.

Once all the cart items have been processed and corresponding order items have been created, the new `CustomerOrder` containing the order items is persisted, in part to acquire a generated value for its `id` field, which is used when generating an e-mail from within the call `sendPOtoMDB()`. The `removeCartItem()` method is then called on each cart item to remove it from the `Customer`.

The non-entity utility class `PurchaseOrder`, which associates a `Customer` object with a specific `CustomerOrder`, is created. This Purchase Order instance is passed as an argument to the `sendPOtoMDB()` method, sending the purchase order to the processing service. Once the call is made, the process becomes asynchronous, and a message is sent back to the client application that the order has been sent for processing.

Since the entire method is executed in a transactional context, changes to the customer object, and any other managed objects, will be persisted when the transaction concludes.

Listing 7-11. The processOrder Business Method

```
public String processOrder(Customer customer) {
  String processStatus = null;
  if (!em.contains(customer)) {
    customer = em.merge(customer);
  }

  if (customer instanceof Individual) {
    if (!performCreditCheck((Individual) customer)) {
      processStatus = "Invalid Credit Card number or credit check failed";
    }
  } else if (customer instanceof Distributor) {
    if (!"APPROVED".equals(((Distributor) customer).getMemberStatus())) {
      processStatus = "Distributor credit check rejected";
    }
  }

  if (processStatus == null) {
    CustomerOrder order = new CustomerOrder();
    order.setCreationDate(new Timestamp(System.currentTimeMillis()));
    em.persist(order);

    List<CartItem> cartItems = customer.getCartItemList();
    if (cartItems != null) {
      List<CartItem> tempCartItems = new ArrayList<CartItem>();
      for (CartItem cItem : cartItems) {
        OrderItem oItem = new OrderItem();
```

```
        int qty = cItem.getQuantity();
        oItem.setQuantity(qty);
        oItem.setOrderDate(new Timestamp(System.currentTimeMillis()));
        oItem.setWine(cItem.getWine());
        Wine tempWine = cItem.getWine();
        Float d = tempWine.getRetailPrice();
        Float price = d * cItem.getQuantity();
        oItem.setPrice(price);
        order.addOrderItem(oItem);
        tempCartItems.add(cItem);
      }
      for (CartItem cartItem : tempCartItems) {
        customer.removeCartItem(cartItem);
        em.remove(cartItem);
      }
    }
    customer.addCustomerOrder(order);

    PurchaseOrder po = new PurchaseOrder();
    po.setCustomer(customer);
    po.setCustomerOrder(order);

    sendPOtoMDB(po);
    processStatus = "Purchase Order sent for processing to the process queue";
  }
  return processStatus;
}
```

Sending a Purchase Order to the Order Processing Service

Listing 7-12 shows the sendPOtoMDB() method in OrderProcessFacadeBean. This
business method makes use of injected Java Messaging Service (JMS) resources for
a topic connection factory and a topic. A connection to a topic connection factory is
created and the connection is started. Once a connection is available, a session is created
and a MessageProducer is created with a topic. An ObjectMessage is created to take the
PurchaseOrder object, and the MessageProducer is used to send the PurchaseOrder to
the topic.

Listing 7-12. The sendPOtoMDB Business Method

```
private void sendPOtoMDB(PurchaseOrder po) {
  //send PO to MDB now
  Connection connection = null;
  Session session = null;
  try {
    connection = poTopicCF.createConnection();
    connection.start();
    session = connection.createSession(false, Session.AUTO_ACKNOWLEDGE);
    MessageProducer producer = session.createProducer(poTopic);
    ObjectMessage objMessage = session.createObjectMessage();
    objMessage.setObject(po);
    producer.send(objMessage);
  } catch (JMSException e) {
    e.printStackTrace();
  } finally {
    if (session != null) {
      try {
        session.close();
      } catch (JMSException ex) {
        Logger.getLogger(OrderProcessFacadeBean.class.getName()).log(Level.
        SEVERE, null, ex);
      }
    }
    if (connection != null) {
      try {
        connection.close();
      } catch (JMSException ex) {
        Logger.getLogger(OrderProcessFacadeBean.class.getName()).log(Level.
        SEVERE, null, ex);
      }
    }
  }
}
```

The complete code for OrderProcessFacadeBean.java is shown in Listing 7-13.

Listing 7-13. OrderProcessFacadeBean.java

```java
@Stateless(name = "OrderProcessFacade", mappedName = "OrderProcessFacade")
public class OrderProcessFacadeBean {
  @PersistenceContext(unitName = "Chapter07-WineAppUnit-JTA")
  private EntityManager em;
  @Resource(mappedName = "poTopicConnectionFactory")
  private TopicConnectionFactory poTopicCF;
  @Resource(mappedName = "PurchaseOrderTopic")
  private Topic poTopic;
  @WebServiceRef(type = CreditService.class)
  CreditService service;

  public Object mergeEntity(Object entity) {
    return em.merge(entity);
  }

  public Object persistEntity(Object entity) {
    em.persist(entity);
    return entity;
  }

  public void createNewOrder(CustomerOrder newOrder) {
    persistEntity(newOrder);
  }

  private boolean performCreditCheck(Individual individual) {
    String ccnum = individual.getCcNum().toString();
    CreditCheckEndpointBean creditService = service.
    getCreditCheckEndpointBeanPort();
    return creditService.creditCheck(ccnum);
  }
```

```java
public String processOrder(Customer customer) {
  String processStatus = null;
  if (!em.contains(customer)) {
    customer = em.merge(customer);
  }

  if (customer instanceof Individual) {
    if (!performCreditCheck((Individual) customer)) {
      processStatus = "Invalid Credit Card number or credit check failed";
    }
  } else if (customer instanceof Distributor) {
    if (!"APPROVED".equals(((Distributor) customer).getMemberStatus())) {
      processStatus = "Distributor credit check rejected";
    }
  }

  if (processStatus == null) {
    CustomerOrder order = new CustomerOrder();
    order.setCreationDate(new Timestamp(System.currentTimeMillis()));
    em.persist(order);

    List<CartItem> cartItems = customer.getCartItemList();
    if (cartItems != null) {
      List<CartItem> tempCartItems = new ArrayList<CartItem>();
      for (CartItem cItem : cartItems) {
        OrderItem oItem = new OrderItem();
        int qty = cItem.getQuantity();
        oItem.setQuantity(qty);
        oItem.setOrderDate(new Timestamp(System.currentTimeMillis()));
        oItem.setWine(cItem.getWine());
        Wine tempWine = cItem.getWine();
        Float d = tempWine.getRetailPrice();
        Float price = d * cItem.getQuantity();
        oItem.setPrice(price);
        order.addOrderItem(oItem);
        tempCartItems.add(cItem);
      }
```

```
      for (CartItem cartItem : tempCartItems) {
        customer.removeCartItem(cartItem);
        em.remove(cartItem);
      }
    }
    customer.addCustomerOrder(order);

    PurchaseOrder po = new PurchaseOrder();
    po.setCustomer(customer);
    po.setCustomerOrder(order);

    sendPOtoMDB(po);
    processStatus = "Purchase Order sent for processing to the process
    queue";
  }
  return processStatus;
}

private void sendPOtoMDB(PurchaseOrder po) {
  //send PO to MDB now
  Connection connection = null;
  Session session = null;
  try {
    connection = poTopicCF.createConnection();
    connection.start();
    session = connection.createSession(false, Session.AUTO_ACKNOWLEDGE);
    MessageProducer producer = session.createProducer(poTopic);
    ObjectMessage objMessage = session.createObjectMessage();
    objMessage.setObject(po);
    producer.send(objMessage);
  } catch (JMSException e) {
    e.printStackTrace();
  } finally {
    if (session != null) {
      try {
        session.close();
      } catch (JMSException ex) {
```

```
          Logger.getLogger(OrderProcessFacadeBean.class.getName()).
          log(Level.SEVERE, null, ex);
      }
    }
    if (connection != null) {
      try {
        connection.close();
      } catch (JMSException ex) {
        Logger.getLogger(OrderProcessFacadeBean.class.getName()).
        log(Level.SEVERE, null, ex);
      }
    }
  }
 }
}
```

The Order Processing Service

The order processing service is an MDB. The idea behind having MDBs in the wine store application is to show how some of the processing in an enterprise application can be done in an asynchronous fashion, and how you can work with the EntityManager, session beans, and other MDBs from an MDB.

Note   Chapter 5, which covers MDBs, describes the asynchronous architecture in detail and gives examples of some possible implementations.

OrderProcessingMDBBean is a plain old Java object (POJO) that is annotated with a class-level @MessageDriven annotation to indicate that it is an MDB. This POJO implements the mandatory onMessage() method to process the incoming messages with the help of a utility method, processOrder(). We will walk through the methods in the MDB from here.

Listing 7-14 shows the code for the onMessage() method. This method checks whether the received message is of ObjectMessage instance type, and the retrieved object is then typecast to the PurchaseOrder utility class. After that, a call to the processOrder() utility method is made to process the received purchase order.

Listing 7-14. The onMessage Method in OrderProcessingMDBBean

```
public void onMessage(Message message) {
  try {
    if (message instanceof ObjectMessage) {
      ObjectMessage objMessage = (ObjectMessage) message;
      Object obj = objMessage.getObject();
      if (obj instanceof PurchaseOrder) {
        po = (PurchaseOrder) obj;
        processOrder(po);
      }
    }
  } catch (JMSException e) {
    e.printStackTrace();
  }
}
```

Listing 7-15 shows the code for the processOrder() method, which begins by opening up the PurchaseOrder to obtain the Customer and CustomerOrder objects. For each order item in the customer order, a corresponding amount of wine is deducted from the inventory tables. To perform this work, the deductInventory() utility method is called.

After the inventory is deducted, it is time to send a status update to the customer. This is done using the e-mail service. The customer's e-mail information and order ID are retrieved from the PO object, the e-mail content is constructed, and a call is made to the sendStatus() utility method.

Listing 7-15. The processOrder Business Method

```
private void processOrder(PurchaseOrder po) {
  Customer customer = po.getCustomer();
  CustomerOrder order = po.getCustomerOrder();

  for (OrderItem oItem : order.getOrderItemList()) {
    Wine wine = oItem.getWine();
    int qty = oItem.getQuantity();
    deductInventory(wine, qty);
  }
```

```
    String from = PopulateDemoData.FROM_EMAIL_ADDRESS;
    String to = customer.getEmail();
    String content =
        "Your order has been processed. "
        + "If you have questions call Beginning EJB Wine Store "
        + "Application with order id # "
        + po.getCustomerOrder().getId().toString();    sendStatus(from, to,
        content);
}
```

Listing 7-16 shows the code for the deductInventory() method. This method makes use of the injected EntityManager to call the query named Inventory.findItemByWine defined in the InventoryItem entity. Once the inventory for the specific wine is retrieved, the quantity is updated using the setQuantity() setter method. The inventory item is managed, so its modifications are synchronized with the database when this CMT method ends, or whenever its context transaction commits.

Listing 7-16. The deductInventory Business Method

```
private void deductInventory(Wine tempWine, int deductQty) {
  InventoryItem iItem =
          em.createNamedQuery("InventoryItem.findItemByWine",
          InventoryItem.class).setParameter("wine", tempWine).
          getSingleResult();
  int newQty = iItem.getQuantity() - deductQty;
  iItem.setQuantity(newQty);
}
```

Listing 7-17 shows the code for the sendStatus() method. This utility method makes use of an injected JMS resource for a topic connection factory and a topic. A connection to a topic connection factory is created and the connection is started. Once a connection is available, a session is created, and a MessageProducer containing the topic is created. A Message object is created, and the JMSType is set to MailMessage. After that, a series of calls to the setStringProperty() method on the Message object is made to create the to, from, subject, and content sections of the e-mail. Once all of the properties are set, the message is sent out to the message topic that will be processed by the e-mail service.

Listing 7-17. The sendStatus() Business Method

```java
private void sendStatus(String from, String to, String content) {
  try {
    System.out.println("Before status TopicCF connection");
    Connection connection = statusMessageTopicCF.createConnection();
    System.out.println("Created connection");
    connection.start();
    System.out.println("Started connection");
    System.out.println("Starting Topic Session");
    Session topicSession =
            connection.createSession(false, Session.AUTO_ACKNOWLEDGE);

    MessageProducer publisher = topicSession.createProducer(statusTopic);
    System.out.println("created producer");
    MapMessage message = topicSession.createMapMessage();
    message.setStringProperty("from", from);
    message.setStringProperty("to", to);
    message.setStringProperty("subject", "Status of your wine order");
    message.setStringProperty("content", content);
    System.out.println("before send");
    publisher.send(message);
    System.out.println("after send");
  } catch (JMSException e) {
    e.printStackTrace();
  }
}
```

The complete code for OrderProcessingMDBBean is shown in Listing 7-18.

Listing 7-18. OrderProcessingMDBBean.java

```java
@MessageDriven(activationConfig = {
  @ActivationConfigProperty(propertyName = "destinationType", propertyValue =
  "javax.jms.Topic")},
    mappedName = "PurchaseOrderTopic")
public class OrderProcessingMDBBean implements MessageListener {
  private PurchaseOrder po;
```

```java
  @PersistenceContext(unitName = "Chapter07-WineAppUnit-JTA")
  private EntityManager em;
  @Resource(mappedName = "StatusMessageTopicConnectionFactory")
  private TopicConnectionFactory statusMessageTopicCF;
  @Resource(mappedName = "StatusMessageTopic")
  private Topic statusTopic;

  public void onMessage(Message message) {
    try {
      if (message instanceof ObjectMessage) {
        ObjectMessage objMessage = (ObjectMessage) message;
        Object obj = objMessage.getObject();
        if (obj instanceof PurchaseOrder) {
          po = (PurchaseOrder) obj;
          processOrder(po);
        }
      }
    } catch (JMSException e) {
      e.printStackTrace();
    }
  }

  private void processOrder(PurchaseOrder po) {
    Customer customer = po.getCustomer();
    CustomerOrder order = po.getCustomerOrder();
for (OrderItem oItem : order.getOrderItemList()) {
      Wine wine = oItem.getWine();
      int qty = oItem.getQuantity();
      deductInventory(wine, qty);
    }
String from = PopulateDemoData.FROM_EMAIL_ADDRESS;
    String to = customer.getEmail();
    String content =
        "Your order has been processed. "
        + "If you have questions call Beginning EJB Wine Store "
        + "Application with order id # "
```

```
            + po.getCustomerOrder().getId().toString();
        sendStatus(from, to, content);
    }
    private void deductInventory(Wine tempWine, int deductQty) {
        InventoryItem iItem =
            em.createNamedQuery("InventoryItem.findItemByWine",
            InventoryItem.class).setParameter("wine", tempWine).
            getSingleResult();
        int newQty = iItem.getQuantity() - deductQty;
        iItem.setQuantity(newQty);
    }
    private void sendStatus(String from, String to, String content) {
        try {
            System.out.println("Before status TopicCF connection");
            Connection connection = statusMessageTopicCF.createConnection();
            System.out.println("Created connection");
            connection.start();
            System.out.println("Started connection");
            System.out.println("Starting Topic Session");
            Session topicSession =
                connection.createSession(false, Session.AUTO_ACKNOWLEDGE);
MessageProducer publisher = topicSession.createProducer(statusTopic);
            System.out.println("created producer");
            MapMessage message = topicSession.createMapMessage();
            message.setStringProperty("from", from);
            message.setStringProperty("to", to);
            message.setStringProperty("subject", "Status of your wine order");
            message.setStringProperty("content", content);
            System.out.println("before send");
            publisher.send(message);
            System.out.println("after send");
        } catch (JMSException e) {
            e.printStackTrace();
        }
    }
}
```

The E-Mail Service

The e-mail service is an MDB. This MDB processes the incoming messages by sending out e-mails using an e-mail resource that is injected as a resource reference.

Listing 7-19 shows the code for the onMessage() method in the StatusMailerBean MDB. We will start by retrieving all of the properties from the message, and then we will create an object of javax.mail.Message using the injected mail resource reference mailSession. Then the message is decorated with relevant e-mail information, and the send() method is called to send the e-mail message.

Listing 7-19. The onMessage Method in the StatusMailer MDB

```
public void onMessage(Message message) {
  try {
    if (message instanceof MapMessage) {
      MapMessage orderMessage = (MapMessage) message;
      String from = orderMessage.getStringProperty("from");
      String to = orderMessage.getStringProperty("to");
      String subject = orderMessage.getStringProperty("subject");
      String content = orderMessage.getStringProperty("content");
      javax.mail.Message msg = new MimeMessage(mailSession);
      msg.setFrom(new InternetAddress(from));
      InternetAddress[] address = {new InternetAddress(to)};
      msg.setRecipients(RecipientType.TO, address);
      msg.setSubject(subject);
      msg.setSentDate(new java.util.Date());
      msg.setContent(content, "text/html");
      System.out.println("MDB: Sending Message from " + from + " to " + to
      + "...");
      Transport.send(msg);
      System.out.println("MDB: Message Sent");
    } else {
      System.out.println("Invalid message ");
    }
```

```
  } catch (Exception ex) {
    ex.printStackTrace();
  }
}
```

The complete code for StatusMailerBean is shown in Listing 7-20.

Listing 7-20. StatusMailerBean.java

```java
@MessageDriven(activationConfig = {
  @ActivationConfigProperty(propertyName = "destinationName",
                            propertyValue = "StatusMessageTopic"),
  @ActivationConfigProperty(propertyName = "destinationType",
                            propertyValue = "javax.jms.Topic")
}, mappedName = "StatusMessageTopic")
public class StatusMailerBean implements MessageListener {
  @Resource(name = "mail/wineappMail")
  private Session mailSession;

  public void onMessage(Message message) {
    try {
      if (message instanceof MapMessage) {
        MapMessage orderMessage = (MapMessage) message;
        String from = orderMessage.getStringProperty("from");
        String to = orderMessage.getStringProperty("to");
        String subject = orderMessage.getStringProperty("subject");
        String content = orderMessage.getStringProperty("content");
        javax.mail.Message msg = new MimeMessage(mailSession);
        msg.setFrom(new InternetAddress(from));
        InternetAddress[] address = {new InternetAddress(to)};
        msg.setRecipients(RecipientType.TO, address);
        msg.setSubject(subject);
        msg.setSentDate(new java.util.Date());
        msg.setContent(content, "text/html");
        System.out.println("MDB: Sending Message from " + from + " to " +
        to + "...");
```

```
      Transport.send(msg);
      System.out.println("MDB: Message Sent");
    } else {
      System.out.println("Invalid message ");
    }
  } catch (Exception ex) {
    ex.printStackTrace();
  }
}
}
```

The Credit Service

The credit service is a stateless session bean that is published as a Web service using JSR 181 (Web Services Metadata for the Java Platform) annotations. The idea behind creating this Web service is twofold:

- It shows how you can expose a stateless session bean as a Web service.

- It shows how you can consume a Web service from an EJB application.

This Web service is consumed by OrderProcessFacadeBean to check the customer's credit card. We are going to use the credit service that we developed in Chapter 6.

The Database Schema

The Wines Online application uses a single database schema to store all of the information related to customers, orders, inventory, and so on. Figure 7-5 shows a database diagram with all of the tables and relationships. The schema is designed to accommodate or showcase most of the O/R (object/relational) mappings in the JPA specification that are covered in this book, including the different types of inheritance strategies between entities. Not shown are the tables dedicated to ID generation for each root entity in an inheritance hierarchy (for example, BUSINESS_CONTACT_ID_GEN) or entity not involved in inheritance (for instance, ADDRESS_ID_GEN).

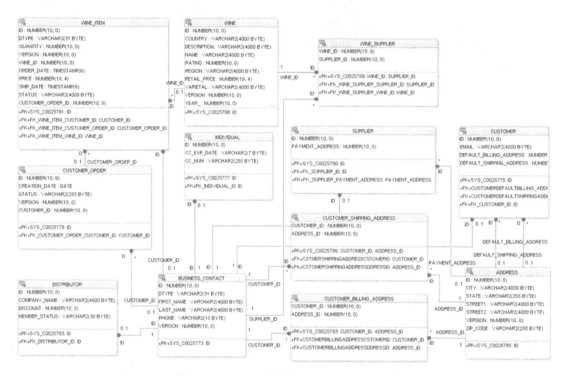

Figure 7-5. *Database diagram for the Wines Online application*

Building, Deploying, and Testing the Application

EJBs need to be packaged into EJB JAR (Java Archive) files before they are assembled
into EAR (Enterprise Archive) files that hold all of the required modules and libraries
for the application. Most application servers provide deployment utilities or Ant tasks
to facilitate deployment of EJBs to their containers. Java integrated development
environments (IDEs) like NetBeans, JDeveloper, and Eclipse provide graphical
deployment tools that allow developers to package, assemble, and deploy applications
to application servers. There is no requirement that EJBs have to be packaged into EJB
JAR files and assembled into EAR files. You can also deploy the EJB JAR files themselves.
In this chapter, we will assemble them into EAR files so that we can make the persistence
unit a shared module (in its own JAR file), and also to set the stage for Chapter 12, in
which we will be building client applications for the wine store back end that we have
just developed. We will also package the EJB/WebService module from Chapter 6 into
this EAR file, along with a Web module that contains a simple test servlet that drives the
test scenario.

Packaging, assembly, and deployment aspects are covered in detail in Chapter 11. In this chapter, we have developed the wine store application back end using session beans, MDBs, JPA entities, and Web services. Using NetBeans and deploying to GlassFish, we will perform the following steps to package, assemble, deploy, and test the services defined in this chapter.

Prerequisites

Before performing any of the steps detailed in the next sections, complete the "Getting Started" section of Chapter 1, which will walk you through the installation and environment setup required for the samples in this chapter.

Creating the Database Connection

The samples in this chapter require a database connection, and for these tests we will use the Derby database that is bundled with NetBeans and Glassfish. If you have not already created the WineApp database, also used for the Chapter 3 and Chapter 4 examples, click on the Services tab, expand the Databases icon, and invoke "Create Database..." on the Java DB node. Create a database named "WineApp" with username and password wineapp/wineapp, as shown in Figure 7-6.

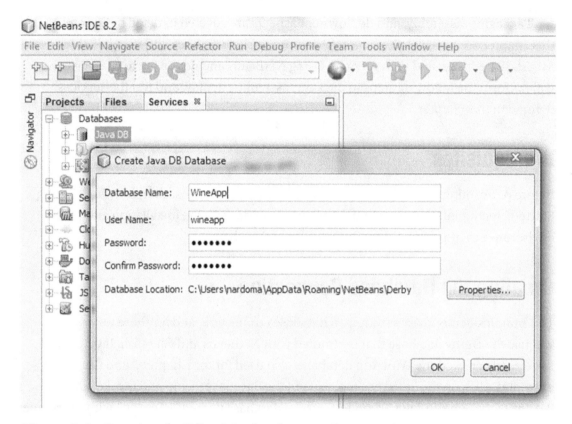

Figure 7-6. *Creating the WineApp database and connection*

This last step created a database connection, which is referenced from the persistence units in the `persistence.xml` files found in both the JPA and EJB projects. While it is possible to pre-create the database objects (tables, sequences, key constraints, and so on), we will let JPA create these database objects automatically the first time they are needed by each persistence unit.

Note   The samples for this chapter, like those for Chapter 3, include a JDBC data source that references these connection details. If you choose to use different credentials, make sure that you update the `persistence.xml` files, as well as the data source defined in the `glassfish-resources.xml` file in the `Chapter07-IntegratedServices-ejb` project.

Creating the JMS and JavaMail Resources

The MDBs in this integrated application require JMS resources. In Chapter 5, we created a JMS topic connection factory and a JMS topic, and we will create an additional one of each that will be consumed by the MDBs. Initially, OrderProcessFacadeBean sends a message to the queue that is consumed by OrderProcessingMDBBean. In turn, OrderProcessingMDBBean uses a JMS topic connection factory to send a message to the queue that will be used by StatusMailerBean to send out e-mail messages to the customer. Each of our topic connection factories also requires a JMS topic to be defined.

If you have not completed the samples in Chapter 5 (EJB Message-Driven Beans), follow the steps in that chapter in the section "Creating the JMS and JavaMail Resources." In addition to the resources created for that chapter's samples, you will need to create an additional TopicConnectionFactory and Topic. Chapter 5 will guide you in creating these additional resources using the GlassFish admin console.

The new resources you will need to create are a TopicConnectionFactory named poTopicConnectionFactory and a Topic named PurchaseOrderTopic.

Opening the Sample Application

Before performing the next step, you may wish to close any existing projects in NetBeans to avoid clutter. Open Chapter07-ServiceIntegration using the File ➤ Open Project menu, as shown in Figure 7-7. Make sure that the 'Open Required Projects' check box is checked.

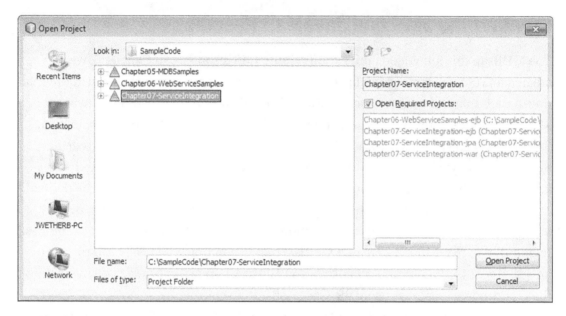

Figure 7-7. *Opening the Chapter07-ServiceIntegration project*

Note that this will open the `Chapter06-WebServiceSamples-ejb` project as well, since it is used directly by the Chapter 7 samples. Some of the source files will initially be flagged with warnings because they are missing dependencies until the EJB Web Service has been configured in the next step.

Configuring the EJB Web Service

We have built our wine store back-end application on top of the work we did in Chapter 6, in which we implemented the credit service.

1. The application in this chapter will not compile until you follow the steps in Chapter 6 to deploy the Web Service and create the Web service client. These steps are outlined here, but you may wish to refer to Chapter 6 for more comprehensive instructions for performing these operations. Right-click on the `Chapter06-WebServiceSamples-ejb` project, and choose 'Clean and Build' followed by 'Deploy.'

2. In the `Chapter06-WebServiceSamples` project, open the 'Web
    Services' section, right-click on `CreditCheckEndpointBean,` and
    choose 'Test Web Service.' When the Web page comes up, click on
    'WSDL File' link, and then copy the browsers URL for the `.wsdl`
    file (typically, `http://localhost:8080/CreditService/CreditCh`
    `eckEndpointBean?Tester`).

3. Now right-click on the `Chapter06-WebServiceSamples-ejb`
    project again, and choose 'New | Web Service Client.' In the
    wizard, select the 'WSDL URL' radio button and paste the `.wsdl`
    URL you copied in step 2. Set the package to '`com.apress.ejb.`
    `chapter06.services.client`' and choose Finish. This will
    complete the Web Service configuration required to run the
    Chapter 7 samples.

A quick look at the modules included in this example reveals that, in addition to
the EJB/WebServices module from Chapter 6, we have another EJB module containing
Session bean facades and MDBs, a number of JPA entities that comprise a JPA
persistence unit, and a Web module containing a test servlet.

The wineapp@yahoo.com Account
and the user.properties File

We have set up a Yahoo! mail account, `wineapp@yahoo.com`, that you may use for testing
purposes. The password is: `wine_app`. All samples in this book that involve a JavaMail
Session default to this account. You are free to use it, or you may prefer to send and
receive e-mail through your own mail server (for example, if you are behind a firewall)
using your own e-mail account(s).

In the `Chapter07-ServiceIntegration-jpa` project, you will find a `user.properties`
file in the root source directory. This file allows you to specify the From: and To: e-mail
addresses for the e-mail generated by this sample. It is shown in Listing 7-21:

Listing 7-21. The `user.properties` file found in the source root of the
`Chapter07-ServiceIntegration-jpa` project

```
# Specify the From: and To: email accounts that will be shown
# in the mail header that is sent from the JavaMail Session
# named 'mail/wineappMail' and configured in Chapter 5. Note
```

```
# that although the email header may appear to be from the
# From account below, it will originate from the account
# configured in the 'mail/wineappMail' JavaMail Session.
from_email_address = wineapp@yahoo.com
to_email_address = wineapp@yahoo.com
```

To change the To: and/or From: e-mail addresses, feel free to edit this plaintext file. Also, refer to the Readme.txt file for guidance with proxy servers and other issues resulting from non-default installation environments.

Building, Deploying, and Executing the Sample Application

With all of the configuration steps completed, you are now ready to build, deploy, and run this chapter's WineApp application through its simple servlet client. To ensure that any previous artifacts are removed, begin by selecting all five NetBeans projects and invoking the 'Clean' operation, shown in Figure 7-8.

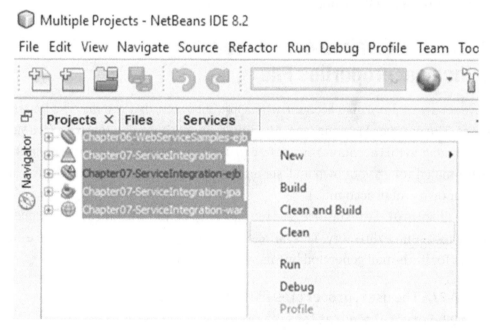

Figure 7-8. *Cleaning the Chapter07-ServiceIntegration project*

Note If GlassFish is running already, and you get errors while building because .jar files cannot be deleted, try shutting down GlassFish and re-invoking the 'Clean' operation.

The next steps are to build, package, and deploy the EJB, JPA, and Web modules and run the servlet client. All of these steps are performed automatically when invoking the 'Run' operation shown in Figure 7-9. NetBeans is able to track the state of the projects and perform any required work prior to executing the ShoppingCartClient servlet.

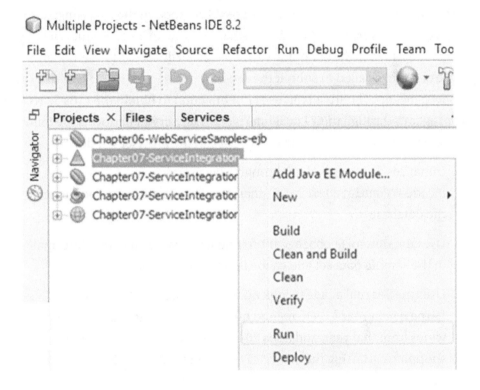

Figure 7-9. Running the Chapter07-ServiceIntegration project, which executes the servlet ShoppingCartClient found in the Chapter07-ServiceIntegration-web module

Client applications and different application architectures will be discussed in detail in Chapter 12. In order to test the deployed wine store application, we have provided a simple servlet client. GlassFish injects the ShoppingCart and SearchFacade session beans into the servlet to search the wines, add items to the shopping cart, and finally submit the order.

Listing 7-22 shows the code for the servlet client. To begin, the client looks up the SearchFacadeBean session bean and calls the findWineByYear() method, which returns a list of wines. In order to add wines to the shopping cart, the client program looks up the ShoppingCart session bean and calls the findCustomer() method. Once the customer has been found, the client goes into a while loop and adds the list of wines retrieved from SearchFacadeBean using the addWineItem() method in the ShoppingCart bean. To keep the client simple, the quantity of each wine is set to 20. Once the client finishes adding all of the wines to the shopping cart, the sendOrderToOPC() method in the ShoppingCart bean is called to submit the order.

The ShoppingCartClient servlet uses EJB injection to obtain the EJBs SearchFacade and ShoppingCart through their Local interfaces. This servlet performs the following steps, logging its progress by sending HTML back to the browser window:

- Initializes the sample data through a Java service façade— PopulateDemoData—that uses the JPA entities to populate the database

- Uses the stateful ShoppingCart to find an existing customer by e-mail in the sample data set and cache it in the session bean

- Uses the SearchFacade to look up the wines from 2004 using the "Wine.findByYear" JPQL named query, displays information about wines from that year, and adds 20 bottles of each to the customer's shopping cart using the addWineItem() method in the ShoppingCart bean

- Once the client finishes adding all of the wines to the shopping cart, the sendOrderToOPC() method in the ShoppingCart bean is called to submit the order

Listing 7-22 shows the servlet source.

Listing 7-22. The ShoppingCartClient.java servlet

```java
@WebServlet(name = "ShoppingCartClient", urlPatterns = {"/ShoppingCartClient"})
public class ShoppingCartClient extends HttpServlet {
  @EJB
  private SearchFacadeLocal searchFacade;
  @EJB
  private ShoppingCartLocal shoppingCart;

  /**
   * Processes requests for both HTTP
   * <code>GET</code> and
   * <code>POST</code> methods.
   *
   * @param request servlet request
   * @param response servlet response
   * @throws ServletException if a servlet-specific error occurs
   * @throws IOException if an I/O error occurs
   */
  protected void processRequest(HttpServletRequest request,
  HttpServletResponse response)
          throws ServletException, IOException {
    response.setContentType("text/html;charset=UTF-8");
    PrintWriter out = response.getWriter();
    try {
      /* TODO output your page here. You may use following sample code. */
      out.println("<html>");
      out.println("<head>");
      out.println("<title>Servlet ShoppingCartClient</title>");
      out.println("</head>");
      out.println("<body>");
      out.println("<h1>Servlet ShoppingCartClient at " + request.
      getContextPath() + "</h1>");
      out.println("</body>");
      out.println("</html>");
```

```java
      out.print("<h2>Populating Demo Data... ");
      new PopulateDemoData("Chapter07-WineAppUnit-ResourceLocal").resetData();
      out.println("done</h2>");

      out.print("<h2>Calling the ShoppingCart to find and cache customer
      with email address " +
      PopulateDemoData.TO_EMAIL_ADDRESS + "... ");
      final Customer customer = shoppingCart.findCustomer(PopulateDemoData.
      TO_EMAIL_ADDRESS);
      out.println("found " + customer.getFirstName() + " " + customer.
      getLastName() + "</h2>");

      out.println("<h2>Calling the SearchFacade to find wines from 2004</h2>");
      List<Wine> yearWineList = searchFacade.getWineFindByYear(2004);
      if (yearWineList != null) {
        for (Wine wine : yearWineList) {
          shoppingCart.addWineItem(wine, 20);
          out.println("<h3>Added cart item for 20 bottles of " + wine.
          getName() + " " + wine.
          getYear() + "</h3>");
        }
      }

      out.print("<h2>Calling the ShoppingCart to send the order to the
      Order Processing Center... ");
      shoppingCart.sendOrderToOPC();
      out.println("done</h2>");
    } catch (Exception ex) {
      ex.printStackTrace();
    } finally {
      out.close();
    }
  }

  /* HttpServlet methods */
}
```

The Servlet Output

The output from the ShoppingCartClient servlet, logging the high-level operations performed by the client, is shown in Figure 7-10:

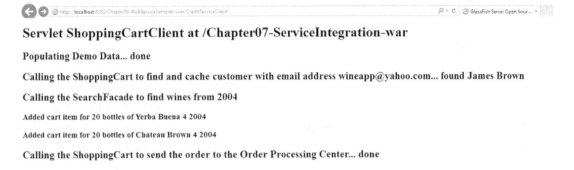

Figure 7-10. *Output from the ShoppingCartClient servlet*

The Resulting E-Mail

The servlet output shown in Figure 7-10 tells only part of the story. The servlet's work ends when the order is sent to the Order Processing Center, in the call to shoppingCart. sendOrderToOPC(). In this sample, the result of a successfully processed order is an e-mail sent from the account configured in the JavaMail session (created in Chapter 5) to the account specified in to_email_account property in the user.properties file. The e-mail that is sent using the default account information is shown in Figure 7-11.

Figure 7-11. *E-mail from wineapp@yahoo.com appearing in the wineapp account's inbox*

If no e-mail appears in the inbox of the account listed in the `to_email_address` property of the `user.properties` file, check the Spam folder for that account or look in the 'GlassFish Server' tab of the Output window in NetBeans for diagnostic information. The `Readme.txt` file in the `Chapter07-ServiceIntegration` project contains additional troubleshooting information should you need it.

Summary

In this chapter, we have covered some ways to integrate different types of EJBs, JPA entities, and Web services with resources like data sources, JMS topics, and JavaMail.

We looked at the conceptual design of our fictitious wine store application, and we laid out the design for the components and services that need to be built. We looked at individual components and services, and we demonstrated how to use different types of EJBs to solve specific application problems.

The wine store application illustrated the various parts of typical back-end applications, which included a comprehensive persistence unit that utilized a range of JPA mappings, session beans that interacted with entities in the persistence unit, MDBs, and Web services using dependency injection.

We also looked at how to inject various types of resources in session beans and MDBs and how to build asynchronicity into the application using the MDBs.

Additionally, we looked into dealing with managed and detached entities from the persistence context and integrating an asynchronous model into a typical back-end application.

Finally, we detailed steps on how you can package individual components and services into modules, assemble them into a Java EE application, and deploy them to the GlassFish server.

In the next chapter, we discuss the transactional services provided by the EJB container and explore the different types of transactional models that you can use in a variety of application architectures.

CHAPTER 8

Transaction Management

Much of the work surrounding the design and development of enterprise applications involves decisions about how to coordinate the flow of persistent data. This includes when and where to cache data, when to apply it to a persistent store (typically the database), how to resolve simultaneous attempts to access the same data, and how to resolve errors that might occur when an action occurs that violates a constraint in the database. A reliable database is capable of handling these issues at a low level—in the database tier—but these same issues can exist in the middle (application server) and client tiers as well, and typically require special application logic. For example, a database provides built-in concurrency control through pessimistic locking support, whereas an application may choose to use an optimistic locking strategy to achieve a result more optimized for performance.

One of the principal benefits of using EJB is its support for enterprise-wide services like transaction management and security control. In this chapter, we will explore how EJB offers transaction services and how you can leverage them to meet your specific requirements.

To illustrate what EJB has to offer and how to use it, we will examine a scenario from our sample Apress Wines Online application that exemplifies the aforementioned data flow issues. We will illustrate EJB's transaction support by showing ways to perform tasks that range from simple and concise to slightly more complex but more flexible. Before we dive into the examples, though, we present an overview of some of the important transaction concepts in the EJB transaction realm, including the Java Transaction API (JTA), the many flexible transaction options offered to you by the EJB container through declarative EJB metadata, and a look at how transactions are handled in the persistence tier. EJB has offered these essential transaction services since its inception, so those of you who are comfortable with these concepts can skip ahead to the example section to see how they manifest themselves in an EJB world involving the Java Persistence API (JPA).

© Jonathan Wetherbee, Massimo Nardone, Chirag Rathod, and Raghu Kodali 2018
J. Wetherbee et al., *Beginning EJB in Java EE 8*, https://doi.org/10.1007/978-1-4842-3573-7_8

What Is a Transaction?

In this section, we will explore the following questions:

- What is a transaction, and why is it important to enterprise applications?

- What are the core ACID (atomicity, consistency, isolation, durability) properties that define a robust and reliable transaction?

- What is JTA, what is a distributed transaction, and what is two-phase commit?

A transaction is a group of operations that must be performed as a unit. These operations can be synchronous or asynchronous and can involve persisting data objects, sending e-mail, validating credit cards, and many other events. A classic example is a banking transfer, in which one operation debits funds from one account (i.e., updates a record in a database table), and another operation credits those same funds to another account (updates another row in that same, or a different, database table). From the perspective of an external application querying both accounts, there must never be a time when these funds can be seen in both accounts. Nor can a moment exist when the funds can be seen in neither account. Only when both operations in this transaction have been successfully performed can the changes be visible from another application context. A group of operations that must be performed together in this way, as a unit, is known as a transaction.

The operations in a transaction are performed sequentially or in parallel, typically over a (relatively short) period of time. After they are all performed, the transaction is applied, or committed. If an error or other invalid condition arises during the course of a transaction, the transaction may be cancelled, or rolled back, and the operations that had thus far been performed under that transaction context are undone.

Distributed Transactions

When the operations in a transaction are performed across databases or other resources that reside on separate computers or processes, this is known as a distributed transaction. Such enterprise-wide transactions require special coordination between the resources involved, and they can be extremely difficult to program reliably. This is where JTA comes in, providing the interface that resources can implement and bind to, to participate in a distributed transaction.

The EJB container is a transaction manager that supports JTA, and so it can participate in distributed transactions involving other EJB containers as well as third-party JTA resources, like many database management systems (DBMSs). This takes the complexity of coordinating distributed transactions off the shoulders of business application developers, so that they are free to integrate loosely coupled services and distribute their data across the enterprise however they choose. In addition, as you will see in the following sections, EJB allows developers to choose whether to demarcate transactions explicitly—with calls to begin, commit, or roll back (cancel) a transaction—or to allow the EJB container to automatically perform transaction demarcation along EJB method boundaries.

The ACID Properties of a Transaction

No, not the electric Kool-Aid kind. Transactions come in all shapes and sizes and can involve synchronous and asynchronous operations, but they all have some core features in common, known as their ACID components. ACID refers to the four characteristics that define a robust and reliable transaction: atomicity, consistency, isolation, and durability. Table 8-1 describes these four components.

Table 8-1. *The ACID Properties of a Transaction*

Feature	Description
Atomicity	A transaction is composed of one or more operations that are performed as a group, known as a unit of work. Atomicity ensures that at the conclusion of the transaction, these operations are either all performed successfully (a successful commit), or none of them are performed at all (a successful rollback). At the end of a transaction, atomicity would be violated if some, but not all, of the operations completed.
Consistency	A consistent transaction has data integrity. Consistency ensures that at the conclusion of the transaction, the data is left in a consistent state, so that database constraints or logical validation rules are not left in violation.
Isolation	Transaction isolation specifies that the outside world is not able to see the intermediate state of a transaction. Outside programs viewing the data objects involved in a transaction must not see the modified data objects until after the transaction has been committed. Transaction isolation is a complex science in itself, and it is largely beyond the scope of this discussion, but suffice it to say that EJB server providers typically offer configurable isolation settings that let you choose the degree to which resources within a transaction's scope can see each other's pending changes, and changes that were committed externally but during the course of the context transaction (dirty reads). There is no standard isolation setting, so portable applications should not rely on a particular configuration in their runtime environment.
Durability	Transactions that are performed correctly are permanent and cannot be affected by any failure of the system. Committing the data into a relational database, in which the results may subsequently be queried, typically achieves this requirement.

Naturally, EJB addresses all these requirements, and we will point out how each one is handled in the examples that follow.

The Java Transaction API (JTA)

JTA defines an interface for clients and transaction-aware resource managers to participate in fault-tolerant distributed transactions. EJB automatically binds to these services, so both clients and enterprise beans can conveniently participate in distributed programming without having to explicitly code logic such as the two-phase commit protocol. The primary interface for an EJB into its JTA transaction is through the `javax.transaction.UserTransaction` object interface instantiated by the EJB container and made available either through injection into the enterprise bean class or through a Java Naming and Directory Interface (JNDI) lookup.

The Two-Phase Commit Protocol

If you have programmed logic using relational databases, you may be familiar with the two-phase commit protocol. This strategy gives veto authority to resource managers participating in a distributed transaction, notifying them through a "prepare" command that a commit is about to be issued, and allowing them to declare whether they can apply their changes. Only if all resource managers indicate through unanimous consent that they are prepared to apply their changes does the final word come down from the transaction manager to actually apply the changes. Typically, resource managers perform the bulk of the changes during the "prepare" step, so the final "commit" step is trivial to execute. This reduces the likelihood that errors will occur during the "commit" step. Robust transaction managers and resource managers are capable of handling even this eventuality.

Transaction Support in EJB

This section will explore the following questions:

- What transaction services are available to enterprise bean developers?

- How do session beans, message-driven beans (MDBs), and entities interact in a transactional context?

Much of the infrastructure in the EJB server is dedicated to supporting these services, and for good reason. Not only does EJB provide a robust JTA transaction manager, it makes it accessible through declarative metadata that can be specified on interoperable, portable business components. Virtually all Java EE applications require transaction services, and EJB brings them to the application developer in a very slick package.

From its inception, the EJB framework has provided a convenient way to manage transactions and access control by letting you define the behavior declaratively on a method-by-method basis. Beyond these container-provided services, EJB lets you turn control over to your application to define transaction event boundaries and other custom behavior.

In this chapter, we look at the role transactions play in accomplishing a range of common tasks in your application. In a typical Java EE application, session beans typically serve to establish the boundaries of a transaction and manipulate entities to interact with the database in the transactional context. Our examples mix session bean and entity operations to illustrate both the built-in (declarative) and manual behavior provided by EJB. In the spirit of the simplified development model, EJB provides a lot of its most useful features by default, so it should come as no surprise that the default transaction options are both useful and powerful.

EJB Transaction Services

The EJB transaction model is built on this JTA model, in which session beans or other application clients provide the transactional context in which enterprise services are performed as a logical unit of work. Enterprise services in the Java EE environment that typically operate in a transactional context include creating, retrieving, updating, and deleting entities; sending JMS messages to the queue; executing MDBs; firing e-mail requests; invoking Web services; executing JDBC operations; and much more.

EJB provides a built-in JTA transaction manager, but the real power lies in the declarative services that EJB offers to bean providers. Using metadata tags instead of programmatic logic, EJB developers can seamlessly participate in JTA transactions and declaratively control the transactional behavior of each business method on an enterprise bean.

EJB extends this programming model by providing explicit support for both JTA transactions and non-JTA (resource-local) transactions. Resource-local transactions are restricted to a single resource manager, such as a database connection, but may result in a performance optimization by avoiding the overhead of a distributed transaction monitor.

In addition, application builders may leverage the container-provided services for automatically managing transactions, or they may choose to take control of the transaction boundaries and handle the transaction begin, commit, and rollback events explicitly. Within a single application, both approaches may be used, in combination if desired. Whereas the choice of whether to have the container or the application itself demarcate transactions is defined on the enterprise bean, the decision of which type of transaction model to use with JPA entities—JTA or resource-local—is determined by how the persistence unit is configured in the persistence.xml file.

The persistent objects in the game—the entities—are entirely, and happily, unaware of their governing transaction framework. The transactional context in which an entity operates is not part of its definition, and so the same entity class may be used in whatever transactional context the application chooses, provided an appropriate EntityManager is created to service the entity's lifecycle events.

If all of this seems a little daunting at this point, fear not. It will all make sense once we walk through some examples in code that demonstrate how all the pieces work together. It is also worth noting that EJB's built-in Container-Managed Transaction (CMT) support is more than adequate for most applications running inside the EJB container. This chapter will let you explore your options—but unless you are writing applications involving entities that live wholly outside of the EJB container, the default support is likely to serve your needs quite nicely.

Session Bean Transactional Behavior in the Service Model

This next section will explore the following questions:

- What declarative transaction support does the EJB container offer to session beans?

- What is the difference between container-managed transaction (CMT) demarcation and bean-managed transaction (BMT) demarcation? When would you choose one approach over the other?

- What are CMT attributes?

- How does EJB support the explicit demarcation of transaction boundaries using bean-managed transaction (BMT) beans?

- What is implicit vs. explicit commit behavior?

The enterprise bean is the heart of the EJB service layer. Through session beans, the EJB container offers declarative demarcation of transaction events, along with the option to demarcate transaction events explicitly in the bean or in the application client code. Let's consider these two approaches separately, beginning with the default option: leveraging container-managed transaction demarcation using declarative markup.

Container-Managed Transaction (CMT) Demarcation

The EJB container provides built-in transaction management services that are available by default to session beans and MDBs. The bean designates transaction characteristics for each of its methods through metadata (using either annotations or XML), and the EJB container follows those directives to determine the transactional action (if any) to perform. Using these directives, the EJB container may automatically begin a new transaction, or suspend or reuse an existing transaction when the method is invoked, and possibly commit the transaction before the method returns to the caller.

Note   Only the bean developer may assign the transaction management type of an enterprise bean. Application assemblers are permitted to override the bean's method-level container-managed transaction attributes through the `ejb-jar.xml` file, but they must use caution to avoid the possibility of deadlock. Application assemblers and deployers are generally not permitted to override the bean's transaction management type.

When an EJB declares its transactional behavior in metadata, the container interposes on calls to the enterprise bean's methods and applies transactional behavior at the session bean's method boundaries, providing a fixed set of options that you can specify for each method. The default behavior provided by the container (i.e., when no other directive is specified) is to check, immediately before invoking the method, whether a transaction context is associated with the current thread. If no transaction context is available, the container begins a new transaction before executing the method. If a transaction is available, the container allows that transaction to be propagated to the method call and made available to the method code. Then, upon returning from the method invocation, the container checks again. If the container was responsible for creating a new transaction context, it automatically commits that transaction after the method is exited. If it didn't create the transaction, then it allows the transaction to continue unaffected. By interposing on the bean's method calls, the EJB container is able to apply transactional behavior at runtime that was specified declaratively at development time.

The default behavior, described in the previous paragraph, is but one of six CMT demarcation options provided by the container. You can attribute any one of these six demarcation options to any method on a session bean. Some of the attribute values require specific conditions to be met; when they are not met, an exception is thrown. These six attributes are listed in Table 8-2.

Table 8-2. *Container Transaction Attribute Definitions*

Transaction Attribute	Behavior
MANDATORY	A transaction must be in effect at the time the method is called. If no transaction is available, a `javax.ejb.EJBTransactionRequired` exception is thrown. This transaction remains in effect while the method is executed, and it is left active upon returning control to the caller.
REQUIRED	This is the default transaction attribute value. Upon entering the method, the container interposes to create a new transaction context if one is not already available. If the container created a transaction upon entering the method, it commits that transaction when the method call completes. If a transaction was already in effect, the container does not commit it before returning control to the client.
REQUIRES_NEW	The container always creates a new transaction before executing a method thusly marked. If a transaction context is already available when the method is invoked, then the container suspends that transaction by dissociating it from the current thread before creating the new transaction. The container then reassociates the original transaction with the current thread after committing the intervening one.
SUPPORTS	This option is basically a no-op, resulting in no additional work by the container. If a transaction context is available, it is used by the method. If no transaction context is available, then the container invokes the method with no transaction context. Upon exiting the method, any preexisting transaction context remains in effect.
NOT_SUPPORTED	The container invokes the method with an unspecified transaction context. If a transaction context is available when the method is called, then the container dissociates the transaction from the current thread before invoking the method, and then it reassociates the transaction with the thread upon returning from the method.
NEVER	The method must not be invoked with a transaction context. The container will not create one before calling the method, and if one is already in effect, the container throws `javax.ejb.EJBException`.

Note   In general, transaction attributes may be specified on a session bean's business interface methods or Web service endpoint interface, or on an MDB's listener method, but some additional restrictions apply for specific cases. Such details are beyond the scope of this book but may be found in the EJB *Core Contracts and Requirements* spec.

All six attributes are typically available for session bean methods, though certain attributes are not available on a session timeout callback method, or when the session bean implements javax.ejb.SessionSynchronization. MDBs support only the REQUIRED and NOT_SUPPORTED attributes. Here is an example of how you would specify the transaction behavior on a session bean method to override the transaction behavior specified (or defaulted) at the bean level:

```
@TransactionAttribute(TransactionAttributeType.SUPPORTS)
public CustomerOrder createCustomerOrderUsingSupports(Customer customer)
  throws Exception { ... }
```

Table 8-3 illustrates an EJB's transactional behavior, dependent on its transaction attribute and the presence or absence of a transactional context at the time the session method is called. For each transaction attribute, we list on separate rows the method body and resource transactional context when a client transaction is absent (None), and when a client transaction is present (Tc). Whenever a new transaction is created for the duration of the method (Tm), it is always committed by the EJB container before control is returned to the caller. Both the transaction associated with the method body code and the transaction associated with resources that are used by the method are shown.

Table 8-3. *Client and Bean Transaction States for Each of the Six Transaction Attributes*

Transaction Attribute	Client's Transaction	Transaction Associated with Business Method	Transaction Associated with Resource Managers
MANDATORY	None	Error	N/A
	Tc	Tc	Tc
NEVER	None	None	None
	Tc	Error	N/A
NOT_SUPPORTED	None	None	None
	Tc	None	None
REQUIRED	None	Tm	Tm
	Tc	Tc	Tc
REQUIRES_NEW	None	Tm	Tm
	Tc	Tm	Tm
SUPPORTS	None	None	None
	Tc	Tc	Tc

Table 8-3 illustrates how the container interposes on CMT-demarcated methods to propagate a transactional context differently for each transaction attribute. This table also illustrates that the transactional context used within the bean method is always the one that is in turn propagated to other methods called by that CMT bean method. Note that a client to an enterprise bean may itself be another enterprise bean.

The EJBContext.setRollbackOnly and getRollbackOnly Methods

In the event that an exception or other error condition is encountered in a method on a CMT-demarcated enterprise bean, the bean may wish to prevent the context transaction from being committed.

The `MessageDrivenContext` methods can be used, in the following ways, whenever we use container-managed transactions:

- `setRollbackOnly`: This method can be used for error handling.

- `getRollbackOnly`: This method can be used to test whether the current transaction has been marked for rollback.

The bean is not allowed to roll back the transaction explicitly, but it may obtain the `javax.ejb.EJBContext` resource (through container injection or JNDI lookup) and call its `setRollbackOnly()` method to ensure that the container will not commit the transaction. Similarly, a bean method may at any time call the `EJBContext.getRollbackOnly()` method to determine whether the current transaction has been marked for rollback, whether by the current bean or by another bean or resource associated with the current transaction.

Bean-Managed Transaction (BMT) Demarcation

For some enterprise beans, the declarative CMT services may not provide the demarcation granularity that they require. For instance, a client may wish to call multiple methods on a session bean without having each method commit its work upon completion. In this case, the client has several options: it can either instantiate its own JTA (or resource-local) transaction and thus control the transaction begin/end boundaries explicitly; it can write a custom CMT session bean to wrap the work inside a transactional bean method and perform the steps inside the container-managed transaction; or it can control the transaction demarcation explicitly by using a transaction resource available through the EJB context.

EJB offers the latter option—known as bean-managed transaction (BMT) support to enterprise beans as a convenient way to handle their demarcation of transaction events. To turn off the automatic CMT demarcation services, enterprise beans simply specify the `@TransactionManagement(TransactionManagementType.BEAN)` annotation or assign the equivalent metadata to the session bean in the `ejb-jar.xml` file. With BMT demarcation, the EJB container still provides the transaction support to the bean, through a `UserTransaction` object available through the bean's `EJBContext` object. The primary difference is that the bean code makes explicit calls to begin, commit, and roll back transactions instead of using CMT attributes to declaratively assign transactional behavior to its methods. The container does not interpose on BMT methods to begin and commit transactions, and it does not propagate transactions begun by a client to beans that elect to demarcate their own transactions. While any given enterprise bean must choose one plan or the other (CMT vs. BMT demarcation) for its methods, both types of beans may interact with each other within a single transaction context.

To demarcate transactions, an enterprise bean obtains an EJBContext (that is, SessionContext for a session bean, or MessageDrivenContext for an MDB) resource through injection:

```
@Resource
SessionContext sessionContext;
```

and then acquires a JTA javax.transaction.UserTransaction instance through this resource:

```
UserTransaction txn = sessionContext.getUserTransaction();
```

This EJB container-provided UserTransaction interface provides begin(), commit(), and rollback() transaction demarcation methods to the bean. Similarly, non–enterprise bean clients may acquire a UserTransaction resource from a JTA server other than the EJB container to demarcate transactions from an application client environment, or they may use a non-JTA resource-local EntityTransaction obtained through an EntityManager (see below). Regardless of how they begin a transaction, though, it becomes the transaction in context when they invoke a session bean method, and the rules from Table 8-3 apply.

In the example we will examine shortly, a stateful session bean using an EXTENDED persistence context and BMT demarcation initiates a transaction in one method that is then propagated to subsequent method calls until the transaction is finally committed in a separate method. This behavior could not be specified with the same method structure by calling these methods separately on a CMT session bean, although it would be possible to achieve the same results by wrapping these separate calls inside a single CMT-demarcated custom method on a CMT session bean.

Note   How does the EJB server wire up a transaction context? You may be curious as to how the EJB server is able to automatically enlist database connections, and other resources obtained programmatically inside an enterprise bean, with the transaction context. Since the EJB server is providing the context for executing bean methods, it is able to interpose on these requests and perform this side-effect logic without interrupting the flow of execution within the method. That is, it intercepts the method invocation before it is performed; does some extra work (like checking the state of the transaction context, possibly creating a new transaction, and associating the enterprise bean with that context); and then invokes the bean method. Upon returning from the bean method invocation, it again has an opportunity to perform extra logic, such as committing the transaction that was created when the method was called, before returning control to the client that invoked the bean method in the first place.

When we use bean-managed transactions, the delivery of a message to the onMessage method takes place outside the JTA transaction context.

The transaction will:

- begin when we call the `UserTransaction.begin` method within the onMessage method, and

- end when we call `UserTransaction.commit` or `UserTransaction.rollback`.

Notice that any call to the `Connection.createSession` method should take place within the transaction.

Implicit Commit vs. Explicit Commit

When using CMT, the container requires that any transaction that it begins when a method is called will be concluded when the method returns to the caller. This is known as implicit commit behavior, or sometimes referred to as auto-commit behavior. The container must enforce this rule or run the risk of losing track of the transaction as control passes up the process stack. While you can still use the container-managed transactions with CMT to allow multiple methods to be called within a single transaction, you must do this by wrapping your method calls within an outer container-managed method. From the perspective of a client, this still appears to be a single method call, to the wrapper method.

When using BMT with stateful session beans, you have the flexibility to achieve an explicit commit model, where the bean or the client can control the beginning and end of a transaction and call multiple methods explicitly during that time before concluding with an explicit call to commit or roll back the work. This puts the burden on the client, or on the bean developer, to ensure that transactions are not left dangling. With proper care, however, this is a powerful tool when the application requires this behavior. As mentioned earlier, EJB provides a built-in transaction for session beans and MDBs to use for this–the `javax.transaction.UserTransaction`–which the bean can access through its injected `javax.ejb.EJBContext` property (as either a `SessionContext` or a `MessageDrivenContext` instance).

We will further explore both implicit and explicit commit behavior in the sample app at the end of this chapter.

Using Transactions with JPA Entities

This section will discuss the following questions:

- How are transactions managed in the persistence layer?

- What options does the persistence framework offer for controlling transactions involving entities?

- What is the role of the persistence context in a transaction?

- How do entities become associated with, and dissociated from, a transactional context?

If you recall from Chapter 3, a persistence unit defines a set of entity classes, and a persistence context is a managed set of entity instances from a single persistence unit. At any point in time, across multiple applications executing in an application server, many persistence contexts may be actively associated with any given persistence unit, but each persistence context is associated with, at most, one transaction context.

Relationship Between Entities and a Transaction Context

From the preceding discussion about how the EJB server acts as a transaction coordinator in associating resources with a transaction context, you may have realized that the persistence context is the resource that gets associated with a transaction.

In this way, a persistence context is propagated through method calls so that entities in a persistence unit can see each other's intermediate state, through their common persistence context, whenever they are associated with the same transaction context. Also, the restriction that only one persistence context for any given persistence unit must be associated with a given transaction context ensures that for any entity of type T with identity I, its state will be represented by only one persistence context within any transaction context.

Within an application thread, only one transaction context is available at any moment, but the EJB server is free to dissociate one persistence context from that thread and associate a new persistence context for the same persistence unit to satisfy transaction isolation boundaries. When the EJB server does this, the newly instantiated persistence context is not able to see the intermediate changes made to any entities associated with the suspended persistence context.

Container-Managed vs. Application-Managed Persistence Context

The persistence services in EJB let you opt out of container-managed persistence contexts altogether and manage the life cycles of your persistence context explicitly within your application code. When an `EntityManager` instance is injected (or acquired through JNDI), it comes in as a container-managed persistence context. The container automatically associates container-managed persistence contexts with any transaction that happens to be in context at the time that the `EntityManager` is used, and it destroys the persistence context when the transaction concludes (with one caveat—see extended persistence contexts, below). Should an application wish to control how or whether its persistence contexts are associated with transactions, and whether it survives past transactional boundaries, it may obtain an `EntityManagerFactory` (again, through container injection or JNDI lookup) and explicitly create the `EntityManager` instances that manage their persistence contexts. An application-managed persistence context is used when the `EntityManager` is obtained through an `EntityManagerFactory`—a requirement when running outside the Java EE container. For more information on using an application-managed `EntityManager` outside of a Java EE container, as in a pure Java SE environment, please see Chapter 4.

Transaction-Scoped Persistence Context vs. Extended Persistence Context

A persistence context that is created when a transaction is created, and destroyed when the transaction ends, is known as a transaction-scoped persistence context. This is the behavior of persistence contexts associated with all EntityManagers used on a stateless session bean.

For stateful session beans, there exists a special form of container-managed EntityManager that is not bound to the life of a transaction, but it is instead bound to the life of a stateful session bean itself. This is known as an extended `EntityManager`, and it behaves much like an application-managed persistence context but the EJB container conveniently manages its life cycle. Because an extended persistence context is not destroyed at the conclusion of each transaction as is a transaction-scoped persistence context, entities can remain in a managed state even after they have been synchronized with the database. In some cases, this avoids the need to re-query them or otherwise obtain a managed instance if you wish to continue working with them after a commit. In a conversational environment, such as a Web application, this can be very useful. An extended persistence context stays open until its context stateful session bean is destroyed. Only stateful session beans may use extended persistence contexts. At the time an `EntityManager` instance is created, its persistence context type is defined, and it may not be changed during the `EntityManagers` lifetime. The default type is transaction scoped; to inject an `EntityManager` by specifying an extended persistence context, you may specify the injection directive with the following:

```
@PersistenceContext(unitName="WineAppUnit", type = PersistenceContextType.
EXTENDED)
private EntityManager em;
```

or you may define a `persistence-context-ref` element in the XML descriptor.

In the transaction examples at the end of this chapter, we will compare the behavior of a stateless session bean using a transaction-scoped persistence context with a stateful session bean that uses an extended persistence context.

JTA vs. Resource-Local EntityManagers

An EntityManager may be defined to participate in either a JTA transaction or a
non-JTA (resource-local) transaction. The features of JTA—most notably, support for
distributed transactions—have been described previously, along with usage of the bean's
interface to a JTA transaction, javax.transaction.UserTransaction. Resource-local
EntityManagers service transactions using the javax.persistence.EntityTransaction
interface available to clients through the EntityManager.getEntityTransaction()
method. This interface exposes the expected transaction demarcation methods begin(),
commit(), and rollback(), along with getRollbackOnly() and setRollbackOnly()
methods that are equivalent to the EJBContext and UserTransaction methods available
to enterprise beans described previously, and an isActive() method to indicate
whether a transaction is currently in progress.

Container-managed EntityManagers must be JTA EntityManagers. Application-
managed EntityManagers may be either JTA or resource-local, but they may only be JTA
EntityManagers if the EntityManager resides in the Java EE environment.

One reason you might want to use a resource-local EntityManager is that while JTA
provides the infrastructure for distributed transactions, resource-local transactions can
provide a performance optimization by eliminating the overhead of this infrastructure.
Another reason is you may wish to use your JPA entities in a stand-alone Java SE
environment where JTA or/or data-source resources are not supported.

We will examine use of the EntityTransaction when we dissect a Java façade in the
sample application later in this chapter.

Two Sample Scenarios

The following two sample scenarios use the entities in the persistence unit defined for
the Wines Online application, which we examined in Chapter 7. The first scenario uses
a stateless CMT session bean, leveraging the declarative transaction services provided
by the EJB container. The second scenario shows how transactions can be managed
explicitly by both the bean and the client when using a stateful BMT session bean. At
the end of this chapter you will find step-by-step instructions for building, deploying,
and testing these samples in GlassFish using NetBeans. For now, we will examine the
source files and discuss the different ways EJB and JPA can interact in a transactional
environment.

Stateless Session Beans with CMT Demarcation

We begin with a default, straightforward, implementation of a stateless session bean, OrderProcessorCMTBean.java (shown in Listing 8-1). This session bean uses CMT demarcation to leverage EJB's declarative transaction support. It is followed by a simple servlet client, OrderProcessorCMTClient.java (shown in Listing 8-2).

Listing 8-1. OrderProcessorCMTBean.java, a Stateless Session Bean Using CMT Demarcation

```java
@Stateless(name = "OrderProcessorCMT", mappedName = "Chapter08-
TransactionSamples-OrderProcessorCMT")
public class OrderProcessorCMTBean {
  @Resource
  SessionContext sessionContext;
  @PersistenceContext(unitName = "Chapter08-TransactionSamples-JTA")
  private EntityManager em;

  /**
   * Remove any existing Customers with email 'wineapp@yahoo.com' and any
     existing Wine with
   * country 'United States'. The EJB container will ensure that this work
     is performed in
   * a transactional context.
   */
  public String initialize() {
    StringBuffer strBuf = new StringBuffer();
    strBuf.append("Removed ");
    int i = 0;

    // Filter the data by removing any existing Customers with email
    // 'wineapp@yahoo.com' (or whatever is defined in the user.properties file).
    for (Customer customer :
        getCustomerFindByEmail(PopulateDemoData.TO_EMAIL_ADDRESS)) {
      em.remove(customer);
      i++;
    }
```

```java
    strBuf.append(i);
    strBuf.append(" Customer(s) and ");

    //  Remove any existing Wine with country 'United States'
    i = 0;
    for (Wine wine : getWineFindByCountry("United States")) {
      em.remove(wine);
      i++;
    }
    strBuf.append(i);
    strBuf.append(" Wine(s)");
    return strBuf.toString();
  }

  /**
   * Create a new CustomerOrder from the items in a Customer's cart.
     Creates a new CustomerOrder
   * entity, and then creates a new OrderItem entity for each CartItem
     found in the Customer's cart.
   *
   * Using CMT w/ the default REQUIRED xaction attribute, if this method is
     invoked without a
   * transaction context, a new transaction will be created by the EJB
     container upon invoking the
   * method, and committed upon successfully completing the method.
   *
   * @return a status message (plain text)
   */
  public CustomerOrder createCustomerOrder(Customer customer) {
    return createCustomerOrderUsingSupports(customer);
  }

  @TransactionAttribute(TransactionAttributeType.SUPPORTS)
  public CustomerOrder createCustomerOrderUsingSupports(Customer customer)
{

    if (customer == null) {
```

```
      throw new IllegalArgumentException("OrderProcessingBean.
      createCustomerOrder(): Customer not specified");
    }

    if (!em.contains(customer)) {
      customer = em.merge(customer);
    }

    final CustomerOrder customerOrder = new CustomerOrder();
    customer.addCustomerOrder(customerOrder);

    final Timestamp orderDate = new Timestamp(System.currentTimeMillis());
    final List<CartItem> cartItemList =
            new ArrayList(customer.getCartItemList());
    for (CartItem cartItem : cartItemList) {
      //  Create a new OrderItem for this CartItem
      final OrderItem orderItem = new OrderItem();
      orderItem.setOrderDate(orderDate);
      orderItem.setPrice(cartItem.getWine().getRetailPrice());
      orderItem.setQuantity(cartItem.getQuantity());
      orderItem.setStatus("Order Created");
      orderItem.setWine(cartItem.getWine());
      customerOrder.addOrderItem(orderItem);

      //  Remove the CartItem
      customer.removeCartItem(cartItem);
    }

    return persistEntity(customerOrder);
  }

  public <T> T persistEntity(T entity) {
    em.persist(entity);
    return entity;
  }

  public <T> T mergeEntity(T entity) {
    return em.merge(entity);
  }
```

```java
  public <T> void removeEntity(T entity) {
    em.remove(em.merge(entity));
  }

  public <T> List<T> findAll(Class<T> entityClass) {
    CriteriaQuery cq = em.getCriteriaBuilder().createQuery();
    cq.select(cq.from(entityClass));
    return em.createQuery(cq).getResultList();
  }

  public <T> List<T> findAllByRange(Class<T> entityClass, int[] range) {
    CriteriaQuery cq = em.getCriteriaBuilder().createQuery();
    cq.select(cq.from(entityClass));
    Query q = em.createQuery(cq);
    q.setMaxResults(range[1] - range[0]);
    q.setFirstResult(range[0]);
    return q.getResultList();
  }

  /**
   * <code>select o from Customer o where o.email = :email</code>
   */
  @TransactionAttribute(TransactionAttributeType.NOT_SUPPORTED)
  public List<Customer> getCustomerFindByEmail(String email) {
    return em.createNamedQuery("Customer.findByEmail", Customer.class).
    setParameter("email", email).getResultList();
  }

  /**
   * <code>select object(wine) from Wine wine where wine.country =
:country</code>
   */
  @TransactionAttribute(TransactionAttributeType.NOT_SUPPORTED)
  public List<Wine> getWineFindByCountry(String country) {
    return em.createNamedQuery("Wine.findByCountry", Wine.class).
    setParameter("country", country).getResultList();
  }
}
```

Listing 8-2. OrderProcessorCMTClient.java, a Servlet That Drives the
OrderProcessorCMT Session Bean

```java
@WebServlet(name = "OrderProcessorCMTClient", urlPatterns = {"/
OrderProcessorCMTClient"})
public class OrderProcessorCMTClient extends HttpServlet {
  @EJB
  OrderProcessorCMTBean orderProcessorCMT;

  /**
   * Processes requests for both HTTP
   * <code>GET</code> and
   * <code>POST</code> methods.
   *
   * @param request servlet request
   * @param response servlet response
   * @throws ServletException if a servlet-specific error occurs
   * @throws IOException if an I/O error occurs
   */
  protected void processRequest(HttpServletRequest request,
  HttpServletResponse response)
          throws ServletException, IOException {
    response.setContentType("text/html;charset=UTF-8");
    response.setContentType("text/html;charset=UTF-8");
    OutputStream rOut = response.getOutputStream();
    PrintStream out = new PrintStream(rOut);
    try {
      /* TODO output your page here. You may use following sample code. */
      out.println("<html>");
      out.println("<head>");
      out.println("<title>Servlet OrderProcessorCMTClient</title>");
      out.println("</head>");
      out.println("<body>");
      out.println("<h1>Servlet OrderProcessorCMTClient at " + request.
      getContextPath() + "</h1>");
      out.println("</body>");
```

```
out.println("</html>");

//  Create and persist a bunch of JPA entities, populating the
    database with data
out.print("<h2>Populating Demo Data... ");
PopulateDemoData.resetData("Chapter07-WineAppUnit-ResourceLocal",
System.out);
out.println("done</h2>");

//  Filter the data by removing any existing Customers with email
//  'wineapp@yahoo.com' (or whatever is defined in the user.
    properties file).
//  The first call to a transactional method on OrderProcessorBMT
    will begin a
//  transaction.
out.print("<h2>Filtering Demo Data... ");
System.out.println(orderProcessorCMT.initialize());
out.println("done</h2>");

//  Create a Customer and add some CartItems and their associated Wines
Individual customer = new Individual();
customer.setFirstName("Transaction");
customer.setLastName("Head");
customer.setEmail(PopulateDemoData.TO_EMAIL_ADDRESS);
for (int i = 0; i < 5; i++) {
  final Wine wine = new Wine();
  wine.setCountry("United States");
  wine.setDescription("Delicious wine");
  wine.setName("Xacti");
  wine.setRegion("Dry Creek Valley");
  wine.setRetailPrice(new Float(20.00D + i));
  wine.setVarietal("Zinfandel");
  wine.setYear(2000 + i);
  orderProcessorCMT.persistEntity(wine);

  final CartItem cartItem = new CartItem();
  cartItem.setCreatedDate(new Timestamp(System.currentTimeMillis()));
```

```
      cartItem.setCustomer(customer);
      cartItem.setQuantity(12);
      cartItem.setWine(wine);

      customer.addCartItem(cartItem);
    }

    //  Persist the Customer, relying on the cascade settings to persist all
    //  related Wine and CartItem entities as well. After the call, the
       Customer
    //  instance will have an ID value that was assigned by the EJB container
    //  when it was persisted.
    orderProcessorCMT.persistEntity(customer);

    //  Create a customer order and create OrderItems from the CartItems
    final CustomerOrder customerOrder =
      orderProcessorCMT.createCustomerOrder(customer);

    out.print("<h2>Retrieving Customer Order Items... ");
    for (OrderItem orderItem: customerOrder.getOrderItemList()) {
      final Wine wine = orderItem.getWine();
      out.println(wine.getName() + " with ID " + wine.getId());
    }
    out.println("done</h2>");
  } finally {
    rOut.close();
    out.close();
  }
}

/*  HttpServlet Methods */
}
```

Transaction Analysis

The following sections will analyze this test run from a transaction perspective.

Populating Test Data Through a Transactional Java Façade

The servlet client begins by wiping the slate clean. The client of a CMT bean does not create transactions, or otherwise concern itself with transactional details. It delegates all work to the CMT session bean and (indirectly to) a Java façade, and relies on them to perform their work in a transactional context. The client first calls the PopulateDemoData class from the Chapter 7 sample application, which is a helper class that delegates to a Java façade that uses an application-managed EntityManager, to reset the demo data to prepare for a new test run. We offer this example first, to see a raw use of transactions in an application-managed EntityManager context. We will examine EJB session bean behavior in a moment.

```
//  Create and persist a bunch of JPA entities, populating the database
with data
out.print("<h2>Populating Demo Data... ");
PopulateDemoData.resetData("Chapter07-WineAppUnit-ResourceLocal", System.out);
out.println("done</h2>");
```

The PopulateDemoData class is shown in Listing 8-3:

Listing 8-3. PopulateDemoData.java, a utility class resets the sample data by delegating to a transactional Java façade over JPA entities

```
public class PopulateDemoData {
  public static final String FROM_EMAIL_ADDRESS;
  public static final String TO_EMAIL_ADDRESS;

  static {
    Properties properties = new Properties();
    InputStream is = null;
    try {
      is = PopulateDemoData.class.getClassLoader().getResourceAsStream
      ("user.properties");
      properties.load(is);
      FROM_EMAIL_ADDRESS = properties.getProperty("from_email_address");
      TO_EMAIL_ADDRESS = properties.getProperty("to_email_address");
    } catch (IOException e) {
      throw new RuntimeException(e);
```

```
    } finally {
      if (is != null) {
        try {
          is.close();
        } catch (IOException ex) {

          Logger.getLogger(PopulateDemoData.class.getName()).log(Level.
          SEVERE, null, ex);
        }
      }
    }
  }

  private JavaServiceFacade facade;

  public static void main(String[] args) {
    PopulateDemoData.resetData("Chapter07-WineAppUnit-ResourceLocal",
    System.out);
  }

  public static void resetData(String persistenceUnit, PrintStream out) {
    PopulateDemoData pdd = null;
    try {
      pdd = new PopulateDemoData(persistenceUnit);

      out.println("Reporting existing data...");
      pdd.showDataCount(out);

      out.println("Removing data...");
      pdd.removeAllDemoData(out);

      out.println("Reporting data after removal...");
      pdd.showDataCount(out);

      out.println("Populating data...");
      pdd.populateDemoCustomer();
      pdd.populateWines();

      out.println("Reporting final data...");
```

```
      pdd.showDataCount(out);
    } finally {
      if (pdd != null) {
        pdd.releaseEntityManager();
      }
    }
  }

  private PopulateDemoData(String persistenceUnit) {
    facade = new JavaServiceFacade(persistenceUnit);
  }

  private void removeAllDemoData(PrintStream out) {
    removeAll(OrderItem.class, out);
    removeAll(CustomerOrder.class, out);
    removeAll(Individual.class, out);
    removeAll(Distributor.class, out);
    removeAll(Supplier.class, out);
    removeAll(InventoryItem.class, out);
    removeAll(CartItem.class, out);
    removeAll(Wine.class, out);
  }

  private <T> void removeAll(Class<T> entityClass, PrintStream out) {
    int i = 0;
    for (T entity : facade.findAll(entityClass)) {
      facade.removeEntity(entity);
    }
    out.println("Removed " + i + " " + entityClass.getSimpleName() + " instances");
  }

  private Customer populateDemoCustomer() {
    Address a = new Address("Redwood Shores", "CA", "200 Oracle Pkwy",
    null, "94065");
    Individual i = new Individual("James", "Brown", "800.888.8000",
    TO_EMAIL_ADDRESS, a, a, "04/14", "123");
    facade.persistEntity(i);
```

```
    return i;
  }

  private InventoryItem populateWines() {
    InventoryItem ii = null;
    for (int i = 0; i < 6; i++) {
      Wine w = new Wine("USA", "Fine Wine - ranked #" + i, "Yerba Buena " +
      i, 90, "Napa Valley", new Float(10 + i), "Zinfandel", 2000 + i);
      facade.persistEntity(w);
      ii = new InventoryItem(10 + i, w, new java.util.Date(System.
      currentTimeMillis()), new Float(1 + i));
      facade.persistEntity(ii);
    }
    for (int i = 4; i < 10; i++) {
      Wine w = new Wine("France", "Fine Wine - ranked #" + i, "Chateau
      Brown " + i, 90, "Loire Valley ", new Float(10 + i), "Zinfandel",
      2000 + i);
      facade.persistEntity(w);
      ii = new InventoryItem(10 + i, w, new java.util.Date(System.
      currentTimeMillis()), new Float(1 + i));
      facade.persistEntity(ii);
    }

    return ii;
  }

  public void showDataCount(PrintStream out) {
    out.println(facade.getCount(Address.class) + " Addresses found");
    out.println(facade.getCount(BusinessContact.class) + " Business
    Contacts found");
    out.println(facade.getCount(CustomerOrder.class) + " Customer Orders found");
    out.println(facade.getCount(Wine.class) + " Wines found");
    out.println(facade.getCount(WineItem.class) + " Wine Items found");
  }
```

```
    private void releaseEntityManager() {
      if (facade != null) {
        facade.close();
      }
    }
}
```

Notice that instead of injecting an EJB façade using the @EJB notation, we instantiate the Java façade (JavaServiceFacade) through its constructor and pass it the name of a RESOURCE_LOCAL persistence unit, which we can see from the original call is "Chapter07-WineAppUnit-ResourceLocal". This helper class is calling operations like persistEntity() and removeCustomerOrder() on the façade without explicitly calling for the operation to be committed, which is an indication that the façade uses implicit commit behavior.

We also take care to ensure that the façade is notified, through its own close() method, after it is used. This allows it to release its own resources: notably, its EntityManagerFactory and EntityManager resources. These are housekeeping items you don't need to worry about with EJBs, since the EJB container handles this level of resource management for you.

Java Façade Using Application-Managed EntityManager

This brings us to the details of the Java façade itself. This façade was actually quietly introduced in Chapter 7, where it is bundled with the common persistence archive we are sharing from that chapter. We will now see how this is handled, by now examining the JavaServiceFacade class in Listing 8-4:

Listing 8-4. JavaServiceFacade.java, a transactional Java façade over JPA entities, exhibiting implicit commit behavior

```
public class JavaServiceFacade {
  private final EntityManagerFactory emf;
  private final EntityManager em;

  public JavaServiceFacade() {
    this("Chapter13-EmbeddableEJBTests-ResourceLocal");
  }
```

```java
public JavaServiceFacade(String persistenceUnit) {
  emf = Persistence.createEntityManagerFactory(persistenceUnit);
  em = emf.createEntityManager();
}

public void close() {
  if (em != null && em.isOpen()) {
    em.close();
  }
  if (emf != null && emf.isOpen()) {
    emf.close();
  }
}

/**
 * All changes that have been made to the managed entities in the
   persistence context are applied
 * to the database and committed.
 */
private void commitTransaction() {
  final EntityTransaction entityTransaction = em.getTransaction();
  if (!entityTransaction.isActive()) {
    entityTransaction.begin();
  }
  entityTransaction.commit();
}

public <T> T persistEntity(T entity) {
  em.persist(entity);
  commitTransaction();
  return entity;
}

public <T> T mergeEntity(T entity) {
  entity = em.merge(entity);
  commitTransaction();
  return entity;
}
```

```java
public <T> void removeEntity(T entity) {
  em.remove(em.merge(entity));
  commitTransaction();
}

public <T> List<T> findAll(Class<T> entityClass) {
  CriteriaQuery cq = em.getCriteriaBuilder().createQuery();
  cq.select(cq.from(entityClass));
  return em.createQuery(cq).getResultList();
}

public <T> int getCount(Class<T> entityClass) {
  CriteriaQuery cq = em.getCriteriaBuilder().createQuery();
  Root<T> rt = cq.from(entityClass);
  cq.select(em.getCriteriaBuilder().count(rt));
  javax.persistence.Query q = em.createQuery(cq);
  return ((Long) q.getSingleResult()).intValue();
}

/**
 * <code>select object(wine) from Wine wine where wine.year = :year</code>
 */
public List<Wine> getWineFindByYear(int year) {
  return em.createNamedQuery("Wine.findByYear", Wine.class).
  setParameter("year", year).getResultList();
}

/**
 * <code>select object(wine) from Wine wine where wine.country =
   :country</code>
 */
public List<Wine> getWineFindByCountry(String country) {
  return em.createNamedQuery("Wine.findByCountry", Wine.class).
  setParameter("country", country).getResultList();
}

/**
```

```
 *  <code>select object(wine) from Wine wine where wine.varietal =
    :varietal</code>
 */
public List<Wine> getWineFindByVarietal(String varietal) {

  return em.createNamedQuery("Wine.findByVarietal", Wine.class).
  setParameter("varietal", varietal).getResultList();
 }
}
```

This façade obtains its `EntityManager` from an `EntityManagerFactory`, and so the life cycle of this `EntityManager` is now the responsibility of the façade is now the responsibility of the façade instead of the container. An application-managed `EntityManager` is bound to a persistence context cache that can exist outside of a transactional context, and live through multiple transactions, which is essentially the same as an EXTENDED persistence context for a stateful session bean. This allows calls such as `EntityManager.persist()` to be made before a transaction has been started. Such an out-of-transaction call would add a new entity to the persistence context but would not immediately result in an SQL call to update the database.

Note   Even before an EntityManager transaction is begun, the persistence context quietly begins its own private transaction, as needed, to service any ID generator requests when EntityManager.persist( ) is called. Because we have bound the PK fields of our entities to a @GeneratedValue ID generator, these IDs are actually eagerly obtained and assigned to the entities during the persist( ).

The persistence context cache is not flushed to the database until the transaction is actually begun, through an `EntityTransaction.begin()` call, which could be immediately before an `EntityTransaction.commit()` call is performed. That is, you have the choice to begin the transaction before any changes are applied to the persistence context or defer the beginning of the transaction until you are ready to commit. In our sample, we defer the `begin()` call to inside the `commitTransaction()` method:

```
private void commitTransaction() {
  final EntityTransaction entityTransaction = em.getTransaction();
  if (!entityTransaction.isActive()) {
```

```
    entityTransaction.begin();
  }
  entityTransaction.commit();
}
```

Contrast this behavior with a stateless session bean using the default CMT behavior of `TransactionAttributeType.REQUIRED`, which implicitly begins a transaction when a session bean method call is made, and it commits the work to the database upon returning from that method call. The transaction begins and ends within the boundaries of that method call, and such CMT beans would never expose `commitTransaction()` or `rollbackTransaction()` methods to their clients, as we will see in the BMT example next. The implicit commit behavior avoids leaving uncommitted data hanging around in a cache, vulnerable to loss due to hardware or network failure. However, it also incurs additional back-end processing to complete the work and commits it each time an atomic operation is performed (not to mention, a persistence context cache is created and destroyed with each call), which can affect performance.

A RESOURCE_LOCAL `EntityManager` provides its clients with an `EntityTransaction` object for managing transactions. The `commitTransaction()` method in Listing 8-4 demonstrates its use, and the implicit behavior of this façade is achieved by the policy of calling `commitTransaction()` at the end of every method that updates the persistence context (through a persist, merge, or remove operation).

Filtering Test Data Using a CMT Session Bean

After using the Java façade (through a utility class) to populate the demo data, the servlet client then calls a stateless CMT session bean, `OrderProcessorCMTBean`, to filter this data remove `Customer` and `Wine` entities that might have been created from previous invocations. We could have both data population and data filtering with a single façade tied to a single persistence unit, but we are deliberately mixing and matching options here to show how they can interact. What allows this to work is that both persistence units, one RESOURCE_LOCAL and one JTA, both point to the same database connection.

```
//  Filter the data by removing any existing Customers with email
'xaction.head@yahoo.com'
//  and any existing Wine with country 'United States'.
out.print("<h2>Filtering Demo Data... ");
System.out.println(orderProcessorCMT.initialize());
out.println("done</h2>");
```

The stateless session bean OrderProcessorCMTBean does not explicitly declare its transactional behavior, and so it assumes the default TransactionManagement value—CMT—which is the equivalent of annotating the bean:

```
@TransactionManagement(TransactionManagementType.CONTAINER)
```

Because the initialize() method is not annotated with a TransactionAttribute override, and OrderProcessorCMTBean does not override the default TransactionAttribute value for all its methods at the bean level, it assumes the default transaction attribute value, the equivalent of the following:

```
@TransactionAttribute(TransactionAttributeType.REQUIRED)
```

Since the client has neither begun nor inherited a transaction, one is created and begun by the EJB container for the duration of the initialize() method, and all changes are committed upon successful completion of this method. CMT beans will always exhibit implicit commit behavior, because the container will not allow a transaction that it begins to continue after the method has completed. The implicit commit causes any changes made during the course of that method to be made persistent, and they are applied to the database so that the changes are visible to all clients henceforth.

Creating New Customer and CartItem Entity Instances in the Client

The next step for the client is to create a new Customer entity instance (actually, the concrete Individual entity subclass of the abstract Customer entity), create some Wine instances, and add some bottles of wine represented by CartItem instances, to the customer's cart:

```java
// Create a Customer and add some CartItems and their associated Wines
Individual customer = new Individual();
customer.setFirstName("Transaction");
customer.setLastName("Head");
customer.setEmail(PopulateDemoData.TO_EMAIL_ADDRESS);
for (int i = 0; i < 5; i++) {
  final Wine wine = new Wine();
  wine.setCountry("United States");
  wine.setDescription("Delicious wine");
  wine.setName("Xacti");
  wine.setRegion("Dry Creek Valley");
  wine.setRetailPrice(new Float(20.00D + i));
  wine.setVarietal("Zinfandel");
  wine.setYear(2000 + i);
  orderProcessorCMT.persistEntity(wine);

  final CartItem cartItem = new CartItem();
  cartItem.setCreatedDate(new Timestamp(System.currentTimeMillis()));
  cartItem.setCustomer(customer);
  cartItem.setQuantity(12);
  cartItem.setWine(wine);

  customer.addCartItem(cartItem);
}
```

Note that during this stage, only the wine instances are persisted explicitly. All other entities that are created are associated, directly or indirectly, with the customer instance, and they exist only in the servlet's method context. No transaction is involved in this process of creating these entity objects, assigning their ordinary properties, and associating them with each other. The wine instances are deliberately not associated with the other object through cascade rules, so they must be persisted explicitly.

Persisting the Customer

Having created the Customer and associated CartItem objects, the client passes the Customer to the OrderProcessorCMT bean's persistEntity() method. Because the relationships on the Customer and CartItem entities are annotated cascade = {CascadeType.ALL}, the act of persisting the Customer entity is cascaded to all associated entities, and so they are all persisted as well. This method call will begin a transaction, persist the customer and related objects to the database, and commit the work:

```
//  Persist the Customer, relying on the cascade settings to persist all
//  related CartItem entities as well. After the call, the Customer
//  instance will have an ID value that was assigned by the EJB container
//  when it was persisted.
orderProcessorCMT.persistEntity(customer);
```

Also note that because we set up an ID generator on the base class for each of the entities in our persistence unit, their id fields are auto-populated at the time they are persisted, and foreign key columns mapped to entity relationships will be wired up properly as well. For the BusinessContext class, which uses a table generator, the ID generator for its id field is defined like this:

```
@Id
@Column(nullable = false)
@GeneratedValue(strategy = GenerationType.TABLE, generator =
"BusinessContact_ID_Generator")
private Integer id;
```

The Customer instance we pass to persistEntity() is updated to become both managed and persisted. Were we calling persistEntity() through a remote interface on OrderProcessorCMTBean, the invocation would use pass-by-value semantics, and we would need to capture the updated Customer instance in the method result. Since we're calling the session bean using local mode from within the Java EE tier, we are using pass-by-reference semantics, so the Customer instance is updated directly.

At the conclusion of the persistEntity() call, the Customer (Individual) and all associated data is now applied to the database and available to all clients, including our own.

Creating the CustomerOrder

An instance of a Customer entity now exists as a persistent row in the database, so we can call createCustomerOrder() with customer to create a new CustomerOrder, and create an OrderItem for each CartItem on the Customer:

```
// Create a customer order and create OrderItems from the CartItems
final CustomerOrder customerOrder =
  orderProcessorCMT.createCustomerOrder(customer);
```

Here again, the createCustomerOrder() method definition is not annotated with a transaction attribute, so it defaults to REQUIRED, and the EJB container creates and begins a new transaction for the duration of that method, and then commits it upon returning control to the client. Note that the implementation of the createCustomerOrder() method delegates to another method, createCustomerOrderUsingSupports(), which is annotated as follows:

```
@TransactionAttribute(TransactionAttributeType.SUPPORTS)
public CustomerOrder createCustomerOrderUsingSupports(Customer customer) {...}
```

This delegation exists purely to allow us to illustrate the transaction behavior involved when calling a method marked SUPPORTS from a method marked REQUIRED. The method called from the client, createCustomerOrder(), causes a transaction to be created that is propagated to its delegate, createCustomerOrderUsingSupports(). This latter method inherits the transaction context created by the EJB container for its caller. Had the client called createCustomerOrderUsingSupports() directly, an exception would have been thrown during its execution, when the remove() and persist() operations were called outside a transaction context.

A lot is going on inside the createCustomerOrderUsingSupports() method. Because the customer argument might be detached (in our case it isn't, since our servlet is running within a local Java EE environment), it needs to be turned into a managed instance. If it is already managed, this precaution is unnecessary but not harmful:

```
if (!em.contains(customer)) {
  customer = em.merge(customer);
}
```

Next, the CustomerOrder instance is created and added to the Customer. Our implementation of the addCustomerOrder() method adds the CustomerOrder to the Customer's customerOrderList property and also assigns the customer back-pointer property on CustomerOrder, effectively wiring up the bidirectional relationship:

```
final CustomerOrder customerOrder = new CustomerOrder();
customer.addCustomerOrder(customerOrder);
```

and the CustomerOrder is then populated with new OrderItems to match each CartItem in the Customer's shopping cart. We copy the customer's CartItem list into an ArrayList so we can iterate over it and remove each CartItem from the Customer after a corresponding OrderItem has been created in the CustomerOrder, without causing a concurrency exception:

```
final Timestamp orderDate = new Timestamp(System.currentTimeMillis());
final List<CartItem> cartItemList =
        new ArrayList(customer.getCartItemList());
for (CartItem cartItem : cartItemList) {
  // Create a new OrderItem for this CartItem
  final OrderItem orderItem = new OrderItem();
  orderItem.setOrderDate(orderDate);
  orderItem.setPrice(cartItem.getWine().getRetailPrice());
  orderItem.setQuantity(cartItem.getQuantity());
  orderItem.setStatus("Order Created");
  orderItem.setWine(cartItem.getWine());
  customerOrder.addOrderItem(orderItem);

  // Remove the CartItem
  customer.removeCartItem(cartItem);
}
```

As each OrderItem is created, its CartItem is removed from the Customer. An orphanRemoval=true property on the @OneToMany relationship annotating Customer. orderItemList ensures that after each CartItem is removed from the Customer, it will be automatically removed from persistent storage as well when the context transaction is committed.

At last, the newly populated CustomerOrder is persisted and returned to the caller:

```
return persistEntity(customerOrder);
```

The transaction is not committed until after the createCustomerOrderUsingSupports() method has completed and control is returned from the wrapper createCustomerOrder() method. Assuming that we are using a JTA transaction that uses a two-phase commit (for instance, a container-managed transaction created by the EJB container), should anything go wrong in the course of either of these methods, the entire transaction will be rolled back, and neither this client nor any outside application will ever be aware that a CustomerOrder was created.

Does This Pass the ACID Test?

Have the core ACID requirements that characterize a valid transaction been met? Let's look at how EJB addresses each one.

Atomicity

The EJB container ensures that whenever a stateless CMT method marked REQUIRED or REQUIRES_NEW is called, if the container interposes to create a new transaction (this will always happen with REQUIRES_NEW), it will resolve that transaction upon exiting the method. If the method completes successfully, and if the bean code did not call EJBContext.setRollbackOnly(), the transaction will be committed. If the method throws an exception, or if EJBContext.setRollbackOnly() is called, the transaction will be rolled back. These two transaction attributes are the only ones for which the container may interpose to create a new transaction. For all other transaction attributes, either an externally managed transaction is involved (in which case the container will not interpose to commit it when the method is exited), or the method is called with no transaction context. In the latter case, because we are using a transaction-scoped persistence context and there is no transactional context, calls to persist(), merge(), or remove() will cause a javax.persistence.TransactionRequiredException. Were we to be using a stateful session bean with an extended persistence context, these changes would be tracked by the persistence context, even outside of a transaction, and applied should a transaction be subsequently created (and associated with this persistence context) and committed.

Consistency

Any database constraints or concurrency conditions (whether enforced in the database or in the EJB container) are guaranteed to be satisfied when a transaction is committed through the EJB services. Violations will result in exceptions being thrown from the EJB container, and the transaction will automatically be rolled back. A successful commit indicates that all defined constraint conditions have been met.

Isolation

This requirement is largely the responsibility of the underlying JTA resources. Each resource may expose its own configurable isolation level settings to provide varying degrees of consistency to the resources involved in a transaction. Isolation levels determine the extent to which resources within the transaction are able to see the partial (in-transaction) state of other resources involved in the transaction, and largely translate into cache consistency settings within the resource. Isolation also determines that the transaction should not see uncommitted data of another transaction. To remain database neutral, our example did not attempt to configure these settings.

Durability

This is also largely the responsibility of the underlying JTA resources involved in the transaction (e.g., the database or mail server). At the conclusion of a JTA transaction, any such resources are expected to be able to show the new state of the data when queried. We demonstrated this by querying the details of the new `CustomerOrder` from the client after the `createCustomerOrder()` method, and its transaction encapsulated within, had completed.

Benefits of This Approach

A principal benefit of using a default stateless session bean with CMT demarcation is that the client does not need to be concerned about beginning, ending, or otherwise coordinating the transaction logic. Also, any transaction context currently in effect on the thread in which the bean method is called is automatically propagated to that method call (if the transaction attribute is `REQUIRED` or `SUPPORTS`). Each call it makes to the `OrderProcessorCMT` bean either completes successfully (in which case it can be assumed that the work has been applied persistently) or results in an exception (whereupon the work performed in that method is completely rolled back). It's a very simple model.

Limitations of This Approach

In general, simple is good, but sometimes it is too limiting. While this example allows the client to create and manipulate new entity instances in the client tier, as when it created the `Customer`, `Wine` and `CartItem` instances, the client must rely on the EJBs to ensure that the updates it makes to the entity model are persisted to the database within a transaction, since transactions are always begun and terminated by the EJB container before control is handed back to the client.

In the next example, we will show how using stateful session beans, coupled with BMT and an extended persistence context, empowers the client with greater flexibility (and with it, responsibility) over the transactional behavior of the application.

Note   There has been a popular conception among EJB users that stateful session beans should be avoided for performance reasons. The performance tests that we have done strongly suggest that stateful session beans have been falsely maligned, and that when correctly used, they can actually boost performance. Furthermore, in EJB, their value is increased, since they provide you this `PersistenceContext.EXTENDED` option, allowing entity instances to be cached for use across transactions.

Stateful Session Beans with BMT Demarcation and Extended Persistence Context

To illustrate extending the reach of EJB's transaction support, here is the same application written using a stateful BMT session bean, `OrderProcessorBMTBean.java`. This BMT example also leverages EJB's built-in transaction support, but instead of relying on the container to manage transaction demarcation at method boundaries, shows how to demarcate transactions explicitly, inside the enterprise bean code and controlled from the client as well.

There is no requirement that you use BMT demarcation when using stateful session beans, and in fact this option is not typically used. We show it here in Listing 8-5 to illustrate how you would use it, should you be so inclined.

Listing 8-5. OrderProcessorBMTBean.java, a Stateful Session Bean Using BMT Demarcation and an Extended Persistence Context

```
@Stateful(name = "OrderProcessorBMT", mappedName = "Chapter08-
TransactionSamples-OrderProcessorBMT")
@TransactionManagement(TransactionManagementType.BEAN)
@Interceptors(OrderProcessorBMTBeanTxnInterceptor.class)
```

```java
public class OrderProcessorBMTBean {
  @Resource
  SessionContext sessionContext;
  @PersistenceContext(unitName = "Chapter08-TransactionSamples-JTA",
  type = PersistenceContextType.EXTENDED)
  private EntityManager em;

  /**
   * Remove any existing Customers with email 'wineapp@yahoo.com' and any
   * existing Wine with country 'United States'
   */
  public String initialize() throws HeuristicMixedException,
      HeuristicRollbackException,
      RollbackException,
      SystemException {
    StringBuffer strBuf = new StringBuffer();
    strBuf.append("Removed ");
    int i = 0;

    // Filter the data by removing any existing Customers with email
    // 'wineapp@yahoo.com' (or whatever is defined in the user.properties file).
    // The first call to a transactional method on OrderProcessorBMT will
       begin a
    // transaction.
    for (Customer customer
        : getCustomerFindByEmail(PopulateDemoData.TO_EMAIL_ADDRESS)) {
      em.remove(customer);
      i++;
    }
    strBuf.append(i);
    strBuf.append(" Customer(s) and ");

    // Remove any existing Wine with country 'United States'
    i = 0;
    for (Wine wine : getWineFindByCountry("United States")) {
      em.remove(wine);
      i++;
```

```
    }
    strBuf.append(i);
    strBuf.append(" Wine(s)");

    // Apply these changes, committing the entity removal operations
    commitTransaction();

    return strBuf.toString();
}

/**
 * Create a new CustomerOrder from the items in a Customer's cart. Creates a
 * new CustomerOrder entity, and then creates a new OrderItem entity for each
 * CartItem found in the Customer's cart.
 *
 * Using CMT w/ the default Required xaction attribute, if this method is
 * invoked without a transaction context, a new transaction will be created by
 * the EJB container upon invoking the method, and committed upon successfully
 * completing the method.
 *
 * @return a status message (plain text)
 */
public CustomerOrder createCustomerOrder(Customer customer) throws Exception {
    if (customer == null) {
        throw new IllegalArgumentException("OrderProcessingBean.
        createCustomerOrder(): Customer not specified");
    }

    // Ensure we are working with a managed Customer object
    customer = em.find(Customer.class, customer.getId());

    CustomerOrder customerOrder = new CustomerOrder();
    customer.addCustomerOrder(customerOrder);
    final Timestamp orderDate = new Timestamp(System.currentTimeMillis());
    // Clone the CartItem list so we remove the CartItem entries from the
        Customer
    // without causing a ConcurrentModificationException on the iterator.
```

```
    final List<CartItem> cartItemList = new ArrayList(customer.getCartItemList());
    for (CartItem cartItem : cartItemList) {
      // Create a new OrderItem for this CartItem
      final OrderItem orderItem = new OrderItem();
      orderItem.setOrderDate(orderDate);
      orderItem.setPrice(cartItem.getWine().getRetailPrice());
      orderItem.setQuantity(cartItem.getQuantity());
      orderItem.setStatus("Order Created");
      orderItem.setWine(cartItem.getWine());
      customerOrder.addOrderItem(orderItem);

      // Remove the CartItem. Note that the 'orphanRemoval' flag will ensure
      // that the cartItem is removed from the database once it is disassociated
      // from a customer.
      customer.removeCartItem(cartItem);
    }

    // The Cascade rules on Customer will cause the CustomerOrder to be
    // persisted when the Customer is merged
    em.merge(customer);

    return customerOrder;
  }

  @ExcludeClassInterceptors
  public void commitTransaction() throws HeuristicMixedException,
  HeuristicRollbackException, RollbackException, SystemException {
    final UserTransaction txn = sessionContext.getUserTransaction();
    if (txn.getStatus() == Status.STATUS_ACTIVE) {
      txn.commit();
    }
  }

  @ExcludeClassInterceptors
  public void rollbackTransaction() throws SystemException {
    final UserTransaction txn = sessionContext.getUserTransaction();
    if (txn.getStatus() == Status.STATUS_ACTIVE) {
      txn.rollback();
```

```java
    }
}

@ExcludeClassInterceptors
public boolean isTransactionDirty() throws SystemException {
  final UserTransaction txn = sessionContext.getUserTransaction();
  return Boolean.valueOf(txn.getStatus() == Status.STATUS_ACTIVE);
}

@ExcludeClassInterceptors
public Object queryByRange(String jpqlStmt, int firstResult, int
maxResults) {
  Query query = em.createQuery(jpqlStmt);
  if (firstResult > 0) {
    query = query.setFirstResult(firstResult);
  }
  if (maxResults > 0) {
    query = query.setMaxResults(maxResults);
  }
  return query.getResultList();
}

public <T> T persistEntity(T entity) {
  em.persist(entity);
  return entity;
}

public <T> T mergeEntity(T entity) {
  return em.merge(entity);
}

public <T> void removeEntity(T entity) {
  em.remove(em.merge(entity));
}

@ExcludeClassInterceptors
public <T> List<T> findAll(Class<T> entityClass) {
  CriteriaQuery cq = em.getCriteriaBuilder().createQuery();
```

```
    cq.select(cq.from(entityClass));
    return em.createQuery(cq).getResultList();
  }

  @ExcludeClassInterceptors
  public <T> List<T> findAllByRange(Class<T> entityClass, int[] range) {
    CriteriaQuery cq = em.getCriteriaBuilder().createQuery();
    cq.select(cq.from(entityClass));
    Query q = em.createQuery(cq);
    q.setMaxResults(range[1] - range[0]);
    q.setFirstResult(range[0]);
    return q.getResultList();
  }

  /**
   * <code>select o from Customer o where o.email = :email</code>
   */
  @ExcludeClassInterceptors
  public List<Customer> getCustomerFindByEmail(String email) {
    return em.createNamedQuery("Customer.findByEmail", Customer.class).
    setParameter("email", email).getResultList();
  }

  /**
   * <code>select object(wine) from Wine wine where wine.year = :year</code>
   */
  @ExcludeClassInterceptors
  public List<Wine> getWineFindByYear(Integer year) {
    return em.createNamedQuery("Wine.findByYear", Wine.class).
    setParameter("year", year).getResultList();
  }

  /**
   * <code>select object(wine) from Wine wine where wine.country = :country
     </code>
   */
```

```java
@ExcludeClassInterceptors
public List<Wine> getWineFindByCountry(String country) {
  return em.createNamedQuery("Wine.findByCountry", Wine.class).
  setParameter("country", country).getResultList();
}

/**
 * <code>select object(wine) from Wine wine where wine.varietal =
   :varietal</code>
 */
@ExcludeClassInterceptors
public List<Wine> getWineFindByVarietal(String varietal) {
  return em.createNamedQuery("Wine.findByVarietal", Wine.class).
  setParameter("varietal", varietal).getResultList();
}

/**
 * <code>select o from InventoryItem o where o.wine = :wine</code>
 */
@ExcludeClassInterceptors
public List<InventoryItem> getInventoryItemFindItemByWine(Object wine) {
  return em.createNamedQuery("InventoryItem.findItemByWine",
  InventoryItem.class).setParameter("wine", wine).getResultList();
}
}
```

Coupled to this stateful session bean is an Interceptor class that serves to interpose on each method that applies changes through the EntityManager to automatically begin a transaction. This pattern is similar to SQL's transactional model, where a transaction is implicitly begun each time a DML operation like INSERT, UPDATE, or DELETE is called. Hence, the client is responsible only for calling COMMIT or ROLLBACK to conclude the transaction, but there is no explicit call to begin the transaction. The Interceptor class is shown here, in Listing 8-6.

Listing 8-6. OrderProcessorBMTBeanTxnInterceptor.java, an Interceptor
used by OrderProcessorBMTBean to begin a JTA transaction, using the
UserTransaction from the BMT bean's SessionContext, each time a method is
called which applies changes through the EntityManager

```
class OrderProcessorBMTBeanTxnInterceptor {
  public OrderProcessorBMTBeanTxnInterceptor() {
  }

  @AroundInvoke
  Object beginTrans(InvocationContext invocationContext) throws Exception {
    final OrderProcessorBMTBean orderProcessorBMTBean =
    (OrderProcessorBMTBean) invocationContext.getTarget();
    final UserTransaction txn = orderProcessorBMTBean.sessionContext.
    getUserTransaction();
    if (txn.getStatus() == Status.STATUS_NO_TRANSACTION) {
      txn.begin();
    }
    return invocationContext.proceed();
  }
}
```

Listing 8-7 shows `OrderProcessorBMTClient.java`, a servlet client that drives the
`OrderProcessorBMT` session bean to demonstrate EJB's BMT demarcation by calling
through the UserTransaction interface.

Listing 8-7. OrderProcessorBMTClient.java, Our Mock Java SE Client

```
@WebServlet(name = "OrderProcessorBMTClient", urlPatterns = {"/
OrderProcessorBMTClient"})
public class OrderProcessorBMTClient extends HttpServlet {
  @EJB
  OrderProcessorBMTBean orderProcessorBMT;

  /**
   * Processes requests for both HTTP
   * <code>GET</code> and
   * <code>POST</code> methods.
```

```
 *
 * @param request servlet request
 * @param response servlet response
 * @throws ServletException if a servlet-specific error occurs
 * @throws IOException if an I/O error occurs
 */
protected void processRequest(HttpServletRequest request,
HttpServletResponse response)
        throws ServletException, IOException {
  response.setContentType("text/html;charset=UTF-8");
  response.setContentType("text/html;charset=UTF-8");
  OutputStream rOut = response.getOutputStream();
  PrintStream out = new PrintStream(rOut);
  try {
    /* TODO output your page here. You may use following sample code. */
    out.println("<html>");
    out.println("<head>");
    out.println("<title>Servlet OrderProcessorBMTClient</title>");
    out.println("</head>");
    out.println("<body>");
    out.println("<h1>Servlet OrderProcessorBMTClient at " + request.
    getContextPath() + "</h1>");
    out.println("</body>");
    out.println("</html>");

    out.print("<h2>Populating Demo Data... ");
    PopulateDemoData.resetData("Chapter07-WineAppUnit-ResourceLocal",
    System.out);
    out.println("done</h2>");

    out.print("<h2>Filtering Demo Data... ");
    StringBuffer strBuf = new StringBuffer();
    strBuf.append("Removed ");
    int n = 0;
```

```
//  Filter the data by removing any existing Customers with email
//  'wineapp@yahoo.com' (or whatever is defined in the user.
    properties file).
//  The first call to a transactional method on OrderProcessorBMT
    will begin a
//  transaction.
for (Customer customer :
     orderProcessorBMT.getCustomerFindByEmail(PopulateDemoData.TO_
     EMAIL_ADDRESS)) {
  orderProcessorBMT.removeEntity(customer);
  n++;
}
strBuf.append(n + " Customer(s) and ");

//  Remove any existing Wine with country 'United States'
n = 0;
for (Wine wine : orderProcessorBMT.getWineFindByCountry("United
States")) {
  orderProcessorBMT.removeEntity(wine);
  n++;
}
strBuf.append(n + " Wine(s)");
out.print(strBuf.toString() + "</h2>");

//  Apply these changes, committing the entity removal operations
orderProcessorBMT.commitTransaction();

//  Create a Customer and add some CartItems and their associated Wines
Individual customer = new Individual();
customer.setFirstName("Transaction");
customer.setLastName("Head");
customer.setEmail(PopulateDemoData.TO_EMAIL_ADDRESS);
for (int i = 0; i < 5; i++) {
  final Wine wine = new Wine();
  wine.setCountry("United States");
  wine.setDescription("Delicious wine");
  wine.setName("Xacti");
```

```
    wine.setRegion("Dry Creek Valley");
    wine.setRetailPrice(new Float(20.00D + i));
    wine.setVarietal("Zinfandel");
    wine.setYear(2000 + i);
    orderProcessorBMT.persistEntity(wine);

    final CartItem cartItem = new CartItem();
    cartItem.setCreatedDate(new Timestamp(System.currentTimeMillis()));
    cartItem.setCustomer(customer);
    cartItem.setQuantity(12);
    cartItem.setWine(wine);

    customer.addCartItem(cartItem);
}

// Persist the Customer, relying on the cascade settings to persist all
// related CartItem entities as well. After the call, the Customer
// instance will have an ID value that was assigned by the EJB container
// when it was persisted.
orderProcessorBMT.persistEntity(customer);

// Create a customer order and create OrderItems from the CartItems
final CustomerOrder customerOrder =
        orderProcessorBMT.createCustomerOrder(customer);

out.print("<h2>Retrieving Customer Order Items... ");
for (OrderItem orderItem : customerOrder.getOrderItemList()) {
  final Wine wine = orderItem.getWine();
  out.println(wine.getName() + " with ID " + wine.getId());
}
out.println("done</h2>");

// Commit the order, applying all of the changes made thus far
orderProcessorBMT.commitTransaction();
} catch (Exception ex) {
ex.printStackTrace();
if (orderProcessorBMT != null) {
  try {
```

```
        orderProcessorBMT.rollbackTransaction();
      } catch (Exception e) {
        e.printStackTrace();
      }
    }
  } finally {
    rOut.close();
    out.close();
  }
}

/* HTTPServlet methods... */
}
```

Transaction Analysis

The following sections will analyze this second example from a transactional
perspective. We have empowered the session bean with state (i.e., Stateful), giving it
control over the demarcation of its transactions, and allowed its associated persistence
context to survive from one transaction to the next.

Session Bean Declaration

These features have arisen through the combination of annotations and code. You'll
notice that this session bean is annotated:

```
@Stateful(name = "OrderProcessorBMT", mappedName = "Chapter08-
TransactionSamples-OrderProcessorBMT")
@TransactionManagement(TransactionManagementType.BEAN)
@Interceptors(OrderProcessorBMTBeanTxnInterceptor.class)
public class OrderProcessorBMTBean {
  @Resource
  SessionContext sessionContext;
  @PersistenceContext(unitName = "Chapter08-TransactionSamples-JTA",
  type = PersistenceContextType.EXTENDED)
  private EntityManager em;
  ...
}
```

It injects both a `SessionContext` and an `EntityManager`. Being stateful allows the enterprise bean to retain state from one client invocation to the next. In this case, that state is the persistence context and the associated transaction, which must survive through multiple method invocations. The BMT declaration means that the container should not automatically interpose on method boundaries to demarcate transactions. Attempts to add `TransactionAttribute` qualifiers to methods on a BMT session bean will be caught and raise an exception at deployment time.

The `@PersistenceContext` annotation holds a `type` property with value `PersistenceContextType.EXTENDED`, meaning that it persists from one transaction to the next, and allows associated entities to remain managed even after the transaction in which they were created has ended. The `UserTransaction` object available through the `sessionContext` property is this BMT bean's interface onto the EJB container's JTA transaction manager, and exposes the `begin()`, `commit()`, and `rollback()` transaction demarcation methods.

Removing Previous Test Data

We could have populated the test environment through a session bean method call, as we did for the preceding CMT example. However, using BMT offers us the option of performing this work interactively, in the client. This is because the `OrderProcessorBMT` bean's persistence context is `EXTENDED`, allowing the entities to remain associated with a persistence context even after control has been returned from the enterprise bean to the client.

```
//  Filter the data by removing any existing Customers with email
//  'wineapp@yahoo.com' (or whatever is defined in the user.properties file).
//  The first call to a transactional method on OrderProcessorBMT will begin a
//  transaction.
for (Customer customer :

  orderProcessorBMT.getCustomerFindByEmail(PopulateDemoData.TO_EMAIL_ADDRESS)) {
  orderProcessorBMT.removeEntity(customer);
  n++;
}
strBuf.append(n + " Customer(s) and ");
```

```
// Remove any existing Wine with country 'United States'
n = 0;
for (Wine wine : orderProcessorBMT.getWineFindByCountry("United States")) {
  orderProcessorBMT.removeEntity(wine);
  n++;
}
strBuf.append(n + " Wine(s)");
out.print(strBuf.toString() + "</h2>");

// Apply these changes, committing the entity removal operations
orderProcessorBMT.commitTransaction();
```

Each call to removeEntity() is performed in the transaction that was begun on the OrderProcessorBMT bean through its Interceptor, and puts the entity in the "removed" state in its persistence context. At the conclusion of these steps, the client calls commitTransaction() to actually perform the DBMS DELETE operations in the database and commit the transaction.

Creating New Customer and CartItem Entity Instances in the Client

As with the preceding stateless session example, the step of instantiating the Customer and its CartItem entity instances and wiring them all together involves no transactions, and they can be carried out entirely within the client:

```
// Create a Customer and add some CartItems and their associated Wines
Individual customer = new Individual();
customer.setFirstName("Transaction");
customer.setLastName("Head");
customer.setEmail(PopulateDemoData.TO_EMAIL_ADDRESS);
for (int i = 0; i < 5; i++) {
  final Wine wine = new Wine();
  wine.setCountry("United States");
  wine.setDescription("Delicious wine");
  wine.setName("Xacti");
  wine.setRegion("Dry Creek Valley");
  wine.setRetailPrice(new Float(20.00D + i));
```

```
wine.setVarietal("Zinfandel");
wine.setYear(2000 + i);
orderProcessorBMT.persistEntity(wine);

final CartItem cartItem = new CartItem();
cartItem.setCreatedDate(new Timestamp(System.currentTimeMillis()));
cartItem.setCustomer(customer);
cartItem.setQuantity(12);
cartItem.setWine(wine);

customer.addCartItem(cartItem);
}
```

It is worth noting that prior to JPA, this work would have required much more effort and expended more resources. With EJB 2.x entity beans, the client developer had two main options. Under one approach, the developer could create data transfer objects (DTOs) or follow some other similar pattern to simulate the task of creating and associating the entity objects through proxies. This network of DTO classes would then be passed into the session bean layer, as we did previously; but inside the session bean, actual entity beans would have to be explicitly created and initialized from the DTO objects.

A second approach, updating the entity beans directly from the client, is simpler to code, but potentially at the expense of higher performance costs. If the client exists outside the Java EE tier, each method call would incur the overhead of RMI/IIOP (remote method invocation over the Internet inter-ORB protocol) marshalling to communicate with the actual EJB object residing in the EJB container. Much of this overhead is removed when the client lives in the Java EE tier, since it could use local entity bean interfaces to communicate directly with the live entity bean; but Java SE clients were forced to use remote interfaces onto the entity beans. On top of that, container-managed relationships (CMRs) are only supported on local component interfaces; so direct entity bean relationship lookups and updates were not even available to Java SE clients in the EJB 2.x world.

Persisting the Customer

Although we chose in this example to embed the transaction begin() operation inside the Interceptor class that interposes on the BMT session bean's methods, we could have exposed a beginTransaction() call to the client as well. Because we have chosen the approach we did, all that is required is the call to persistEntity() that now implicitly begins the transaction (but does not commit it):

```
//  Persist the Customer, relying on the cascade settings to persist all
//  related CartItem entities as well. Reassign the customer
//  to pick up the ID value that was assigned by the EJB container when
//  it was persisted.
orderProcessorBMT.persistEntity(customer);
```

The transaction context does not extend to the client thread itself; it exists only in the session bean's thread. The call to UserTransaction.begin() that occurs inside the Interceptor establishes a transaction context on that thread that is then available to the session bean when its persistEntity() method is called.

Creating the CustomerOrder

Our transaction, now in effect, continues through the step of creating the customer order. This stage is similar to the stateless CMT example except that the transaction has already been created and must be explicitly committed at the conclusion.

```
//  Create a customer order and create OrderItems from the CartItems
final CustomerOrder customerOrder =
        orderProcessorBMT.createCustomerOrder(customer);

out.print("<h2>Retrieving Customer Order Items... ");
for (OrderItem orderItem : customerOrder.getOrderItemList()) {
  final Wine wine = orderItem.getWine();
  out.println(wine.getName() + " with ID " + wine.getId());
}
out.println("done</h2>");

//  Commit the order, applying all of the changes made thus far
orderProcessorBMT.commitTransaction();
```

Should the client wish to cancel the order at this stage, perhaps through interactive confirm/cancel buttons exposed in a client panel, the BMT option provides this possibility even after the `CustomerOrder` has been created.

Benefits of This Approach

The benefit of using explicit transaction demarcation is the additional degree of flexibility that it offers. The EJB server is still acting in its capacity as transaction manager, only it exposes the transaction demarcation control to the enterprise bean instead of automating this demarcation based on the `@TransactionAttribute` settings on each method. While the stateless example could have prompted the user *before* creating the `CustomerOrder`, this approach allows the `CustomerOrder` to be created and validated— for example, before being submitted to the user for confirmation. BMT must be used with caution, however, for the reasons mentioned in the following section.

Limitations of This Approach

It can be argued that the additional degree of flexibility is typically outweighed by the additional burdens of tracking the transaction state and avoiding misuse by session bean clients. Leaving the process of beginning and ending transactions to the mercy of the order in which clients call the session bean methods offers the possibility of dangling transactions. The client, in coordination with the bean itself, has the responsibility of cleanly ending—whether committing or rolling back—each transaction that has begun. This may be a reasonable risk if you can control how clients will use the bean—but session beans are openly published, and it may be difficult to anticipate who might use them, and how.

BMT session beans can be written to safeguard against misuse, but this safeguard code is probably going to leave the bean with behavior similar to CMT beans anyway, in which case little is gained for your efforts.

Building, Deploying, and Testing: A Transactional Scenario from the Wines Online Application

Now that we've examined many of the details of transaction support offered by EJB, let's execute the test cases we just covered.

For both the CMT and BMT scenarios, we invoke a servlet client that creates a new customer, builds up a shopping cart consisting of cart item entries, and then creates a customer order consisting of order items based on the cart items in the cart. We chose these examples for this chapter because they involve multiple operations that can be partitioned into transactional work units of greater or less granularity depending on the requirements of the client.

To illustrate the default support provided by EJB, we use the example we explored first: a standard stateless session bean implementation that uses the default CMT demarcation. In our second example, we demonstrate the client taking some responsibility for managing the transaction, using a stateful session bean using BMT demarcation and an extended persistence context.

Prerequisites

Before performing any of the steps detailed in the next sections, complete the "Getting Started" section of Chapter 1. This section will walk you through the installation and environment setup required for the samples in this chapter.

Opening the Sample Application

This chapter's root project holds a dependency on the JPA persistence unit defined in Chapter07-ServiceIntegration-jpa. Launch the NetBeans IDE, and open the Chapter08-TransactionSamples project using the File ➤ Open Project menu. Make sure that the 'Open Required Projects' check box is checked. See Figure 8-1.

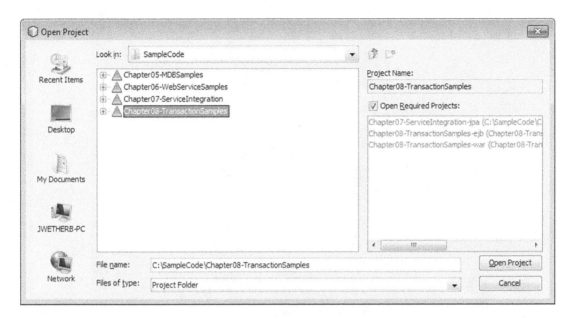

Figure 8-1. *Opening the Chapter08-TransactionSamples project*

This application consists of three modules: a JPA persistence unit taken directly from Chapter 7; an EJB module containing CMT and BMT session beans explored in this chapter; and a Web module containing the two servlet clients that we also examined. See Figure 8-2.

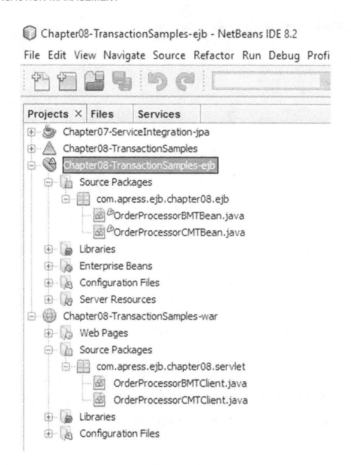

Figure 8-2. *Observing the structure of the Chapter08-TransactionSamples application*

Creating the Database Connection

The samples in this chapter require a database connection, and for these tests we will use the Derby database that is bundled with NetBeans and Glassfish. If you have already created the WineApp database, also used for the examples in Chapter 3, Chapter 4, and Chapter 7, continue to the next step. Otherwise, click on the Services tab, expand the Databases icon, and invoke "Create Database..." on the Java DB node. Create a database named "WineApp" with username and password wineapp/wineapp as shown in Figure 8-3.

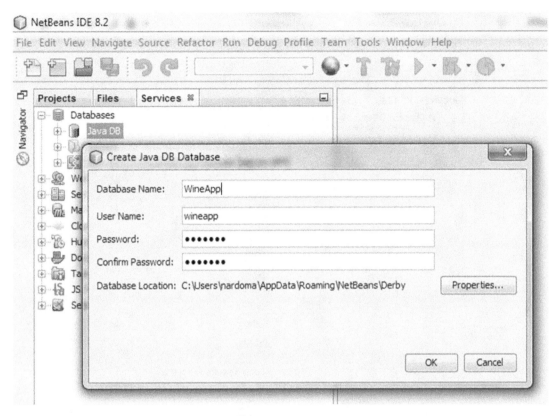

Figure 8-3. *Creating the WineApp database and connection*

This last step created a database connection, which is referenced from the persistence units in the persistence.xml files found in both the JPA and EJB projects. While it is possible to pre-create the database objects (tables, sequences, key constraints, etc.), we will let JPA create these database objects automatically the first time they are needed by each persistence unit.

Compiling the Sources

After the WineApp database has been created, invoke the context menu on Chapter08-TransactionSamples node, and build the application by selecting the Clean and Build menu option as shown in Figure 8-4.

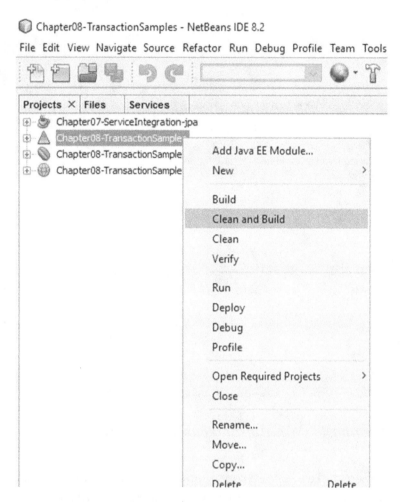

Figure 8-4. *Building the application*

Deploying and Running the Client Programs

Once the project sources have built successfully, invoke the same menu and choose
Deploy as shown in Figure 8-5.

Figure 8-5. *Deplyiong the application*

When that completes, invoke either the Run or Debug menu item to launch the OrderProcessorCMTClient servlet. We have preconfigured the Chapter09-TransactionSamples project to run this servlet by default. The servlet will display the output from the example using the default browser configured for NetBeans a shown in Figure 8-6.

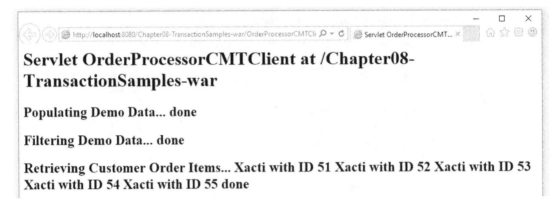

Figure 8-6. *Output from running the OrderProcessorCMTClient servlet*

If you choose to debug, feel free to add some breakpoints to the
OrderProcessorCMTBean.java session bean, the OrderProcessorCMTClient.java
servlet, the JPA entities, or any of the other source files in the application.

Next, launch the second example, the OrderProcessorBMTClient servlet. To do
this, you may either update your browser URL to replace CMT with BMT or update the
properties of the Chapter09-TransactionSamples project. Just re-deploy the project
using the OrderProcessorCMTBean.java session bean and then selecting the Run
category. The result is shown in Figure 8-7.

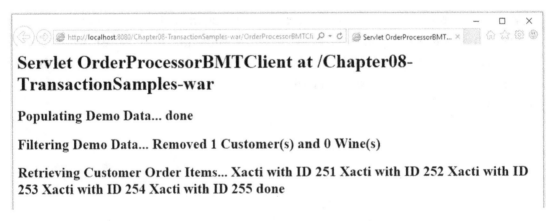

Figure 8-7. *Configuring the Chapter09-TransactionSamples project's Run target*

Summary

This chapter has defined the concepts essential to all transaction behavior and explored the transactional features offered by the EJB server and interfaces accessible to the enterprise bean developer.

We began by exploring the core ACID characteristics that define a transaction—atomicity, consistency, isolation, and durability. We introduced JTA and described the features and benefits of its distributed transaction model, including the behavior of the essential two-phase commit protocol.

We looked at how the EJB server acts as a JTA transaction manager, allowing EJBs to participate seamlessly in distributed transactions, and alleviating bean developers of the need to explicitly bind persistence or other transactional operations with transactional resources. We also detailed EJB's declarative support for these transaction services to enterprise bean developers, exploring both CMT and BMT demarcation–supported enterprise beans, and using both implicit and explicit commit models. For CMT beans, we described the behavior and implications of each of the six transaction attributes that may be used to define the transactional behavior of a CMT bean method. In the JPA realm, we explored the relationship between transactions and persistence contexts and explained how extended persistence contexts may be used with stateful session beans to support entities in resolving relationships with other entities, even outside of a transactional context.

The chapter then examined some live examples based on a scenario taken from the Wines Online application. These examples illustrated the use of CMT and BMT demarcation, extended persistence context on stateful session beans, rollback scenarios, client-controlled transactions, interactions with entities outside a transactional context using a BMT bean, and transaction context propagation between methods on a CMT bean.

We concluded with steps for running the CMT and BMT example applications that we examined.

In the next chapter, we will explore some techniques you can use to analyze the EJB-specific performance of your applications. Using a couple of common examples, we will demonstrate how you can set up your own tests to analyze your specific application components.

CHAPTER 9

EJB Performance and Testing

As developers, we are always trying to find the most efficient way to write code that delivers the highest performance. Over the years, we have learned that some of the assumptions we make are not always right and that certain programming models and techniques that we use do not achieve the expected level of performance. The surprise here is that most of the time, our expectations are defeated with models and techniques that our logic and gut feelings tell us are best.

Performance of computer systems is a very complex issue. Just think about the following: We are programming a piece of Java code that takes advantage of an infrastructure called Java Enterprise Edition (Java EE), which happens to run on top of a Java Virtual Machine (JVM). In this book we will utilize the Java EE version 8. The virtual machine is hosted on an operating system, which runs on a computer that interacts with other computers using networks composed of hardware and software components. Each of these layers—the network, the computer, the operating system, the JVM, and the Java EE server—has a number of knobs that can be used to configure and optimize behavior. Each of them will present a different behavior under various usage conditions, which will inevitably impact the behavior of the other layers. Within this rather complex context, it becomes a little easier to understand why our logic will not always work.

The bottom line is that we just cannot generalize when making performance statements. The only way that we can find out what performance to expect from our system is to test it in conditions as close as possible to the ones in which the code will run when in the production environment.

Every software application is unique. In order to understand the performance of your own application, you must test it yourself, according to your own definition of performance. In some situations, good performance will mean the ability to support a

© Jonathan Wetherbee, Massimo Nardone, Chirag Rathod, and Raghu Kodali 2018
J. Wetherbee et al., *Beginning EJB in Java EE 8*, https://doi.org/10.1007/978-1-4842-3573-7_9

large number of users; in others (for example, when the user load is small), it will simply mean being able to run as fast as possible.

In this chapter, we describe a methodology that you can use to test the performance of your systems in a consistent way. We also present tools that you can use to conduct these tests. Finally, we carry out a performance test to illustrate the methodology and the usage of the tools. The methodology and toolkit are useful in two basic situations:

- Performance testing a complete application

- Designing for performance (examining the performance costs of various aspects of the Java EE API and how certain design decisions will impact overall performance)

In the first scenario, we treat the application like a black box. We test the application under various user loads and investigate the performance of every request made by the users. The data is analyzed—we search for requests that don't meet the required criteria, and opportunities for improving performance are identified.

While the aforementioned is useful, our advice is to performance test as early in the development cycle as possible. This way, you can use the methodology and the data you obtain from it to help you design for performance, rather than performance testing after the fact.

The example presented in this chapter focuses on designing for performance, rather than testing a complete application. If you are interested in learning more about the methodology of testing an application and performance testing in general, you can refer to *J2EE Performance Testing with BEA WebLogic Server* by Peter Zadrozny (Apress, 2003). In this chapter, we present an adaptation of the methodology presented in Zadrozny's book, which is narrowly focused on the example at hand.

The Testing Methodology

The focus of the testing methodology is consistency of data measurement. The following list provides a high-level overview of the steps that are involved in the methodology. We present them and describe them in the logical order in which they will be carried out when performing each test:

1. *Define the performance criteria.* We must define the relevant performance metrics for the specific application in question and set a realistic target for that metric (for instance, a maximum acceptable response time).

2. *Accurately simulate the application usage.* The key aspect of this is the definition of the test scripts. These are configuration files that contain a set of requests that represent typical usage profiles of the application.

3. *Define the test metrics.* These include the duration of the tests, the size of the sample, the amount of initial data to exclude, and others.

4. *Perform the tests.*

Performance Criteria

Depending on the type of application, your focus will vary between two basic performance indicators: response time and throughput.

When working with synchronous interactive applications, we define a maximum acceptable response time. This is the maximum amount of time that we are willing to wait before we get a response from the application.

For a batch or back-end application, we define the minimum acceptable throughput, typically as transactions per second (TPS), but this has to be based on a solid understanding of exactly how a transaction will be defined in your system.

Each of these metrics is inextricably linked to one another; however, we have not been able to find any mathematical or geometrical relation between them.

Our advice is to define your performance metrics clearly and unambiguously and to test to well-defined requirements. Not doing so is an open invitation to test and tune endlessly.

As we will be collecting data during the performance test runs, we need to have a clear understanding of the basic statistics, so let's examine them in more detail.

For the purposes of this book, we define *response time* as the length of time a client has to wait from the moment it sends a request to the moment it receives the last byte of the response from the application.

The sets of data that we collect from a performance test run consist of the individual response times of every request that makes up the test script. Each request in a test script is executed one after another, by each simulated user for a certain period of time. Our base measurement of analysis is the arithmetic mean of the response times for all users of a particular request: the average response time (ART).

Aggregate average response time (AART) is a measurement that we use extensively when analyzing performance data, and we define it as the sum of the ARTs of every individual request in a test script, divided by the number of requests in that test script.

Admittedly, AART has no real meaning in terms of how an application is performing, but it does provide an excellent indicator of how loaded the entire system is. As such, we sometimes refer to this measurement as the *load factor*. A typical AART curve when plotted against the number of simultaneous users looks like the one presented in Figure 9-1.

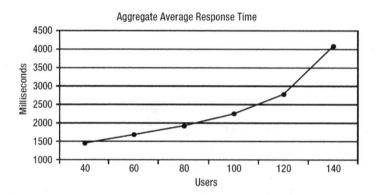

Figure 9-1. *A typical AART curve*

Throughput is not a clear-cut metric in the same way as is response time. The standard way of expressing throughput is in TPS, and it is vital to understand what a transaction represents in the application being tested. It might be a single query or a specific group of queries. In a messaging system, it might be a single message; and in a servlet-based application, it might be a request. Even when there is consensus as to exactly what is being measured, the values obtained for throughput can often be misinterpreted. The reason for this is that many people regard this metric in much the same way as they regard "miles per hour": as a measurement of speed. In fact, throughput is a measure of capacity.

We can attempt to explain how throughput works in terms of a supermarket analogy. Imagine that a supermarket runs a promotion whereby 10 shoppers will get for free everything they can put in their shopping carts in 15 minutes. The supermarket is the application, the shoppers are analogous to the requests (or messages), and the supermarket staff who are restocking the shelves are analogous to the components of your system that are working to cope with the demand.

Even if all 10 shoppers reach capacity (by completely filling their carts in 15 minutes), it doesn't necessarily mean that they've taken everything available in the supermarket. However, as we increase the number of shoppers, we will reach a point where there are enough shoppers to empty the supermarket in that time. We call this the point of saturation, as there are no more resources available. As we increase the number of shoppers beyond this point, crowding in the aisles causes reduced shopper mobility (longer response times) and, ultimately, an actual drop in throughput.

Similar to ART, our base measurement of analysis is the arithmetic mean of the requests per second for all users of a particular request. We call this TPS.

For the purposes of analyzing performance data, and independently of the definition of throughput used for a specific performance test, we use the concept of total transactional rate (TTR). TTR is the addition of the TPS measurements of each request in a test script. TTR provides us with an excellent indicator of system capacity. Figure 9-2 shows a typical TTR curve, which reaches the point of saturation at about 100 users. At that point, it starts dropping (due to, for example, too many shoppers).

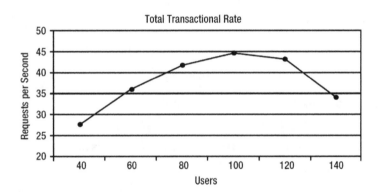

Figure 9-2. *A typical TTR curve*

The AART curve presented in Figure 9-1 is the result of data collected from the same test run as the TTR curve presented in Figure 9-2. If you review the AART curve, you can see that the response time increases in a linear fashion until it reaches 100 users. After that, the increase is more dramatic. This coincides with the TTR curve, in which the saturation point is reached at 100 users. After that, the performance of the application in general degrades. Analyzing these two curves, you can state that the application has an upper limit of 100 users under the conditions of the performance test.

Simulating Application Usage

The objective of this section of the methodology is to ensure that we are collecting our performance data in test conditions that mimic reality as closely as possible. This applies more so when performance testing whole applications, and less so when designing for performance.

For every application, there will be a number of different profiles of use that will be run concurrently. Sometimes, we will be able to simulate usage with a single test script and a single request. In other cases, it can take a dozen or so profiles, each with a different amount of requests.

A special note has to be made regarding *think time*, also known as *sleep time*. This is the amount of time that elapses between the executions of each individual request in a test script. In real life, think time can be highly variable. It can be as little as a few seconds (for example, when clicking a button that will take us to the next page), or as much as 5 to 10 minutes (for instance, when examining the transactions we made in our bank account over the last month). For the performance tests, we have adopted two basic strategies:

- *Using the real think time*: This case is used when doing a performance test of a complete, working application.

- *Using zero think time*: This case is used when performing more general investigative measurements, such as comparing programming techniques. The consequence of this is that we are not testing under realistic conditions. However, we can perform accurate comparative measurements, and once we have chosen the best scenario from these results, we can then perform tests with realistic think times.

Defining Test Metrics

The methodology is based on using a fixed number of users per test run. A performance test is made up by a number of test runs, usually increasing the user load with each subsequent test run. Some people are interested in ramping up the number of users during a single test run. We believe that this introduces a new variable that can have negative effects on the results, and it is statistically incorrect from the standpoint of finding a maximum user load.

The first step is finding a representative number of simultaneous users (the lower limit) that can be increased in a regular fashion until reaching the saturation point of the application (the upper limit). We typically have a couple of additional test runs over the upper limit, just to understand better the behavior (or misbehavior) of the application.

Unfortunately, there is no exact science for choosing the upper limit up front. We usually select a random number of users and perform a couple of test runs in which the number of users is higher and lower than that initial random choice, and we analyze the results to determine the direction we should pursue—either increasing or decreasing the number of users.

The second step is defining the sample size: that is, the length of time for which the test run will execute. To choose the actual sample size, we have to reach a compromise between two divergent interests. The first is that we want to have enough data so that the sample is statistically significant. The second is the desire to make the tests as short as possible, since we will have many test runs to do and we don't want to spend too much time on them.

To figure out the sample size, we perform a test run using the upper limit of users, for a longer-than-usual period of time. We then plot the AART against time and analyze the curve. We are looking for a segment of the curve that is pretty much stable.

Another point that has to be made is that of data exclusion. When you first start a test, the response times are usually higher than normal. This is because all of the subsystems that make up the application take a little while to get up to speed. For example, the optimizer in the JVM needs a couple of minutes to optimize the running code. The same goes for the cache of the database, which will take a little time before it is useful (and so on with other components of the application).

These unusually high response times that are seen initially only affect the first few users on a production application that will typically run for weeks. However, in our case, in which we will be testing for just a few minutes, these results will negatively skew our sample results. Because of this, we exclude the first few sets of data we collect, and we start the sample when the curve has stabilized.

Thus, the sample size will start at a certain time after the actual test run has started, and it will last for a certain period that provides us with enough data to deem it statistically significant.

Next is the issue of assessing the accuracy of the test results. Depending on the kind of performance test that is being conducted, you can use two different ways to measure accuracy with a high level of certainty.

For performance tests that deal with a complete application, we usually calculate the following metric, which we call the *quality of a sample*:

$$quality = standard\ deviation\ /\ arithmetic\ mean$$

We usually apply this formula to the AART data collected.

Tip   Based on our experience, acceptable quality numbers lie in the range of 0.06 to 0.2. When the quality number exceeds 0.25, we carefully analyze all of the available data to find out the reason for such a low-quality sample. Sometimes, this can lead us to discard the data generated by the test run in question.

When doing tests focused on designing for performance and, more specifically, when the think time is zero, we use another method called *calibration*. Here we perform three test runs with the upper limit of users. We then compare the AART and TTR results of each test run against each other. The comparison is done as a percentage, and the greatest difference of all values is taken as the margin of error for the performance test.

Now that we have described all the preparation work, we can move on to describe the actual test runs that will provide us with the data that we need to perform the analysis and to make the conclusions of the performance test. The actual test runs are rather mechanical and boring procedures in which you start with a test run using the lower limit of users, increase the number of users, perform another test run, and so on until you reach the upper limit. As mentioned earlier, you will probably want to have a couple of additional test runs in which the upper limit is exceeded.

Because the base of the methodology is consistency, you will have to reset or restart every component or subsystem that makes up the application. In our case, that will be the database and the Java EE server.

We will go over a practical example of implementing the methodology later in this chapter to illustrate how to use it.

The Grinder

The Grinder is a Java-based load-testing framework that is freely available under a BSD-style open source license. *The Grinder*, along with its source code, documentation, ancillary modules, test scripts, and much more, can be found at `http://grinder.sourceforge.net`. There are also some mailing lists that you can join in order to participate in the Grinder community.

Please remember that the Grinder version 3 is required for Java EE 8.

The Grinder is extremely powerful, yet it's easy to use and is a lightweight toolkit. It allows you to simulate users and behaviors via test scripts across a number of machines. It consists of the following:

- A worker process that interprets the test scripts written in Jython and performs the tests using a number of worker threads, each of which simulates a user.

- An agent process that manages the worker processes. If you are running the simulated users on more than one computer, you will need one agent process for every computer.

- The console, which collates and displays statistics while coordinating the other processes.

The grinder process is shows in Figure 9-3.

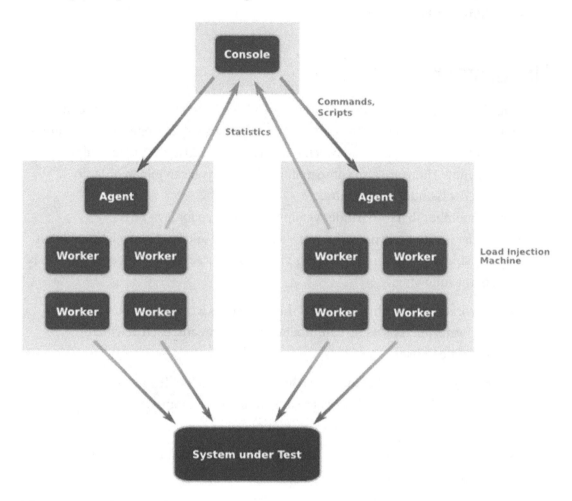

Figure 9-3. *The Grinder Process*

A *performance test* using *The Grinder* is a collection of test runs that can include one or more *test scripts*. A *test run* is the continuous sequential execution of test scripts. The test runs can last either a specific number of cycles or a specific period of time. A *cycle* is a single execution of a test script.

Note   What we call a *cycle* is defined in the documentation of *The Grinder* as a *run,* which we find confusing.

Test scripts are used to simulate the application usage. Test scripts represent the usage profiles that you want to simulate. A test script contains one or more *requests*, which resemble the typical interaction that a user of a specific profile would have with the application.

Note   Again, to avoid confusion, we use the word *request* instead of *test*, as defined in the documentation of *The Grinder*.

A Grinder test script is a Jython program that can contain certain logic to modify the default behavior, which is the sequential execution of the requests (for example, to execute certain requests based on the response of an already executed request).

A test script can be written by hand or, if the simulated user interacts with the application via an HTML interface, it can be recorded. The TCP Proxy module can be used to accomplish this. This module is part of *The Grinder* distribution. The HTML plug-in filter of the proxy allows your interaction with an application through a Web browser to be recorded. For details on how to use this functionality, please refer to the documentation.

In addition to executing URLs, *The Grinder* can also execute Java code as part of a request in a test script. This gives you the flexibility of simulating heavy clients, such as Swing-based clients.

Each agent process sets up a connection with the console to receive commands (such as start, stop, and reset), which it passes on to its worker processes. Each worker process sets up a connection to the console to report statistics.

In addition to the statistics presented on the console, for each test run, every worker process writes logging information and a final statistics summary to a file with a name that starts with the word out. Errors are written to a file with a name that starts with the word error. If no errors occur during a test run, no error file will be created. Detailed statistical information for every request executed is written to a file with a name that starts with the word data. These files follow a naming convention that, in addition to the words we described, also contain the name of the computer hosting the worker process and the number of the working process, as you can have more than one.

Modifying values in the `grinder.properties` configuration easily alters the behavior of *The Grinder*. Very likely, the most common properties you will be modifying are the following:

- `grinder.threads`: This property specifies the number of simulated users that will execute the specified test script.

- `grinder.runs`: This property specifies the number of times a simulated user will sequentially execute the test script (cycles). If the value is zero, it will execute forever.

- `grinder.consoleHost`: This is the name or IP address of the computer running the Grinder console.

- `grinder.logProcessStreams`: Set to `true`, this property will provide extremely detailed information about the execution of every simulated user. This information appears in the `out` file. It is useful during the preliminary runs, but we strongly suggest that you set it to `false` for all of the other runs, as it will degrade the performance of the test runs.

- `grinder.logDirectory`: This property specifies the directory in which you want to place the three log files described earlier.

- `grinder.script`: This is the file name of the test script to be executed.

There are many more properties available. Please consult the Grinder documentation for a full list of properties.

The Test Application

The test application that we have used for performance testing is a subset of the integrated Wines Online back-end application developed in Chapter 7. The user interface is developed using JavaServer Faces (JSF).

The latest JSF specifications can be found in this web page:

`https://javaee.github.io/javaserverfaces-spec/`

JavaServer Faces (JSF) is a Java Community Process (JCP) Standard technology for authoring component-based user interfaces on the Java EE platform.

Please notice that the JSF available by the time this manuscript was written was version 2.3, which was part of Java EE 8 in April 2017.

The executable implementations of the JSF 2.3 can be found in the javax.faces repository:

https://maven.java.net/content/repositories/releases/org/glassfish/
javax.faces/2.3.0/

Please refer to the NetBeans Introduction to JavaServer Faces 2.x on the NetBeans web page:

https://netbeans.org/kb/docs/web/jsf20-intro.html

Figure 9-4 displays the JSF page, which shows the catalog of all available wines in a list box. Users can a select wine items of their choice, enter the quantity in the input text box, and click the "Add to Cart" button. Users can repeat the same process to add more wines, and finally they can click the "Submit Order" button.

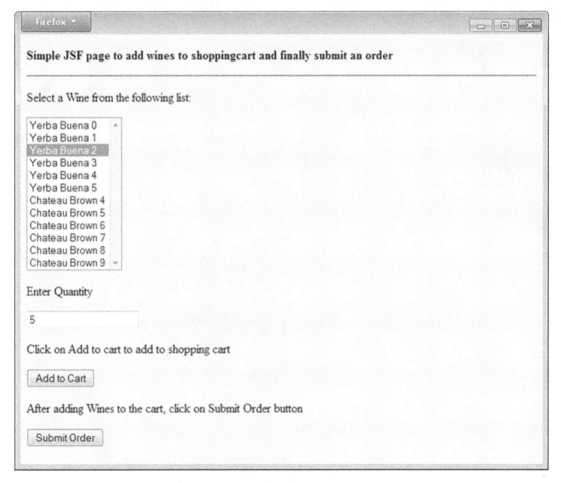

Figure 9-4. *The wine store JSF application*

Figure 9-5 shows the interaction between the JSF application and the back-end wine store application. When the JSF application is launched from the browser, a call to the getWineDisplayList() method (which uses an injected EJB in the managed bean) is made. This retrieves a list of all available wines using the findAll() method on the injected WineFacade EJB. The initial JSF page displays the retrieved list of wines. When the user adds a wine item and clicks the "Add to Cart" button, the addWineToCart() method in the ShoppingCart session bean is invoked, creating a new customer and adding the wine to the customer's cart items. Adding a customer only happens when the addWineToCart() item is called for the first time. When the user finally submits the order from the client application, the processOrder() method in the ShoppingCart session bean is invoked, which creates a new customer order, adds all the cart items to the order as order items, deletes the items in the cart, and finally deducts the inventory.

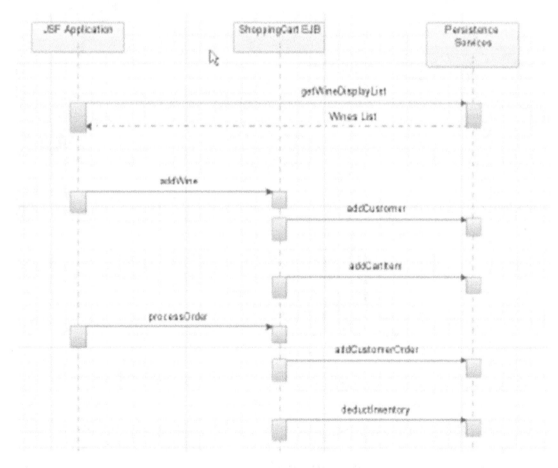

Figure 9-5. *The wine store application components and services interaction*

Figure 9-6 illustrates the Java Persistence API (JPA) entities, the inheritance model between the Java classes, and the relationships between them. The `BusinessContact` entity is inherited by the `Customer` and `Supplier` entities. The `Customer` entity is inherited by the `Individual` and `Distributor` entities. The `InventoryItem`, `CartItem`, and `OrderItem` entities inherit the `WineItem` entity. The wine store persistence unit also contains different types of relationships between these entities (including one-to-one, one-to-many, and many-to-many) that are exercised in the test application. Relationship fields whose names end in `List` are 0..* properties; all others are single-value properties. The relationship mappings used in these entities were covered in Chapter 3 and Chapter 4.

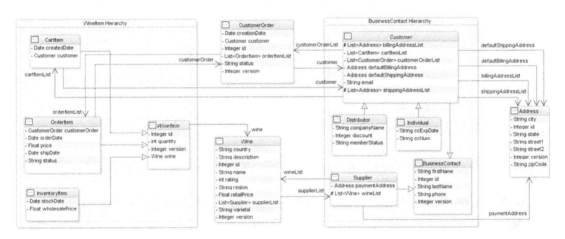

Figure 9-6. *The wine store domain model*

For the performance tests that we are going to run, all of the previously discussed components (the JSF application, the `ShoppingCart` and `WineFacade` session beans, and the Java classes in the persistence unit) remain exactly the same. The only differences between the two tests are the object/relational (O/R) mapping annotations specified in the JPA entities of the domain model and the database schema to which these Java classes are mapped. The first test uses a `JOINED` entity inheritance strategy in which the two root entities (`BusinessContact` and `WineItem`) map to the root table in the hierarchy, and the tables for all the subentities join to that table. Figure 9-7 shows the database schema used for mapping the persistent Java classes using a `JOINED` inheritance strategy.

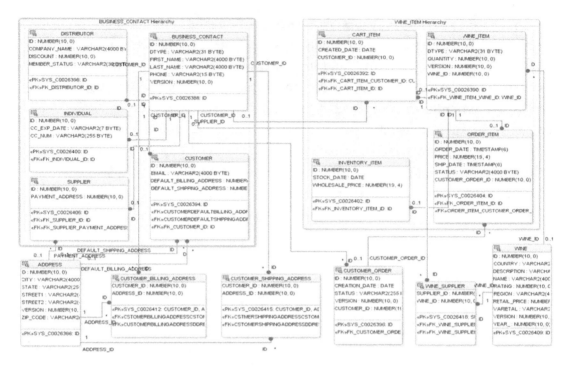

Figure 9-7. *The database schema for the JOINED entity inheritance strategy*

In the second test, we use a SINGLE_TABLE entity inheritance strategy in which the entities in each class hierarchy all map onto a single table. Figure 9-8 shows the database schema that is used to map the second test case.

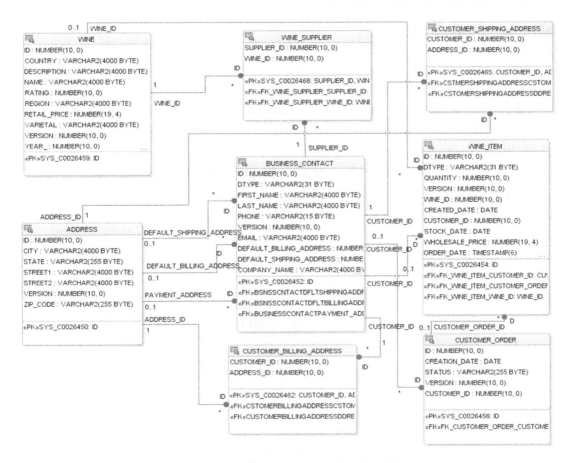

Figure 9-8. *The database schema for the SINGLE_TABLE entity inheritance strategy*

Note   Inheritance strategies are explained in detail in Chapter 4.

The Performance Test

Following the methodology described earlier, and using the test program just described, we will get on with the task of comparing the inheritance models to find out which one is best under the following conditions.

The Test Environment

We have set up a test machine in the cloud, which has eight cores and 8GB of memory. It runs an instance of the GlassFish server (in this book version 4.1.1). The test application uses the Derby database, which is also running on this server. We run *The Grinder* from our laptop, which is not in the data center where we have the test machine running, so all the traffic is going over the Internet. Normally, we would not do this, as we prefer to work in so-called sterile conditions; that is, the only traffic on the test network is the one generated by the tests. However, after doing many preliminary tests, we found that the margin of error of the tests to be so very low (1%), that we decided to continue working this way.

The test computer runs only the corresponding software required for the tests, besides the default processes of the operating systems. We use the default settings on all of the software involved. We realize that better performance can be obtained by fine-tuning these components, but that would be beyond the scope of this book.

The Test Script

As mentioned earlier in this chapter, the idea is to create a test script that resembles as closely as possible the usage of the application in real life. Since this is a design-for-performance test, we use a test script that loosely resembles the typical usage profile of the application:

1. The user goes to the wine application website (home).

2. The user selects a couple of bottles of one type of wine.

3. The user selects a few bottles of another type of wine.

4. The user checks out.

Since, in this example, we are comparing a couple of different inheritance models to understand which one applies best to our circumstances (design for performance), we use a zero think time.

Admittedly, running this set of performance tests using Derby is not very realistic, but the intent here is to provide an example on how to use the methodology. Our intention is that readers will apply this process to testing their own application, in their own application environment.

The output of the TCP Proxy module can be redirected to a file. This output is a Jython program that contains a high-level flow of the recorded tests, and it is easily readable by humans. This is where we modify or remove the `grinder.sleeptime` directives to eliminate the think time, or where we change the name or IP address of the target machine running the application. We review in detail the actual `wine.py` test script in the next section.

Setup

The installation of GlassFish was explained in the Getting Started section of Chapter 1, so we won't go over that here. You just need to make sure that the GlassFish server is up and running, and that the application is deployed with the necessary resources (JDBC connection pool and resource). One way to start the GlassFish server is to change directories to `%GLASSFISH_HOME%/bin` in a command shell and issue the following command:

```
asadmin start-domain
```

To stop the GlassFish server, you issue the following command:

```
asadmin stop-domain
```

Throughout the performance tests, we restart the GlassFish server with:

```
asadmin restart-domain
```

The Database

Each of the two tests requires its own database connection to ensure that your DB schemas don't collide. The tables mapped by each inheritance schema use similar names but have different structures. To minimize the installation requirements, we used the Derby database supplied with GlassFish for our tests. The projects are preconfigured for Derby, and to run them out of the box you will need to create the Derby databases. Refer to the Creating the Database Connection and Sample Schema section in Chapter 3 for steps on how to create a new database (and associated connection) in Derby. For these tests, you will need to create a `WineAppJoin` database with user `wineapp_join/wineapp_join` and a `WineAppST` database with user `wineapp_st/wineapp_st`.

Configuring Connections to Your Own Database

You may wish to use Oracle or some other production database when running your tests. To do so, you would update the `persistence.xml` file in the JPA project for each test (`Chapter09-PerformanceJoined-jpa` and `Chapter09-PerformanceSingleTable-jpa`) to modify the connection and information to point to your database. First create a separate database connection for each test, as we did for Derby above. For Oracle, we suggest that you begin by creating new DB users `wineapp_join/wineapp_join` and `wineapp_st/wineapp_st` in your database. Then go to the Services tab in NetBeans, right-click on Databases, and choose New Connection... to create a new database connection for each user.

Once your test database connections are created, you can edit the `persistence.xml` file in each JPA project through its Design editor tab by selecting the appropriate Joined or SingleTable connection through the JDBC Connection combo.

Similarly, you would need to update the `<property>` entries of the `<jdbc-connection-pool>` entry in the `glassfish-resources.xml` file inside the EJB project for each test (`Chapter09-PerformanceJoined-ejb` and `Chapter09-PerformanceSingleTable-ejb`) to update the connection information. (NetBeans 7.2.1 doesn't provide an editor to do this through a drop-down list, but you can easily cut/paste the `<property>` elements that specify the connection details.) Be sure to preserve the `<jdbc-resource>` jndi-name property as `jdbc/wineAppJoin, or jdbc/wineAppST` for the `SINGLE_TABLE` test, since this resource is referenced by name from the persistence units in the EJB projects.

The Grinder

The next step is to install *The Grinder* on the computer dedicated to creating the simulated user load. Once you have downloaded *The Grinder* from `http://grinder.sourceforge.net`, all you need to do is to unzip it in the desired directory.

The Grinder version 3.11 was installed for this testing in the C:\grinder-3.11 r directory of our laptop. Once you've done that, you can extract the Grinder-related files from the download package. These are in the `grinder` directory. We installed these files in the `C:\SampleCode` directory. There are three files needed for our example: `grinder.properties, joined.py, and single.py`. The last two files are the actual test scripts.

Refer to the Grinder.properties web page for additional information about how to configure this file:

http://grinder.sourceforge.net/g3/properties.html

Let's start by reviewing the first script, grinder.properties, shown in Listing 9-1.

Listing 9-1. grinder.properties

```
# Beginning EJB in Java EE 8
# Chapter 9: EJB Performance and Testing

# The number of worker processes
grinder.processes=1

# Number of simulated users
grinder.threads=140

# Run forever
grinder.runs=0

# Name of the machine where the console runs
grinder.consoleHost=localhost

# We don't want a full detailed log file
grinder.logProcessStreams=false

# Place the log files in this directory
grinder.logDirectory=log

# Start all the simulated users at the same time
grinder.initialSleepTime=0

# properties file. The default is "helloworld.py".
# Execute the test script called joined.py
grinder.script=joined.py
```

The comments in this properties file are pretty clear. You will just be changing the number of simulated users (grinder.threads) and the number of cycles that the test script will run (grinder.runs). Just make sure that you have the correct name or IP address of the machine on which the Grinder console will be running. Other than that, you really don't need to change anything else in this properties file.

The Test Script

In Listing 9-2 we present the core of the Jython program generated by the HTTP Proxy when we recorded the session with a joined tables inheritance scheme. The think time statements, which appear in bold, normally will present the amount of time it took you to go from one request to the next while recording the test script, as measured in milliseconds. As mentioned earlier, we replaced the original values with zero, but you can also just delete that line (see Listing 9-2).

Listing 9-2. Main Section of the Test Script

```
def __call__(self):
  """Called for every run performed by the worker thread."""
  self.page1()     # GET WineStoreJoined.jsp (request 101)

  grinder.sleep(0)
  self.page2()     # POST WineStoreJoined.jsp (request 201)

  grinder.sleep(0)
  self.page3()     # POST WineStoreJoined.jsp (request 301)

  grinder.sleep(0)
  self.page4()     # POST WineStoreJoined.jsp (request 401)
```

As an example of the page methods, we present in Listing 9-3 the one for page 1, the first request of the test script, along with a few definitions that happen before the first page method.

Listing 9-3. Example of the page method

```
url0 = 'http://glassfish:8080'
request101 = createRequest(Test(101, 'GET WineStoreJoined.jsp'), url0)
class TestRunner:
  """A TestRunner instance is created for each worker thread."""
```

```
# A method for each recorded page.
def page1(self):
  """GET WineStoreJoined.jsp (request 101)."""
  result = request101.GET('/Chapter09-PerformanceJoined-war/faces/
  WineStoreJoined.jsp')
  self.token_j_id_id17 = \
    httpUtilities.valueFromHiddenInput('j_id_id17') # 'j_id_id17'
  self.token_javaxfacesViewState = \
    httpUtilities.valueFromHiddenInput('javax.faces.ViewState')
    # '9131085258160566843:4053788772783974794'

  return result
```

Running the Simulated Users

You will have to modify the classpath of the following command according to where you installed the Grinder software. To execute the grinder, though, all you need is the following simple command. Just don't launch it before you start the Grinder console.

```
java -classpath \grinder\lib\grinder.jar net.grinder.Grinder
```

The Grinder Console

As an alternate way to start the console, all we do is change the directory to `C:\grinder\lib` and issue the following command to bring up the console:

```
java -classpath grinder.jar net.grinder.Console
```

Figure 9-9 shows the Grinder console.

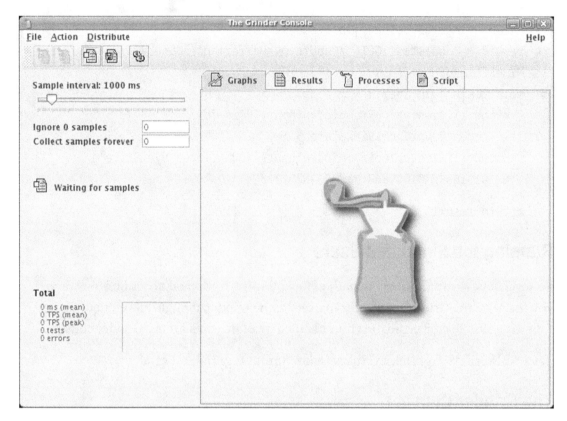

Figure 9-9. *The Grinder console*

The console has a couple of buttons on the top-left side that are used to indicate the Grinder agent to start or reset the worker threads: that is, the simulated users. When you hover over them, it will present a description of the function of the button. Figure 9-10 shows the Grinder console during the execution of a performance test and the information it normally displays.

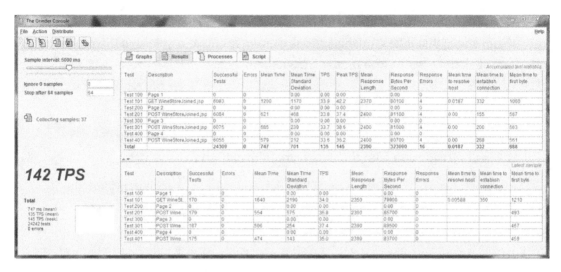

Figure 9-10. *Performance test with the Grinder*

Just to make sure that things are working fine, go ahead and do a quick test with only one simulated user for one cycle (after configuring the database; see "The Database" section, above). The steps are as follows:

1. Use the following URL to reset the database: `http://yourserver:port/Chapter09-PerformanceJoined-war/ResetJoinedData`

2. Reset the Glassfish server.

3. Start the Grinder console: `java -classpath` <classpath_to_the_grinder> `net.grinder.Console`

4. Edit the `grinder.properties` file, and verify that you have only one user and one cycle.

5. Start the grinder agent and the grinder console by typing the following commands: `java -classpath` <classpath_to_the_grinder> `net.grinder.Grinder.`

6. Click the start button on the Grinder console. No results will be displayed on the console because it will run for only one cycle.

459

7. Check the window where you started the Grinder agent. When it states that it has finished and is waiting for the console signal, click the reset button on the Grinder console.

8. Go to the log directory, and review the file that starts with the word out. This file contains a summary of the whole test run, including statistics. If there is a problem, this file and the error file will provide you with the necessary information to solve it.

After you have run these steps once for each test, you may want to update the persistence.xml file in both the JPA projects of each test app to turn off table generation. We left this flag on so that the tables would be created the first time you ran the ResetJoinedData/ResetSingleTableData servlets. After you have run each script once to create the tables for your persistence unit, you can avoid the overhead (and the warnings issued) due to the tables already existing for each subsequent run.

Now that everything is set and ready, you can go on to the next step.

Preliminary Tests

The objective of this first set of tests is to get familiar with the application and its behavior, as well as to discover any potential problems we might have with the test script or the application. As we're testing two different implementations of inheritance, it really doesn't matter which implementation we use for these preliminary tests, so we choose to conduct our initial tests with the implementation that uses multiple tables. We already performed one test run with one user for one cycle. Now we can move on to a test run for unlimited cycles and let it run for a couple of minutes. Then we'll move on to test with multiple simultaneous users for one cycle. This is done to make sure that the application and the test script can handle concurrency correctly. We will typically choose 10 users. After that, we'll test 10 users for unlimited cycles for a couple of minutes. Once these tests have completed successfully, we'll know that the test script and application are working fine, and we'll be ready for the next step.

We're looking to select a representative number of users for about half a dozen quick test runs that can clearly show us how the application behaves as we increase the user load.

When dealing with performance tests of full applications, we typically look for the upper limit of users when the maximum acceptable response time is reached or exceeded. Since this is a design-for-performance test, and we are not using any think time in the test script, we are going to focus on finding the number of users for which the saturation point of the application is reached. The strategy, as much as it can be called that, is to pick a number of users at random.

The test runs are short, since we don't need an exact upper limit number, just an approximation. In this case, we choose to start with 100 simultaneous users, and we will collect data from the test runs for 2.5 minutes. Since we are using a sample interval of 5 seconds, we just type **30** in the Grinder console's "Collect samples forever" box. The title to the box will change to "Stop after 30 samples" after we type 30. To keep things simple, we will not exclude the initial data. We do this by typing **0** in the Grinder console's "Ignore samples" box. The collected statistics will present values that are a little higher than normal. This is not an issue, as these tests are just preliminary. Following best practices, we reset the database and the Glassfish server for every performance test.

We start our first test run, and we obtain an AART of 737 milliseconds.

Note   You can find this information on the bottom part of the left column of the console (to the left of the square that graphically presents the TPS) with the title "(mean)".

The TTR is 137 (you can find this information in the same place that you found the AART, with the title "TPS (mean)"). Next, we will try again with 120 users. For this, we modify the grinder.properties file by changing the grinder.threads property to 120. We perform the next run and obtain an AART of 911 milliseconds and a TTR of 133. As the TTR for 120 users is lower than that for 100 users, we know that the saturation point is at about 100 or fewer users, so our next test run will be with 80 users.

After changing the number of users in the grinder.properties file, we start the test run. We obtain an AART of 593 milliseconds and a TTR of 136. These results indicate that the saturation point is somewhere around the 100-user mark, so we will use this as the upper limit. (Talk about a lucky guess in choosing 100 users as the initial test point!)

Based on this information, we choose to select 40 users as the lower limit and 100 users as the upper limit. The test runs will be done with 40, 60, 80, 100, 120, and 140 users. This will provide us with six reference points, which should clearly show us the behavior of the application.

Sample Size

Now that we have chosen the upper and lower limits of simultaneous users, we want
to figure out how long the tests should run. This is rather simple. All we need to do is to
perform a test run that will execute for a longer period of time than the 2.5 minutes we
chose earlier. Our experience with this kind of test tells us that about 7 minutes is typically
a good choice. The test run will be performed with the upper limit, which is 100 users.

Once we have concluded the test run, we take the data file generated by *The Grinder*
that contains the individual response times for every simulated user for every test. This
file can be found in the log directory with a file name that starts with the word data. Next
we plot a curve that presents the AART over the time period of the test. The results of
this test run are presented in Figure 9-11. Here we can see that the response time curve
stabilizes at about 60 seconds into the test run.

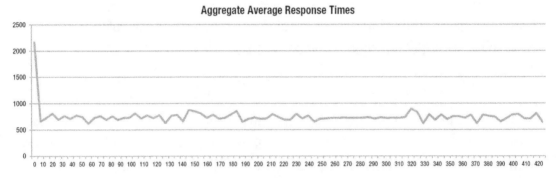

Figure 9-11. *Sample size analysis chart, plotting AARP over time period of the test*

We can also see that the curve remains fairly stable after the 60-second mark and
extremely stable after the 240-second mark. Therefore, we decide the test runs will last
240 seconds (4 minutes—nice and short), of which we will ignore the first 60 seconds. As
we have defined the sample size in the Grinder console to be 5 seconds; this means that
we will ignore 12 samples and collect 36 samples.

Calibration

Now we proceed to find out the accuracy of our performance test. Since this will be done
based on three test runs using the upper limit, we only have to do two additional runs.
We can use the appropriate data from the previous run to determine the sample size.

Tip   It has been our experience that typical margins of error using this method are between 5 and 10 percent. They tend to increase when there are think times in the test scripts. In these cases, it's not unusual to find numbers as high as 30 percent.

Table 9-1 and Table 9-2 show the differential of the results collected from the test runs for the AART and the TTR.

Table 9-1. *Margin of Error (AART)*

AART	Run 1	Run 2	Run 3
Run 1		100.1 percent	100.0 percent
Run 2	99.9 percent		100.0 percent
Run 3	99.9 percent	100.0 percent	

Table 9-2. *Margin of Error (TTR)*

TTR	Run 1	Run 2	Run 3
Run 1		99.3 percent	100.0 percent
Run 2	100.7 percent		100.0 percent
Run 3	100.7 percent	100.0 percent	

The biggest differences in these tables are 100.7 percent (for instance, run 2 vs. run 1 in the TTR table), and 99.9 percent (for example, run 3 vs. run 1 in the AART table). Thus. the official margin of error of this performance test is 0.7 percent, which is a very good number.

The Actual Test Runs

Now that we have completed all of the preparations, we are ready to start running the formal tests that will give us a picture as to which inheritance model behaves best under extremely stressful conditions.

This part of the performance tests is mechanical and rather boring. The initial step is to start the Grinder console and make sure that the parameters for our tests are set correctly. First, we verify that the sample interval is set to 5,000 milliseconds. Next, we check that we ignore 12 samples (of 5 seconds each, totaling the 60 seconds that we chose earlier). Then we choose to stop collecting data after 36 samples (of 5 seconds each, totaling the 180 seconds that we chose earlier).

The steps to follow for each test run are as follows:

1. Reset the database using the corresponding URL depending on the inheritance model:

    ```
    http://yourserver:port/Chapter09-PerformanceJoined-war/
    ResetJoinedData
    ```

    ```
    http://yourserver:port/Chapter09-PerformanceSingleTable-war/
    ResetSingleTableData
    ```

2. Restart the GlassFish server.

3. Edit the grinder.properties file, and modify the number of users.

4. Click the "Start to capture statistics" button on the Grinder console. This will clear out all the results of the previous run.

5. Click the "Start processes" button on the Grinder console.

6. Wait for the data collection to complete. A good indicator is when the line on the center of the left panel goes from stating "Collecting samples: XX" in green to stating "Ignoring samples: XX" in red.

7. Click the "Reset processes" button on the Grinder console. This step actually stops the execution of the simulated users.

8. Click the "Save results" button. Provide a descriptive file name, and save the results displayed on the console for later analysis.

9. Start over again at the beginning of this list.

Once you have finished with all of the test runs for the JOINED table inheritance strategy, you can proceed to do all of the preparations for the set of test runs for the SINGLE_TABLE inheritance scheme.

As explained in the earlier sections, the differences between our two tests are O/R mapping annotations and the database schema. Once the application is ready for the next set of test runs, just repeat the steps you did for the previous set of test runs.

Analyzing the Results

We have to start by stating that the results presented in this chapter are not meant to endorse one inheritance method over another. They are provided only to illustrate how to apply the methodology and how to use the Grinder toolkit. Because of this, we have gone into this performance test with no expectations about which inheritance model will work better.

We start our analysis by reviewing the results of the test run of the multiple-table inheritance with 100 users. These results are shown in Table 9-3.

Table 9-3. *Multiple-Table, 100-User Results*

100 Users	ART	TPS
Request 1	1,240	34.1
Request 2	594	34.1
Request 3	549	34.1
Request 4	543	34.1
Total	732	136

Two things should quickly come to your attention. The first is that the time required to obtain the home page of the application was long—a little over 1 second—especially when compared to all of the other response times in the test script. This can be explained because in setting up the main page, although simple, it involves sending data from the server to the browser, which in general is considered a more expensive operation than updating a shopping cart. The next thing that should catch your eye is that the checkout process lasts less than 1 second. While this is an ideal time for a process that verifies inventory and that performs other actions associated with a checkout, the truth is that there is not much of an inventory on this test system.

Looking at the results from the test run of the single-table inheritance model with 100 users (shown in Table 9-4), you can see a similar pattern of behavior, so at least it's consistent.

Table 9-4. *Single-Table, 100-User Results*

100 Users	ART	TPS
Request 1	1,320	33.4
Request 2	580	33.4
Request 3	540	33.5
Request 4	543	33.6
Total	745	134

This part of the analysis is limited to reviewing every individual request, and it is usually done with the results collected from the test run with the upper limit of users. The next step is to analyze the AART and TTR for all of the user loads that we selected. We start with the results from using the multiple-table inheritance model, which is shown in Table 9-5.

Table 9-5. *Multiple-Table, All-User Results*

Users	AART	TTR
40	291	137
60	438	137
80	584	137
100	732	136
120	919	130
140	1,120	125

From this table, it can be seen that the saturation point is reached from the beginning of the performance tests, which is quite unusual. This means that the inheritance model is gobbling up all of the resources available from the beginning.

Let's review the results for the single-table inheritance model so that we can do some comparisons. They are presented in Table 9-6.

Table 9-6. *Single-Table, All-User Results*

Users	AART	TTR
40	296	135
60	446	135
80	592	134
100	745	134
120	908	132
140	1,120	125

Once again, we see the same pattern of saturation from the beginning. This could be attributed to the Derby database and memory usage. What can also be seen is that both the Total Transactional Rate and the Aggregate Average Response Times are slightly lower than those of the multiple-table inheritance model.

This comparison can be seen more clearly in the charts presented in Figure 9-12, which contains a comparison of both sets of results for the AART; and Figure 9-13, which contains the comparison for the TTR.

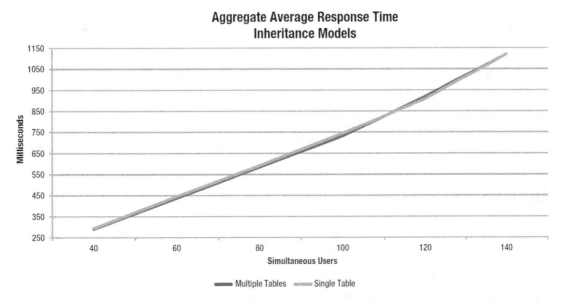

Figure 9-12. *AART comparison*

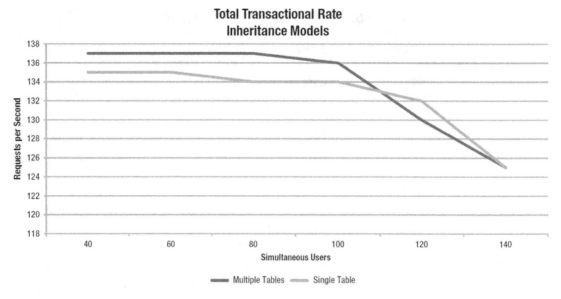

Figure 9-13. *TTR comparison*

In Figure 9-12, the Aggregate Average Response Times (AART) are pretty much the same, so we will have to look carefully at the Total Transactional Rate (TTR) to try to understand which model is more beneficial under the conditions of the performance tests we are doing.

In Figure 9-13, not only does the single-table model reach the saturation point faster than the multiple-table model, but the Total Transactional rate is slightly lower than that of the multiple-table model. As you can see, the single-table model starts degrading at 60 concurrent users, whereas the multiple-table model does so at 80 concurrent users. The big drop, however, happens earlier for the multiple-table model. Based on the data collected, we can conclude that the JOINED, or multiple-table, inheritance model presents a slightly better performance under highly stressful conditions.

Summary

In this chapter, we have presented *The Grinder*, a methodology to conduct performance tests, and a toolkit to generate the load for the performance tests. We went through an example of a performance test that used the methodology and the toolkit. In particular, we discussed performance criteria, with a review of the two performance indicators: response time and throughput. We covered the simulation of application usage, with a discussion about test scripts and think times. We also covered the defining of test metrics, such as the number of users, sample size, and exclusion of data, as well as how to determine the accuracy of the performance test.

To illustrate the use of this methodology, we presented a detailed case study using the application we created in the previous chapters and compared two inheritance strategies.

In the next chapter, we will look into Contexts and Dependency Injection (CDI) and how it can be used to enhance EJBs and the application development experience.

CHAPTER 10

Contexts and Dependency Injection

In this chapter, we will discuss *Contexts and Dependency Injection* (CDI). CDI provides powerful services to *glue* the various tiers of the Java EE framework together. The first public draft of *Java Contexts and Dependency Injection for the Java EE Platform*, as defined in JSR 299, was made public in 2008. During the initial development phase, the JSR 299 specification was called *Web Beans*. After the specification was renamed to Contexts and Dependency Injection, the initial reference implementation was given the name *Web Beans*. The use of the same name, Web Beans, in two different contexts created some confusion among the community members, and this led to the renaming of the reference implementation from Web Beans to *Weld*. Notice that Weld 3.0, the reference Implementation of CDI, will be integrated with the upcoming GlassFish 5.

CDI builds upon the Interceptor Specification (JSR 318), the Managed Bean Specification (JSR 316), and the Dependency Injection for Java Specification (JSR 330).

You might be wondering why we have included a chapter on CDI in this book. There are two reasons for this: First, the dependency injection behavior first introduced in EJB is enhanced in CDI; and second, CDI supplements EJB by providing the *contextual* functionality to an application. EJB complements CDI by providing enterprise services like security, transaction management, and scalability to an application. If an application developer *wisely* decides when to use CDI, EJB, or both, then the resulting application will be both nimble and scalable.

After you have finished this chapter, you will gain an insight into the following areas:

- CDI basics

- Relationship of CDI with EJB

- Deploying and executing CDI clients

© Jonathan Wetherbee, Massimo Nardone, Chirag Rathod, and Raghu Kodali 2018
J. Wetherbee et al., *Beginning EJB in Java EE 8*, https://doi.org/10.1007/978-1-4842-3573-7_10

What Is CDI?

Before the arrival of CDI on the Java EE scene, there was no easy way for the three tiers of Java EE technology—namely, the Web tier, the business tier, and the persistence tier—to interact with each other in a loosely coupled but typesafe manner. The Web tier did not have a proper mechanism to support transactions because it focused on presenting the content and had limited access to transactional resources.

CDI was mainly introduced to help with:

- Life cycle for stateful objects bound to lifecycle contexts

- Typesafe dependency injection mechanism

- Event notification

- Integration with the Unified Expression Language (EL)

CDI services help in unifying Enterprise JavaBeans (EJB) and JavaServer Faces (JSF) programming models. CDI services allow Enterprise JavaBeans to be used as the Managed Beans in JavaServer Faces framework. CDI also provides a good support for accessing transactional resources, which facilitates an easy creation of Web applications using Java Persistence API. CDI bridges this gap. Using CDI, the Web tier can directly interact with the beans in the business and persistence tiers. This is the reason why CDI was initially named Web Beans.

Contexts and Dependency Injection for Java EE (CDI) 1.0 (JSR-299) was first introduced as part of the Java EE 6 platform including:

- A well-defined life cycle for stateful objects bound to lifecycle contexts

  - Where the set of contexts is extensible

- A typesafe dependency injection mechanism without verbose

- Configuration

  - Dependencies can be selected at development or deployment time

- Typesafe decorators and interceptors

- An event notification model

- An SPI allowing portable extensions to integrate cleanly with the container

Then CDI 1.1/1.2 (JSR-346) was developed, including the following:

- Add automatic enablement of CDI in Java EE (beans.xml is not required)

- Add introspection with event, bean, decorator, and interceptor metadata

- Ease access to bean manager from outside CDI with CDI class

- Add global enablement of interceptors using the @Priority annotation

- Add unmanaged allowing easy access to non-contextual instances

- Spec clarification of CDI Life Cycle and Events

- Reworking Bean defining annotation to avoid conflict with other JSR 330 frameworks

- Clarification on conversation resolution

- OSGi official support in the API

Finally, CDI 2.0 (JSR-365), completed in May 2017, is a major evolution of the CDI 1.2 (JSR 346) specification lead by Antoine Sabot-Durand (Red Hat Inc.).

The Java EE 8 platform requires CDI 2.0, which comes with the following new features:

- Built-in annotation literals that can be used for creating instances of annotations

- An API which can be used for bootstrapping a CDI container in Java SE 8

- Some new configurators interfaces, which can be used for dynamically defining as well as modifying CDI objects

- Support for observer ordering, which is used to determine the order in which the observer methods for a particular event are invoked

- Support for firing events asynchronously

- Spec was split into three parts

- Java SE Support, using CDI outside Java EE

- Alignment on Java 8 features (streams, lambdas, repeating qualifiers)

- Event enhancement

- Configurators for major SPI elements

- Possibility to apply interceptor on producers

The CDI 2.0 specification was split into three parts such as Java SE, Java EE, and CDI Core. The main reason for splitting was:

- To align on many other Java EE specs that support Java SE bootstrapping

  - JAX-RS, JPA, etc.

- To boost CDI adoption for Spec and Frameworks

  - Java SE has been already supported by Weld, Apache OpenWebBeans, Apache DeltaSpike, and so on, but API is different from each implementation.

  - Programming model should be defined to avoid user confusion.

- To provide a mean of building new stacks out of Java EE (MicroProfile)

After the splitting, the specification name was also changed from "Contexts and Dependency Injection for Java EE (JSR 346)" to "Contexts and Dependency Injection for Java (JSR 365)."

Note   Custom libraries using CDI 1.x might be built again to align with CDI 2.0

Information about CDI be found at: `http://www.cdi-spec.org/`

The CDI specification can be found at: `http://docs.jboss.org/cdi/spec/2.0/cdi-spec.html`

Figure 10-1 shows the architecture of a Java EE application before the arrival of CDI on the Java EE scene, and Figure 10-2 shows how the Web tier and the business tier interact after the arrival of CDI.

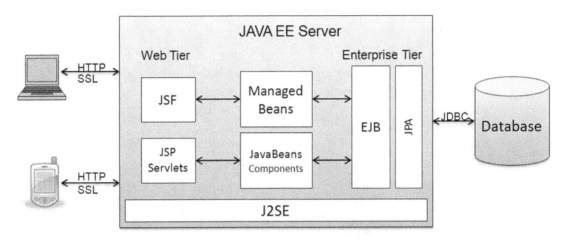

Figure 10-1. *Java EE Application Architecture before CDI*

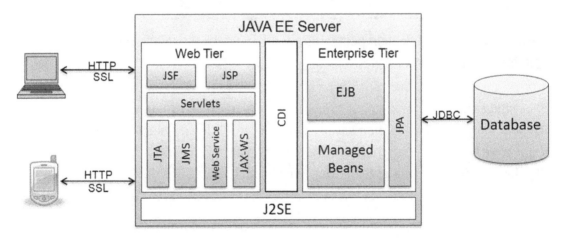

Figure 10-2. *CDI Application Architecture*

The two important features provided by CDI are a part of its name:

- **Contexts**: Deals with binding the stateful components (like stateful session beans) to a well-defined scope. Stateful components are those that retain information across their invocations. A CDI container associates stateful components with a definite scope—creating them when required and destroying them when they are out of scope. As a result, the client is not burdened with managing the life cycle of the stateful components.

- **Dependency Injection**: Deals with injecting the components into an application in a loosely coupled but typesafe way. The injected components are instantiated by the container, which means users don't need to create an instance of the component using *new*. Users can use the interface instead of the actual implementation of the interface for injection. This allows users to defer selection of a specific implementation, of a bean type that needs to be injected, to deploy at runtime.

Note   We can use injection points only in a CDI-enabled application, and Java EE 8 platform requires Dependency Injection for Java 1.0.

Listings 10-1, 10-2, and 10-3 demonstrate the concepts of "Contexts" and "Dependency Injection" in their simplest form. In the following sections of this chapter, we will build upon this example to demonstrate the various features of CDI. Listing 10-1 defines a Wine interface that is implemented by the RedWine class, as shown in Listing 10-2.

Listing 10-1. Wine.java

```
package com.apress.ejb.chapter10;

public interface Wine {
    public String getColor();
}
```

The RedWine class demonstrates the "Context" aspect of CDI. It has the ApplicationScoped annotation, which means that an instance of RedWine will be created only once when the application is instantiated, and that instance will be destroyed when the application is shut down. During the lifetime of the application, this instance will be shared across the application. We will learn more about scopes later in this chapter.

Listing 10-2. RedWine.java demonstrates the Context aspect

```
package com.apress.ejb.chapter10;

import javax.enterprise.context.ApplicationScoped;

@ApplicationScoped
public class RedWine implements Wine {
    public String getColor() {
        return "Red";
    }
}
```

The client shown in Listing 10-3 injects the field newWine using the @Inject annotation. Fields injected using the @Inject annotation are instantiated by the container, which means that users do not need to create an instance of the object using *new, nor do they need a compile-time dependency on the actual implementation class.* An important thing to observe here is that the newWine field is of type Wine. In this particular case, the container automatically uses the RedWine implementation for instantiation. If we had to instantiate RedWine in the classical way, then we would have to use the RedWine implementation instead of the Wine interface. As a result, there would have been a tight coupling between the client and the Wine object that could not be changed either at deploy time or at runtime. We will learn more about how the CDI container *knows* which implementation to inject when we discuss dependency injection later in this chapter.

Listing 10-3. WineClient.java demonstrates the Dependency Injection Aspect

```
package com.apress.ejb.chapter10;

import javax.inject.Inject;

public class WineClient {
```

```
    // Instantiating the classical way
    private Wine oldWine = new RedWine();

    // Instantiating via field dependency injection
    @Inject
    private Wine newWine;
}
```

For reference, the CDI specification also defines the following services. A more detailed explanation of these advanced CDI topics is outside the scope of this chapter, but you are encouraged to refer to the CDI spec for additional information.

- Integration of the Web tier with contextual objects via Unified Expression Language (EL)

- Decorators that implement beans and can intercept the invocation of those beans by business methods

- Interceptors for separating business logic from cross-cutting concerns

- Event notification model that defines the interaction between beans in a loosely coupled manner

- Ability to interact cleanly with the container via Portable Extensions

Relationship with EJB

CDI bridges the gap between the Web tier consisting of Servlets, JSP, and JSF and the enterprise tier consisting of EJB and JPA. Servlets, JSP, and JSF are responsible for content presentation but do not have transaction management and persistence functionality. EJB and JPA, support database-related operations like commit, rollback, and other transaction management functionality. Using CDI, Web applications can perform database-related operations supported by JPA using session beans as a *façade*.

Session Beans participate in the CDI life cycle like *managed beans*. Session Beans can be injected into other session beans and managed beans. Managed Beans can be injected into session beans. Users should be careful while deciding whether to use session beans or managed beans. Session Beans should be used when the application requires the following advanced enterprise services:

- Role-based security

- Transaction management

- Scalability through instance pooling

- Concurrency

- Events and timers

Managed beans will suffice for applications that require dependency injection, lifecycle management, and interceptors. Managed Beans can be easily upgraded to session beans by adding `@Stateless`, `@Stateful`, or `@Singleton` annotation.

Note   Message-Driven Beans and Entities are non-contextual objects and may not be injected into other objects. Message-Driven Beans take advantage of a few CDI features, like interceptors and decorators, as the container performs injection on all managed bean instances including the noncontextual ones.

CDI Concepts

Now that we have a basic understanding of CDI, its place in the Java EE stack, and its relationship with EJB, let us take a detailed look at Contexts and Dependency Injection.

Beans and beans.xml

Beans are container-managed components that contain business logic: for example, managed beans and session beans. It is important for readers to note that CDI does *not* introduce a new bean type called a "CDI Bean" with its own unique component model. CDI provides a set of services that can be consumed by managed beans and EJBs that are defined by their existing component models. The process that the CDI container undergoes of identifying beans found in the various deployment modules is called *bean discovery*. The beans discovered by the container via bean discovery participate in the CDI life cycle. The life cycle of these beans is managed by the container as per the CDI specification.

Note   Throughout this chapter, the word "bean" implies Java beans participating in the CDI life cycle unless specified otherwise.

The beans within a module participate in the CDI life cycle if the container detects a `beans.xml` file in the `WEB-INF` directory of a WAR file or the `META-INF` directory of a JAR file. Presence of `beans.xml` within a module aids the container to isolate quickly the CDI-related modules, making bean discovery quicker. CDI does *not* require the `beans.xml` to declare the beans available in the module; `beans.xml` can be empty. CDI artifacts like alternatives, interceptors, and stereotypes are declared in the `beans.xml` if required.

The CDI container provides the following services to its beans:

- Transparent creation, destruction, and scoping

- Typesafe-scoped resolution via qualifiers when injected into Java clients

- Typesafe-scoped resolution via name when used in Unified EL Expressions for JSF clients

- Lifecycle callbacks

- Automatic injection of other bean instances

- Interception and decoration

- Event notification

Beans are injected into other beans and clients by declaring a class-level field and annotating it with the `javax.inject.Inject` annotation. Beans can also be used with Web tier technologies like JSP and JSF via Unified EL Expressions, by annotating them with the `javax.inject.Named` annotation.

Scope

The scope of an object determines the life span of individual instances of that object. An application containing stateful object instances needs these instances to hold their state for a defined period. The scope dictates when a bean instance should be created and when the container should destroy it.

CDI has the following five types of scopes.

Application Scope

The state of an application-scoped bean is shared across all of the users of the application. An application-scoped object is created only once during the lifetime of the application—the first time it is injected—and is destroyed only when the application is shut down. An application scope is declared using the @javax.enterprise.context.ApplicationScoped annotation.

Request Scope

The state of a request-scoped bean is shared by all of the beans involved in a single request. A request-scoped bean is created once per request and destroyed upon completion of that request. A request scope is declared using the @javax.enterprise.context.RequestScoped annotation.

Session Scope

The state of a session-scoped bean is shared across multiple requests within the same HTTP session. A session-scoped bean is created when the HTTP session begins and is destroyed when the HTTP session closes or times out. A session scope is declared using the @javax.enterprise.context.SessionScoped annotation.

Conversation Scope

The state of a conversation-scoped bean is shared across all of the standard lifecycle phases of a JSF faces or non-faces request. One JSF request is associated with only one conversation. Any conversation can be either in *transient* state or in *long-running* state. Transient is the default state for a conversation. A conversation is marked long running by calling Conversation.begin(), and it is marked as transient by calling Conversation.end(). At the end of a JSF request, a conversation-scoped object has to be in transient state to be destroyed. A conversation scope is declared using the @javax.enterprise.context.ConversationScoped annotation.

Dependent Pseudo-Scope

The dependent scope is the default scope, and the container applies it when no scope is explicitly defined. The instances of beans with a dependent scope are bound to only one object. Instances of such beans are created and destroyed in sync with the creation and destruction of the associated object. These bean instances are not shared between the client applications. The dependent scope is declared using the `@javax.enterprise.context.Dependent` annotation.

Note   Users can define custom scopes by using the `@javax.inject.Scope` annotation.

Dependency Injection with @Inject

Before the publication of JSR 330, which introduced Dependency Injection, a client requiring services of a dependent class either had to instantiate a concrete instance of that class or rely upon an outside module to wire up the dependency before it was required. This created either a tightly coupled compile-time dependency between the client and the dependent class or reliance by the client on an outside process to "configure" the client appropriately. With dependency injection, the contract between the client and the dependent class became decoupled, and the client gained some control over how it was initialized. The client could request a resource to be injected by its interface and relied on the container to inject an acceptable instance of some concrete implementation class deliberately unknown to the client. CDI extends the power of the client to control its configuration by introducing a way (Qualifiers, see below) for the client to tell the container which abstract characteristics it requires of the injected class. The container uses these requirements to decide, at runtime, which dependent class to inject. This creates an even more loosely coupled system whereby the injected class requirements are configured declaratively and dynamically in the client and bound to an implementation class by the container at runtime.

The `@javax.inject.Inject` annotation defines an injection point, and there are three locations in a bean where injection can be performed by the CDI container: to initialize parameter values on a constructor declaration, to initialize parameter values on a method declaration, and to initialize a class member in a field declaration. We will examine each of these next.

482

Bean Constructor Parameter Injection

A CDI bean designates a single one of its constructors to be its *bean constructor*. This is the constructor that the CDI container uses to instantiate the bean. Bean constructor parameter injection occurs when we add an @javax.inject.Inject annotation to a bean constructor with one or more parameters. If a bean constructor has more than one parameter, then all of the parameters are valid injection points, which means that the container must provide values for all the parameters of a bean constructor. If the bean class does not have a bean constructor with an @Inject annotation, then the default (parameterless) constructor is used as the bean constructor.

It is possible for a client application to bypass the container and directly instantiate the bean. The obvious result in such cases is that the returned object is not bound to any context and the life cycle of the new instance is not managed by the container.

Listing 10-4 shows how the beanConstParaInjVintage field in the WineCellarClient class can be initialized with a vintage Wine type using a bean constructor parameter injection.

Note   The CDI container will choose the default implementation of the Wine interface and pass an instance of that implementation onto the WineCellarClient bean constructor.

Listing 10-4. WineCellarClient.java

```
package com.apress.ejb.chapter10;

import javax.inject.Inject;

public class WineCellarClient {
    private Wine beanConstParaInjVintage;

    @Inject
    WineCellarClient(Wine vintage)
    {
        this.beanConstParaInjVintage = vintage;
    }
}
```

Initializer Method Parameter Injection

CDI can also initialize a bean's properties afterward by calling methods on the bean that have been annotated @javax.inject.Inject. A bean method with an @javax.inject.Inject annotation is called an *initializer method*. An initializer method must be nonabstract, nonstatic, and nongeneric. An initializer method can have zero or more parameters. If an initializer method has multiple parameters, then all of the parameters are valid injection points and the CDI container must be able to supply values for all of the parameters. It is legal for a bean class to declare multiple initializer methods.

It is possible for a client application to bypass the container and directly call the initializer method. Again, the obvious result in such cases is that the container will pass no parameters to the method.

Listing 10-5 shows how the WineCellarClient class can be modified to use the initializer method parameter injection instead of bean constructor parameter injection to achieve the same result.

Listing 10-5. WineCellarClient.java

```java
package com.apress.ejb.chapter10;

import javax.inject.Inject;

public class WineCellarClient {
    private Wine initParaInjVintage;

    WineCellarClient()
    {
    }

    @Inject
    public void setVintageWine(Wine vintage)
    {
        this.initParaInjVintage = vintage;
    }
}
```

Field Injection

Finally, a CDI container can instantiate a class-level field by selecting an unambiguous implementation of the field's interface type. A class-level field can be injected by annotating it with the @Inject annotation. An injected field must be a nonstatic, nonfinal field of a bean class or of any Java EE component class supporting injection.

Listing 10-6 shows how field injection simplifies initialization of the fieldInjVintage.

Listing 10-6. WineCellarClient.java

```java
package com.apress.ejb.chapter10;

import javax.inject.Inject;

public class WineCellarClient {
    @Inject
    private Wine fieldInjVintage;
}
```

Dependency Resolution

The CDI specification guarantees loosely coupled and typesafe resolution of injected beans. The CDI container can unambiguously select an implementation of a bean type (class or interface) with exactly one implementation. But it is possible for a bean type to have multiple implementations. For example, we can add another class WhiteWine, as shown in the Listing 10-7, that implements the interface Wine that we created in Listing 10-1.

Listing 10-7. WhiteWine.java

```java
package com.apress.ejb.chapter10;

public class WhiteWine implements Wine {
    public String getColor() {
        return "White";
    }
}
```

After introduction of the `WhiteWine` implementation, our `WineClient`, in which `Wine` is injected, needs to distinguish between the two implementations of `Wine`: that is, `RedWine` and `WhiteWine`. The CDI container raises an *unsatisfied or ambiguous dependency* deployment time error when it is not able to isolate one bean class that needs to be injected at a given injection point. This ambiguous dependency issue can be resolved by using any one of the following three solutions:

- Qualifiers (for compile-time resolution)

- Alternatives (for deployment-time resolution)

- Producers (for runtime resolution)

Qualifiers

A qualifier type enables CDI components to interact in a loosely coupled way by providing polymorphism at compile time and dynamic binding at runtime. A qualifier type allows the client to specify the desired characteristics of the instance to be injected without having to know which concrete implementation class is being chosen.

Let us try and understand qualifiers using an example. The addition of `WhiteWine` class in Listing 10-7 forced the container to raise an error, as the container could not decide whether to instantiate the `RedWine` or the `WhiteWine` implementation. We will use a qualifier to resolve this dependency. Listing 10-8 shows a user-defined qualifier named Red.

Listing 10-8. Red.java

```
package com.apress.ejb.chapter10;

import static java.lang.annotation.ElementType.TYPE;
import static java.lang.annotation.ElementType.FIELD;
import static java.lang.annotation.ElementType.PARAMETER;
import static java.lang.annotation.ElementType.METHOD;
import static java.lang.annotation.RetentionPolicy.RUNTIME;
import java.lang.annotation.Retention;
import java.lang.annotation.Target;
import javax.inject.Qualifier;

@Qualifier
```

```
@Retention(RUNTIME)
@Target({METHOD, FIELD, PARAMETER, TYPE})
public @interface Red {
}
```

We will augment the RedWine class shown in Listing 10-2 with the Red qualifier, as shown in Listing 10-9.

Listing 10-9. RedWine.java

```
package com.apress.ejb.chapter10;

import javax.enterprise.context.ApplicationScoped;

// Instance will be created only once, will be shared
// across the application and will be destroyed on
// application shutdown
@ApplicationScoped
@Red
public class RedWine implements Wine {
    public String getColor() {
        return "Red";
    }
}
```

Introducing this custom qualifier allows us to resolve the ambiguous dependency error. WineClient, as coded in Listing 10-3, will now instantiate WhiteWine, as WhiteWine has the @Default qualifier, and the injection point also has the same @Default qualifier. Listing 10-10 shows how we can instantiate the newWine field with RedWine implementation by adding the @Red qualifier at the injection point.

Listing 10-10. WineClient. java

```
package com.apress.ejb.chapter10;

import javax.inject.Inject;

public class WineClient {
    // Instantiating in classic way
    // private Wine oldWine = new RedWine();
```

```
// Instantiating via field dependency injection
@Inject
@Red
private Wine newWine;
}
```

Now that we have a basic understanding of how qualifiers help us in resolving ambiguity, we will look into the four types of CDI qualifiers.

@Default

When a bean or an injection point does not explicitly define a qualifier, the CDI container assumes the qualifier as @javax.enterprise.inject.Default. If the CDI bean has only one implementation, then the CDI container can easily select that implementation for injection, as there is no ambiguity. The @Default is a built-in qualifier that informs the CDI container to inject a single, default bean implementation when no other qualifier (other than @Named, see below) is specified. The WhiteWine class in Listing 10-7 has the @Default qualifier and can be written, as shown in Listing 10-11, without any change in behavior.

Listing 10-11. WhiteWine.java

```
package com.apress.ejb.chapter10;
import javax.enterprise.inject.Default;
@Default
public class WhiteWine implements Wine {
    public String getColor() {
        return "White";
    }
}
```

@Any

Just like the @Default qualifier, all beans implicitly have the @Any qualifier. We can add an @javax.enterprise.inject.Any annotation to the WhiteWine class, as shown in Listing 10-11, alongside @Default without any change in behavior. An @Any qualifier at an injection point is useful for iterating over all of the implementations of a bean type.

Listing 10-12 shows how a @Any qualifier can be used to iterate over all of the implementations of Wine.

Listing 10-12. AllWinesClient.java

```
package com.apress.ejb.chapter10;

import javax.enterprise.inject.Any;
import javax.enterprise.inject.Instance;
import javax.inject.Inject;

public class AllWinesClient {
    @Inject
    @Any
    private Instance<Wine> allWines;

    private void printAllWineColors(){
        for (Wine wine : allWines){
            System.out.println(wine.getColor());
        }
    }
}
```

@Named

The @Named built-in qualifier is used by the beans that are required to be made accessible to the Web tier through the Unified Expression Language (EL). By default, the bean name with its first letter in lowercase is used to access the bean. A non-default name can be passed as an argument to the @Named qualifier.

@New

The @New qualifier disassociates an instance of the bean from its declared scope. An application can obtain the bean instances that are not bound to the declared scope by using the @New qualifier. The @New qualifier forces the container to create a new instance of the bean that is not bound to the specified CDI contextual life cycle.

For example, an instance of newWine, as shown in Listing 10-10, will be application scoped as it is qualified with the @Red annotation and the RedWine bean is application scoped. If we update the client to include the @New annotation, as shown in Listing 10-13, then the newWine instance will be dependent scoped—adopt the life cycle of its normal Java context—and not application scoped.

Listing 10-13. WineClient.java

```
package com.apress.ejb.chapter10;

import javax.enterprise.inject.New;
import javax.inject.Inject;

public class WineClient {
    // Instantiating in classic way
    // private Wine oldWine = new RedWine();

    // Instantiating via field dependency injection
    @Inject
    @Red
    @New
    private Wine newWine;
}
```

User-defined qualifiers can be created using the @Qualifier annotation, as shown in Listing 10-8.

Alternatives

Alternatives enable the CDI components to interact in a loosely coupled way by providing polymorphism at deployment time. An alternative bean is declared by annotating the bean class with an @Alternative annotation. An alternative bean must be explicitly declared in the beans.xml file if it has to be available for lookup, injection, or EL resolution. When an ambiguous dependency exists at an injection point, the container attempts to resolve the ambiguity by looking for the available alternative among the beans that could be injected.

Alternatives use the information supplied in beans.xml to select the implementation that needs to be instantiated. As the responsibility of choosing the implementation is shifted out of the Java code and into a deployment descriptor, recompilation of the Java code is not warranted if we decide to choose a different implementation.

To resolve a dependency at deploy time using alternatives, add the @javax.enterprise.inject.Alternative annotation to the RedWine and the WhiteWine implementations mentioned in Listing 10-2 and Listing 10-7, respectively. Then update the beans.xml with the implementation class that should be instantiated, as shown in Listing 10-14. The CDI container will instantiate the RedWine class in this case. Recompilation of the client is not required if we decide to instantiate the WhiteWine class later. We only need to update the beans.xml descriptor accordingly. If at deployment time the beans.xml contains more than one implementation class or with a class name that cannot be resolved, the container automatically detects the problem and treats it as an error.

Listing 10-14. beans.xml

```xml
<?xml version="1.0" encoding="UTF-8"?>
<beans xmlns="http://java.sun.com/xml/ns/javaee"
    xmlns:xsi="http://www.w3.org/2001/XMLSchema-instance"
    xsi:schemaLocation="http://java.sun.com/xml/ns/javaee
    http://java.sun.com/xml/ns/javaee/beans_1_0.xsd">

    <alternatives>
        <class>com.apress.ejb.chapter10.RedWine</class>
    </alternatives>
</beans>
```

Producers

We have seen how to use the @Inject annotation to inject beans and to resolve ambiguous dependencies that we face during injection using qualifiers and alternatives. Using producers, we can inject any object in any other object provided that *we produce* the object that needs to be injected. A producer method acts as a source of objects that need to be injected. The objects that need to be injected need not be instances of a bean, and the concrete type of the object that needs to be injected can be decided at runtime. This provides a loosely coupled but typesafe polymorphism at runtime. One of the practical uses of producers is to inject Java EE resources like EntityManager, QueueConnetion, QueueSession, and so on. CDI also provides the @Dispose annotation, which we can use to free up the resources by closing them when they go out of scope.

Producer Field is a simpler alternative to Producer Methods.

Listing 10-16 shows how a producer method can be used to select which implementation of the Wine interface is chosen for dependency injection. The decision to choose the exact implementation for injection is taken at runtime. The qualifier RandomSelector defined in Listing 10-15 is similar to the qualifier Red defined in Listing 10-8.

Listing 10-15. RandomSelector.java

```
package com.apress.ejb.chapter10;

import static java.lang.annotation.ElementType.TYPE;
import static java.lang.annotation.ElementType.FIELD;
import static java.lang.annotation.ElementType.PARAMETER;
import static java.lang.annotation.ElementType.METHOD;
import static java.lang.annotation.RetentionPolicy.RUNTIME;
import java.lang.annotation.Retention;
import java.lang.annotation.Target;
import javax.inject.Qualifier;

@Qualifier
@Retention(RUNTIME)
@Target({METHOD, FIELD, PARAMETER, TYPE})
public @interface RandomSelector {
}
```

Listing 10-16 shows the WineSelector class that has a getWine method that returns an instance of Wine. The important thing to note here is the exact instance of Wine (RedWine or WhiteWine) that will be returned is decided at the runtime. In this case, that decision is based on the number generated by the random number generator.

Listing 10-16. WineSelector.java

```
package com.apress.ejb.chapter10;

import java.util.Random;
import javax.enterprise.inject.New;
import javax.enterprise.inject.Produces;
```

```java
public class WineSelector {
    @Produces
    @RandomSelector
    public Wine getWine(@New RedWine rw, @New WhiteWine ww) {
        final int wineNumber = new Random().nextInt(2);
        if (wineNumber == 0) {
            return rw;
        }
        else if (wineNumber == 1) {
            return ww;
        }
        else{
            return null;
        }
    }
}
```

Listing 10-17 shows the WineClient class that uses the RandomSelector qualifier to instantiate the randomWine field based on the random number generated in Listing 10-16.

Listing 10-17. WineClient.java

```java
package com.apress.ejb.chapter10;

import javax.inject.Inject;

public class WineClient {
    @Inject
    @RandomSelector
    private Wine randomWine;
}
```

Interaction with Session Beans

CDI enhances the functionality provided by the session beans by associating them with a definite scope and creating a loosely coupled typesafe ecosystem that resolves ambiguity through injection at compile time, deploy time, or runtime. In return, managed beans can be annotated with a @Stateful, @Stateless, or @Singleton annotation enhancing them with declarative enterprise features like role-based security, transaction management, scalability, and concurrency in a multiuser environment.

Session Bean Scope

Session beans participate in the contextual life cycle provided by the CDI container like any other bean. A session bean can be associated with CDI scopes by adding CDI-specific scope annotations (@ApplicationScoped, @RequestScoped, @SessionScoped, or @ConversationScoped). As a result, the container automatically creates a session bean instance when it is needed by the client and, when no longer in scope, the container automatically destroys the instance.

By default, all generic session beans have @Dependent pseudo-scope, and hence they cannot be shared between the client applications. Inherently, some types of session beans play well with specific types of scopes. For example, a singleton session bean can have only one instance that exists during the entire life of an application. This property of the singleton session bean compliments the property of an application-scoped bean. Adding an @ApplicationScoped annotation to a stateless session bean does not make sense as a stateless session bean instance is associated with a client only for the duration of its invocation and does not maintain a conversational state with the client.

As a result, users must follow the rules mentioned in Table 10-1 while applying the CDI scopes to a session bean. If a session bean specifies an illegal scope, the container automatically detects the problem and treats it as a definition error.

Table 10-1. *Session Bean to CDI Scope Mapping*

Session Bean Type	Scope
@Singleton	@ApplicationScoped or @Dependent
@Stateless	@Dependent
@Stateful	@ApplicationScoped, @RequestScoped, @SessionScoped, @ConversationScoped, or @Dependent

Resolving Session Bean Ambiguity

Just like any other bean, session beans participating in the CDI life cycle can encounter the "unsatisfied or ambiguous dependency" error when the CDI container is not able to isolate one session bean that can be injected at a given injection point. These ambiguities can be resolved by applying qualifiers, alternatives, or producers to the participating session bean.

Session beans participating in a CDI life cycle use qualifiers (@Default, @Any, @New, @Named, or user defined) to resolve ambiguous dependencies at compile time, just like any other bean.

If an ambiguous dependency needs to be resolved at deployment time, then an alternative session bean must be declared explicitly in beans.xml. Once declared in beans.xml, it is automatically available for lookup, injection, or EL resolution.

The producer method of a session bean must be either a business method of the EJB or a static method of the bean class. If this is not the case, the container automatically detects the problem and treats it as a definition error. Similarly, the producer field must be a static field of the bean class.

Users can use qualifiers, alternatives, and producers with session beans in exactly the same way they use them with other beans.

Limitations

While CDI and session beans are great companions with each filling the gap that was left by the other, session beans participating in the CDI life cycle do have some limitations. For example, remote interfaces of session beans are not included in set of bean types and cannot participate in the CDI life cycle.

Compiling, Deploying, and Testing the CDI Application

Unlike EJB, CDI doesn't define any special deployment archive. CDI beans can be packaged within a JAR, EJB-JAR, or WAR file. The only condition is that the archive must be a *bean archive*, which means that the archive must include the beans.xml descriptor. The location of CDI beans within an archive is dependent on the location of its beans.xml.

- If the beans.xml is located in the META-INF directory of the archive, then the CDI beans must be packaged in a library JAR, an EJB JAR, or a RAR archive.

- If the beans.xml is located in the WEB-INF directory of the WAR file, then the CDI beans must be packaged in WEB-INF/classes directory of a WAR file.

In the case of some CDI containers, packaged CDI archives need to be assembled into an Enterprise Archive (EAR) file before deployment. Application servers provide deployment utilities or Ant tasks to facilitate deployment of CDI beans. Java IDEs (integrated development environments) like JDeveloper, NetBeans, and Eclipse also provide deployment features that allow developers to package and deploy CDI beans to an application server.

Throughout this chapter, we have used code snippets that demonstrate the two core aspects of CDI: scope and dependency injection. We started with developing a simple Wine interface and then went on to create two implementations of it – RedWine and WhiteWine. We learned about the various scopes and added the application scope to the RedWine implementation. We also saw examples that resolved ambiguous dependency by using qualifiers, alternatives, and producers. The WineClient client that we listed in the chapter until now demonstrates how clients can potentially interact with the CDI beans, but it is not a full-fledged executable client. We will now convert the WineClient client into a servlet client and test the CDI beans using it by deploying them on the GlassFish application server. The following sections will walk you through the steps necessary to compile, deploy, and test these CDI beans using their corresponding servlet clients.

Prerequisites

Before performing any of the steps detailed in the next sections, complete the "Getting Started" section of chapter 1. This section will walk you through the installation and environment setup required for the samples in this chapter.

Note   While creating a *new* NetBeans project, make sure that you have selected the "Enable Contexts and Dependency Injection" check box on the "Server and Settings" page of the new application wizard. This will create a beans.xml and add the CDI-related runtime libraries to your project.

Structure of the Sample Code

We have divided the samples into the following four packages, and all the artifacts within those packages have the package-private scope. We do this separation so that the CDI objects and their clients do not interfere with each other, and we can observe their behavior in isolation.

- com.apress.ejb.chapter10.userdefinedqualifier

- com.apress.ejb.chapter10.anyqualifier

- com.apress.ejb.chapter10.alternatives

- com.apress.ejb.chapter10.producers

Compiling the CDI Beans and Their Clients

Copy the Chapter10-CDISamples directory and its contents into a directory of your choice. Run the NetBeans IDE, and open the Chapter10-CDISamples project using the File ➤ Open Project menu, as shown in Figure 10-3.

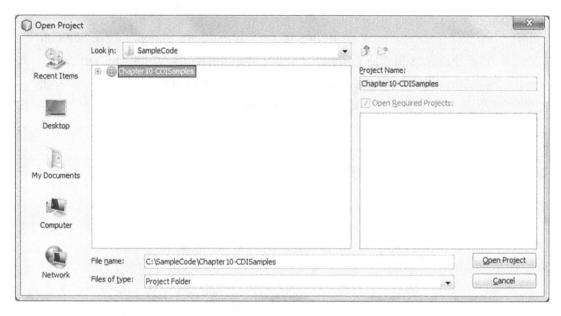

Figure 10-3. *Opening the Chapter10-CDISamples project*

Expand the `Chapter10-CDISamples` node and observe that the various packages listed above appear under the `Source Packages` section as shown in Figure 10-4.

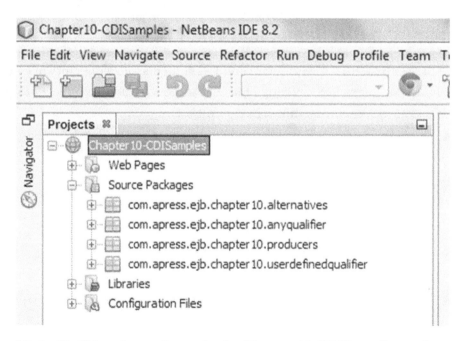

Figure 10-4. *Verifying the packages in the Chapter10-CDISamples project*

Invoke the context menu on the Chapter10-CDISamples node, and build the application by selecting the Clean and Build menu option, as shown in Figure 10-5. The CDI bean and their clients compile without any errors.

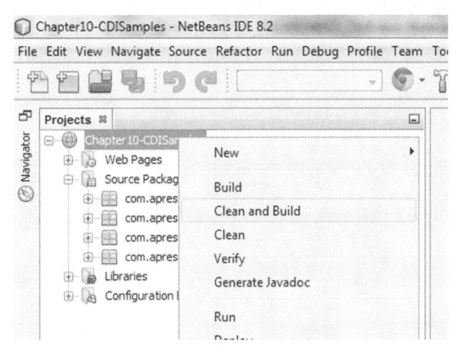

Figure 10-5. *Building the project*

Deploying and Running the CDI Clients

Once we have compiled the CDI project, we can run the clients directly using the Run option available on the context menu of each of the servlet clients. When we *run* the servlet client the NetBeans IDE will automatically package the CDI beans and their clients and deploy them to the integrated GlassFish application server.

Testing the User-Defined Qualifier Client

We will start with testing and experimenting with the user-defined qualifier Red, which we created in Listing 10-8 and used in Listings 10-9 and 10-10.

In addition to the Red qualifier, we have also created the White qualifier that we have added to the WhiteWine implementation of the Wine interface. Expand the com.apress.ejb.chapter10.userdefinedqualifier package, and right-click on the

UsrDefQlfWineClient servlet to invoke the context menu, as shown in Figure 10-6. Next select the Run option to execute the servlet client.

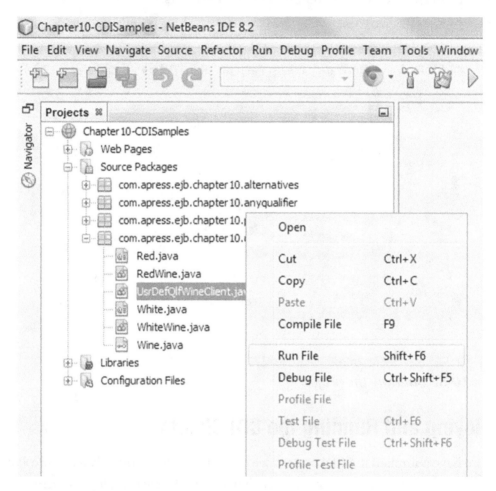

Figure 10-6. *Running the User-Defined Qualifier Client*

Even though there are two implementations of the Wine interface—RedWine and WhiteWine—the CDI container is able to resolve the ambiguous dependency by using the @Red annotation on injected newWine field. The result of the executed servlet is shown in Figure 10-7.

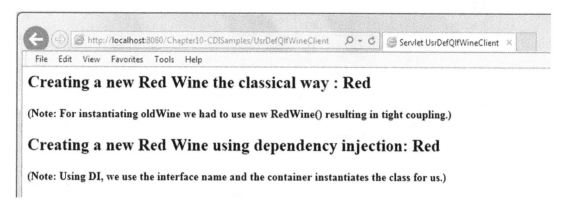

Figure 10-7. *Results from the User-Defined Qualifier servlet*

You can try to run the client again with the following changes and observe the difference in the output:

- Replace the @Red annotation on the injected newWine field with the @White annotation.

- Remove both @Red and @White annotations on the injected newWine field, and execute the servlet client.

Testing the Any Qualifier Client

Next, we will test the Any qualifier, demonstrated in Listing 10-12, which will return the list of all the implementations of the Wine interface.

In addition to the RedWine and WhiteWine implementations, we have also created the SparklingWine implementation along with its Sparkling qualifier. Expand the com.apress.ejb.chapter10.anyqualifier package, and right-click on the AnyWineClient servlet to invoke the context menu, as shown in Figure 10-8. Select the Run option to execute the servlet client.

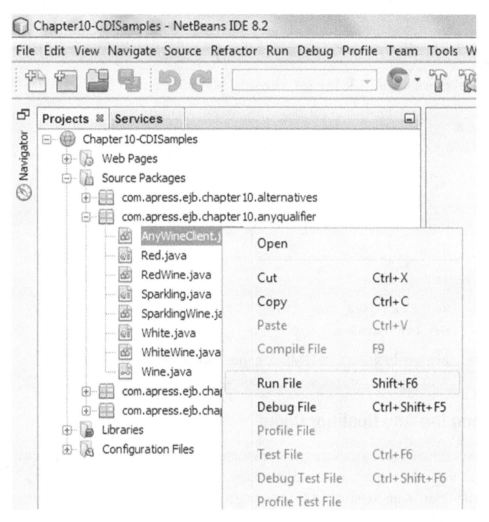

Figure 10-8. *Running the Any qualifier client*

By using the @Any qualifier, the container is able to determine all the implementations of the Wine interface. The result of the executed servlet is shown in Figure 10-9.

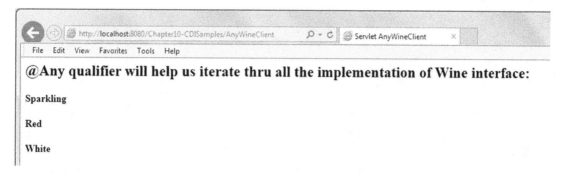

Figure 10-9. *Result from the Any qualifier client servlet*

You can try to run the client again with the following changes and observe the difference in the output:

- Create a RoseWine implementation along with its Rose qualifier in the same package, and rerun the servlet client.

- Remove the @Any annotation present on the injected allWines field, and execute the servlet client.

Testing the Alternatives Client

After seeing the qualifiers in action, we will look at how we can resolve ambiguous dependencies at deploy time using alternatives. We saw how to declare alternatives in beans.xml in Listing 10-14.

Expand the com.apress.ejb.chapter10.alternatives package, and right-click on the AlternativesWineClient servlet to invoke the context menu, as shown in Figure 10-10. Select the Run option to execute the servlet client.

Figure 10-10. *Running the Alternatives client*

The CDI container instantiates the `RedWine` class using the `<alternatives>` declaration in the `beans.xml`. The output of the execution is shown in Figure 10-11.

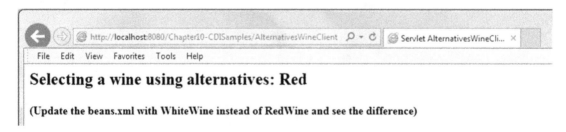

Figure 10-11. *Result from the Alternatives client*

You can try and run the client again with the following changes and observe the difference in the output:

- Update the beans.xml with WhiteWine, and rerun the servlet client.

- Remove the @Alternative annotation present on RedWine or WhiteWine implementation, and execute the servlet client.

Testing the Producers Client

Finally, we will see the producers in action. We saw how to declare a producer method in Listing 10-16. Expand the com.apress.ejb.chapter10.producers package, and right-click on the ProducerWineClient servlet to invoke the context menu, as shown in Figure 10-12. Select the Run option to execute the servlet client.

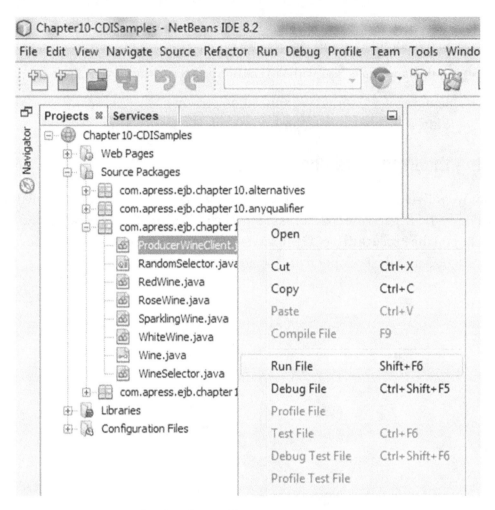

Figure 10-12. *Running the Producer client*

The WineSelector class declares a producer method named getWine. In the getWine method, we generate a random number that is greater than or equal to 0 and less than 4. The getWine method returns an instance of an implementation of the Wine interface based on the generated random number. The output is shown in Figure 10-13.

Figure 10-13. *Result from Producers client*

You can try to run the client again with the following changes and observe the difference in the output:

- Re-deploy and rerun the client servlet a couple of times, and observe the difference in output.

- Comment out the @Produces annotation present on the getWine method, and execute the servlet client.

Summary

In this chapter, we covered Contexts and Dependency Injection (CDI) version 2.0. We looked at the place that CDI occupies within Java EE framework and the benefits it provides by gluing Web and business tiers. We especially learned that we can now use CDI 2.0 on Java EE as well as Java SE as well as how the CDI 2.0 new features help increase developer productivity. We explained the two main components of CDI framework, namely, contexts and dependency injection. We also looked at the contextual life cycle of stateful components participating in the CDI life cycle and discussed different types of scopes. Using examples, we also looked at different ways that dependency can be injected and how ambiguous dependency issues can be resolved at compile time, deploy time, or runtime. We discussed the relationship between CDI and EJB, specifically with session beans. Finally, we deployed and executed the sample CDI client program using the GlassFish application server and experimented with the sample code to see how changes to the code affect the output.

CHAPTER 11

EJB Packaging and Deployment

Until now, we have focused on how to build EJBs, Java Persistence API (JPA) entities, and their clients, for exploiting the surrounding enterprise services offered by the EJB container. In Java EE parlance, these tasks fall under the role of Application Component Provider, which is simply referred to as the Provider. In this chapter, we explore the topics that surround the process of packaging your components into modules and library components, binding external references declared in your Java EE components to actual resources in your server environment, and sending it all off to an application server so that the components can be executed at runtime by an application. These responsibilities are handled by the Java EE roles of the Application Assembler (the Assembler) and the Application Deployer (the Deployer). While in practice it is common for a single individual to perform one or more of these roles, or for many people to perform any single role, for the purpose of explaining these topics, we will partition the deployment tasks into stages that correspond to these designated roles.

We will emphasize EJB and JPA entity components and also touch upon deployment of the other Java EE module types: Web application modules, application clients, and resource adapters. We will also look at the relationship between the Java EE server and the four Java EE containers that it supports, and we will explore some of the services that are provided by a Java EE server.

Following a brief overview of the deployment tasks in which we introduce much of the deployment terminology, we offer a look at the Java EE infrastructure components—the Java EE server and containers—that support deployment. We will explore the different types of Java EE modules and how they fit together and how you specify the deployment descriptors—metadata files—that define each module. A section on library components is offered, which explains how to declare class-path dependencies between Java EE modules and library components. We then provide a more detailed

509

© Jonathan Wetherbee, Massimo Nardone, Chirag Rathod, and Raghu Kodali 2018
J. Wetherbee et al., *Beginning EJB in Java EE 8*, https://doi.org/10.1007/978-1-4842-3573-7_11

examination of the Assembler and Deployer roles, and we conclude with the deployment requirements that are specific to EJB modules and JPA persistence units.

In the current Java world, it is very important the usage of Java Virtual Machine (JMV). Basically, every Java program requires a JVM running on our machine so that all the Java bytecode is run using that JVM. This means that VM will be not distributed with each program. The same concept is used for Java EE. After reading this chapter, you should understand how to do the following:

- Group your EJB, JPA, and other application components into Java EE modules and library components.

- Resolve naming collisions and redundancies found in external references.

- Package a Java EE application consisting of one or more Java EE modules and library components.

- Declare class-path dependencies between modules and libraries.

- Bind external references to physical resources in the application server environment.

A Note on Deployment Tools

This chapter provides some examples of how to structure your application archives. It assumes that you have access to software tools, typically offered through an integrated development environment (IDE), to assist you in the assembly and deployment of your Java EE applications. There have been efforts in the Java Community Process (JCP) to standardize in this area (see JSR 88, the Java EE Application Deployment API), but deployment inevitably requires application server-specific configuration tasks. Fortunately, application servers generally provide Ant tasks to invoke their own deployment utilities, and you may also use Ant to create the deployable archives. The use of Ant is prevalent in many development environments and is nearly ubiquitous in production environments in which automated scripts are required to deploy the same Java EE applications to multiple Java EE server instances. Many of the customization steps that are described in this chapter require the use of interactive editors, mainly for updating Java EE generic and platform-specific XML deployment descriptors. For these tasks, an IDE can prove invaluable, and many IDEs provide platform-specific deployment support that guides you in packaging, configuring, and deploying your Java EE applications.

Overview of the Packaging and Deployment Processes

Packaging is the process of assembling (or grouping) various Java EE modules into Java EE JAR, WAR, or EAR files. Once packaged in a Java Archive (JAR) file, a Web Archive (WAR) file, or an Enterprise Archive (EAR) file, the Java EE application is ready to be delivered to the application server. *Deployment* is the process of installing Java EE components in an application server so that they can be found and executed when you run your application. This process involves multiple tasks that must be performed, roughly, in sequence. These tasks are summarized in the following sections, and each is described in greater detail and applied specifically to EJB and JPA deployment later in this chapter. Some steps will only need to be performed under special circumstances, so actual deployment may involve only a subset of these tasks.

Major packaging distribution goal is making sure that:

- Not all the libraries needed by the programs will be distributed. Instead it is making sure that they will be downloaded" once in the whole system.

- Not many libraries needed by the programs will be loaded many times into memory. Instead we need to load the shared code once for other programs to use it.

The Provider

Generally speaking, the Provider (there may be many for a given project) produces the Java EE application components as a precursor to deployment. The tasks associated with the Provider, along with the files delivered by this role, are shown in Figure 11-1.

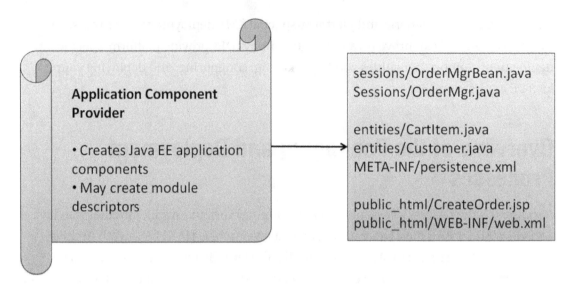

Figure 11-1. *Tasks and deliverables of the Application Component Provider*

The deliverables from the Provider are application components and possibly module descriptors, provided either as files on disk or packaged into Java Archive (JAR) files.

The Assembler

The Assembler takes the output from the Provider, and with it performs the tasks and produces the deliverables illustrated in Figure 11-2.

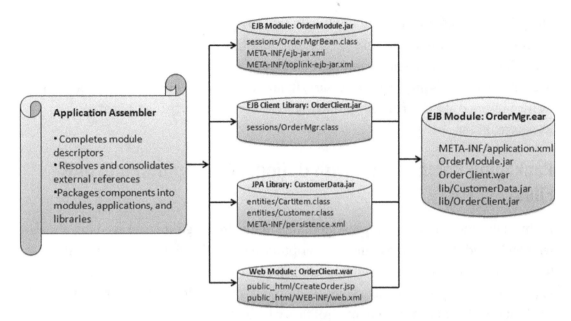

Figure 11-2. *Deployment tasks and deliverables of the Application Assembler*

Grouping Components by Container Type to Produce Java EE Modules

The output of the Provider is a set of Java EE components, such as EJBs, JPA entities, JSF (JavaServer Faces) pages, application client classes, and possibly others. The Provider may also produce non-Java EE components, like ordinary Java classes. The Assembler groups the Java EE components together such that each group contains components of only one Java EE component type. Whenever the Provider has defined a module-level deployment descriptor (XML) file, the Assembler may follow any directives in that file to compose the groups, or the Assembler may choose either to merge or split descriptors to increase or decrease the number of Java EE components in each group. At the end of this process, each resulting group will become a Java EE module. The non-Java EE classes and resources that are left over may be bundled into the Java EE modules or isolated into their own groups to become sharable library components.

Defining Module-Level Deployment Descriptors (Optional)

For each Java EE module that is formed, the Assembler may locate and assign a deployment descriptor to represent that module. Starting with Java EE 5, this step is optional, since annotations now make it possible to identify the module type by analyzing its file contents. For example, you (in the role of either the Provider or the Assembler) are free to define an `ejb-jar.xml` deployment descriptor; but unless you are overriding information that is captured in Java annotations, or you have chosen to not use annotations, it is no longer necessary. In Java EE 5, an EJB module is defined simply by the presence of a class in a file group that is annotated `@Stateless`, `@Stateful`, or `@MessageDriven`.

Packaging Components (with Optional Descriptors) into JAR Files

In this stage, the component groups identified in the first stage are packaged together with their module-level deployment descriptors, if defined, into files using the JAR format. EJB modules are archived into EJB JAR files with a `.jar` extension, Web application modules are archived into Web Archive (WAR) files with a `.war` extension, application clients are archived into JAR files with a `.jar` extension, and so on. JPA persistence units may be archived into their own JAR files (with `.jar` extensions) or archived directly into EJB JAR or WAR files. We'll cover this detail in the "Assembling a Persistence Unit" section later in the chapter.

In addition, non-Java EE components, such as ordinary Java classes, may be added to these Java EE module archives; or the Assembler may archive them into their own JAR files to be deployed as library components.

Creating an Enterprise Archive (EAR) File (Optional)

If you (as the Assembler) have created multiple archives that you want to deploy together as a logical group, you will need to bundle these archives together inside a wrapper JAR file known as an *EAR file*, which uses the suffix `.ear`. This EAR file is referred to as a Java EE application. If you have created only a single EJB JAR or WAR archive, no further packaging is required. You can skip the step of creating a wrapper EAR file, and deploy the EJB JAR or WAR file as a stand-alone module.

An application acts as a packaging boundary, ensuring that the Java EE components in all modules are able to communicate with each other within a single naming context. A Java EE application does not necessarily correspond to an actual end-user application as it may be used by many different client applications, but it allows client applications to connect to the Java EE application once and access the Java EE components in that application from a single context.

An EAR file may contain an application-level deployment descriptor, `application.xml`, in its `META-INF` directory. This file is optional in Java EE 5, since it is now possible to rely on default rules to provide default names and properties for each module. By default, each module name defaults to the short name of its archive file, minus the file suffix (`.jar`, `.war`, and so on). Defining an `application.xml` descriptor allows you to refine the default names and properties and to choose selectively which modules in the EAR file to include in the application for a particular deployment. The Figure 11-3 shows the EAR File Structure.

Note   A WAR file and an EAR file are standard JAR files with a `.war` or `.ear` extension respectively.

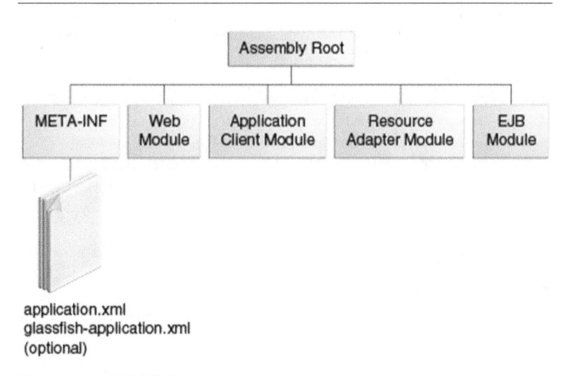

application.xml
glassfish-application.xml
(optional)

Figure 11-3. *EAR File Structure*

Assembler-Specific Tasks

Depending on the completeness and the complexity of the deployment descriptors for each module, the Assembler may be required to complete or refine some of the external references declared by the Provider. In many cases, the modules are sufficiently self-contained and complete so that there is no further work for the Assembler to perform, even when a deployment descriptor is not supplied by the Provider. In more complex deployment scenarios, when Provider-supplied documentation is used (possibly communicated through description properties on either the annotations or in the deployment descriptor), the Assembler may need to consolidate semantically equivalent but disparately named resources into a minimal, distinct set. Conversely, the Assembler may need to avoid resource name collisions by renaming resource references that share the same name but hold different semantics.

For example, if the Assembler is bundling two Java EE modules produced by different providers into a single Java EE application, both providers may reference the same logical EJB but use different names, or they may reference them with the names not yet bound. It is the responsibility of the Assembler to detect cases such as this, using the documentation provided by the Provider(s), and update the EJB references to bind to a single name. This name may be chosen by the Assembler and assigned to the EJB in that application context.

Any changes made by the Assembler are applied only to the module and application deployment descriptor files, and not to the Java source. This process works because of the rules of precedence dictated by Java EE, which in the case where conflicting metadata properties are defined both in the Java annotation source and the XML deployment descriptors, the deployment descriptors will prevail. The Assembler is able to resolve inconsistencies in the Java source by working only with the deployment descriptor files.

The Deployer

The tasks and deliverables of the Deployer are depicted in Figure 11-4.

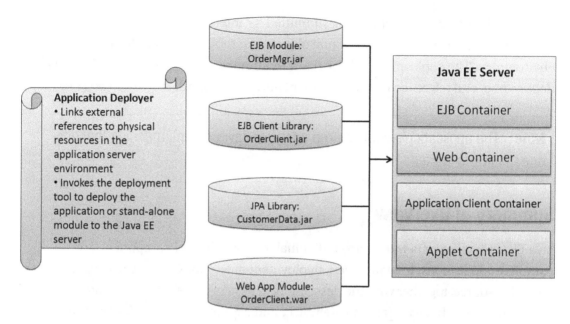

Figure 11-4. *Tasks and deliverables of the Application Deployer*

Deployer-Specific Tasks

Again, using instructions from the Assembler (and Provider)—typically communicated through description properties in the deployment descriptors or source annotations, the Deployer is required to bind all external references onto concrete resources (EJB references, resource references, persistence unit references, and so on) in the target application server environment. Only the Deployer can presume to know about the target server environment, and Java EE has deliberately added a layer of indirection to all resource usage to allow this binding to occur without affecting the work of either the Provider or the Assembler. This is why all resources used by the Java EE components are referred to via indirect references.

As was the case with the Assembler, Java EE policy dictates that the Deployer is allowed to make changes only to the XML deployment descriptor files and not to annotations in the Java source.

Invoking the Application Server-Specific Deployment Tool

Finally, your Java EE module or your Java EE application is ready to be submitted to the application server. Your application server will provide a deployment tool that lets you complete the deployment and install the Java EE components in the application server, ready to be executed by the end-user applications. During this stage, the deployment

517

tool will validate the module(s) being submitted for internal integrity and ensure that all resources can be bound to actual objects that reside in the application server environment. The deployment will fail if any required resources cannot be located at deploy time, or if referenced library components are not found.

Note   The application server will run once per environment, meaning that only one runtime is started.

Summary of Overview

Java EE deployment lets you deploy individual modules, library components, or complete applications. In many cases, deployment may simply involve packaging the compiled source, together with the descriptors (a `persistence.xml` file is mandatory for persistence units, but `ejb-jar.xml`, `web.xml,` and `application.xml` files are optional for an EJB JAR, WAR and EAR modules respectively) and submitting them to a deployment tool. When assembling applications from multiple modules that may have been built by different component providers and may be of differing versions, the Assembler role takes on greater importance.

Java EE Deployment Infrastructure

Now that we have summarized the deployment process, let us explore some areas of the Java EE infrastructure that are central to deployment. An understanding of this topic is useful when it is time to make your own decisions about how to package your code into modules and to resolve and bind external references.

The Java EE Server

The *Java EE server* is the program running inside your application server that provides enterprise services to your Java EE components when they are executed. The Java EE server is also responsible for handling deployment requests and redirecting them to the Java EE containers that it hosts.

The Java EE specification defines the list of core services that must be supported by a Java EE server. These include messaging, database, security, transaction, persistence, and many other services. The Java EE server may also be extended to provide additional services, or alternative implementations of existing services, which are beyond those mandated by the specification. Java EE specification defines how a server may be extended to provide its containers with access to remote and external services by adapting them into the Java EE environment using resource adapters through the Java EE Connector API.

The Java EE Containers

The primary purpose of the Java EE server is to support Java EE containers, which provide various environments in which Java EE components are run.

Containers are the interface between a component and the low-level, platform-specific functionality that supports the component.

Before we can execute it, we must assemble into a Java EE module and deploy into its container the following: a Web, enterprise bean, or application client component, which means that we need to specify the container settings for each component in the Java EE application and for the Java EE application itself.

We must use the Java EE container settings to customize the underlying support provided by the Java EE server, including services as the following:

- The Java EE security model;

- The Java EE transaction model;

- JNDI lookup services;

- The Java EE remote connectivity model.

The Java EE 8 specification stipulates support for the following Java EE containers shown in Figure 11-5 and are the following:

- Java EE server: The runtime portion of a Java EE product.

- EJB container: Manages the execution of enterprise beans for Java EE applications.

- Web container: Manages the execution of web pages, servlets, and some EJB components for Java EE applications.

- Application client container: Manages the execution of application client components.

- Applet container: Manages the execution of applets and consists of a web browser and a Java Plug-in running on the client together.

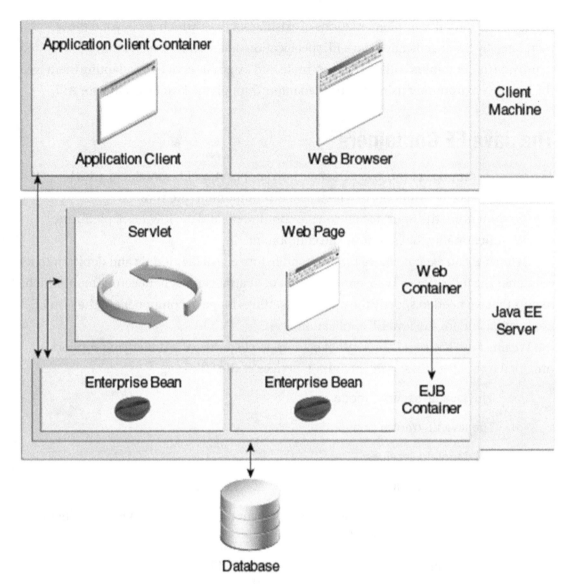

Figure 11-5. *A JAVA EE 8 Container*

While the EJB and Web containers execute in the application server running in the middle tier, the application client container typically executes in a Java SE environment on the client tier, and the applet container typically runs inside a Web browser. Nonetheless, they all rely on their underlying Java EE server for the many enterprise services that they in turn provide—through APIs—to the components that execute inside their container environment. For example, a Java EE server provides native messaging services to a Java EE container, and the container exposes messaging services to its components through the JMS (Java Message Service) API. Similarly, the container exposes database services through Java Database Connectivity (JDBC), transaction services through Java Transaction API (JTA), and so on. The Java EE containers also interpose on all communication between Java EE application components executing in Java EE containers, to provide component and resource injection. This is illustrated in Figure 11-6.

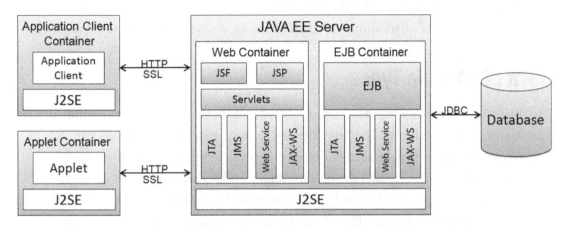

Figure 11-6. *A JAVA EE Server*

In addition to the many built-in services offered to Java EE components by the Java EE containers, Java EE allows for the integration of third-party services—through resource adapters and the Connector API—that are exposed to Java EE components through their containers using the Java EE Service Provider Interface (SPI).

Java EE Deployment Components

The principal building block components of a Java EE deployment are the Java EE application and the Java EE modules. Let's take a look at what defines these components.

The Java EE Application

Java EE lets you deploy both individual Java EE modules and entire Java EE applications to the server. As mentioned in the preceding "Overview of the Packaging and Deployment Processes" section, when deploying an application, you package the individual Java EE modules, together with any associated deployment descriptors and dependent library components, into a wrapper archive JAR file known as an EAR file, which has the suffix .ear. Deploying an individual Java EE module is essentially a shortcut to avoid wrapping one JAR file around another single JAR file.

Apart from its packaging structure, a Java EE application operates, at runtime, as a context in which one or more associated Java EE components, such as EJBs, servlets, and application clients, can operate and communicate with one another using a shared class loader and namespace. It may be useful to think of a Java EE application as a loosely coupled group of Java EE modules that are able to see each other and to share resources.

Java EE Module Types

Java EE defines the following Java EE module types: EJB, Web application, application client, and resource adapter. The first three correspond to their eponymous containers, and their deployment is delegated to these containers. Deploying a resource adapter module installs the resources in the Java EE server and registers these resources for use by Java EE components. Ordinary Java classes and other resources referenced by your Java EE modules may also be included as library components within an EAR file, either packaged as JAR files or stored as directories, and deployed with your Java EE application.

Note that a JPA persistence unit, comprising a set of JPA entities, is not a Java EE module but a library component. We describe some of the reasons for this in the "Persistence Unit" section that follows.

Let's take a closer look at each of the Java EE module types.

EJB Module

An EJB module is comprised of one or more session and/or message-driven beans (MDBs). It is packaged into an EJB JAR file, and if it includes an ejb-jar.xml deployment descriptor (this is optional starting with Java EE 5), it must be located in the META-INF directory in the JAR file. Platform-specific descriptors may also be added to this META-INF directory. If the EJB JAR file doesn't contain an ejb-jar.xml file, the EJB bean classes must identify themselves as EJBs using @Stateless, @Stateful, @Singleton, or @MessageDriven annotations.

In many cases, it is desirable to isolate the client's view of an EJB module into its own archive. When the client communicates only with a session bean's interfaces, it does not need access to the session bean class. In this case, it is good practice to package only the interfaces of the session bean(s), along with any other dependent classes, into a separate EJB client JAR library. This JAR file can be handed to the client, but it can also be referenced from the EJB JAR file so that these interfaces do not need to be duplicated inside the EJB JAR file. To reference the EJB client JAR file, or any other JAR file or directory in the EAR file, the Assembler adds a `Class-Path` entry to the `META-INF/MANIFEST.MF` file in the JAR file that points to these locations:

```
Class-Path: MyEjb-Client.jar
```

Note For further information on the `MANIFEST.MF` file, including usage of the Class-Path and Extension-List entries referred to in this chapter, please see: `http://docs.oracle.com/javase/6/docs/technotes/guides/jar/jar.html`.

More than one JAR file or directory can be referenced in this way by separating the `.jar` and directory entries with a space character. The path of the referenced JAR files is relative to the EJB JAR file itself, which must be located in the root directory of the EAR file. In the preceding example, the `MyEjb-Client.jar` file is also located in the root directory of the EAR file.

An EJB module may also include a persistence unit, which is described in the following section. A persistence unit may only exist in the EJB JAR in expanded form; JAR files may not be nested inside the EJB JAR file. A persistence unit is defined by the presence of a `META-INF/persistence.xml` file in the contents of the EJB JAR file.

An EJB module may be assigned a name using a module declaration inside a `META-INF/application.xml` file. When no `META-INF/application.xml` file is present during deployment, as when the EJB JAR file is deployed stand-alone or within an EAR file that does not include this descriptor, it is assigned a default name. This name is derived from the name of the EJB JAR archive, minus any directory information or the `.jar` suffix. For example, an EJB JAR file may be bundled in an EAR file in the following location:

```
./OrderManagerEJBModule.jar
```

In this case, its default module name would be `OrderManagerEJBModule`.

EJBs in a WAR File

The EJB 3.0 specification simplified the packaging of EJBs by making the packaging of XML descriptors like ejb-jar.xml optional. The EJB 3.1 specification has taken this simplification even further by allowing the packaging of EJBs (POJOs annotated with @Stateless, @Stateful, @Singleton, or @MessageDriven annotations) directly in the WEB-INF/classes directory of the WAR file. Similarly, the ejb-jar.xml descriptor, if present, can be packaged directly into the WEB-INF directory along with web.xml. With this change, users no longer need to create a separate EJB JAR module for packaging the EJBs. Figure 11-7 depicts this new packaging option.

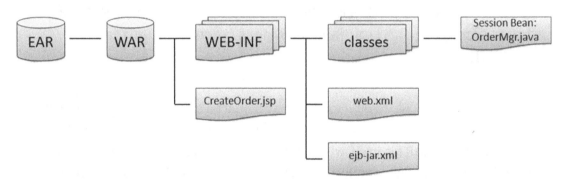

Figure 11-7. *Packaging EJB directly under WEB-INF\classes directory of WAR file*

Persistence Unit

A group of JPA entities, known as a *persistence unit*, is neither strictly a module type nor does it have its own dedicated container. Instead, the Java EE server supports persistence directly as one of the core services it offers to the Java EE containers. This allows JPA entities to behave as persistent objects and interact with Java EE components while executing in the other Java EE container environments. By not being constrained to their own container, JPA entities are also free to execute and demonstrate persistent behavior outside the Java EE environment.

Note   In a deployment context, the term *persistence unit* refers to a group of collocated JPA entities and a corresponding (and mandatory) META-INF/ persistence.xml file. This group of files may be packaged into its own JAR file, or the files may be bundled directly inside an EJB JAR or WAR file. In turn, the persistence.xml file defines one or more <persistence-unit> entries that may further partition the entities in the persistence unit packaging structure. In this chapter, we differentiate these two concepts that share similar names by always using the hyphen (persistence-unit) when describing the `<persistence-unit>` XML element. Thus, any reference to a persistent unit can be assumed to refer to the group of entities Collocated with a `persistence.xml` file.

As mentioned in the preceding note, the packaging of persistence units is different from the packaging of other module types. When packaged in a Java EE application EAR file, a persistence unit is treated as a library component (see the "Library Components" section below). It can be packaged into a JAR file, or its classes can be packaged directly inside an EJB JAR or WAR file. Either way, a `META-INF/persistence.xml` file serves to identify the entities contained in the persistence unit. We will discuss the packaging details in the "Assembling a Persistence Unit" section later in this chapter.

Web Application Module

A Web application module is comprised of servlets, HTML pages, JSF, JSP documents, and any other Web-based files. Its deployment descriptor is the `WEB-INF/web.xml` file and, as with the EJB module, the presence of this file is now optional starting with Java EE 5 since its contents can be derived using default rules. When archived, the contents of a Web application module are packaged into a JAR file with the suffix `.war`. This is commonly referred to as a *WAR file*.

The contents of a WAR file follow a special structure to suit application partitioning in Web browsers better. Of particular relevance when bundling persistence units into a WAR file, Java `.class` files are placed in the `WEB-INF/classes` directory, and dependent JAR files may be added directly to the `WEB-INF/lib` directory.

Similar to an EJB module, a Web module may be assigned a name using a module declaration inside a `META-INF/application.xml` file. When no `META-INF/application.xml` file is present during deployment, as when the WAR file is deployed stand-alone or within an EAR file that does not include this descriptor, it is assigned a default name. This name is derived from the name of the WAR archive, minus any directory information or the `.war` suffix. For example, a WAR file may be bundled in an EAR file in the following location:

`./OrderManagerWebApp.war`

In this case, its default module name would be `OrderManagerWebApp`.

Resource Adapter Module

Resource adapters offer a mechanism for extending a Java EE server. They allow resources and services managed by external systems to be integrated into the Java EE server for use by components executing in the Java EE containers. A resource adapter module contains a set of resource adapters and an optional `META-INF/ra.xml` deployment descriptor.

During deployment, a resource adapter is packaged into a *Resource Archive (RAR) file*, which is a JAR file with the suffix `.rar`.

Application Client Module

An application client module contains Java classes that can be executed in a Java SE environment on the client tier. The application client container is a lightweight Java EE container that supports injection and provides persistence, security, and messaging services, among others. It does not provide many of the services that are available from the middle-tier Java EE containers.

The deployment descriptor for an application client module resides in `META-INF/application-client.xml` and, like the other Java EE module deployment descriptors, is optional starting with Java EE 5.

Security Module

This module will help and allow the developer to configure a web component or enterprise bean so that system resources are accessed only by the authorized users.

As we said, the enterprise tier and web tier applications are made up of components, which are deployed then into various containers. These components, in general, are combined to build a multitier enterprise application. In specific the security for components is provided by their containers, where each container provides two kinds of security such as: declarative and programmatic.

- Declarative security defines a certain application component's security requirements by using either deployment descriptors or annotations.

- Programmatic security, instead, will be embedded in an application and will be used to make security decisions.

Library Components

Shared classes or other resources that your modules require at runtime can be packaged into *library components*. Libraries may either be installed in the application server (the process of installing a library is not described here) or bundled inside your EAR or WAR file. Any JAR-format file embedded inside an EAR, whether a Java EE module or a bundled library archive, may reference a bundled library component using the Class-Path property in the META-INF/MANIFEST.MF file.

Note   Whenever a JAR file is referenced through a Class-Path entry, only the classes in the referenced JAR file are recognized by the deployment tool. Any descriptor files found in the referenced JAR file will be ignored.

Bundled Libraries

Listing 11-1 shows the file contents of a sample EAR file to demonstrate how the Class-Path property references a bundled library. Here we use a shorthand notation to show the Class-Path: myEjb-Client.jar entries that reside in the META-INF/MANIFEST.MF files for their associated JAR and WAR files.

Listing 11-1. Example EAR File Contents Showing Explicit Module Dependencies on a Bundled Library Component

```
myApp.ear:
 META-INF/application.xml
 myEjb.jar Class-Path: myEjb-Client.jar
 myWebApp.war Class-Path: myEjb-Client.jar
 myEjb-Client.jar
```

In this example, the client-side interfaces (remote, local, and Web service endpoint interfaces) have been deliberately stripped from the myEjb.jar EJB module and packaged into the bundled myEjb-Client.jar library component. The META-INF/ejb-jar.xml descriptor in myEjb.jar contains the following entry:

```
<ejb-client-jar>myEjb-Client.jar</ejb-client-jar>
```

This identifies myEjb-Client.jar as the JAR file holding its client-side interfaces. The myEjb.jar EJB module depends on these EJB interfaces, and it declares its dependence through its Class-Path entry referencing the myEjb-Client.jar library. The myWebApp.war Web module references these EJB interfaces, and it declares its dependence on myEjb-Client.jar in the same way. The myEjb-Client.jar library is an ordinary JAR file, and it sits alongside the EJB and WAR files in the EAR file.

An alternative to explicitly declaring dependence on a bundled library component is to use the EAR file's built-in library directory, lib, as shown in Listing 11-2. All JAR files found in the lib directory are automatically added to the class-path of the Java EE modules in the EAR file.

Listing 11-2. Example EAR File Contents Showing Implicit Module Dependencies on a Shared, Bundled Library Component

```
myApp.ear:
 META-INF/application.xml
 myEjb.jar
 myWebApp.war
 lib/myEjb-Client.jar
```

This achieves the same result as Listing 11-1. Assuming application.xml does not specify a <library-directory> element that overrides the default lib directory, the Java EE server will automatically add the myEjb-Client.jar file to the class-paths of the myEjb.jar and myWebApp.war modules.

Libraries may also be bundled in the WEB-INF/lib directory for the JAR files of a WAR file, and in the WEB-INF/classes directory for the unpackaged classes of a WAR file.

Installed Libraries

It is also possible to install libraries in your application server environment and then reference them from the JAR-format files in your EAR file using the Extension-List property in the JAR file's META-INF/MANIFEST.MF file. This is an efficient means of sharing libraries across Java EE applications since it avoids having to bundle the libraries redundantly in multiple EAR files. The installed libraries are stored on disk by the application server instance, and typically a shared library entry in one of the application server's configuration files links the name of the installed library with its JAR file or files. Java EE applications may then refer to this installed library by name without having to know about the JAR file contents of the library.

An example of using an installed library is shown in Listing 11-3.

Listing 11-3. Example EAR File Contents Showing Usage of an Installed Library

```
myApp.ear:
 META-INF/MANIFEST.MF:
  Extension-List: commonUtils
  commonUtils-Extension-Name: com/apress/ejb/ch11/commonUtils
  commonUtils-Extension-Specification-Version: 1.4
 META-INF/application.xml
 myEjb.jar
```

In this example, the EAR file's `META-INF/MANIFEST.MF` file is used to declare a reference to an installed library named `commonUtils`, version 1.4. This gives all the JAR files inside the EAR file access to the contents of the `commonUtils` library, satisfying the `myEjb.jar` module's dependence on the contents of this library. The reference could have been defined on `myEjb.jar` instead, in which case only `myEjb.jar` would be given access to this library. Either way, the installed library must have been installed prior to deployment of `myEjb.jar`.

The `META-INF/MANIFEST.MF` file for the JAR file contained in our `commonUtils` library is shown in Listing 11-4.

Listing 11-4. Contents of an Installed Library's JAR File

```
commonUtils.jar:
 META-INF/MANIFEST.MF:
  Extension-Name: com/apress/ejb/ch11/commonUtils
  Specification-Title: Utils for implementing common patterns
  Specification-Version: 1.4
```

Versioning of Libraries

Although it is not mandated by the Java EE specification, many application servers support Java EE application isolation levels that allow each Java EE application to have its own class loader. This allows multiple applications running simultaneously in the same Java EE server to reference different versions of the same bundled or installed library component. An example where this is useful is when you wish to migrate a subset of your applications to use a new library version. You can install the new library version in the server and then selectively update the Specification-Version property for any applications that you wish to use the new library version.

Alternatively, Java EE servers with this level of isolation support will allow you to deploy a Java EE application that bundles its own version of a dependent library. The rules of precedence in the Java EE specification dictate that, in the case of a conflict between a bundled library and an installed library with the same Extension-Name, the bundled library will be used. This guarantees that the application will always use its bundled library, regardless of which versions of that library are available in the server's installed library base.

Application Servers and Platform Independence

Java EE has always held a keen eye to portability, although in practice this has often been difficult to achieve. Ideally, all Java EE servers implement the specification as far as it goes and then differentiate themselves both on performance and features, like support for configurable isolation levels and advanced object/relational (O/R) mapping options that are recommended (or hinted at, but not mandated) by the specification.

Application servers are expected to define their own platform-specific descriptors to be used to augment the core requirements of the Java EE specification, and indeed virtually all application server implementations offer such descriptors. Over time (and we have seen this most notably in the area of JPA mapping metadata), features that are found to be lacking in the specification and are solved by vendor implementations, get rolled into the specification and are made generic. For example, EJB 2.1 offered no support or regulations on how to define O/R mappings for entity beans, nor on how to implement an entity inheritance hierarchy. Starting with EJB 3, the JPA has taken many of the best ideas coming out of TopLink, Hibernate, and Java Data Objects (JDO), and rolled them straight into the orm.xml file to offer these features, as well as others.

Deployment Tools

Application server vendors have virtually all standardized on JSR 88, which specifies the use of managed JavaBeans, called *MBeans*, to manage the deployment process. MBeans are self-describing and follow design patterns defined by the Java Management Extensions (JMX) specification to provide an interface between the Java EE server and the application server's deployment tool. The actual interfaces exposed by the Java

EE-deployment MBeans vary from one application server to another; but the fact that all deployment tools now use them, to one degree or another, offers some consistency between vendor deployment tools.

Typically, a vendor's deployment tools will guide the Assembler not only through the process of packaging the Java EE modules, libraries, and application archives, but also through specifying some amount of metadata for populating both the Java EE generic and platform-specific deployment descriptors. The tools will also accept EJB, WAR, or EAR files, and they actually perform the installation and validation deployment tasks in the server itself.

Note   Cargo is a thin wrapper that allows you to manipulate Java EE containers in a standard way. Cargo aims to provide an abstraction API to many of the popular Java EE containers, through the medium of Ant tasks, Maven, and IDE plug-ins. For more information on Cargo, see `http://cargo.codehaus.org`.

The Deployment Plan

Some vendors' application server tools record the Deployer's choices in a document called a *deployment plan*. Since deployment is often an iterative process, especially during the development and testing stages, it is convenient to capture the Deployer's choices so that the Deployer does not have to specify the same information repeatedly.

Currently, there is no standard format for a deployment plan specified in JSR 88 or elsewhere, so it is not a document that can be reused across application server implementations. If you find this inconvenient, get involved in the JCP and form or join a JSR to promote a standard in this area.

Deployment Roles

Any encompassing enterprise service platform is, by its very nature, complex. Recognizing this reality, the architects of Java EE have partitioned the Java EE services into well-defined APIs. Similarly, they have partitioned the tasks associated with the various stages of developing and configuring Java EE applications into well-defined roles. We mentioned that the tasks associated with building the various application components, such as EJBs, entities, servlets, JSF JSPs, and many others, fall under the

Java EE role of Application Component Provider. There are also other roles, such as the System Component Provider, which is responsible for installing resources in the application server that are required by the application components. Among these are database resources, authorization policies, security roles, and many others, including services brought in through resource adapters.

We had previously introduced the roles of Application Assembler and Application Deployer. In this section, however, we will explore these roles in greater depth.

The Application Assembler

Here is what you need to know as an application Assembler.

Defining and Describing External Dependencies

The Provider identifies the external requirements held by its components, either in annotations, deployment descriptors, or both. These dependencies may be on other EJBs, persistence units, environment property values, database connections, or any other object external to that application component. It is the responsibility of the Assembler to describe these external dependencies further such that the Deployer can figure out how to map them to concrete resources in a specific application server environment. External dependencies are defined through <ejb-ref>, <ejb-local-ref>, <resource-ref>, <resource-env-ref>, <security-role-ref>, and <message-destination-ref> entries in annotations or deployment descriptors. The Assembler's job is to analyze these external references and patch them up. This process involves the following steps.

Ensuring That All References Are Complete

It is legal, and common, for the Provider to complete the definition of external references only partially. The Provider may not know, or may attempt to guess, the actual names of the resources being referenced. In such cases, the Provider will spell out the details of the reference—its object type, its internally used name, and a description of the logical behavior of the referenced object. The Assembler takes this information and then links it to a name of a resource that is internally consistent within the application. An example of this is an EJB reference. A web.xml, ejb-jar.xml, or application-client.xml descriptor is allowed to declare EJB references using an <ejb-ref> element. An <ejb-ref> has an ejb-ref-name property that is used by the referencing component (whether a Web

form, another EJB, or an application client), and links it to the actual name assigned to
the EJB during deployment by assigning a value to the ⟨ejb-ref⟩'s ejb-link property.
Listing 11-5 illustrates an ⟨ejb-ref⟩ that has been fully defined by the Assembler.

Listing 11-5. An ejb-ref Descriptor Element that Has Been Properly Linked to a
Named EJB

```
<ejb-ref>
 <description>
  Some description that defines this EJB to the Assembler
 </description>
 <ejb-ref-name>ejb/MyAccountManager</ejb-ref-name>
 <ejb-ref-type>Session</ejb-ref-type>
 <remote>com.apress.ejb.ch11.MyAccountManager</remote>
 <ejb-link>SalesAccountManager</ejb-link>
</ejb-ref>
```

Note   The ⟨home⟩ and ⟨local-home⟩ properties are optional starting with EJB 3.

It is also possible to resolve a reference to an EJB that is packaged in a different EJB
JAR file in the same application. Listing 11-6 illustrates how you would use a special path
notation in the ejb-link value to do this. The ejb-link property value may refer to any
EJB found in an EJB JAR file in the application EAR file.

Listing 11-6. An ejb-ref Descriptor Element that Links to an EJB Residing in a
Different EJB JAR in the Application

```
<ejb-ref>
 <description>
  Some description that defines this EJB to the Assembler
 </description>
 <ejb-ref-name>ejb/MyAccountManager</ejb-ref-name>
 <ejb-ref-type>Session</ejb-ref-type>
 <remote>com.apress.ejb.ch11.MyAccountManager</remote>
 <ejb-link>../salesEjbModule.jar#SalesAccountManager</ejb-link>
</ejb-ref>
```

This example shows how the link would appear if the SalesAccountManager EJB was moved into a peer EJB module named salesEjbModule.jar. Finally, the Assembler may need to resolve EJB references that have been partially declared using @EJB annotations in the Java source, as shown in Listing 11-7.

Listing 11-7. A Partial @EJB Annotation in a Java Source File

```
@EJB(name="AccountManager",
    beanInterface=AccountManager.class,
    description="The Department Account Manager")
private AccountManager acctMgr;
```

The Assembler would add an <ejb-ref> element to complete this reference but would leave the properties that have already been defined intact, as shown in Listing 11-8.

Listing 11-8. An ejb-ref Descriptor Element that Fills in the Missing Properties of an @EJB Annotation

```
<ejb-ref>
 <ejb-ref-name>ejb/MyAccountManager</ejb-ref-name>
 <ejb-link>SalesAccountManager</ejb-link>
</ejb-ref>
```

Note   While it is possible to use JNDI (Java Naming and Directory Interface) to look up EJBs deployed outside the context application, <ejb-ref>, <ejb-local-ref>, and the corresponding @EJB annotation may only be used to access EJBs deployed in the context application.

This process continues until the Assembler has linked all the EJB, resource, resource environment, and any other references that were found dangling.

Resolving Conflicting and Redundant References

The modules presented to the Assembler for assembly into an application may have been built by different Providers, or at different times. In such cases, it is common to find references to the same logical resources but using different names. It is the responsibility of the Assembler to scan both the source annotations and any XML deployment descriptors and rename any redundant references to a common name.

Similarly, the same internal name may be used by application components to refer to logically distinct resources. Using the description properties of these references, found both on annotations and in deployment descriptors, along with any other documentation supplied by the Provider, the Assembler must detect such conflicts and rename these references appropriately.

The Assembler may choose to populate each module descriptor fully by merging Java annotations found in the module source files into the descriptor, whenever it is not in conflict. If the Assembler chooses to perform this task, the descriptor's `metadata-complete` property may be set to `true`. This signals to the Deployer that this descriptor and the Java annotations need not be further analyzed, leading to a speedier deployment.

Packaging

The Assembler performs the packaging stage to bundle application components into container-specific JAR files and component libraries. This packaging process was outlined in the preceding "Overview of the Packaging and Deployment Processes" section. You can use Ant or ZIP utilities to perform these steps of grouping the Java EE components into modules and packaging them into JAR files. However, this is an area that benefits from the use of a visual packaging tool, typically available through an IDE. The Assembler packages EJB and application client modules into JAR files, Web application modules into WAR files, and resource adapters into RAR files.

When assembling a stand-alone Java EE module with no bundled libraries, no further packaging is needed. The module's JAR file is ready to be deployed.

If multiple modules are involved, or if libraries need to be bundled as well, the Assembler creates an EAR file and adds the modules and libraries to this archive. The Assembler may add the modules using an internal directory structure, provided that the `lib` directory, or the directory specified by `<library-directory>` in the `application.xml` file, is honored as the location for implicitly shared libraries.

An optional `application.xml` file in the EAR file's `META-INF` directory may be used to identify the modules explicitly, which are included in the application. This is the way of telling the deployment tool to ignore the modules that are not meant of be part of the application, but for some reason are included as part of the application.

The Application Deployer

The module or package produced by the Assembler is then handed off to the Deployer. The Deployer has intimate knowledge of the target application server environment, including information about all the resources that are currently deployed in that environment.

The Deployer's actual experience differs due to the varying tool sets offered by vendors to accompany their application servers. The logical processes of the deployment state are outlined in the following sections.

Unpackaging the Archive

The EAR file, or stand-alone module JAR file, is unpackaged and its contents are analyzed.

Deriving the Module Descriptors

The Deployer processes the descriptor for each Java EE module. If a descriptor was provided, and if its `metadata-complete` property is set to `true`, then the Deployer can send the module off to the appropriate container. If the descriptor is not supplied, or if `metadata-complete` is not set to `true`, then the Java source contents of that module must be scanned to detect annotations. All metadata properties found by scanning the annotations are coalesced with properties found in the descriptor. During this reconciliation step, Java EE precedence rules dictate that whenever both an annotation and the descriptor provide a value for a given property, the value in the descriptor prevails. The result of this reconciliation state is a completed descriptor for that module.

Binding External References

All external references found are checked for completeness, ensuring that the work of the Assembler was performed. These references are then matched to actual resources in the application server environment. If any resources cannot be bound, an error is reported back to the Deployer so that it can be resolved. As you can imagine, this process greatly benefits from a robust deployment tool set provided by the application server.

Deploying to the Containers

Each completed module can be sent to its corresponding container to be installed and registered. Once complete, the Java EE components in these modules are ready to be accessed by clients.

Assembling an EJB JAR Module

An EJB JAR file is a pretty straightforward archive. The `.class` files are laid out in the JAR file in directories corresponding to their packages, rooted at the top-level directory of the JAR. The `ejb-jar.xml` deployment descriptor, if present, goes in the `META-INF` directory, typically accompanied by any other platform-specific descriptors.

Arbitrary classes may be included alongside the EJB classes and interfaces. It is a common practice to package the shared library JARs in the same EAR file as the EJB JAR file. Libraries bundled in the surrounding EAR file may be referenced using the `Class-Path` property of the EJB JAR file's `META-INF/MANIFEST.MF` file, as described in the preceding "Library Components" section. Similarly, you may reference installed libraries previously deployed but outside the context application by listing them in the `Extension-List` property in the `META-INF/ MANIFEST.MF` file.

When it comes to specifying the metadata for an EJB, the `ejb-jar.xml` descriptor and the Java source annotations are mutually redundant. The decision to use one approach over another is largely a matter of Provider preference, though this decision is also affected by how the application will be edited, assembled, and deployed. However, the top-level settings, (such as `<ejb-client-jar>`) have no corresponding annotations and must be assigned through this descriptor.

Note   Starting with Java EE 5, we have the ability to deploy EJB and WAR modules directly, without packaging them as a Java EE application. This is only appropriate if these modules hold no external dependencies on classes in other JAR files that are not already deployed to the target application server environment.

Naming Scope

Within a Java EE application, no two EJBs may have the same name. It is the Assembler's responsibility to detect this case and rename EJBs appropriately to resolve the conflict.

Assembling a Persistence Unit

A *persistence unit* is a set of JPA entity, mapped superclass, and embeddable classes coupled with a mandatory `META-INF/persistence.xml` file. Java EE offers a fixed set of ways to bundle a persistence unit during deployment. You can package a persistence unit in any of the following ways:

- Into one or more JAR files, which in turn may be packaged within a WAR or an EAR file

- As a set of classes within an EJB-JAR file

- In the `classes` directory of a WAR file

- Or as a combination of the above-mentioned ways

The JAR file or directory where its `META-INF/persistence.xml` file is located is called the *root* of the persistence unit, and it defines the root directory for the classes that comprise the persistence unit. The root of the persistence unit must be one of the following:

- An EJB-JAR file

- The `WEB-INF/classes` directory of a WAR file

- A JAR file in the `WEB-INF/lib` directory of a WAR file

- A JAR file in the library directory of an EAR file

- An application client JAR file

The decision of where you bundle your persistence unit determines which modules will have visibility to it. For instance, adding it to the EAR file's library directory gives access to all other modules in the application. Placing it in the EJB, Web application, or application client JAR limits its scope to that module.

In addition to the `persistence.xml` file, one or more O/R mapping files may be added to the `META-INF` directory to augment or override any annotations that may have been specified in the managed JPA classes. The JPA specifies the default file name to be META-INF/orm.xml, but each `<persistence-unit>` defined in the persistence.xml file may specify its own mapping files, using `<mapping-file>` elements. Notice that Java EE 8 comes with the JPA version 2.2.

Naming Scope

Within a Java EE application, it is possible for two JPA entities to have the same name, but only if they are in separate contexts. For instance, two Web application modules may bundle separate persistence units inside their WEB-INF/lib or WEB-INF/classes directories. In this case, the persistence units are private to each Web application module, and duplicate names between these persistence units will not cause a conflict.

It is the Assembler's responsibility to detect conflicts within the same naming scope and rename entity-name properties appropriately to resolve the conflict.

Summary

This chapter introduced the topic of Java EE deployment, and it covered both general deployment issues and areas of deployment that are specific to EJBs and JPA entities. We began the discussion with an overview of the tasks that are performed during deployment, noting that, depending on the complexity of the Java EE modules being deployed, some steps may not be required. This overview section also explained the roles of the Assembler and Deployer, and it explained the deployment tasks in the context of these two roles.

To provide some background into the deployment infrastructure (knowledge that will assist you when choosing how to partition your applications and resolve external references), we explored the Java EE server and the four Java EE containers: EJB, Web, application client, and applet. This led to a discussion of the corresponding Java EE module types, and the definition of a Java EE application. We also explained how to use library components to package your JPA persistence units and non-Java EE components.

The remainder of the chapter provided a more in-depth look at the roles of the Assembler and Deployer, and it concluded with further specifics on how to deploy EJB modules and JPA persistence units.

In the next chapter, we explore how to build clients that are capable of interacting with EJB components in a multiuser, distributed environment.

CHAPTER 12

EJB Client Applications

So far in our journey, we have covered, in detail, session beans, entities using the Java Persistence API (JPA), message-driven beans (MDBs), publishing stateless session beans as Web services, and integrating all of these components. On top of this, we have covered specific details on transactions and performance. While we have been developing simple servlets as our client applications to illustrate how the components work, we haven't thoroughly discussed the different types of EJB client applications and how to develop them. In this chapter, we will discuss different application architectures in which client applications can be involved, and we will build the common ones.

Application Architecture

The Java EE platform provides flexibility on how components can be distributed across different tiers and architectures. You can choose the right architecture and programming model based on the application or configuration requirements. In this section, we will look at the different architectures and programming models that you can use.

Figure 12-1 shows the architectural layout for Web-based applications. This architecture is typically front ended by a Web application running in a browser. These days, other types of client devices (such as smartphones, tablets, cell phones, and telnet devices) are also being used to run these applications. The Web application running in a browser or mobile device renders the user interface using Web technologies such as JavaServer Pages (JSP), JavaServer Faces (JSF), or Java Servlets. Typical user actions, such as entering search criteria or adding items to a shopping cart, will invoke/call session beans running in an EJB container via one of the aforementioned Web technologies. Once the session beans are invoked, they process the requests, and responses are sent back.

541

© Jonathan Wetherbee, Massimo Nardone, Chirag Rathod, and Raghu Kodali 2018
J. Wetherbee et al., *Beginning EJB in Java EE 8*, https://doi.org/10.1007/978-1-4842-3573-7_12

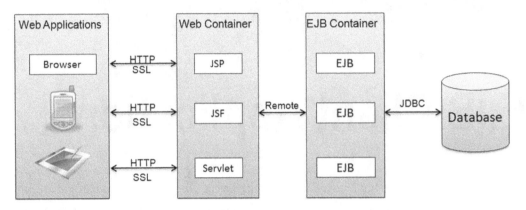

Figure 12-1. *A Web-based application architecture*

This architecture allows you to leverage all of the benefits of session beans, such as encapsulating interactions with entities, managing transactions and security, and so on. The downside is that you need an EJB container or an application server to deploy and run the session beans. Another thing to note in this architecture is that you can run the Web and EJB containers on two different physical machines or on two separate Java Virtual Machines (JVMs) on the same physical machine. The pros and cons of this approach were discussed in Chapter 2.

A slight modification of this architecture is shown in Figure 12-2, in which the Web and EJB containers are collocated in the same JVM. In this architecture, Web components interact with EJB components in local mode. The pros and cons of this approach were also discussed in Chapter 2.

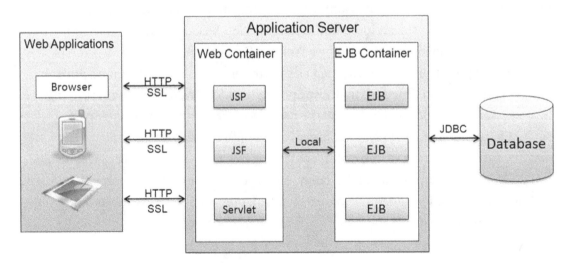

Figure 12-2. *A Web-based application architecture with local invocation*

The JPA specification provides a lightweight persistence object model with plain old Java objects (POJOs) and annotations for object/relational (O/R) mapping. This is drastically different from what the earlier EJB specifications were doing for persistence. The lightweight nature of this persistence model makes it possible to have application architectures that allow Web applications to interact directly with persistence object models or JPA entities. Figure 12-3 shows the architectural layout for this kind of programming model. In this architecture, the Web components will interact with entities using the EntityManager to perform CRUD (create, retrieve, update, delete) operations and queries to retrieve data.

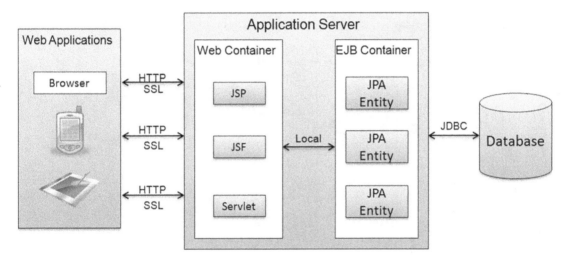

Figure 12-3. *A Web-based application architecture using JPA entities*

The upside of this programming model is that you can run your Web applications on any standard lightweight Web container (such as Tomcat). You don't need any EJB containers or application servers, as you aren't using session beans or MDBs. This architecture is widely used with other O/R frameworks, such as TopLink and Hibernate, on which the JPA specification is based. The downside is that you lose some of the services provided by EJB containers (such as transactions and security).

The preceding three architectures are most commonly used when building Web applications with EJBs or entities. Other variants of these architectures are possible, but we will not be drilling down into all of the options.

The next two architectures are programming models in which the client applications are of the desktop variety, which provide rich UI functionality for data entry purposes.

Figure 12-4 shows an architecture in which a client application running on the desktop invokes a remote session. The client application running on the desktop has data entry screens used by the end users (such as customer service representatives and bank tellers). These client applications can be developed using Java Swing technology in Java SE or using plain Java classes (POJOs) that are run from the command line. Generally, the end users launch the client application from their desktop, enter some data, and trigger an event by pressing some onscreen UI component (such as a Submit button).

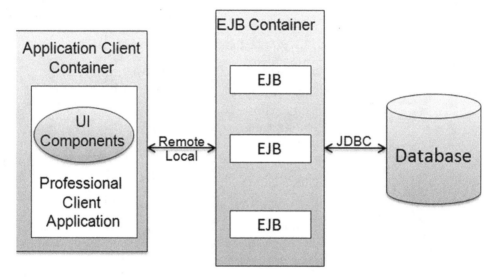

Figure 12-4. *A professional desktop client application architecture*

Client applications can either be installed on the desktop machine or downloaded from a server using technologies like Java Web Start. In this architecture, there will always be remote invocation of the session beans from the client applications, as the session beans will be running on a remote server. This architecture can leverage the benefits of session beans, as is the case with Web applications.

Figure 12-5 shows an architecture that uses JPA entities directly instead of going through the session beans. In this programming model, the client application and entities packaged in a persistence unit are collocated and assembled as a single application unit. The client application makes use of the `EntityManager` to perform CRUD operations and queries to retrieve the data.

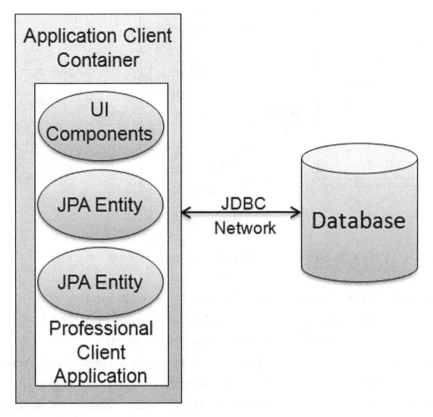

Figure 12-5. *A professional client application architecture using JPA entities*

The upside of this programming model is that you can run your applications in a standard Java SE environment without using an EJB container, but the obvious downside is that you will lose the services like security and transaction management that are provided by the EJB container.

As described in Chapter 6, stateless session beans can be published as Web services. Once a stateless session bean is published as a Web service, any Web service client application that can assemble and send a Simple Object Access Protocol (SOAP) message can invoke the published Web service. Figure 12-6 shows this architecture.

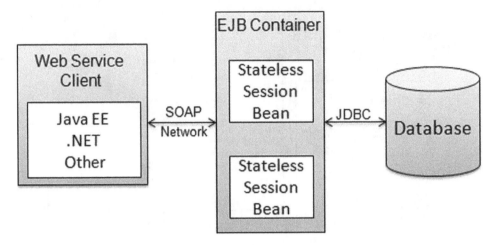

Figure 12-6. *A Web service client application architecture*

Enterprises typically have several business processes that interact with heterogeneous back-end systems or services. *Business Process Execution Language (BPEL)* is a standard markup language that allows you to assemble discrete Web services as a single business process. BPEL-based business processes use standard Web services architecture and infrastructure to invoke one or more Web services. Figure 12-7 shows an architecture in which a BPEL-based business process invokes a stateless session bean published as a Web service. For example, Chapter 6 demonstrated how to create and publish a credit service that checks the validity of a credit card. In the context of an order-processing business process, this credit service may be one of several services with which the business process interacts to fulfill the order process.

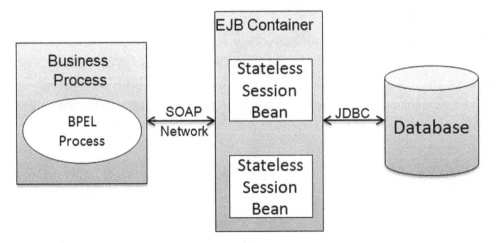

Figure 12-7. *A business process as a client application*

So far, we have looked at the possible architectures and programming models that involve EJB or JPA components. In the next sections, we will drill down into the Web-based application architecture shown in Figure 12-2 and demonstrate how you can expand on the integrated back-end application developed for the Wines Online application in Chapter 7. We chose this architecture because it is commonly used and helps us illustrate the usage of container services.

JSF

JavaServer Faces technology establishes the standard for building server-side user interfaces for Java EE. JavaServer Faces (JSF) custom tags libraries for expressing UI components within a view and for wiring components to server-side objects. The JSF version 2.3 was used during the writing of this manuscript.

In this section, we will look at developing a Web application that uses JavaServer Faces (JSF) to talk to an integrated EJB back-end application using the architecture shown in Figure 12-2. We will start with a brief introduction to several concepts of JSF to prepare you to develop a full-fledged Web application. JSF was first introduced in 2002 and requires JDK 1.5 or higher, so the very first requirement is to have JDK installed on your machine.

Mainly JSF will help us to do the following:

- Drop components onto a page by adding component tags,

- Wire component-generated events to server-side application code,

- Bind UI components on a page to server-side data,

- Construct a UI with reusable and extensible components,

- Save and restore UI state beyond the life of server requests.

In this manuscript, the JSF version 2.3 was used including new features include like these:

- The CDI alignment improvements;

- JSF 2.3 artifacts can now be easily injected into Java classes and EL expressions;

- Improvement of WebSocket, which is a protocol that provides full duplex bidirectional communication over TCP;

- Date-Time API improvements;

- API enhancements including UIData, UIRepeat, etc.

Note   This section by no means provides a comprehensive discussion of JSF. As with any other Java EE technology, detailed information about JSF can be found at: `https://myfaces.apache.org/jsfintro.html`

JSF Views include:

- Tree of Components

- Facelets or HTML

- Expression Language

- Mix with JSTL and other tab libraries, as needed

- Component Libraries

Here is what's new in JSF 2.3 in Java EE 8:

- Two feature drivers: Oracle & Community

- Feature clean-up

- Small new feature set based upon community requests

- Mature standard for building Java EE applications

JSF 2.3 New Features include:

- Inject ViewMap

  - @ViewMap

  - @Inject

  - Map viewMap;

- Inject UiViewRoot @Inject

  - UIViewRoot viewRoot;

- #1332 - Let CDI handle #{view}

- #1331 - Let CDI handle #{application}

- #1254 - Contracts attribute too restrictive

- #1328 - Let CDI handle #{session} EL resolving

- #1325 - Let CDI handle #{applicationScope}

- #1311 - Let CDI handle #{facesContext} EL resolving

- #1323 - Support @Inject for the applicationMap @ApplicationMap

  - @Inject

  - Map applicationMap;

  - Map applicationMap;

- #1322 - Simplify #{externalContext} to use ExternalContextProducer

- #1309 - Support @Inject for ExternalContext

  - @Inject ExternalContext externalContext;

- #527 - Support @Inject for FacesContext

  - @Inject FacesContext facesContext;

- javax.faces.bean.ManagedProperty Replacement

- #1396 - f:socket for SSE and WebSocket

Evolution of Java EE Web Technologies

Java EE technologies have evolved to deliver a mature, reliable, and stable platform that allows developers to build enterprise-scale applications. The platform has evolved significantly in the Web technologies space as well. Figure 12-8 shows the evolution of Web technologies in the Java EE platform.

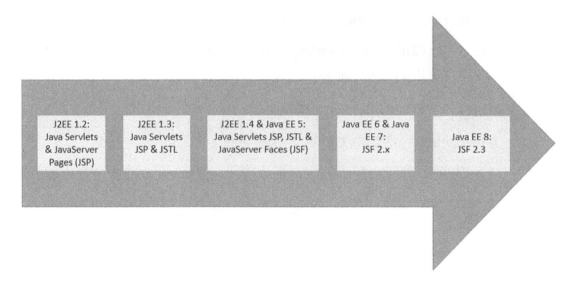

Figure 12-8. *The evolution of Java EE Web technologies*

Prior to the arrival of Java Servlets, CGI scripts were used to generate dynamic Web content. CGI scripts had their own limitations, including the scripts being run as individual processes, which led to scalability issues.

After CGI scripts, Java Servlets became the basis of all Web technologies in the Java EE platform. Java Servlets provided a great start for developing standards-based Web components and applications that are portable across Web containers. One of the disadvantages of Java Servlets was they were code intensive—all of the HTML was printed out using `println()` methods. Servlets did not provide a bridge between the graphic designers who created the design of the pages and the Java programmers who created the dynamic content.

JSP was next in the evolution of Web technologies; it bridged the gap between graphic designers and Java programmers. Based on Java Servlets technology, JSP pages are HTML pages with embedded Java code. This model allowed graphic designers to create JSP pages, which programmers could then make dynamic by adding Java code or *scriplets*. When compiled, JSP pages become Java servlets.

While the advent of JSP pages was nice, many developers now had to deal with mundane tasks like iterating over collections of data. This led to the creation of the JSP Standard Tag Library (JSTL), which automated some of these tasks.

While all of these advances in technologies simplified the building of Web applications, there was no standard component model for developing them. On top of this, development of Web applications with reusable components in fourth-generation languages (4GLs) like Visual Basic, Oracle Forms, and PowerBuilder weren't available yet either.

JSF is the latest Java EE Web technology. With the component model, it addresses the issues of reusable components and ease of building Web applications. The reusable component model is not the only thing that JSF provides, though. We will look into some of the other features and benefits of JSF in the following sections.

The Model-View-Controller Pattern

During the early phases of Java EE Web technology development, most of the Web applications were built using the so-called Model-I approach. The basic idea of Model-I is that the Web technology that renders the dynamic Web content is closely intertwined with the business logic of the back-end systems. There was no separation of concerns in this approach, which led to application maintenance issues. The Model-II approach (also known as the Model-View-Controller [MVC] pattern) was a follow-up to the Model-I approach. The key to this approach is the clean separation between the view layer and the model layer that supplies the data and business logic.

Major Model-View-Controller benefits include:

- Action-oriented framework layered on top of JAX-RS

- Manual controller logic... you control your own destiny

- No UI Components

- You choose your front-end technology

The MVC pattern isn't specific to the Java language as such; it dates back to languages like Smalltalk. In this approach, the model layer is used for the business logic and data, the view is used to render the user interface, and the controller is used for application flow and event handling. While the Java EE platform had been evolving with respect to the model and view-side technologies, it didn't include a built-in framework that could be used on the controller side. Instead, many developers built homegrown controllers using Java Servlets technology. Many others turned to Apache Struts, which provided an alternative to writing homegrown controllers. Apache Struts is a widely used open source framework that has become the de facto controller framework for Web applications.

Finally, JSF technology standardized the controller aspect of the MVC pattern by providing a controller as part of the framework.

MVC 1.0 controllers benefits include:

- Controls the request-processing for an MVC application

- JAX-RS Implementation

- Class annotated with @Controller either at class level or method level

- Must be CDI Managed

- Possible to create hybrid classes (@Controller at method level)

- Four return types: String, void, Response, Viewable

    - String: returns path to view

    - Void: requires @javax.mvc.View annotation

      Response: typical javax.ws.rs.core.Response, providing full access to the response

      Viewable: javax.mvc.Viewable containing information about the view and how to process

- Default response type text/html, but can be modified with @Produces

The MVC 1.0 includes models to utilize entity classes for data, or store into a CDI bean. Two ways to work with models include:

- javax.mvc.Models class

- CDI-Based Models

JSR 371: Model-View-Controller 1.0 Specification can be found at:
`https://www.mvc-spec.org/`

Here are the major differences between JSF and MVC:
JSF:

- Component Based

- Controller Logic

- Automates Processing

- Facelets

- Rapid Development

- Works well with REST

- Stateful… remains across requests

MVC:

- Action Based

- Layered on Top of JAX-RS

- Manual Validations/Conversions

- Many Different View Options

- Fine Control Request/Response

- Great fit for REST

- No State Across Requests

JSF Architecture

Figure 12-9 shows the simplified JSF architecture. JSF has a front controller servlet called
`FacesServlet`. `FacesServlet` performs the role of brokering the incoming requests
from clients to the right places. As mentioned earlier, JSF comes with reusable Web
components that can be used to develop user interfaces. These UI components can be
associated with objects called *managed beans*. These managed beans handle the logic
for the application and interact with back-end systems or components like EJBs. Each
UI component in JSF can be associated with a different render kit that can generate
different markup, such as HTML or WML (Wireless Markup Language), onto different
types of devices.

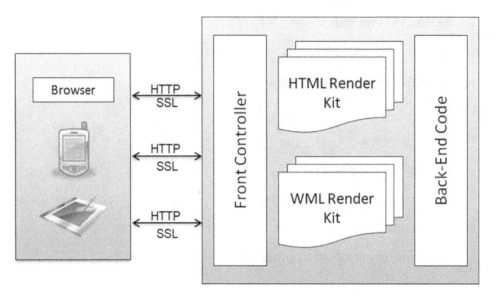

Figure 12-9. *JSF architecture*

The JSF Life Cycle

Figure 12-10 shows the JSF life cycle that handles the initial requests, as well as the *postbacks* from the client application or user interface. The following list describes the lifecycle phases:

- *Restore view*: If the incoming request is an initial request, the JSF implementation creates the view. During the view creation, the UI objects for each UI component are created and stored in a component tree. The state of the UI view is then saved for subsequent requests. If the incoming request is a postback, the JSF implementation restores the saved UI to process the current request.

- *Apply request values*: In this phase, the data that was sent as part of the request is used to update the UI objects that are part of the view.

- *Process validation*: In this phase, the data that has been submitted is validated.

- *Update model*: In this phase, the back-end objects are updated with the validated data from the request. Conversion of received data also happens in this phase.

- *Invoke application*: In this phase, the back-end application is invoked to complete the processing of the request, and the response is rendered back to the client.

- *Render response*: In this phase of the life cycle, the UI components are rendered, and the response is sent back to the client.

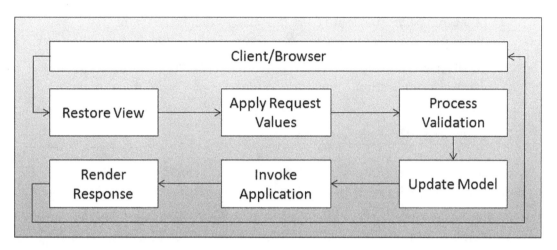

Figure 12-10. *The JSF life cycle*

The JSF Application

A typical JSF application consists of the following:

- *JSP pages or Facelets*: The JSP pages or Facelets in the application contain the JSF UI components that are encapsulated in the JSP tags. Each JSF component is a building block that is markup agnostic. It contains three major pieces: a UIComponent, a renderer, and a tag handler. The UIComponent defines the behavior of the component (for example, the behavior of a UI component like a radio group or a menu). It is also associated with a specific renderer at runtime. The renderer is in charge of what markup is being rendered to the client. A *tag handler* is a JSP tag that allows for usage of JSF UI components in JSP.

- *Navigation model*: The information about how the control flows through the application is defined in an XML deployment descriptor called `faces-config.xml`. This file can hold several other types of information, such as validators, converters, and lists of managed beans. Each JSF application can contain more than one `faces-config.xml` file.

- *Managed beans*: These are plain Java classes that facilitate the application logic. They can be used as bindings to the data coming from a back-end component, or to invoke a business method in the back-end application.

JSF Tools and Components

Having a standard doesn't always help. Support from developer communities and vendors plays an important role in making a technology successful. While the goal of JSF is to simplify drastically Web application development, this goal cannot be reached with standardization alone. We need the full range of available UI components for developers to build applications, as well as the full range of development tools to assist in the application-building process. In the last couple of years, development tools such as JDeveloper, Java Studio Creator, and Eclipse have provided support for building JSF applications. Apache MyFaces, an open source implementation of the JSF framework, offers components that provide more functionality than those from the JSF reference implementation. Oracle has also released more than 100 standard Faces components under the umbrella of ADF Faces. These ADF Faces components have been donated to the Apache Software Foundation, and are now part of the MyFaces project, A.K.A. *Trinidad*. All of these factors have significantly contributed to the success of the JSF technology and its adoption by developers.

Note   Information about the MyFaces project can be found at: `http://myfaces.apache.org`.

Developing Web Applications Using JSF and EJB

A significant amount of work was done in Chapter 7 to integrate different types of EJBs (session beans, MDBs, entities, and Web services) to develop a full-fledged EJB back-end infrastructure for the Wines Online application. In this section, we will develop a JSF client application that will work on top of the EJB back-end application, as shown in Figure 12-11.

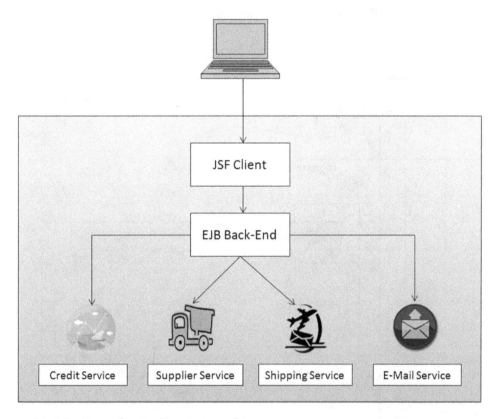

Figure 12-11. *Sample application architecture*

The main goal of this section is to show you how to develop a set of JSF pages and wire them to EJB components in the back-end application. With this in mind, we'll start with the ways in which the user would navigate through a set of Web pages to perform the following operations:

- Register as a new customer

- Log in

- Search wines based on different criteria

- Add wines to the shopping cart

- View the contents of the shopping cart

- Submit orders

Figure 12-12 shows the application flow, and it illustrates a set of JSF pages that allows the user to perform the aforementioned actions. We will build one page at a time, wire each page to the EJB back-end application as needed, and complete the application.

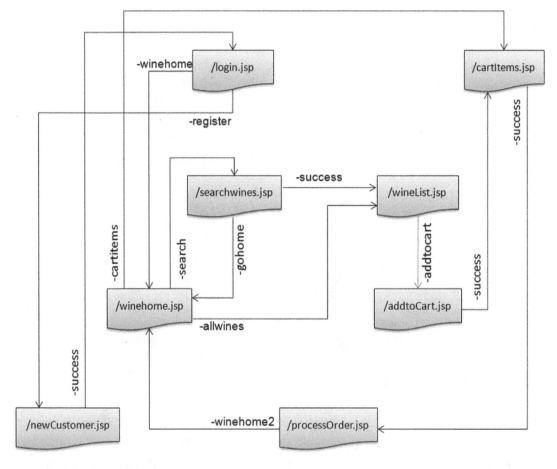

Figure 12-12. *JSF application page flow*

We'll start with a simple login page.

The Login Page

To simplify the login process, we will use the e-mail address of the customer to authenticate and authorize the order. Email is one of the mapped fields in the Customer entity of the persistence unit used in Chapter 7. Listing 12-1 shows the code for login. jsp. To begin, there are two tag library directives, some standard HTML tags, and some tags to render the JSF UI components. Any page that includes JSF elements must have the f:view tag as the outermost JSF tag. The h:form tag creates an HTML form, the h:inputText tag creates an input text field, and the h:commandButton tag creates a Submit button in the form. As you may notice, the value attributes for h:inputText have a different syntax from the ones used in HTML. We are using the Expression Language (EL) syntax — #{}. The expression #{Login.email} means that the JSP page wants to access the e-mail property from the Login object. The Login object is a *managed bean*, which will be discussed shortly. Similar to a HTML form, there is an action attribute for h:commandButton. The EL syntax used for action is #{Login.processLogin}, which means that when the user hits the Submit button, a POST operation will trigger the processLogin method in the Login managed bean.

Listing 12-1. login.jsp

```
<!DOCTYPE HTML PUBLIC "-//W3C//DTD HTML 4.01 Transitional//EN"
"http://www.w3.org/TR/html4/loose.dtd">
<%@ page contentType="text/html;charset=windows-1252"%>
<%@ taglib uri="http://java.sun.com/jsf/html" prefix="h"%>
<%@ taglib uri="http://java.sun.com/jsf/core" prefix="f"%>
<f:view>
  <html>
    <head>
      <meta http-equiv="Content-Type"content="text/html;
      charset=windows-1252"/>
      <title>Login Page</title>
    </head>
    <body>
      <h:form>
        <h3> Beginning EJB: Wine Store Application </h3>
        <h5> Enter Email address: </h5>
```

```
    <p>  <h:inputText value="#{Login.email}"/> </p>
    <p>  <h:commandButton value="Login" action="#{Login.processLogin}"/> </p>
  </h:form>
 </body>
</html>
</f:view>
```

Figure 12-18, shown in the "Compiling, Deploying, and Testing the JSF Application" section later in the chapter, shows the login.jsp page rendered in the browser.

The next step is to create a Login managed bean that will be used with login.jsp. Managed beans are JavaBeans that are used by JSF applications. These objects are managed by the JSF implementation, and the properties and methods in these objects can be referenced from JSP pages using value-binding and method-binding expressions. Listing 12-2 shows the Login managed bean. Login has three property fields along with their accessor: email, customer, and shoppingCart. We have an @EJB annotation on top of the setShoppingCart() method. We are using setter injection to inject the stateful session bean ShoppingCart that we had developed in Chapter 7. We have one additional method processLogin() in our bean that calls the findCustomer(String email) business method using the injected shoppingCart stateful session bean. This business method returns a Customer object if the e-mail ID exists in our customer database. Additional logic is incorporated to return a string value stored in the faces-config.xml file, for use in our navigation model. We will discuss this shortly.

Listing 12-2. Login.java

```java
package com.apress.ejb.chapter12.view.managed;

import com.apress.ejb.chapter07.ejb.ShoppingCartLocal;
import com.apress.ejb.chapter07.entities.Customer;
import javax.ejb.EJB;

public class Login
{
  public Login() {
  }
  String email;
  Customer customer;
  ShoppingCartLocal shoppingCart;
```

```java
  public void setEmail(String email) {
    this.email = email;
  }

  public String getEmail() {
    return email;
  }

  public String processLogin() {
    String navigation = null;
    customer = (Customer)shoppingCart.findCustomer(email);

    if (customer != null) {
      navigation = "winehome";
    }
    else {
      navigation = "register";
    }
    return navigation;
  }

  public void setCustomer(Customer customer) {
    this.customer = customer;
  }

  public Customer getCustomer() {
    return customer;
  }

  @EJB
  public void setShoppingCart(ShoppingCartLocal shoppingCart) {
    this.shoppingCart = shoppingCart;
  }

  public ShoppingCartLocal getShoppingCart() {
    return shoppingCart;
  }
}
```

The deployment descriptor faces-config.xml has information on page navigation, managed beans, and so on. Listing 12-3 shows the faces-config.xml with control flow to and from login.jsp. It also shows the Login class being registered as a managed bean. We have set the scope of the Login managed bean to session. This allows us to store information about the customer and shopping cart through the session so that we don't have to re-query our back-end application for the same information. This also facilitates the usage of this information across other pages and invokes other business methods on the ShoppingCart stateful session bean without having to look up the bean again. Additionally, we have created three navigation rules:

- From login.jsp to winehome.jsp, with the value winehome: This will be used if the login is successful.

- From login.jsp to newCustomer.jsp, with the value register: This will be used if the login fails and the customer wants to register as a new customer.

- From newCustomer.jsp to login.jsp, with the value success: This will be used to navigate the customer back to the login page after successful registration.

Listing 12-3. faces-config.xml

```xml
<?xml version="1.0" encoding="windows-1252"?>
<!DOCTYPE faces-config PUBLIC
  "-//Sun Microsystems, Inc.//DTD JavaServer Faces Config 1.1//EN"
  "http://java.sun.com/dtd/web-facesconfig_1_1.dtd">

<faces-config xmlns="http://java.sun.com/JSF/Configuration">

  <managed-bean>
    <managed-bean-name>Login</managed-bean-name>
    <managed-bean-class>com.apress.ejb.chapter12.view.managed.Login
    </managed-bean-class>
    <managed-bean-scope>session</managed-bean-scope>
  </managed-bean>
```

```
<navigation-rule>
  <from-view-id>/login.jsp</from-view-id>
  <navigation-case>
    <from-outcome>winehome</from-outcome>
    <to-view-id>/winehome.jsp</to-view-id>
  </navigation-case>
  <navigation-case>
    <from-outcome>register</from-outcome>
    <to-view-id>/newCustomer.jsp</to-view-id>
  </navigation-case>
</navigation-rule>

<navigation-rule>
  <from-view-id>/newCustomer.jsp</from-view-id>
  <navigation-case>
    <from-outcome>success</from-outcome>
    <to-view-id>/login.jsp</to-view-id>
  </navigation-case>
</navigation-rule>

</faces-config>
```

So far, we have shown you how to get started with a JSF application with a simple login page that can look up EJBs and invoke business methods. In the next few sections, we will continue on our venture to complete the remaining wine store JSF application pages.

The New Customer Registration Page

Listing 12-4 shows the code for the newCustomer.jsp JSF page. This page is very similar to the login.jsp page created earlier, except that it has more input fields that capture the customer information. All input fields in the JSP page (First Name, Last Name, Phone, Email, Street 1, Street 2, City, State, Zip Code, Credit Card, and Credit Card Expiration date) have value-binding expressions that map to properties in the NewCustomer managed bean. It also has a Submit button whose action is mapped to the AddNewCustomer() method in the managed bean using the expression #{NewCustomer. AddNewCustomer}.

Listing 12-4. newCustomer.jsp

```
<!DOCTYPE HTML PUBLIC "-//W3C//DTD HTML 4.01 Transitional//EN"
"http://www.w3.org/TR/html4/loose.dtd">
<%@ page contentType="text/html;charset=windows-1252"%>
<%@ taglib uri="http://java.sun.com/jsf/html" prefix="h"%>
<%@ taglib uri="http://java.sun.com/jsf/core" prefix="f"%>
<f:view>
  <html>
    <head>
      <meta http-equiv="Content-Type" content="text/html; charset=windows-1252"/>
      <title>New Customer Page</title>
    </head>
    <body>
      <h:form>
        <h1> Beginning EJB: Wine Store Application </h1>
        Enter the following information to register as a new customer:
        <table cellspacing="2" cellpadding="3" border="1" width="100%">
          <tr>
            <td width="33%">First Name</td>
            <td width="67%"> <h:inputText value="#{NewCustomer.
            firstName}"/> </td>
          </tr>
          <tr>
            <td width="33%">Last Name</td>
            <td width="67%"> <h:inputText value="#{NewCustomer.lastName}"/> </td>
          </tr>
          <tr>
            <td width="33%">Phone</td>
            <td width="67%"> <h:inputText value="#{NewCustomer.phone}"/> </td>
          </tr>
          <tr>
            <td width="33%">Email</td>
            <td width="67%"> <h:inputText value="#{NewCustomer.email}"/> </td>
          </tr>
          <tr>
```

```
            <td width="33%">Street 1</td>
            <td width="67%"> <h:inputText value="#{NewCustomer.streetOne}"/> </td>
         </tr>
         <tr>
            <td width="33%">Street 2</td>
            <td width="67%"> <h:inputText value="#{NewCustomer.streetTwo}"/> </td>
         </tr>
         <tr>
            <td width="33%">City</td>
            <td width="67%"> <h:inputText value="#{NewCustomer.city}"/> </td>
         </tr>
         <tr>
            <td width="33%">State</td>
            <td width="67%"> <h:inputText value="#{NewCustomer.state}"/> </td>
         </tr>
         <tr>
            <td width="33%">Zip Code</td>
            <td width="67%"> <h:inputText value="#{NewCustomer.zipCode}"/> </td>
         </tr>
         <tr>
            <td width="33%">Credit Card </td>
            <td width="67%"> <h:inputText value="#{NewCustomer.ccnum}"/> </td>
         </tr>
         <tr>
            <td width="33%">Credit Card Expiry date</td>
            <td width="67%"> <h:inputText value="#{NewCustomer.ccexpDate}"/> </td>
         </tr>
      </table>
      <h1>
         <h:commandButton value="Submit" action="#{NewCustomer.
         AddNewCustomer}"/>
      </h1>
    </h:form>
  </body>
 </html>
</f:view>
```

Figure 12-19 (in the "Compiling, Deploying, and Testing the JSF Application" section) shows the newCustomer.jsp page being rendered in the browser.

After the newCustomer.jsp page is created, we will create the NewCustomer managed bean. Listing 12-5 shows the code for this managed bean that has getter and setter methods for all of the properties referred by the newCustomer.jsp page. In addition, the class injects the CustomerFacade stateless session bean using the @EJB annotation. Finally, the AddNewCustomer() method creates a new Individual entity instance using the getter methods of the properties and calls the AddCustomer() business method in CustomerFacade. Upon successful execution, this method returns a success string that navigates the user to the login page.

Listing 12-5. NewCustomer.java

```
package com.apress.ejb.chapter12.view.managed;

import com.apress.ejb.chapter07.ejb.CustomerFacadeLocal;
import com.apress.ejb.chapter07.entities.Address;
import com.apress.ejb.chapter07.entities.Individual;
import javax.ejb.EJB;

public class NewCustomer
{
  private String firstName;
  private String lastName;
  private String phone;
  private String email;
  private String streetOne;
  private String streetTwo;
  private String city;
  private String state;
  private String zipCode;
  private String ccnum;
  private String ccexpDate;

 @EJB
 CustomerFacadeLocal customerFacade;

  public NewCustomer() {
  }
```

```
public void setFirstName(String firstName) {
  this.firstName = firstName;
}

public String getFirstName() {
  return firstName;
}

public void setLastName(String lastName) {
  this.lastName = lastName;
}

public String getLastName() {
  return lastName;
}

public void setPhone(String phone) {
  this.phone = phone;
}

public String getPhone() {
  return phone;
}

public void setEmail(String email) {
  this.email = email;
}

public String getEmail() {
  return email;
}

public void setStreetOne(String streetOne) {
  this.streetOne = streetOne;
}

public String getStreetOne() {
  return streetOne;
}
```

```java
  public void setStreetTwo(String streetTwo) {
    this.streetTwo = streetTwo;
  }

  public String getStreetTwo() {
    return streetTwo;
  }

  public void setCity(String city) {
    this.city = city;
  }

  public String getCity() {
    return city;
  }

  public void setState(String state) {
    this.state = state;
  }

  public String getState() {
    return state;
  }

  public void setZipCode(String zipCode) {
    this.zipCode = zipCode;
  }

  public String getZipCode() {
    return zipCode;
  }

  public void setCcnum(String ccnum) {
    this.ccnum = ccnum;
  }

  public String getCcnum() {
    return ccnum;
  }
```

```java
  public void setCcexpDate(String ccexpDate) {
    this.ccexpDate = ccexpDate;
  }

  public String getCcexpDate() {
    return ccexpDate;
  }

  public String AddNewCustomer() {
    Individual customer = new Individual();
    customer.setFirstName(firstName);
    customer.setLastName(lastName);
    customer.setPhone(phone);
    customer.setEmail(email);

    Address address = new Address();
    address.setStreet1(streetOne);
    address.setStreet2(streetTwo);
    address.setState(state);
    address.setCity(city);
    address.setZipCode(zipCode);

    customer.setDefaultBillingAddress(address);
    customer.setCcNum(ccnum);
    customer.setCcExpDate(ccexpDate);

    if (customerFacade != null) {
      customerFacade.registerCustomer(customer);
    }

    return "success";
  }
}
```

Note   Chapter 7 provides the details on all the EJBs and business methods available for the clients.

Now we need to update the `faces-config.xml` file shown in Listing 12-3 by adding the `NewCustomer` as a managed bean. Listing 12-6 shows the snippet of XML that needs to be added. Unlike the `Login` managed bean, we are going to set the scope of this bean to `request`, as we don't need to store the customer registration information across the session.

Listing 12-6. faces-config.xml, with the NewCustomer Managed Bean

```
<managed-bean>
  <managed-bean-name>NewCustomer</managed-bean-name>
  <managed-bean-class>com.apress.ejb.chapter12.view.managed.NewCustomer
  </managed-bean-class>
  <managed-bean-scope>request</managed-bean-scope>
</managed-bean>
```

Note   We have already added the navigation case from `newCustomer.jsp` to `login.jsp` in Listing 12-3.

We have finished the login and new customer registration tasks. The next step is to allow the user to search for wines based on different criteria. We will start by creating a simple JSF page that will provide the links to different options available to the user.

The Links Page

Listing 12-7 shows the code for the `winehome.jsp` JSF page. This page uses an `h:commandLink` JSF UI component that allows you to embed output text that should be displayed when the page is rendered. It also includes a live link that the user can click to navigate to the next page. This page provides three options to the user:

- A complete list of available wines

- The ability to search wines by year, country, or varietal

- The ability to view the shopping cart and submit orders

Listing 12-7. winehome.jsp

```jsp
<!DOCTYPE HTML PUBLIC "-//W3C//DTD HTML 4.01 Transitional//EN"
"http://www.w3.org/TR/html4/loose.dtd">
<%@ page contentType="text/html;charset=windows-1252"%>
<%@ taglib uri="http://java.sun.com/jsf/html" prefix="h"%>
<%@ taglib uri="http://java.sun.com/jsf/core" prefix="f"%>
<f:view>
  <html>
    <head>
      <meta http-equiv="Content-Type" content="text/html; charset=windows-1252"/>
      <title>Wine Home Page</title>
    </head>
    <body>
      <h:form>
        <h1> Beginning EJB: Wine Store Application </h1>
        <p>
          <h:commandLink action="#{WineList.findAllWines}">
            <h:outputText value="Complete List of Wines"/>
          </h:commandLink>
        </p>
        <p>
          <h:commandLink action="search">
            <h:outputText value="Search by Year or Country or Varietal"/>
          </h:commandLink>
        </p>
        <p>
          <h:commandLink action="cartitems">
            <h:outputText value="View shopping cart and submit order"/>
          </h:commandLink>
        </p>
      </h:form>
    </body>
  </html>
</f:view>
```

We can specify the action attribute with the h:commandLink component that can be an expression based on a method or property in a managed bean. Alternatively, the action attribute can be the name of the navigation case that is defined in faces-config. xml. We are going to use the method-binding expression #{WineList.findAllWines} as an action property value for the "Complete List of Wines" option, and we will use the names of the navigation case for the remaining two options.

Figure 12-21 (in the "Compiling, Deploying, and Testing the JSF Application" section) shows the winehome.jsp page rendered in a browser.

The next step is to define the WineList managed bean that will talk to the back-end EJB to get the list of all wines. Listing 12-8 shows the code for the WineList bean. We will start by injecting the SearchFacade EJB using the @EJB annotation. The findAllWines() method in the bean class makes use of the injected SearchFacade stateless session bean and calls the getWineFindAll() business method that returns the list of available wines. The returned list of wines is stored in the winesList property of the managed bean, and the allwines string is returned as the navigation case.

Listing 12-8. WineList.java

```java
package com.apress.ejb.chapter12.view.managed;

import com.apress.ejb.chapter07.ejb.SearchFacadeLocal;
import com.apress.ejb.chapter07.entities.Wine;
import java.util.ArrayList;
import java.util.List;
import javax.ejb.EJB;
import javax.faces.application.Application;
import javax.faces.component.html.HtmlDataTable;
import javax.faces.context.FacesContext;
import javax.faces.el.ValueBinding;

public class WineList
{
  public WineList() {
  }

  @EJB
  private SearchFacadeLocal searchFacade;
  private List<Wine> winesList = new ArrayList();
```

```
public String findAllWines() {
  if (searchFacade == null) {
    return "gohome";
  }
  else {
    winesList = searchFacade.getWineFindAll();
    return "allwines";
  }
}

public void setWinesList(List<Wine> winesList) {
  this.winesList = winesList;
}

public List<Wine> getWinesList() {
  return winesList;
}
}
```

To finish the work for this page, we will extend the faces-config.xml file with the details shown in Listing 12-9. We have defined WineList as a managed bean and added three more navigation rules that create the following links:

- From winehome.jsp to searchwines.jsp, to take the user to the search page

- From winehome.jsp to wineList.jsp, after executing the findAllWines() method provided in the managed bean

- From winehome.jsp to cartItems.jsp, to show the list of all items in the shopping cart

Listing 12-9. faces-config.xml, with the WineList Managed Bean

```
<managed-bean>
  <managed-bean-name>WineList</managed-bean-name>
  <managed-bean-class>com.apress.ejb.chapter12.view.managed.WineList
  </managed-bean-class>
  <managed-bean-scope>session</managed-bean-scope>
</managed-bean>
```

```
<navigation-rule>
  <from-view-id>/winehome.jsp</from-view-id>
  <navigation-case>
    <from-outcome>search</from-outcome>
    <to-view-id>/searchwines.jsp</to-view-id>
  </navigation-case>
  <navigation-case>
    <from-outcome>allwines</from-outcome>
    <to-view-id>/wineList.jsp</to-view-id>
  </navigation-case>
  <navigation-case>
    <from-outcome>cartitems</from-outcome>
    <to-view-id>/cartItems.jsp</to-view-id>
  </navigation-case>
</navigation-rule>
```

We will work on the three pages to which we are navigating in the next sections.

The Search Page

Listing 12-10 shows the code for the searchwines.jsp JSF page. This page allows the user to search for the wines by year, country, or varietal. We are using the h:selectOneListBox components that are populated with a static list of values for each of the search criteria. The value selected from the list box is stored in the properties of the SearchWines managed bean using the value-binding expressions specified in the value attribute of the h:selectOneListBox component. We have also provided three Submit buttons whose action attributes have method-binding expressions, such as #{WineList.searchByYear}, to trigger a method in the WineList managed bean that will retrieve the results from the EJB back-end application.

Listing 12-10. searchwines.jsp

```
<!DOCTYPE HTML PUBLIC "-//W3C//DTD HTML 4.01 Transitional//EN"
"http://www.w3.org/TR/html4/loose.dtd">
<%@ page contentType="text/html;charset=windows-1252"%>
<%@ taglib uri="http://java.sun.com/jsf/html" prefix="h"%>
<%@ taglib uri="http://java.sun.com/jsf/core" prefix="f"%>
```

```
<f:view>
  <html>
    <head>
      <meta http-equiv="Content-Type" content="text/html; charset=windows-1252"/>
      <title>Search Wines Page</title>
    </head>
    <body>
      <h:form>
        <h2> Beginning EJB: Wine Store Application </h2>
        <h4> Search Wines </h4>
        <table cellspacing="2" cellpadding="3" border="1" width="100%">
          <tr>
            <td><h:outputText value="Year"/></td>
            <td>
              <h:selectOneListbox value="#{SearchWines.year}">
              <f:selectItem itemLabel="2001" itemValue="2001"/>
              <f:selectItem itemLabel="2002" itemValue="2002"/>
              <f:selectItem itemLabel="2003" itemValue="2003"/>
              <f:selectItem itemLabel="2007" itemValue="2007"/>
              <f:selectItem itemLabel="2008" itemValue="2008"/>
              <f:selectItem itemLabel="2009" itemValue="2009"/>
              </h:selectOneListbox>
            </td>
            <td><h:commandButton value="Go" action="#{WineList.
            searchByYear}"/></td>
          </tr>
          <tr>
            <td><h:outputLabel value="Country"/></td>
            <td>
              <h:selectOneListbox value="#{SearchWines.country}">
              <f:selectItem itemLabel="USA" itemValue="USA"/>
              <f:selectItem itemLabel="France" itemValue="France"/>
              <f:selectItem itemLabel="Australia" itemValue="Australia"/>
              </h:selectOneListbox>
            </td>
```

575

```
            <td><h:commandButton value="Go" action="#{WineList.
            searchByCountry}"/></td>
         </tr>
         <tr>
           <td><h:outputLabel value="Varietal"/></td>
           <td><h:selectOneListbox value="#{SearchWines.varietal}">
             <f:selectItem itemLabel="Zinfandel" itemValue="Zinfandel"/>
             </h:selectOneListbox>
           </td>
           <td><h:commandButton value="Go" action="#{WineList.
           searchByVarietal}"/></td>
         </tr>
       </table>
     </h:form>
   </body>
 </html>
</f:view>
```

Figure 12-22 (in the "Compiling, Deploying, and Testing the JSF Application" section) shows the searchwines.jsp page rendered in a browser.

The next step is to add new methods to the WineList managed bean and define a new managed bean called SearchWines. Listing 12-11 shows the SearchWines managed bean that has three properties (year, varietal, and country) and their accessors. User-selected values in the searchwines.jsp page are stored in these properties, which can be retrieved by the WineList managed bean.

Listing 12-11. SearchWines.java

```java
package com.apress.ejb.chapter12.view.managed;

public class SearchWines
{
  public SearchWines() {
  }

  public String year;
  public String varietal;
  public String country;
```

```
public void setYear(String year) {
  this.year = year;
}

public String getYear() {
  return year;
}

public void setVarietal(String varietal) {
  this.varietal = varietal;
}

public String getVarietal() {
  return varietal;
}

public void setCountry(String country) {
  this.country = country;
}

public String getCountry() {
  return country;
}
}
```

We have to add new functionality to the WineList managed bean created earlier (see Listing 12-8) by adding three more methods that are bound in the method-binding expressions of the searchwines.jsp JSF page. Listing 12-12 shows the three methods: searchByYear(), searchByCountry(), and searchByVarietal(). Each of these methods needs the value of the properties from the SearchWines managed bean. JSF provides access to the requested data and data from other objects through the FacesContext object. Once we have the reference to FacesContext, we can get access to the application and the managed beans. All methods use the technique of getting the Application from FacesContext and calling the createValueBinding() method with the value-binding expression to retrieve the value of the relevant property from the SearchWines managed bean. Once the value of the property is retrieved from SearchWines, the method calls the business methods in the SearchFacade EJB by passing in the parameters that match the search criteria to retrieve the list of wines. The retrieved list of wines is stored in the winesList property that is of java.util.List type.

Listing 12-12. WineList.java, with Search Methods

```java
public String searchByCountry() {
  FacesContext ctx = FacesContext.getCurrentInstance();
  Application app = ctx.getApplication();
  ValueBinding wineyear = app.createValueBinding("#{SearchWines.country}");
  String country = wineyear.getValue(ctx).toString();
  if (searchFacade == null) {
    return "gohome";
  }
  else {
    winesList = searchFacade.getWineFindByCountry(country);
    return "success";
  }
}

public String searchByVarietal() {
  FacesContext ctx = FacesContext.getCurrentInstance();
  Application app = ctx.getApplication();
  ValueBinding wineyear = app.createValueBinding("#{SearchWines.varietal}");
  String varietal = wineyear.getValue(ctx).toString();
  if (searchFacade == null) {
    return "gohome";
  }
  else {
    winesList = searchFacade.getWineFindByVarietal(varietal);
    return "success";
  }
}

public String searchByYear() {
  FacesContext ctx = FacesContext.getCurrentInstance();
  Application app = ctx.getApplication();
  ValueBinding wineyear = app.createValueBinding("#{SearchWines.year}");
  String year = wineyear.getValue(ctx).toString();
  if (searchFacade == null) {
```

```
      return "gohome";
  }
  else {
    winesList = searchFacade.getWineFindByYear(new Integer(year));
    return "success";
  }
}
```

All of the methods return a value of success that will be used as a navigation case. We need to add this navigation case into faces-config.xml and also register SearchWines as a managed bean. Listing 12-13 shows the snippets of XML that need to be added to faces-config.xml. A success value returned by the methods will take the user to wineList.jsp that will display the list of wines. Notice that we have set the scope of the SearchWines managed bean to session, as we are accessing the properties from other managed beans as well.

Listing 12-13. faces-config.xml, with the SearchWines Managed Bean

```xml
<navigation-rule>
  <from-view-id>/searchwines.jsp</from-view-id>
  <navigation-case>
    <from-outcome>gohome</from-outcome>
    <to-view-id>/winehome.jsp</to-view-id>
  </navigation-case>
  <navigation-case>
    <from-outcome>success</from-outcome>
    <to-view-id>/wineList.jsp</to-view-id>
  </navigation-case>
</navigation-rule>

<managed-bean>
  <managed-bean-name>SearchWines</managed-bean-name>
  <managed-bean-class>com.apress.ejb.chapter12.view.managed.SearchWines
  </managed-bean-class>
  <managed-bean-scope>session</managed-bean-scope>
</managed-bean>
```

So far, we have completed the following tasks:

- Creating the login page

- Creating the registration page

- Creating the home page with a list of options

- Creating the search page

We will now work on showing the wine list to the user in the wineList.jsp page.

The Wine List Page

Listing 12-14 shows the code for the wineList.jsp JSF page. In this page, we are using a new UI component called h:dataTable. This component allows collections of data to be rendered from managed bean properties that are of type java.util.List. In the previous sections, we have been storing the retrieved wines in the winesList property. The #{WinesList.winesList} expression is used for the value attribute of h:dataTable to display the list of wines in the table format. Once the list of wines is displayed to the user, the user can select one of the wines displayed in the data table component so that the user can see the details of the wine in a different page and add it to the shopping cart if the user wants to buy it. In order to keep track of the selected wine in the data table component, we have added the binding attribute to h:dataTable. One last thing we need to do is to provide a hyperlink for each row in the data table that the user can click to select the wine. To achieve this, we will wrap the column displaying the wine ID with the h:commandLink component. The value of the h:commandLink action attribute is set to the #{WinesList.invokeAddToCart} expression, which means that we need to extend the WinesList managed bean with a new method: invokeAddToCart().

Listing 12-14. wineList.jsp

```
<!DOCTYPE HTML PUBLIC "-//W3C//DTD HTML 4.01 Transitional//EN"
"http://www.w3.org/TR/html4/loose.dtd">
<%@ page contentType="text/html;charset=windows-1252"%>
<%@ taglib uri="http://java.sun.com/jsf/html" prefix="h"%>
<%@ taglib uri="http://java.sun.com/jsf/core" prefix="f"%>
<f:view>
```

```
<html>
  <head>
    <meta http-equiv="Content-Type" content="text/html; charset=windows-1252"/>
    <title>Wine List Page</title>
  </head>
  <body>
    <h:form>
      <h2> Beginning EJB: Wine Store Application </h2>
      <h:dataTable value="#{WineList.winesList}" var="wines"
                      binding="#{WineList.dataTable1}" id="dataTable1">
        <h:column>
          <f:facet name="header">
            <h:outputText value="Id"/>
          </f:facet>
          <h:commandLink action="#{WineList.invokeAddToCart}">
              <h:outputText value="#{wines.id}"/>
          </h:commandLink>
        </h:column>
        <h:column>
          <f:facet name="header">
            <h:outputText value="Name"/>
          </f:facet>
          <h:outputText value="#{wines.name}"/>
        </h:column>
        <h:column>
          <f:facet name="header">
            <h:outputText value="Varietal"/>
          </f:facet>
          <h:outputText value="#{wines.varietal}"/>
        </h:column>
        <h:column>
          <f:facet name="header">
            <h:outputText value="Country"/>
          </f:facet>
          <h:outputText value="#{wines.country}"/>
```

```
        </h:column>
        <h:column>
          <f:facet name="header">
            <h:outputText value="Year"/>
          </f:facet>
          <h:outputText value="#{wines.year}"/>
        </h:column>
        <h:column>
          <f:facet name="header">
            <h:outputText value="Region"/>
          </f:facet>
          <h:outputText value="#{wines.region}"/>
        </h:column>
        <h:column>
          <f:facet name="header">
            <h:outputText value="Rating"/>
          </f:facet>
          <h:outputText value="#{wines.rating}"/>
        </h:column>
        <h:column>
          <f:facet name="header">
            <h:outputText value="Retail Price"/>
          </f:facet>
          <h:outputText value="#{wines.retailPrice}"/>
        </h:column>
        <h:column>
          <f:facet name="header">
            <h:outputText value="Description"/>
          </f:facet>
          <h:outputText value="#{wines.description}"/>
        </h:column>
        <h:column>
          <h:commandButton value="Add to Cart" action="#{WineList.
          invokeAddToCart}"/>
        </h:column>
```

```
            </h:dataTable>
        </h:form>
    </body>
  </html>
</f:view>
```

Figure 12-23 (in the "Compiling, Deploying, and Testing the JSF Application" section) shows the wineList.jsp page rendered in the browser.

Listing 12-15 shows the new code that we need to add to the WinesList managed bean. We will add a new property, dataTable1, with respective accessor methods and a brand new method, invokeAddToCart(). The new dataTable1 property is used to set the value of the binding attribute in the h:dataTable1 component in wineList.jsp, as shown in Listing 12-14. In the invokeAddToCart() method, we are retrieving the selected row using the getRowData() method of the dataTable1 property and setting it as the value of the selectedWine property in a new managed bean: JSFShoppingCart. We have used the technique of getting the application from FacesContext and setting the value of the property, instead of retrieving the value as we did in the earlier use case. The invokeAddToCart() method returns addtocart on successful execution that we will use as a navigation case.

Listing 12-15. WineList.java, with the invokeAddToCart Method

```
private HtmlDataTable dataTable1;

public void setDataTable1(HtmlDataTable dataTable1) {
  this.dataTable1 = dataTable1;
}

public HtmlDataTable getDataTable1() {
  return dataTable1;
}

public String invokeAddToCart() {
  Wine addWine = (Wine)this.getDataTable1().getRowData();
  FacesContext ctx = FacesContext.getCurrentInstance();
  Application app = ctx.getApplication();
```

```
  ValueBinding binding = app.createValueBinding("#{JSFShoppingCart.
  selectedWine}");
  binding.setValue(ctx, addWine);
  return "addtocart";
}
```

Before we update the faces-config.xml, we need to create a new managed bean, JSFShoppingCart. Listing 12-16 shows the code for this managed bean. We will start with a simple property, selectedWine, with its accessor methods, and then we will extend the bean to meet the new requirements. (These requirements will be discussed in later sections of the chapter.)

Listing 12-16. JSFShoppingCart.java

```
package com.apress.ejb.chapter12.view.managed;

import com.apress.ejb3.wineapp.Wine;

public class JSFShoppingCart {
  public JSFShoppingCart() {
  }

  Wine selectedWine;

  public void setSelectedWine(Wine selectedWine) {
    this.selectedWine = selectedWine;
  }

  public Wine getSelectedWine() {
    return selectedWine;
  }
}
```

We need to update the faces-config.xml by registering JSFShoppingCart as a managed bean and add a new navigation case from wineList.jsp to addtoCart.jsp. Listing 12-17 shows the XML snippets that will go into the faces-config.xml file.

Listing 12-17. faces-config.xml, with the JSFShoppingCart Managed Bean

```
<managed-bean>
  <managed-bean-name>JSFShoppingCart</managed-bean-name>
  <managed-bean-class>com.apress.ejb.chapter12.view.managed.
JSFShoppingCart</managed-bean-class>
  <managed-bean-scope>session</managed-bean-scope>
</managed-bean>

<navigation-rule>
  <from-view-id>/wineList.jsp</from-view-id>
  <navigation-case>
    <from-outcome>addtocart</from-outcome>
    <to-view-id>/addtoCart.jsp</to-view-id>
  </navigation-case>
</navigation-rule>
```

In this particular task, we have displayed the list of wines in a data table component and provided the user with the ability to select one of the wines. The selected wine is stored in the JSFShoppingCart managed bean.

The Display Selected Wine Details Page

Listing 12-18 shows the code for the addtoCart.jsp JSF page. On this particular page, we are going to use the h:outputText component to display the wine information and the h:inputText component to let the user enter the quantity for the selected wine. The value attribute of h:outputText is populated from the selectedWine property in the JSFShoppingCart managed bean developed in the preceding section. The value of h:inputText is set with the expression #{JSFShoppingCart.quantity}; this will be a new property that we need to add to JSFShoppingCart. One last thing to notice in this page is the h:commandButton component that the users will use as a Submit button to add wines to the shopping cart. The value of the action attribute for h:commandButton is set to the #{JSFShoppingCart.addToCart} expression. The addToCart() is a new method that we will have to add to the JSFShoppingCart bean.

Listing 12-18. addtoCart.jsp

```
<!DOCTYPE HTML PUBLIC "-//W3C//DTD HTML 4.01 Transitional//EN"
"http://www.w3.org/TR/html4/loose.dtd">
<%@ page contentType="text/html;charset=windows-1252"%>
<%@ taglib uri="http://java.sun.com/jsf/html" prefix="h"%>
<%@ taglib uri="http://java.sun.com/jsf/core" prefix="f"%>
<f:view>
  <html>
    <head>
      <meta http-equiv="Content-Type" content="text/html; charset=windows-1252"/>
      <title>Add To Cart Page</title>
    </head>
    <body>
      <h:form>
        <h3>Beginning EJB: Wine Store Application</h3>
        <h5>Selected Wine - Enter Quantity and press AddtoCart button</h5>
        <table cellspacing="3" cellpadding="2" border="1" width="100%">
          <tr>
            <td>Wine ID</td>
            <td> <h:outputText value="#{JSFShoppingCart.selectedWine.id}"/> </td>
          </tr>
          <tr>
            <td>Name</td>
            <td> <h:outputText value="#{JSFShoppingCart.selectedWine.
            name}"/> </td>
          </tr>
          <tr>
            <td>Description</td>
            <td> <h:outputText value="#{JSFShoppingCart.selectedWine.
            description}"/> </td>
          </tr>
          <tr>
            <td>Country</td>
```

```
      <td> <h:outputText value="#{JSFShoppingCart.selectedWine.
      country}"/> </td>
    </tr>
    <tr>
      <td>Rating</td>
      <td> <h:outputText value="#{JSFShoppingCart.selectedWine.
      rating}"/> </td>
    </tr>
    <tr>
      <td>Region</td>
      <td> <h:outputText value="#{JSFShoppingCart.selectedWine.
      region}"/> </td>
    </tr>
    <tr>
      <td>Retail Price</td>
      <td> <h:outputText value="#{JSFShoppingCart.selectedWine.
      retailPrice}"/> </td>
    </tr>
    <tr>
      <td>Varietal</td>
      <td> <h:outputText value="#{JSFShoppingCart.selectedWine.
      varietal}"/> </td>
    </tr>
    <tr>
      <td>Year</td>
      <td>
        <h:outputText value="#{JSFShoppingCart.selectedWine.year}"/>
      </td>
    </tr>
    <tr>
      <td>Quantity</td>
      <td> <h:inputText value="#{JSFShoppingCart.quantity}"/> </td>
    </tr>
</table>
<p>
```

```
            <h:commandButton value="Add to cart" action="#{JSFShoppingCart.
            addToCart}"/>
        </p>
      </h:form>
    </body>
  </html>
</f:view>
```

Figure 12-24 (in the "Compiling, Deploying, and Testing the JSF Application" section) shows the addtoCart.jsp page rendered in the browser.

We will update the JSFShoppingCart managed bean with a new Quantity property and an addToCart() method. Listing 12-19 shows the code snippets for these two things. The Quantity property has the accessor methods, and the addToCart() method uses the technique of getting the application from FacesContext and retrieving the instance of the ShoppingCart stateful EJB from the Login managed bean. Once that is done, the addWineItem() business method is invoked to add the selected wine and quantity to the list of cart items in the ShoppingCart EJB. The addToCart() method returns a value of success that will be used as a navigation case.

Listing 12-19. JSFShoppingCart.java, with the addToCart Method

```
String Quantity;

public void setQuantity(String quantity) {
  this.Quantity = quantity;
}

public String getQuantity() {
  return Quantity;
}

public String addToCart() {
  Integer qty = new Integer(Quantity);
  FacesContext ctx = FacesContext.getCurrentInstance();
  Application app = ctx.getApplication();

  //check whether customer has already logged in.
  ValueBinding customerBinding = app.createValueBinding("#{Login.customer}");
  if (customerBinding.getValue(ctx) == null) {
```

```
      return "success";
   }
   else {
      ValueBinding shoppingCartBinding = app.createValueBinding("#{Login.
      shoppingCart}");
      shoppingCart = (ShoppingCartLocal)shoppingCartBinding.getValue(ctx);
      shoppingCart.addWineItem(selectedWine, qty.intValue());
      return "success";
   }
}
```

To complete this task, we need to add one navigation case to the faces-config.xml. Listing 12-20 shows the XML snippet. When a wine is successfully added to the shopping cart, the user is taken to a new page, cartItems.jsp, which displays the list of all items in the cart.

Listing 12-20. faces-config.xml, with the addtoCart Navigation Rule

```
<navigation-rule>
   <from-view-id>/addtoCart.jsp</from-view-id>
   <navigation-case>
      <from-outcome>success</from-outcome>
      <to-view-id>/cartItems.jsp</to-view-id>
   </navigation-case>
</navigation-rule>
```

The Display Cart Items Page

Listing 12-21 shows the cartItems.jsp JSF page. In this page, we want to display all of the items in the shopping cart using a data table component. The #{JSFShoppingCart.cartItems} expression is used as a value-binding expression for the h:dataTable1 component. This means that again we have to update our JSFShoppingCart managed bean with code that will populate the cartItems property. Finally, the JSF page has a h:commandButton component that the user will use as a Submit button to complete the order. #{JSFShoppingCart.ProcessOrder} is a method-binding expression used for the Submit button.

Listing 12-21. cartItems.jsp

```
<!DOCTYPE HTML PUBLIC "-//W3C//DTD HTML 4.01 Transitional//EN"
"http://www.w3.org/TR/html4/loose.dtd">
<%@ page contentType="text/html;charset=windows-1252"%>
<%@ taglib uri="http://java.sun.com/jsf/html" prefix="h"%>
<%@ taglib uri="http://java.sun.com/jsf/core" prefix="f"%>
<f:view>
  <html>
    <head>
      <meta http-equiv="Content-Type" content="text/html;
      charset=windows-1252"/>
      <title>Cart Items Page</title>
    </head>
    <body>
      <h:form>
        <h3>Beginning EJB: Wine Store Application</h3>
        <h4>Shopping Cart</h4>
          <h:dataTable value="#{JSFShoppingCart.cartItems}" var="cartItems">
            <h:column>
              <f:facet name="header">
                <h:outputText value="Id"/>
              </f:facet>
              <h:outputText value="#{cartItems.id}"/>
            </h:column>
            <h:column>
              <f:facet name="header">
                <h:outputText value="Created Date"/>
              </f:facet>
              <h:outputText value="#{cartItems.createdDate}"/>
            </h:column>
            <h:column>
              <f:facet name="header">
                <h:outputText value="Wine"/>
              </f:facet>
              <h:outputText value="#{cartItems.wine.name}"/>
```

```
        </h:column>
        <h:column>
          <f:facet name="header">
            <h:outputText value="Quantity"/>
          </f:facet>
          <h:outputText value="#{cartItems.quantity}"/>
        </h:column>
      </h:dataTable>
      <h:commandButton value="Submit Order" action="#{JSFShoppingCart.
      ProcessOrder}"/>
    </h:form>
  </body>
</html>
</f:view>
```

Figure 12-25 (in the "Compiling, Deploying, and Testing the JSF Application" section) shows the cartItems.jsp page rendered in the browser.

Listing 12-22 shows the code snippets that are used to update the JSFShoppingCart managed bean. We have a property–cartItems–of java.util.List type, with accessor methods. In the getter method, we are retrieving the Customer object and the instance of the ShoppingCart stateful EJB from the Login managed bean, and we are calling the business method getAllCartItems() that returns the list of items in the cart. The second method, ProcessOrder(), also retrieves the instance of the ShoppingCart stateful EJB from the Login managed bean and invokes the ProcessOrder business method on the back-end application to complete the order on the JSF application side. Upon successful execution, the ProcessOrder() method in JSFShoppingCart returns success as a value that is used for navigation back to the home page of the application.

Listing 12-22. JSFShoppingCart.java, with the getCartItems and ProcessOrder Methods

```
List<CartItem> cartItems = new ArrayList();

public void setCartItems(List<CartItem> cartItems) {
  this.cartItems = cartItems;
}
```

```
public List<CartItem> getCartItems() {
  FacesContext ctx = FacesContext.getCurrentInstance();
  Application app = ctx.getApplication();
  ValueBinding customerBinding = app.createValueBinding("#{Login.customer}");
  Individual customer = (Individual)customerBinding.getValue(ctx);
  ValueBinding shoppingCartBinding = app.createValueBinding("#{Login.
  shoppingCart}");
  shoppingCart = (ShoppingCartLocal)shoppingCartBinding.getValue(ctx);
  return shoppingCart.getAllCartItems(customer);
}

public String ProcessOrder() {
  FacesContext ctx = FacesContext.getCurrentInstance();
  Application app = ctx.getApplication();
  ValueBinding shoppingCartBinding = app.createValueBinding("#{Login.
  shoppingCart}");
  shoppingCart = (ShoppingCartLocal)shoppingCartBinding.getValue(ctx);
  shoppingCart.sendOrderToOPC();
  return "success";
}
```

One last thing that we need to do is to add a navigation case to faces-config.xml that will route the user back to the processOrder.jsp notification page as shown in Listing 12-23.

Listing 12-23. faces-config.xml, with the cartItems Navigation Rule

```
<navigation-rule>
  <from-view-id>/cartItems.jsp</from-view-id>
  <navigation-case>
    <from-outcome>success</from-outcome>
    <to-view-id>/processOrder.jsp</to-view-id>
  </navigation-case>
</navigation-rule>
```

The Notification Page

We're almost there! We will add one final JSF page processOrder.jsp that will display an order submission message to the user and provide a link to navigate back to the home page. Listing 12-24 shows the code for processOrder.jsp. As you can see, the page is pretty static—it prints out notification text and uses an h:commandLink component to route the user back to the winehome.jsp page that shows the list of options for searching wines, viewing the contents of the shopping cart, and so on.

Listing 12-24. processOrder.jsp

```
<!DOCTYPE HTML PUBLIC "-//W3C//DTD HTML 4.01 Transitional//EN"
"http://www.w3.org/TR/html4/loose.dtd">
<%@ page contentType="text/html;charset=windows-1252"%>
<%@ taglib uri="http://java.sun.com/jsf/html" prefix="h"%>
<%@ taglib uri="http://java.sun.com/jsf/core" prefix="f"%>
<f:view>
  <html>
    <head>
      <meta http-equiv="Content-Type" content="text/html; charset=windows-1252"/>
      <title>Process Order Page</title>
    </head>
    <body>
      <h:form>
        <p> <strong>Beginning EJB: Wine Store Application</strong> </p>
        <p> <strong>Your order has been submitted, you will receive an
        email with order id and details.</strong> </p>
        <p>
          <h:commandLink value="Back to Home" action="winehome2">
            <h:outputText value="Back to wine search"/>
          </h:commandLink>
        </p>
      </h:form>
    </body>
  </html>
</f:view>
```

Figure 12-26 (in the "Compiling, Deploying, and Testing the JSF Application" section) shows the processOrder.jsp page being rendered in the browser.

To complete the process, we will add one final navigation case into faces-config. xml, as shown in Listing 12-25.

Listing 12-25. faces-config.xml, with the processOrder Navigation Rule

```
<navigation-rule>
  <from-view-id>/processOrder.jsp</from-view-id>
  <navigation-case>
    <from-outcome>winehome2</from-outcome>
    <to-view-id>/winehome.jsp</to-view-id>
  </navigation-case>
</navigation-rule>
```

With that, we have completed the JSF application with the control flow shown previously in Figure 12-12. Now we will look at deploying and executing the completed application and walk through the screens that we have developed, which access the EJB back-end application.

Compiling, Deploying, and Testing the JSF Application

JSF applications need to be packaged into Web Archive (WAR) files before they're assembled into Enterprise Archive (EAR) files that hold all of the required modules and libraries for the application. Most application servers provide deployment utilities or Ant tasks to facilitate deployment of EJBs to their containers. Java-integrated development environments (IDEs) like JDeveloper, NetBeans, and Eclipse also provide deployment features that allow developers to package, assemble, and deploy applications to application servers.

Packaging, assembly, and deployment aspects are covered in detail in Chapter 11. In this chapter, we have developed a JSF application that accesses the back-end application built in Chapter 7. We will perform the following steps to deploy and test the JSF application.

Prerequisites

Before performing the steps detailed in the next sections, complete the "Getting Started" section of Chapter 1, which will walk you through the installation and environment setup required for the samples in this chapter. Since we have built our JSF application on top of the work we have done in Chapter 7, you will need to make sure that you have completed the following steps:

- You must have created the resources detailed in the "Creating Data Sources, JMS Resources, and Mail Resources" section of Chapter 7.

- You must have successfully deployed the application as detailed in the "Deploying the Application" section of Chapter 7.

Note   The sample code of Chapter 7 is dependent on Chapter 6. Hence, make sure that you have completed both Chapter 6 and Chapter 7 before you proceed further. Refer to the Readme.txt bundled with the sample code in case you face any problems in executing the sample code.

Compiling the JSF Application

Copy the Chapter12-JSFClientSamples directory and its contents into a directory of your choice. As the sample code of this chapter references the artifacts of Chapter 6, make sure that you have the Chapter06-WebServiceSamples directory alongside the Chapter12-JSFClientSamples directory. Run the NetBeans IDE, and open the Chapter12-JSFClientSamples file using the File ➤ Open Project menu, as shown in Figure 12-13.

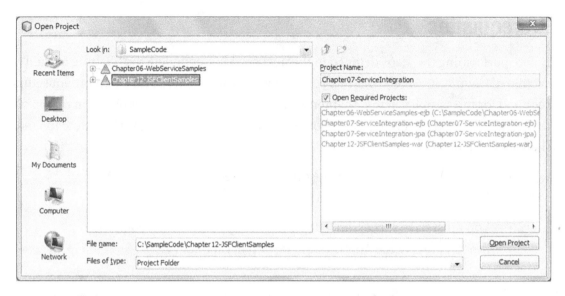

Figure 12-13. *Opening the Chapter12-JSFClientSamples file*

Note   Before you open the `Chapter12-JSFClientSamples` file within NetBeans, make sure you have closed the `Chapter07-ServiceIntegration` project and `Chapter06-WebServiceSamples` from the NetBeans IDE. The sample code of Chapter 12 is built on top of Chapter 6 and Chapter 7, and having these projects open within NetBeans will result in compilation errors. NetBeans will automatically open the required projects when `Chapter12-JSFClientSamples` is opened.

Expand the `Chapter12-JSFClientSamples-war` node, and observe that all of the JSF files and managed beans discussed in this chapter are listed as shown in Figure 12-14.

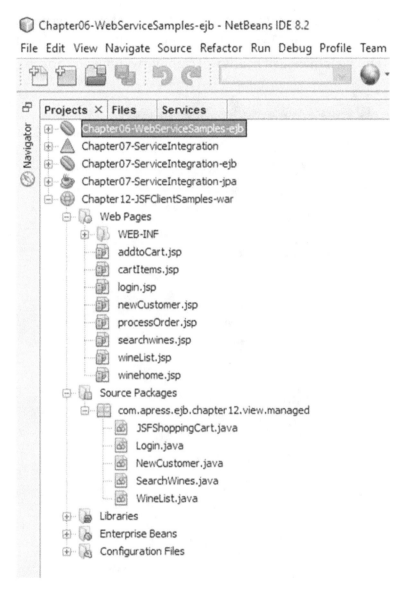

Figure 12-14. *Verifying the packages in the Chapter12-JSFClientSamples-war project*

Invoke the context menu on the Chapter07-ServiceIntegration node, and build the application by selecting the Clean and Build menu option, as shown in Figure 12-15. The JSF pages and their managed beans will compile without any errors.

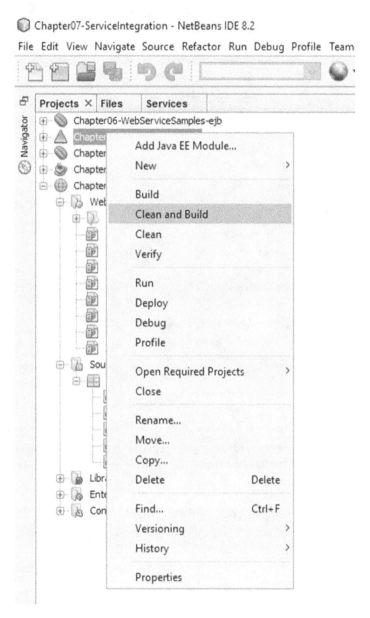

Figure 12-15. *Building the project*

Deploying and Running the Wine Store Application

Once the JSF pages and managed beans are successfully compiled, we need to set the run target that we wish to execute. To set the run target, invoke the context menu on Chapter07-ServiceIntegration node, and select the Properties menu option. As shown in Figure 12-16, select the Run category, enter the run target as faces/login.jsp in Relative URL text field, and click OK.

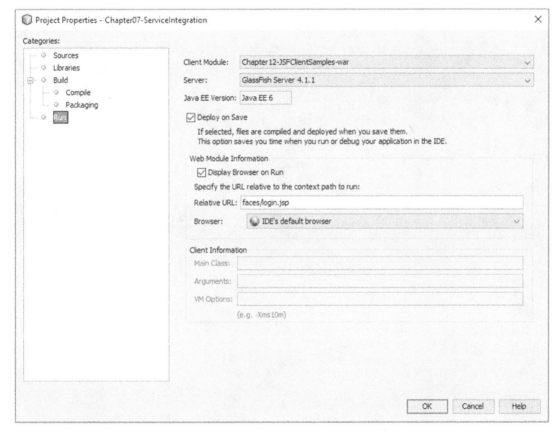

Figure 12-16. *Setting the run target*

Now you are ready to run the wine store application with the JSF user interface. To run the application, invoke the context menu on Chapter07-ServiceIntegration node and select the Run menu option, as shown in Figure 12-17. Running the application will deploy the application on the integrated GlassFish application server and launch the wine store application in your default browser.

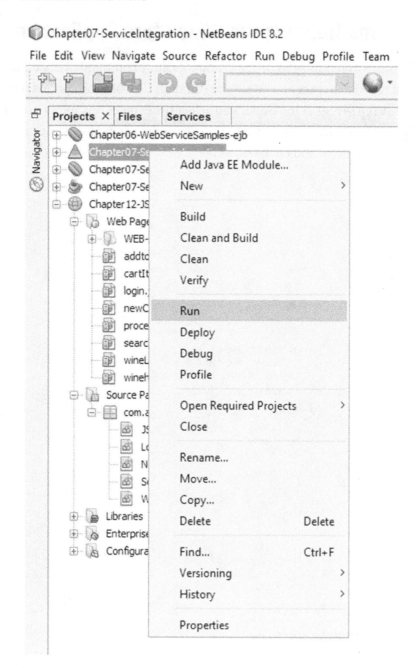

Figure 12-17. *Running the wine store application*

Upon startup, the login page rendered as shown in Figure 12-18.

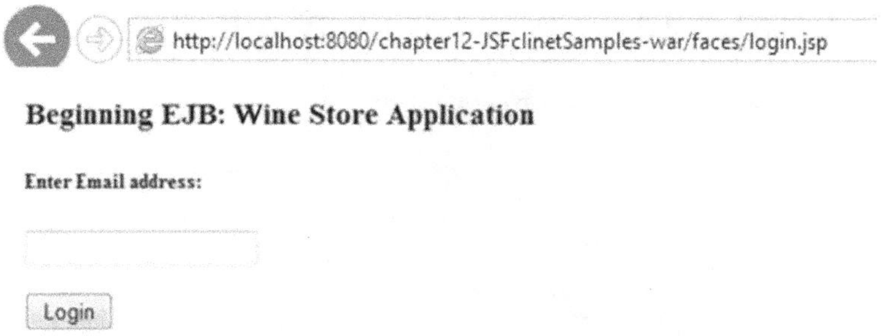

Figure 12-18. *The wine store application login page*

Note   As the aim of this sample application is solely to learn the technology, its code does not have the required data validations entry that you would normally find in enterprise applications. Thus, make sure you enter valid values for the given text fields.

Enter your e-mail in the "Enter Email address" text field, and click the "Login" button. Since you haven't registered as a customer yet, and your e-mail does not exist in the customer database, you will be redirected to the customer registration page, as shown in Figure 12-19. Enter the relevant values in the input fields as shown, and click the "Submit" button.

Beginning EJB: Wine Store Application

Enter the following information to register as a new customer:

First Name	Wine
Last Name	User
Phone	88888888
Email	wineapp@yahoo.com
Street 1	Wine Street
Street 2	Wine Street 2
City	Wine City
State	Wine State
Zip Code	39855
Credit Card	434612345678901234
Credit Card Expiry date	1212

Submit

Figure 12-19. *The customer registration page*

Upon successful registration, you will be routed back to the login page. On the login page, enter the e-mail address that you have used in the registration process and click the "Login" button, as shown in Figure 12-20.

Beginning EJB: Wine Store Application

Enter Email address:

wineapp@yahoo.com

Login

Figure 12-20. *The wine store application login page*

After the e-mail address is validated, you will be routed to the wine store home page that will show you a list of options, as shown in Figure 12-21.

Beginning EJB: Wine Store Application

Complete List of Wines

Search by Year or Country or Varietal

View shopping cart and submit order

Figure 12-21. *The wine store home page*

We will walk you through the search use case. Click the link that reads, "Search by year, country, or varietal." You will be routed to the search page, as shown in Figure 12-22.

Figure 12-22. *The search page*

Select "Zinfandel" as the varietal, and click the "Go" button. Figure 12-23 shows the list of wines that satisfy the search criteria.

Beginning EJB: Wine Store Application

Id	Name	Varietal	Country	Year	Region	Rating	Retail Price	Description	
301	Yerba Buena 0	Zinfandel	USA	2000	Napa Valley	90	10.0	Fine Wine - ranked #0	Add to Cart
302	Yerba Buena 1	Zinfandel	USA	2001	Napa Valley	90	11.0	Fine Wine - ranked #1	Add to Cart
303	Yerba Buena 2	Zinfandel	USA	2002	Napa Valley	90	12.0	Fine Wine - ranked #2	Add to Cart
304	Yerba Buena 3	Zinfandel	USA	2003	Napa Valley	90	13.0	Fine Wine - ranked #3	Add to Cart
305	Chateau Brown 4	Zinfandel	France	2004	Loire Valley	90	14.0	Fine Wine - ranked #4	Add to Cart
306	Chateau Brown 5	Zinfandel	France	2005	Loire Valley	90	15.0	Fine Wine - ranked #5	Add to Cart
307	Chateau Brown 6	Zinfandel	France	2006	Loire Valley	90	16.0	Fine Wine - ranked #6	Add to Cart
308	Chateau Brown 7	Zinfandel	France	2007	Loire Valley	90	17.0	Fine Wine - ranked #7	Add to Cart
309	Chateau Brown 8	Zinfandel	France	2008	Loire Valley	90	18.0	Fine Wine - ranked #8	Add to Cart
310	Chateau Brown 9	Zinfandel	France	2009	Loire Valley	90	19.0	Fine Wine - ranked #9	Add to Cart

Figure 12-23. *The wine list page*

In the wine list page, click the "Add to Cart" button for the wine that you wish to add to the shopping cart. This will bring you to the JSF page, as shown in Figure 12-24, which shows the details of the wines and a text box for entering the quantity.

http://localhost:8080/chapter12-JSFclinetSamples-war/faces/wineList.jsp

Beginning EJB: Wine Store Application

Selected Wine - Enter Quantity and press AddtoCart button

Wine ID	301
Name	Yerba Buena 0
Description	Fine Wine - ranked #0
Country	USA
Rating	90
Region	Napa Valley
Retail Price	10.0
Varietal	Zinfandel
Year	2000
Quantity	10

Add to cart

Figure 12-24. *The wine details page*

Enter "10" for quantity, and click the "Add to cart" button. You will be routed to the shopping cart page. At this stage, you can either submit your order by pressing the "Submit Order" button or use your browser's back button to go to the page that lists the wines and add more wines to your shopping cart. As shown in Figure 12-25, the shopping cart page shows all of the items in the shopping cart.

Beginning EJB: Wine Store Application

Shopping Cart

Id	Created Date	Wine	Quantity
1155	2013-02-07 16:23:11.04	Yerba Buena 0	10
1156	2013-02-07 16:23:23.613	Chateau Brown 9	5

Submit Order

Figure 12-25.   *The shopping cart page*

The shopping cart page provides a "Submit Order" button for submitting the order. Click this button, and the order will be processed by the EJB back-end application. You will then be shown a notification page, as shown in Figure 12-26.

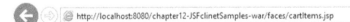

Beginning EJB: Wine Store Application

Your order has been submitted, you will receive an email with order id and details.

Back to HomeBack to wine search

Figure 12-26.   *The notification page*

Once the order has been processed, you will receive an e-mail notification, as shown in Figure 12-27.

Figure 12-27. *The notification e-mail*

The Application Client Container

We have mentioned and used the application client container in earlier chapters, and we have shown a couple of application architectures in Figure 12-4 and Figure 12-5. Application clients or client programs that are developed using technologies like Java Swing can be run in stand-alone Java SE environments. Application client containers provide additional system services (such as security and deployment) that client programs can use during execution.

An application client can leverage authentication services provided by the application client container for authenticating its users. The container's service may be integrated with the native platform's authentication system to provide single sign-on capability to the enterprise users.

Client programs using an application client container can invoke EJBs. Similar to other Java EE components, programs running in a client container can use the Java Naming and Directory Interface (JNDI) to look up EJBs or resources like Java Message Service (JMS) and JavaMail. Application client containers also provide injection facilities to client programs. Since application client containers do not create instances of an application client, static fields and methods should be used for injecting any resources.

Application clients are packaged into JAR files. If an application client container is used to run the client programs, then you will have to bundle or package the application client container along with the application so that you can run it on individual desktop machines.

Summary

In this chapter, we introduced different application architectures that you can use to meet different requirements, as well as the programming models that go along with them. We looked at architectures that are useful for Web and desktop applications, and we also looked at Web service client applications and business process services that can make use of EJBs published as Web services.

We discussed how Java EE based Web technologies have evolved, resulting in significantly simplified Web application development.

We drilled down into JSF architecture, the JSF life cycle, and JSF applications, as well as the current state of tools and UI components for JSF.

Ultimately, we built a comprehensive JSF application to communicate with the integrated EJB back-end application developed in Chapter 7. During the development process, we illustrated several programming techniques for sharing the data in the JSF application and looking up and invoking business methods in the back-end application.

Finally, we examined the application client container, including the services that it provides to client programs running on desktop machines.

The last chapter of this book will detail the various EJB testing scenarios and will guide you on using JUnit to test EJB components (and JPA entities) in GlassFish's Embeddable EJB Container.

## CHAPTER 13

Testing in an Embeddable EJB Container

As with all mission-critical software, EJB components must be well tested before they are deployed into a production environment. The finest level of granularity in an EJB is its method; so proper unit tests must test each method of each EJB in isolation. For stateless Session beans, this is typically sufficient. Because a stateful Session bean may also contain state, full coverage additionally requires inclusion of more coarse-grained scenarios as well, involving sequences of method calls. When a stateless Session bean effectively stores "state" information in a database, as through JPA entities, multistep test scenarios are generally also required. In this chapter, we will look at both single-method and multi-method tests, covering stateless and stateful Session beans serving primarily as service interfaces for JPA-based operations.

Test Clients

Thus far, the examples in this book have largely used servlets as clients to call EJB methods. Using test frameworks, such as ServletUnit, servlets can serve as a viable unit test bed for testing EJBs. Similarly, JSF clients that call EJBs can be unit tested using the HttpUnit framework, which allows you to record user interactions with JSF clients running in a browser and then compare the actual screen results with expected screen results. However, both approaches must be executed within a full Java EE application server. In this chapter, we will explore a lightweight option for testing EJBs running in a pure Java SE environment.

EJB Lite

EJB Lite was introduced in EJB 3.1 and further enhanced in EJB 3.2, and it is specified to be a minimal subset of the full EJB Container functionality. Recognizing that many enterprise applications require only a subset of the full EJB API, EJB Lite includes many of the most important features of EJB but with a smaller footprint. Implementations of EJB Lite include the Embeddable EJB Container, described below; and the Java EE Web Profile.

Because EJB Lite is a strict subset of the EJB API, any application that is compliant with EJB Lite will also run in a full EJB Container within a Java EE server. That is, EJB Lite does not explicitly support any behavior that is outside of the EJB API.

Embeddable EJB Container

An *Embeddable EJB Container* is essentially a Java library that provides the services defined by the EJB Lite specification. It emulates an EJB Container running in a Java EE environment, but it runs in a Java SE environment. In fact, attempting to instantiate an Embeddable EJB Container from within a Java EE environment is restricted. This embeddable container provides an operating environment for EJBs, supplying injected resources, security, and a JTA transactional interface so that EJBs can be tested in a controlled environment.

How This Chapter Is Organized

In this chapter, we explore some of the principle concepts around unit testing. We then look at how to set up, execute, and debug JUnit tests using an Embeddable EJB Container, drawing from a handful of scenarios in our WineApp application. We will next take a close look at the services offered by EJB Lite, uncover its strengths and limitations, and show some useful shortcuts to isolate the EJB and JPA components being tested while reducing complexity in the test environment.

After we examine the JUnit test code that enables you to work with EJBs in the Embeddable EJB Container, we will look at some of the configuration options that you can leverage that are particularly well suited for a test environment. At the conclusion of the chapter, we will walk you through step-by-step instructions on how to set up and configure a JUnit environment in NetBeans, and then execute and debug the tests.

Concepts

Let's take a closer look at some of the principal concepts that we'll be covering in this chapter.

JUnit

JUnit is a test framework widely used for testing Java classes of all forms. *Test classes* are ordinary Java classes that have been annotated to identify methods that serve special purposes. A method annotated as @Test identifies a single unit test. The test invokes one or more methods on a class being tested, obtains the results from calling those methods, and compares the actual with the expected results. When they differ, the test reports a failure, and the tester is alerted that a test needs attention.

By writing JUnit tests that comprehensively test the behavior of one or more classes, the tester can then execute those tests each time changes are made to the code being tested or to any code that is called indirectly. Any failures indicate that the expected behavior is no longer occurring. Furthermore, because a unit test typically targets a very specific bit of functionality, the failed test can clearly identify to the tester the specific code area that caused the disruption.

Because an EJB is a component that honors a public interface, it lends itself well to this form of unit testing. The introduction to EJB 3.1 of EJB Lite and Embeddable EJB Containers formally allows EJBs to be unit tested, without modification, through the JUnit testing framework in a pure Java SE environment.

EJB Lite

Let us take a closer look at the subset of features that comprise EJB Lite. Table 13-1 shows which of the major features of EJB 3.2 are included in EJB 3.2 Lite.

Table 13-1. *The features of EJB 3.2 that are part of EJB 3.2 Lite*

EJB 3.2 Feature	Included in EJB 3.2 Lite
Session Beans (stateless, stateful, and singleton)	Yes
Message-Driven Beans (MDBs)	No
Entity Beans (EJB 2.x)	No
Java Persistence API (JPA) 2.0	Yes
No Interface	Yes
Local business interface	Yes
Remote interface	No
Embeddable API	Yes
JAX-WS Web Service End Point	No
JAX-RPC Web Service End Point	No
Nonpersistent EJB Timer Service	Yes
Persistent EJB Timer Service	No
Local asynchronous session bean invocations	Yes
Remote asynchronous session bean invocations	No
Interceptors	Yes
RMI-IIOP Interoperability	No
Container-managed transactions	Yes
Bean-managed transactions	Yes
Declarative Security	Yes
Programmatic Security	Yes

Most notably, in EJB 3.2 Lite all forms of Local session beans are supported, but Remote session beans, MDBs, and EJBs as Web Services are not. Security and JTA support is in EJB Lite, including support for BMT and CMT. Finally, support for EntityManager and EntityManagerFactory injection is offered for JPA.

Embeddable EJB Container Client

A client using the Embeddable EJB Container looks up EJBs through JNDI instead of through injection since a Java EE server provides client injection, which is absent in this environment. EJBs themselves may be injected with other EJBs, however, along with other resources that are provided by their EJB Container.

In the JUnit examples shown later in this chapter, the JUnit test classes themselves are the clients of the Embeddable EJB Container. They instantiate the container directly through a static factory method, optionally initializing the container with configuration properties. The container then provides an InitialContext to the client that can be used to look up EJB and other resources through a JNDI namespace. The Embeddable EJB Container is capable of supporting EJBs at runtime, injecting session beans with resources, providing a JTA context for performing transactions, and all other services specified in EJB Lite that are listed in Table 13-1.

When the Embeddable EJB Container is instantiated in an environment where the GlassFish Embeddable Server (which also runs in a Java SE environment) is present, GlassFish augments the experience by providing services to the Embedded EJB Container.

JUnit Tests

Having explored the core concepts of this chapter, let us now look at some examples in the code. Like the Embeddable EJB Container, JUnit is essentially a Java library that you include in the class-path to enable functionality in your application. While it is beyond the scope of this chapter to describe all of the features of JUnit (including grouping tests into Suites, defining initialization Parameters, and so on), for the purposes of our example, it is useful to view the basic task of writing and executing JUnit classes as follows:

- Write test classes that follow JUnit patterns to initialize the test environment.

    - Write one or more methods that perform a specific unit test by calling one or more methods on an EJB, obtain the results from those method calls, and compare the results with previously defined expected results.

- At a per-class level, instantiate the Embeddable EJB Container the first time that any test method in the class is invoked, and close the container to release resources after the last test method is invoked.

- At a per-test level, initialize the database connection used by the JPA persistence unit to remove any existing data, and reset the state to a properly configured one.

- Invoke the JUnit test runner, passing as arguments the names of test classes you wish to execute and adding the following to the class-path:

    - The JUnit classes (.jar file(s))

    - The JUnit classes you wrote (optionally in .jar file(s))

    - The EJB .jar file(s) for EJBs you are testing, along with any dependent .jar files (like JPA persistence units)

    - An Embeddable EJB Container .jar, along with any dependent .jar files it needs

An IDE like NetBeans, JDeveloper, or Eclipse greatly simplifies the invocation process, as you will see later in the chapter, and it will even set up a lot of the basic plumbing in your JUnit test classes. This leaves you with the core task of writing just the code specific to each unit test.

Let us now dissect a JUnit test class we have written against the EJBs in our WineApp sample application to test a handful of scenarios.

WineAppServiceTest: A JUnit Test Class for the WineAppService EJB

For this chapter's example, we offer in Listing 13-1 a JUnit test class that contains all of the elements required to unit test EJBs in the Embeddable EJB Container.

Listing 13-1. WineAppServiceTest.java, a JUnit class for testing EJBs in the WineApp application

```
public class WineAppServiceTest {
  private static EJBContainer ejbContainer;
  private static NetworkServerControl derbyServer;
```

```java
public WineAppServiceTest() {
}

@BeforeClass
public static void setUpClass() throws Exception {
  PrintWriter pw = new PrintWriter(System.out);

  //  Start the Derby Database server, waiting until it is responsive
  //  before continuing
  try {
    derbyServer = new org.apache.derby.drda.NetworkServerControl();
    derbyServer.start(pw);
    int i = 50;
    while (--i > 0) {
      try {
        derbyServer.ping();
        break;
      } catch (Exception ex) {
        System.out.println("Derby Server started; waiting for
        response...");
      }
      Thread.sleep(100);
    }
  } finally {
    pw.close();
  }

  //  Instantiate an Embeddable EJB Container
  ejbContainer = javax.ejb.embeddable.EJBContainer.createEJBContainer();
}

@AfterClass
public static void tearDownClass() throws Exception {
  //  Close the Embeddable EJB Container, releasing all resources
  ejbContainer.close();

  //  Shutdown the Derby Database server
  derbyServer.shutdown();
}
```

```
@Before
public void setUp() {
  //  Inititalize the data in the domain model
  PopulateDemoData.resetData("Chapter13-EmbeddableEJBTests-
  ResourceLocal", System.out);
}

@After
public void tearDown() {
}

/**
 * Test findCustomerByEmail on WineAppService.
 *
 * Assert that the Customer returned is named "James Brown".
 *
 * @throws Exception
 */
@Test
public void testFindCustomerByEmail() throws Exception {
  System.out.println("findCustomerByEmail");
  WineAppService wineAppSvcFacade =
      (WineAppService) ejbContainer.getContext().lookup("java:global/
      classes/WineAppService");
  Customer customer =
      wineAppSvcFacade.findCustomerByEmail(PopulateDemoData.TO_EMAIL_
      ADDRESS);
  assertEquals("WineAppServiceFacade.findCustomerByEmail(): Checking
  customer name",
      "James Brown",
      customer.getFirstName() + " " + customer.getLastName());
}

/**
 * Test createIndividual() on WineAppService and findCustomerByEmail() on
 * CustomerFacade.
 *
```

```
 * Assert that the Individual instance created in createIndividual() has the
 * expected email property.
 * Assert that the Customer retrieved in
 * findCustomerByEmail() has the expected name.
 * Assert that the shippingAddress property is in a managed state after
   merge
 */
@Test
public void testCreateIndividual() throws Exception {
  System.out.println("createIndividual");
  WineAppService wineAppSvcFacade =
      (WineAppService) ejbContainer.getContext().lookup("java:global/
      classes/WineAppService");
  String email = "drwho@yahoo.com";
  Individual individual =
      wineAppSvcFacade.createIndividual("Adam", "Beyda", email);
  assertEquals("WineAppServiceFacade.createIndividual(): Checking
  Individual.email prop",
      email, individual.getEmail());

  CustomerFacade custFacade =
      (CustomerFacade) ejbContainer.getContext().lookup("java:global/
      classes/CustomerFacade");
  Customer customer = custFacade.findCustomerByEmail(email);
  assertEquals("CustomerFacade.findCustomerByEmail(): Checking Customer.
  email prop",
      "Adam Beyda", customer.getFirstName() + " " + customer.
      getLastName());

  // Managed/detached entity state check
  Address shippingAddress = new Address("San Mateo", null, null, null,
  null);
  customer.setDefaultShippingAddress(shippingAddress);
  customer = custFacade.merge(customer);
  assertNotNull("customer.getDefaultShippingAddress().getId() is null",
      customer.getDefaultShippingAddress().getId());
```

```
  assertNotNull("shippingAddress.getId() is null",
      shippingAddress.getId());
}

/**
 * Test createIndividual() and createCustomerOrder() on WineAppService,
 * getWineFindByYear() on WineFacade, and merge() on CustomerFacade.
 *
 * Assert that the total value of the created order is 110.
 * Assert that the customerOrder and customer objects are in a managed
 state
 */
@Test
public void testCreateCustomerOrder() throws Exception {
  System.out.println("createCustomerOrder");
  Context context = ejbContainer.getContext();
  WineAppService wineAppSvcFacade =
      (WineAppService) context.lookup("java:global/classes/
      WineAppService");
  WineFacade wineFacade =
      (WineFacade) context.lookup("java:global/classes/WineFacade");
  CustomerFacade custFacade =
      (CustomerFacade) context.lookup("java:global/classes/
      CustomerFacade");

  //  Add CartItems to the Customer's cart and merge the customer changes
  final String email = "drwho@yahoo.com";
  Customer customer = wineAppSvcFacade.createIndividual("Adam", "Beyda",
  email);
  for (Wine wine : wineFacade.getWineFindByYear(2005)) {
    customer.addCartItem(new CartItem(10, wine));
  }
  customer = custFacade.merge(customer);

  CustomerOrder customerOrder = wineAppSvcFacade.
  createCustomerOrder(customer);
  Float total = new Float(0);
```

```
for (OrderItem orderItem : customerOrder.getOrderItemList()) {
    total += orderItem.getQuantity() * orderItem.getPrice();
}
assertEquals("Checking that customer order totals $270", total, new
Float(270));

//  Query the latest state of our customer from the persistence context
//  (using a new transaction, courtesy CMT) and check whether it
    contains a
//  customer order with a populated 'id' field
CustomerOrder customerOrder1 =
    wineAppSvcFacade.findCustomerByEmail(email).getCustomerOrderList().
    get(0);
assertNotNull("customerOrder1.getId() is null", customerOrder1.
getId());

//  Check whether our original customer order has had its 'id' field
    auto-populated
assertNotNull("customerOrder.getId() is null", customerOrder.getId());

//  Check whether the customer order referenced by our customer
//  has had its 'id' field auto-populated
CustomerOrder customerOrder2 = customer.getCustomerOrderList().get(0);
assertNotNull("customerOrder2.getId() is null", customerOrder2.
getId());
    }
}
```

When this test class is executed in the JUnit tester, each method marked @Test is run in isolation as its own unit test. However, before any of these methods is executed, JUnit performs some initialization steps to instantiate the Embeddable EJB Container and initialize the data in the persistence unit. We will explore the elements of this JUnit class next, beginning with the initialization steps.

Instantiating the Embeddable EJB Container and Starting Derby

Before any test in this class is executed, we want to initialize the Embeddable EJB Container. Because this is a somewhat resource-intensive operation (albeit not as expensive as launching a full-blown GlassFish server), we would like to do this only once each time the JUnit tester is launched. JUnit lets you annotate static methods with @BeforeClass, and it executes these methods once per JUnit session, before the first unit test method is executed on that class. Our class-level setup method is as follows:

```java
@BeforeClass
public static void setUpClass() throws Exception {
  PrintWriter pw = new PrintWriter(System.out);

  // Start the Derby Database server, waiting until it is responsive
  // before continuing
  try {
    derbyServer = new org.apache.derby.drda.NetworkServerControl();
    derbyServer.start(pw);
    int i = 50;
    while (--i > 0) {
      try {
        derbyServer.ping();
        break;
      } catch (Exception ex) {
        System.out.println("Derby Server started; waiting for
        response...");
      }
      Thread.sleep(100);
    }
  } finally {
    pw.close();
  }
```

```
//  Instantiate an Embeddable EJB Container
ejbContainer = javax.ejb.embeddable.EJBContainer.createEJBContainer();
}
```

We begin by starting up the Derby database to allow our persistence unit to connect to a running server. Because the `org.apache.derby.drda.NetworkServerControl.` `start()` method is asynchronous, we have to assume that the server might not be available for connections right away, so we ping it in a loop, sleeping briefly between iterations, until it is ready or we decide to time out.

Once Derby is available for connections, we create the Embeddable EJB Container through the `javax.ejb.embeddable.EJBContainer.createEJBContainer()` call. Our `WineAppServiceTest` class is called from the JUnit tester, and NetBeans launches the tester with a class-path containing the JPA persistence unit `.jar` file (from Chapter 7) along with the EJBs defined in our Chapter 13 EJB jar and all of the necessary Java libraries required to run the JUnit framework and instantiate the Embeddable EJB Container. The current (at the time of this writing) GlassFish implementation links to a GlassFish server installation area to provide the services an EJB Container generally requires from its host Java EE server environment. Again, because we are running in a Java SE environment, the Java EE GlassFish server is not actually started, but classes required by the Embeddable EJB Container are loaded as needed from the Java libraries that comprise GlassFish.

At the conclusion of the JUnit session, the Embeddable EJB Container and the Derby Database server must be closed properly to release any resources that they may continue to hold. JUnit invokes methods annotated `@AfterClass` at this time, and our method `tearDownClass()` performs these tasks:

```
@AfterClass
public static void tearDownClass() throws Exception {
    //  Close the Embeddable EJB Container, releasing all resources
    ejbContainer.close();

    //  Shutdown the Derby Database server
    derbyServer.shutdown();
}
```

Initializing Data in the Persistence Unit

Whereas steps such as starting the Derby and Embeddable EJB Container need to be performed only once per JUnit test session, other initialization steps must be executed prior to every JUnit test. Per-test initialization steps goes in a method (or methods) annotated @Before, like this:

```
@Before
public void setUp() {
  //  Inititalize the data in the domain model
  PopulateDemoData.resetData("Chapter13-EmbeddableEJBTests-ResourceLocal",
System.out);
}
```

For our tests, we want to ensure that each unit test begins with the same data in the database, so we execute a script that initializes the database and resets the data to the desired state. You may be familiar with this static PopulateDemoData.resetData() method from when it was used in other chapters. Note that we pass the name of a persistence unit so that we can reuse it in different application contexts. The JPA persistence unit in the Chapter07-ServiceIntegration-jpa project defines its own persistence.xml file, and within it a <persistence-unit> named Chapter07-WineAppUnit-ResourceLocal. The <persistence-unit> we are using for our JUnit tests is "Chapter13-EmbeddableEJBTests-ResourceLocal" and it is defined in our context project, Chapter13-EmbeddedEJBTests, in the "Configuration Files" section. Since the entity classes in our JPA persistence unit are visible to our Test/EJB module, we are free to define additional persistence units that reference these same entity classes. JPA is happy to let you define multiple persistence units for the same entity classes, using multiple persistence.xml files if desired, allowing each persistence unit to specify a different database connection, schema generation plan, persistence provider, or any other configuration option. We define a new persistence unit in this case so that we can map them to a database connection that is suited to testing purposes. This connection is described next.

Using the "jdbc/__default" Connection

GlassFish comes preconfigured with a connection well suited for use by the Embeddable EJB Container. It is created automatically when requested, and it is deleted automatically when the Embedded Glassfish Server closes. It is available to clients as a data-source resource named `jdbc/__default`, and it is used by both our JTA and RESOURCE_ LOCAL persistence units defined in the `persistence.xml` file found in `Chapter13-EmbeddableEJBTests` and shown in Listing 13-2.

Listing 13-2. persistence.xml, containing the two persistence units used by our tests

```
<?xml version="1.0" encoding="UTF-8"?>
<persistence version="2.0" xmlns="http://java.sun.com/xml/ns/persistence"
xmlns:xsi="http://www.w3.org/2001/XMLSchema-instance"
xsi:schemaLocation="http://java.sun.com/xml/ns/persistence
http://java.sun.com/xml/ns/persistence/persistence_2_0.xsd">
  <persistence-unit name="Chapter13-EmbeddableEJBTests-ResourceLocal"
  transaction-type="RESOURCE_LOCAL">
    <provider>org.eclipse.persistence.jpa.PersistenceProvider</provider>
    <non-jta-data-source>jdbc/__default</non-jta-data-source>
    <class>com.apress.ejb.chapter07.entities.Address</class>
    <class>com.apress.ejb.chapter07.entities.BusinessContact</class>
    <class>com.apress.ejb.chapter07.entities.CartItem</class>
    <class>com.apress.ejb.chapter07.entities.Customer</class>
    <class>com.apress.ejb.chapter07.entities.CustomerOrder</class>
    <class>com.apress.ejb.chapter07.entities.Distributor</class>
    <class>com.apress.ejb.chapter07.entities.Individual</class>
    <class>com.apress.ejb.chapter07.entities.InventoryItem</class>
    <class>com.apress.ejb.chapter07.entities.OrderItem</class>
    <class>com.apress.ejb.chapter07.entities.Supplier</class>
    <class>com.apress.ejb.chapter07.entities.Wine</class>
    <class>com.apress.ejb.chapter07.entities.WineItem</class>
    <exclude-unlisted-classes>true</exclude-unlisted-classes>
    <properties>
      <property name="eclipselink.ddl-generation" value="drop-and-create-
      tables"/>
    </properties>
  </persistence-unit>
  <persistence-unit name="Chapter13-EmbeddableEJBTests-JTA" transaction-
  type="JTA">
```

```
      <provider>org.eclipse.persistence.jpa.PersistenceProvider</provider>
      <jta-data-source>jdbc/__default</jta-data-source>
      <class>com.apress.ejb.chapter07.entities.Address</class>
      <class>com.apress.ejb.chapter07.entities.BusinessContact</class>
      <class>com.apress.ejb.chapter07.entities.CartItem</class>
      <class>com.apress.ejb.chapter07.entities.Customer</class>
      <class>com.apress.ejb.chapter07.entities.CustomerOrder</class>
      <class>com.apress.ejb.chapter07.entities.Distributor</class>
      <class>com.apress.ejb.chapter07.entities.Individual</class>
      <class>com.apress.ejb.chapter07.entities.InventoryItem</class>
      <class>com.apress.ejb.chapter07.entities.OrderItem</class>
      <class>com.apress.ejb.chapter07.entities.Supplier</class>
      <class>com.apress.ejb.chapter07.entities.Wine</class>
      <class>com.apress.ejb.chapter07.entities.WineItem</class>
      <exclude-unlisted-classes>true</exclude-unlisted-classes>
   </persistence-unit>
</persistence>
```

The two persistence units are nearly identical but for their transactional and schema generation behavior. The first persistence unit, `Chapter13-EmbeddableEJBTests-ResourceLocal`, references `jdbc/__default` as a `non-jta-data-source`, and it is used by our non-EJB Java façade inside the `PopulateDemoData.resetData()` operation. Since we know our tests will execute this operation prior to each test, we configure its persistence unit always to drop and re-create the schema objects required by the entities in that unit. This is reflected in the property defined for that unit:

```
<property name="eclipselink.ddl-generation" value="drop-and-create-tables"/>
```

Note   In JPA 2.0 and earlier, schema generation options were not defined in the spec, and users had to rely on platform-specific support for this, like the EclipseLink property shown above. JPA 2.1 introduces support for schema generation through a number of standard configuration properties, including a parallel property to the one above: "`javax.persistence.schema-generation-action`". Currently the Java EE 8 provides the JAP version 2.2 but for compatibility with JPA 2.0 libraries, for now we use the EclipseLink property in our examples.

The second persistence unit in our `persistence.xml` file, Chapter13-EmbeddableEJBTests-JTA, can assume that the schema has already been created, so we deliberately do not enlist a schema generation option for this persistence unit.

If we needed to free up resources acquired during the individual unit tests runs, we could free them up using a method annotated @After. In our example, we don't need to do this, so we leave the method body empty.

The Unit Test Methods

Having now covered the test initialization steps, we turn our attention to the unit tests themselves. Each unit test is annotated @Test to differentiate it from ordinary methods that might also be on the class, and we include three test methods.

The first test, `findCustomerByEmail()`: executes a single method `findCustomerByEmail()` on the `WineAppService` EJB, which returns a `Customer` instance. It then asserts that the firstname + lastName is "James Brown," the expected result. Our test class controls the state of the data in the persistence unit, and so it knows what to expect.

```
/**
 * Test findCustomerByEmail on WineAppService.
 *
 * Assert that the Customer returned is named "James Brown".
 *
 * @throws Exception
 */
@Test
public void testFindCustomerByEmail() throws Exception {
  System.out.println("findCustomerByEmail");
  WineAppService wineAppSvcFacade =
      (WineAppService) ejbContainer.getContext().lookup("java:global/
      classes/WineAppService");
  Customer customer =
      wineAppSvcFacade.findCustomerByEmail(PopulateDemoData.TO_EMAIL_
      ADDRESS);
  assertEquals("WineAppServiceFacade.findCustomerByEmail(): Checking
  customer name",
```

```
        "James Brown",
        customer.getFirstName() + " " + customer.getLastName());
}
```

EJB Lookup Through JNDI

EJB injection is not available to us from the JUnit test class, since it is running in an ordinary Java SE environment and not inside the Embeddable EJB Container. Thus we use JNDI through the `javax.naming.Context` API provided by our `EJBContainer` object to get references to the EJBs we are testing. There are several ways to look up an EJB, depending on whether it is global to the application or local to your context module. In this example, our EJBs are registered globally to the application, and we can use the global namespace to find them, using a URL such as `"java:global/classes/WineAppService."`

The second test, `testCreateIndividual()`, is a superset of the first test, but it does not rely on any side effects of the first test:

```
/**
 * Test createIndividual() on WineAppService and findCustomerByEmail() on
 * CustomerFacade.
 *
 * Assert that the Individual instance created in createIndividual() has the
 * expected email property.
 * Assert that the Customer retrieved in
 * findCustomerByEmail() has the expected name.
 */
@Test
public void testCreateIndividual() throws Exception {
  System.out.println("createIndividual");
  WineAppService wineAppSvcFacade =
      (WineAppService) ejbContainer.getContext().lookup("java:global/
classes/WineAppService");
  String email = "drwho@yahoo.com";
  Individual individual =
      wineAppSvcFacade.createIndividual("Adam", "Beyda", email);
  assertEquals("WineAppServiceFacade.createIndividual(): Checking
  Individual.email prop",
      email, individual.getEmail());
```

```
CustomerFacade custFacade =
    (CustomerFacade) ejbContainer.getContext().lookup("java:global/
    classes/CustomerFacade");
Customer customer = custFacade.findCustomerByEmail(email);
assertEquals("CustomerFacade.findCustomerByEmail(): Checking Customer.
email prop",
    "Adam Beyda", customer.getFirstName() + " " + customer.
    getLastName());

// Managed/detached entity state check
Address shippingAddress = new Address("San Mateo", null, null, null,
null);
customer.setDefaultShippingAddress(shippingAddress);
customer = custFacade.merge(customer);
assertNotNull("customer.getDefaultShippingAddress().getId() is null",
    customer.getDefaultShippingAddress().getId());
assertNotNull("shippingAddress.getId() is null",
    shippingAddress.getId());
}
```

This tests our transactional method `createIndividual()` on `WineAppService`, which creates and persists an instance of `Individual`. We then query it through `findCustomerByEmail()` on a separate EJB, `CustomerFacade`, to verify that it can be found.

A secondary step in the test creates a new address and assigns it as the customer's default shipping address. We will return to this when running the tests later in this chapter.

Our third unit test, `testCreateCustomerOrder()`, further tests the app behavior by calling multiple transactional methods on different EJBs and combining test-side and server-side steps that build up a customer cart and process it to create a customer order:

```
/**
 * Test createIndividual() and createCustomerOrder() on WineAppService,
 * getWineFindByYear() on WineFacade, and merge() on CustomerFacade.
 *
 * Assert that the total value of the created order is 110.
 * Assert that the customerOrder and customer objects are in a managed
 *   state
 */
```

```java
@Test
public void testCreateCustomerOrder() throws Exception {
  System.out.println("createCustomerOrder");
  Context context = ejbContainer.getContext();
  WineAppService wineAppSvcFacade =
      (WineAppService) context.lookup("java:global/classes/
      WineAppService");
  WineFacade wineFacade =
      (WineFacade) context.lookup("java:global/classes/WineFacade");
  CustomerFacade custFacade =
      (CustomerFacade) context.lookup("java:global/classes/
      CustomerFacade");

  // Add CartItems to the Customer's cart and merge the customer changes
  final String email = "drwho@yahoo.com";
  Customer customer = wineAppSvcFacade.createIndividual("Adam", "Beyda",
  email);
  for (Wine wine : wineFacade.getWineFindByYear(2005)) {
    customer.addCartItem(new CartItem(10, wine));
  }
  customer = custFacade.merge(customer);

  CustomerOrder customerOrder = wineAppSvcFacade.
  createCustomerOrder(customer);
  Float total = new Float(0);
  for (OrderItem orderItem : customerOrder.getOrderItemList()) {
    total += orderItem.getQuantity() * orderItem.getPrice();
  }
  assertEquals("Checking that customer order totals $270", total, new
  Float(270));

  // Query the latest state of our customer from the persistence context
  // (using a new transaction, courtesy CMT) and check whether it contains a
  // customer order with a populated 'id' field
```

```
CustomerOrder customerOrder1 =
    wineAppSvcFacade.findCustomerByEmail(email).getCustomerOrderList().
    get(0);
assertNotNull("customerOrder1.getId() is null", customerOrder1.getId());

//  Check whether our original customer order has had its 'id' field
    auto-populated
assertNotNull("customerOrder.getId() is null", customerOrder.getId());

//  Check whether the customer order referenced by our customer
//  has had its 'id' field auto-populated
CustomerOrder customerOrder2 = customer.getCustomerOrderList().get(0);
assertNotNull("customerOrder2.getId() is null", customerOrder2.getId());
}
```

This high-level test covers some ground and also exercises a real-world process. It is designed to sniff out any breakages across a relatively large swath of code, and it complements other tests that are designed to pinpoint very specific areas of the code should changes to the app cause these tests to start to fail.

Having examined our JUnit test code in detail, you can now follow the steps outlined in the next section to build and run these tests in NetBeans using JUnit with the Embedded EJB Container.

Building and Testing the Sample Code

Now that we've examined how JUnit tests can be written to execute EJB unit tests against an Embeddable EJB Container, let's execute the test cases we just covered from within NetBeans.

Prerequisites

Before performing any of the steps detailed in the next sections, complete the "Getting Started" section of Chapter 1. This section will walk you through the installation and environment setup required for the samples in this chapter.

Opening the Sample Application

This chapter's root project holds a dependency on the JPA persistence unit defined in `Chapter07-ServiceIntegration-jpa`. Launch the NetBeans IDE, and open the `Chapter13-EmbeddableEJBTests` project using the `File ➤ Open Project` menu. Make sure that the `'Open Required Projects'` check box is checked as shown in Figure 13-1.

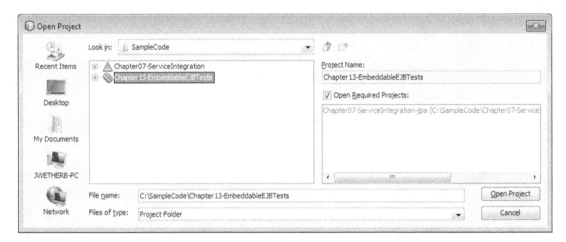

Figure 13-1. *Opening the Chapter13-EmbeddableEJBTests project*

This project is a stand-alone EJB project, a departure from the other Java EE Application projects that we have used for the other chapters. The project consists of a handful of EJBs to be tested, under the `Source Packages` folder; a `persistence.xml` file defining the persistence units used by the EJBs, in the `Configuration Files` folder; and our JUnit test class in the `Test Packages` folder. The structure is shown in Figure 13-2.

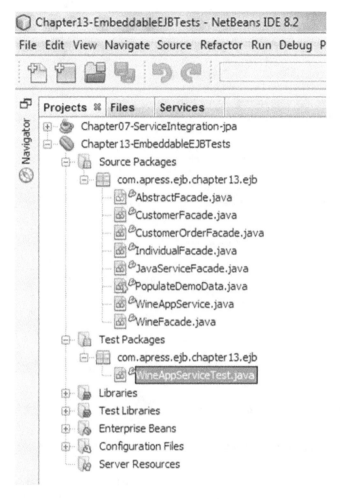

Figure 13-2. *Observing the structure of the Chapter13-EmbeddableEJBTests project*

Compiling the Sources

Invoke the context menu on the Chapter13-EmbeddableEJBTests node, and build the application by selecting the Clean and Build menu option, as shown in Figure 13-3.

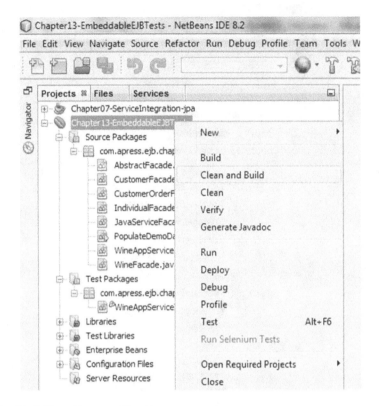

Figure 13-3. *Building the application*

Running the JUnit Tests

There are several ways to launch JUnit tests from NetBeans, but for these tests, you will right-click on the WineAppServiceTest class and choose "Test File," as shown in Figure 13-4.

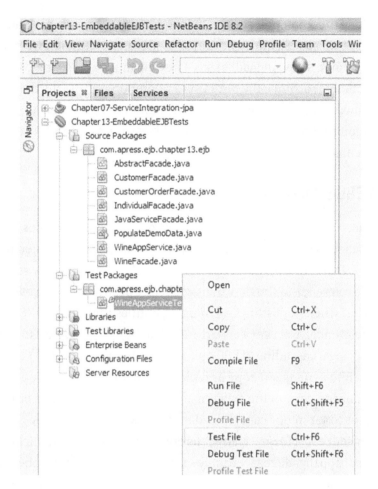

Figure 13-4. *Launching the JUnit Tester to execute the unit tests in WineAppServiceTest.java*

This step instantiates the Embeddable EJB Container, initializes the database, and executes the three unit tests in our class. The results of the test will appear in the Test Results tab.

As you will see, the second and third tests fail due to assertion failures. So let's diagnose these problems.

Fixing the Test Cases

Our first failure occurs in the second unit test – testCreateIndividual() – with the message shippingAddress.getId() is null. Interestingly, the prior assertion check in that unit test—checking the id field on the shippingAddress property currently known to our customer—succeeded. You might be forgiven for thinking that these asserts should be checking the same object—the object that was originally assigned to the customer using setDefaultShippingAddress()—because, although we performed a merge() on customer, shippingAddress is a new instance and so logically it was persisted and not merged. Since the persist() operation transforms the object into a managed instance in-place, without creating a new managed object the way that merge() does, shouldn't our original shippingAddress instance now just be the original instance but in a managed state?

Cascading MERGE Operations

The answer is that a cascade MERGE performs a merge() of new instances as well as of detached and managed ones; new instances in this case are not persisted through a call to persist(). Thus our original shippingAddress reference is now stale, and the customer holds a reference to the new managed copy of shippingAddress. This is an important "gotcha" when persisting and merging entities that cascade MERGE operations to objects they reference. A merge() is performed on both new and existing objects that are found during a cascading MERGE operation. Whereas persist() transforms the original instance into a managed copy and places it in the persistence context, merge() creates a new managed copy of the original and adds that instead. The original object being merged (customer in our case) is updated correctly to refer to the newly managed copy of shippingAddress. However, any references to the original, detached instances—for example, our shippingAddress variable—are now stale and need to be refreshed before they can be used.

Thus to fix this problem, we need to obtain the new managed copy of the shippingAddress object from the EntityManager by calling merge(). If we amend the test code, adding line 124, as shown in Figure 13-5, and rerun the test, this test will now succeed.

```
118    // Managed/detached entity state check
119    Address shippingAddress = new Address("San Mateo", null, null, null, null);
120    customer.setDefaultShippingAddress(shippingAddress);
121    customer = custFacade.merge(customer);
122    assertNotNull("customer.getDefaultShippingAddress().getId() is null",
123        customer.getDefaultShippingAddress().getId());
124    shippingAddress = custFacade.merge(shippingAddress);
125    assertNotNull("shippingAddress.getId() is null",
126        shippingAddress.getId());
```

Figure 13-5. *Updating the test method WineAppServiceTest. testCreateIndividual() to refresh a stale reference*

Returning Managed Objects from EJB Methods

The third test appears to fail with a similar issue. We can fix it in the same way by explicitly merging all of the objects within our test client to obtain managed references after they have been added to the persistence context—whether directly or through a cascading MERGE operation. However, in this case, we are calling an EJB method to assemble a CustomerOrder instead of wiring things up within the test client, and we decide to address this issue in the EJB code itself.

Let's go into the debugger and see if we can see why our customerOrder reference has a null id field when the same customerOrder queried from the database has its id field properly assigned.

Open the WineAppService.java file, and add a breakpoint on the custFacade.merge(customer); call inside createCustomerOrder(), as shown in Figure 13-6.

```
33    public CustomerOrder createCustomerOrder(Customer customer) {
34        // Create a new CustomerOrder from the customer's cart items
35        CustomerOrder customerOrder = new CustomerOrder();
36        for (CartItem cartItem : customer.getCartItemList()) {
37            Wine wine = cartItem.getWine();
38            // Add 10% discount for a wine when buying 10 or more bottles
39            Float discount = cartItem.getQuantity() >= 10 ? wine.getRetailPrice() / 10 : 0f;
40            Float discountPrice = wine.getRetailPrice() - discount;
41            Date date = new Date(System.currentTimeMillis());
42            OrderItem orderItem =
43                new OrderItem(cartItem.getQuantity(), wine, date,
44                                discountPrice, null, null, customerOrder);
45            customerOrder.addOrderItem(orderItem);
46        }
47        customer.addCustomerOrder(customerOrder);
         custFacade.merge(customer);
49
50        return customerOrder;
51    }
```

Figure 13-6. *Setting a breakpoint inside WineAppService.createCustomerOrder()*

With the breakpoint set, right-click on WineAppServiceTest.java, and this time select the item "Debug Test File" to launch the JUnit tester in debug mode.

When our breakpoint is hit, open up the Variables panel and navigate to the customerOrder local variable. Expand customerOrder to view the current values of its properties, navigate to its inherited properties, and observe that its id property is null.

This is to be expected. At this stage in the method, `customerOrder` is a new instance and has not yet been persisted. Thus, its primary key value hasn't been generated or assigned yet to its `id` field.

Step over the line with the breakpoint to perform the `merge()` on `customer`. We know from the cascade rules on `Customer` that when a `Customer` instance (or any of its subtypes) is merged, all referenced `CustomerOrder` instances will be merged as well.

When inspecting `customerOrder` in the Variables window again after executing the merge, we find that its `id` field is still null. The `@GeneratedValue` setting on its `id` field ensures that a value is assigned when it is persisted or merged into the persistence context, so evidently this object is not the managed copy created when `merge()` was called on its `customer` parent. Consequently, the method `createCustomerOrder()` is returning the wrong instance of `customerOrder`. To fix this, edit the return statement to return a managed instance of `customerOrder` instead as shown in Figure 13-7.

```
50           return custOrdFacade.merge(customerOrder);
```

Figure 13-7. *Updating WineAppService.createCustomerOrder() to return a managed instance of customerOrder*

This gets us past the `customerOrder.getId() is null` assertion failure that we were hitting. Running the tests again lands us at the final issue we need to resolve. Our `customer` instance was in a managed state after it was created through `createCustomerOrder()` a few lines previously. However, the assertion failure `customerOrder2.getId() is null` indicates that it is somehow holding onto a stale copy of `customerOrder`. A closer inspection identifies that our copy of `customer` became detached when it was merged inside `createCustomerOrder()`. Because we do not pass the merged copy back to the client, the client is responsible for obtaining the new managed copy. Acquiring this managed copy through another `merge()` call fixes the problem, as shown on line 173 in Figure 13-8.

```
171     // Check whether the customer order referenced by our customer
172     //   has had its 'id' field auto-populated
173     customer = custFacade.merge(customer);
174     CustomerOrder customerOrder2 = customer.getCustomerOrderList().get(0);
175     assertNotNull("customerOrder2.getId() is null", customerOrder2.getId());
```

Figure 13-8. *Updating WineAppServiceTest.testCreateCustomerOrder() to assign a managed instance to the customer variable*

... and with that, our tests now execute successfully.

Beyond exploring the step-by-step process of executing and debugging JUnit tests involving session beans and entities, a key takeaway from this exercise is that merge operations, particularly those involving cascade MERGE, can lead to stale references and this can be difficult to spot in the code. A safe approach is always to persist new entities explicitly if you need to continue to reference them, rather than allow them to be persisted through a cascade merge, which causes the original instances to become detached. Also, remember to merge objects to obtain their current managed state if you have any doubt about their state following a method call where they might have been persisted or merged.

Summary

The chapter began with an introduction to the following key concepts:

- *JUnit*: A framework for unit testing Java classes;

- *EJB Lite*: A minimal subset of the EJB API, which provides essential services to EJBs without the overhead of some of the more resource-intensive features required by a full EJB Container;

- *Embeddable EJB Container*: An implementation of EJB Lite that runs in a pure Java SE environment instead of a Java EE application server, and which provides a lightweight environment for testing EJBs through Junit.

While examining a JUnit test class that was written to test EJB facades over a JPA persistence unit, we dissected the configuration requirements when running tests in an Embeddable EJB Container.

Finally, we walked through the steps for building and executing our JUnit tests in NetBeans against the GlassFish implementation of an Embeddable EJB Server. The tests were preconfigured to fail, and we walked through the process of examining and uncovering the causes of the failures, using the debugger to assist us in arriving at their solutions.

We closed the chapter with an important takeaway about exercising caution when working with references to entities that can become detached when they become merged or persisted due to cascade rules when a related entity is merged.

Index

A

Abstract entity, 159, 191

Advanced persistence features, 16

Aggregate average response time (AART), 438–439, 441–442, 461–463, 466–468

Application Assembler
    creating EAR file, 514–515
    deployment descriptors, 513
    external dependencies
        conflicts and redundant references, 534
        <ejb-ref> descriptor, 533–534
        packaging, 535
        partial @EJB annotations, 534
        responsibility, 532
        web.xml, ejb-jar.xml, and application-client.xml descriptor, 532
    grouping components, 513
    packaging components, JAR files, 514
    specific tasks, 515–516
    tasks and deliverables, 512–513

Application servers
    deployment plan, 531
    deployment tools, 530–531
    platform-specific descriptors, 530

AroundInvoke methods, 55

Atomicity, consistency, isolation, durability (ACID), 369–370, 407–408

Auto-acknowledge, 241

Autogenerated primary key values (@GeneratedValue), 211–213, 227

B

Bean-managed concurrency, 69, 71

Bean-managed transaction (BMT)
    benefits, 425
    CMT services, 379
    creating CustomerOrder, 424–425
    Customer and CartItem entity instances, 422–423
    EJBContext, 380
    limitations, 425
    onMessage method, 381
    OrderProcessorBMTBean.java, 409, 411–415
    OrderProcessorBMTBean TxnInterceptor.java, 416
    OrderProcessorBMTClient.java, 416–420
    persisting customer, 424
    removing test data, 421–422
    session bean declaration, 420–421
    UserTransaction object, 379, 380

Bidirectional relationship, 161

Business Process Execution Language (BPEL), 546

C

D

E